The
Economic
Problem

Student Companion To

The Economic Problem

ROBERT L. HEILBRONER

LESTER C. THUROW

with the assistance of
E. LAWRENCE MINARD

FOURTH EDITION

Prentice-Hall, Inc., Englewood Cliffs, New Jersey

Printed in the United States of America

10   9   8   7   6   5   4   3   2

0-13-226944-9

Prentice-Hall International, Inc., *London*
Prentice-Hall of Australia, Pty. Ltd., *Sydney*
Prentice-Hall of Canada, Ltd., *Toronto*
Prentice-Hall of India Private Limited, *New Delhi*
Prentice-Hall of Japan, Inc., *Tokyo*

Contents

3
MICROECONOMICS:
ANATOMY OF A MARKET SYSTEM

4
PROSPERITY AND RECESSION— THE ECONOMICS OF THE MACROSYSTEM

6

SOCIOMETRIC SYSTEMS

Introduction

Textbooks — no student will believe this — are as great a problem for their authors as for their readers. The problem is how much to say, and when to quit. And the problem about the problem is that there is no satisfactory answer within the confines of the length of a normal textbook and of a normal student's patience.

The solution, to the extent that it exists, lies in supplementing a text with a reader and workbook. There are chapters in the text that ought to be pursued further, through the writings of other people, whether these support or oppose the views of the text. There are certainly chapters that need sheer work to enable a student to familiarize himself or herself with the material. And there are some chapters where *both* readings and working exercises are useful.

At any rate, the purpose of this combined reader and workbook is to help make *The Economic Problem* "sink in." We all know how deceptive the learning process can be. We read a page and everything seems crystal clear. We are asked a simple question about it and the thing twists into a helpless mess. The purpose of readings and writings is to get rid of the twists and to put the material in your mind in that final and decisive manner that the psychologists call the "Aha!" reaction.

Only a few more words of introduction seem necessary. First we should emphasize that many of the readings are shortened considerably. This is not always a loss — not every master of economics is a master of economy when it comes to style-but all too often important subsidiary points or illustrative material have had to be sacrificed to brevity. Thus if an excerpted article fires you to do more reading on your own, *go to the originals first.*

Second, *do all the exercises, even the easy ones.* There is often a tendency in books of exercises to work out a problem or two and to skip those that are a "snap." Don't. Doing easy problems *correctly* reinforces your knowledge and may prevent you from doing harder problems incorrectly.

Third, you will find some questions in the workbook that have no answers to refer to. These are limited to questions whose answers should be crystal clear. The more difficult questions, quizzes, true-false, multiple choice items, and the like, have answers provided at the end of the exercise. The only exception is the "tear out and hand to your instructor" pages. You will have to ask the instructor for the right answers to these questions.

One last word. Inevitably, in setting questions, puzzles, and problems, authors make mistakes. Ambiguities creep in, questions turn out to be harder than they were meant to be, or answers are just plain wrong. We depend on today's students to help us make this book easier for tomorrow's. When you come across something that seems wrong (or something that just irritates or baffles you), drop us a line. We will appreciate hearing from you, will try to answer you, and will certainly correct the error in subsequent printings.

The Economic Problem

THE ECONOMY
IN OVERVIEW

The Economic Problem

The first part of the text gives you a chance to see the woods before the trees close in. Therefore, these first two chapters should be read through fairly rapidly, aiming at the main ideas rather than the subsidiary details. You don't have to master details of economic history or the fine points of Adam Smith: you *should* emerge with some feeling for the "economic problem," for the general historic process that brought market society into being, and for the general nature of the problems that market society presents.

In most of the review chapters of this workbook we will give you a fairly close discussion of the points of the text, followed by a more or less extensive grilling on them. Here, we think it better just to single out a few words and ideas that you might think about, and then go on to some readings that will broaden your exposure to the main ideas of the section.

First the central ideas . . .

1. TRADITION, COMMAND, MARKET

There seems no need to review this main idea of Chapter 1. Instead, we suggest you look at the endpapers of *The Economic Problem,* where the three main systems are indicated on a map of the world. You may disagree with the map, which is necessarily illustrative at best. Do you agree that the portions designated as Traditional display the static properties of traditional economic systems?

2. PRODUCTION AND DISTRIBUTION

Here are the two key aspects of the economic problem — the two essential activities that must be carried out if a society is to assure its own provisioning, to reproduce itself. We will be studying these problems in great detail in subsequent chapters. Make sure that you understand the social, as well as the technical, nature of these problems. Both production and distribution concern *behavior* as well as the physical activities of making or allocating goods.

3. THE DIVISION OF LABOR

Few characteristics of advanced economies are more important, both for production and distribution, than the division of labor. Why? Because the division of labor enormously enhances the productive capacity of labor, as Adam Smith's pin factory illustrates. (Think of an automobile plant!) But the division of labor is also significant for distribution, because it means that no person with his own efforts produces the variety of goods and services he or she needs. Division of labor imposes the need for *exchange* and for a system of distribution that will assure the interchange of the products of specialized labor.

4. SCARCITY

Economics "exists" because goods are scarce. There would be no production or distribution problem if goods were free. Remember, however, that scarcity is not just imposed on us by nature but is also imposed on us by ourselves. That is, our desires create scarcity. If we were content to live as our greatgrandparents did there would be much less scarcity in America today.

Note: There is always a scarcity of some things. There are never enough beautiful women or handsome men. There is never enough love. There are never enough clear days. But these kinds of scarcities do not enter into the production and distribution of goods: they are not *economic* scarcities.

5. THE FACTORS OF PRODUCTION

Here is a phrase we will use repeatedly. It means two things:

a. The *physical agencies* that enter into output. These are usually classified as labor, land, and capital.
b. The existence of land, labor, and capital as *saleable commodities.*

All societies have factors of production in the first sense. Not all have them in the second sense. It is only when the services of land, labor, and capital are freely bought and sold on a vast scale that the market system itself can be said to solve the economic problem.

6. MODELS

We have also seen the first reduction of the complexity of the real economic world to the simplicity of a "model." Remember that models do not attempt to explain all reality, just important events. That is why models *must* be "abstract" — that is, simplifications of reality.

We will be tracing the operations of many such models throughout the chapters to come. But our look into Adam Smith has given us a first insight into the way economics can analyze the trends of a market system, through the use of models.

It will be more than enough if you really understand these few key terms. Rather than give you problems to work with at this stage, we would like to suggest that you browse through a short series of readings whose purpose is to underpin the main lessons of Section 1 of the text. What you will find in the next few selections are excerpts from economic anthropologists and economic historians aimed at underscoring the main themes of the "economic problem" itself.

The reading tells you about traditional societies and how they work. It is helpful because it makes you realize the gulf that lies between these kinds of societies and our own — and because it enables you to see that traditional societies also have economic problems of production and dis-

tribution, although they solve them very differently from the way we do.

Here and there you will find numerals in the margins of the readings. They refer you to comments at the end of each reading, where we offer questions, amplifications, or critiques to matters posed in the text. In a sense they are an economist's commentary on the readings. How many can you anticipate?

There is no special reading devoted to Adam Smith's *Wealth of Nations,* because the text itself covers that central work fairly carefully. If you would like to learn more about Adam Smith, you might look into Chapter 2 of *The Worldly Philosophers* (Robert L. Heilbroner, Simon and Schuster, N.Y., 1972) or the article on Smith in the *Encyclopedia Britannica* (1974). But there is no need to become an expert on Smith. Try, rather, to gain from this first section a real feeling for the economic problem as a whole and for the genesis of that remarkable market system into which we will be inquiring.

WHAT ALL ECONOMIES HAVE IN COMMON

George Dalton

An anthropologist looks at the range of human societies and picks out what is "economic" about them.

Economies exist because people living in societies exist. A society is a group of people who recognize special affinities among themselves — language, religion, citizenship, kinship — compared to outsiders, who interact with one another in frequent and in structured (or "institutionalized") ways, and who share a common location. The United States is a national society,

as is the Soviet Union. Evanston, Illinois is a local society (or community) within the United States. A hunting and gathering band of Australian aborigines is a small society. The Roman Empire was a larger society. (Note that in English we use

Reprinted from George Dalton, "Traditional, Tribal and Peasant Economics," from the McCaleb Anthropology Module (Warner, 1971).

the same words, "economy," "society," and "culture," to describe groupings of enormously varying size.)

Societies are big and small, they rise and fall, sometimes change drastically while remaining intact, and occasionally disappear. But because they consist of people and structured modes of persons and groups living together over long periods of time, they have "economies." We can say this unambiguously because all people and all societies — regardless of time and place — share two basic economic (material) needs: as a biological being, a person needs food, shelter, and, in most parts of the world, clothing, whether he is a Boston banker, a Soviet collective farm worker, or a Trobriand Islander; and, if he is to live, he needs to be provided with these repeatedly, throughout his life. *Individual physical existence requires continual, repetitive (and therefore structured) provisioning of material goods and of services* (such as medical care). This is one reason why the United States, the Soviet Union, and the Trobriand Islands each has an "economy."

But societies are more than persons physically existing and people are more than biological beings. They are also social and psychic beings who require social and psychological nourishment, which, in turn, requires the continual, repetitive provision of material goods and services. These social (public, community) activities and relationships — religion, defense, dispute settlement, marriage — go on in all societies. They require the services (roles and functions) of specialists such as priests and soldiers, food, clothing, and shelter for the specialists, and equipment (churches, crucifixes, bows and arrows, wedding rings, funeral pyres). *Social or community existence requires continual, repetitive provisioning of material goods and services.* This is a second reason why the United States, the Soviet Union, and the Trobriand Islands each has an "economy."

We see, then, that economies exist because of the fundamentally similar biological needs of all people, and the fundamentally similar social needs of communities of people. Both private and public life require the structured provisioning of goods and services.

There is a third point of fundamental similarity: in their provisioning, all societies make use of *human labor, natural resources, technology* of some sort (tools and knowledge, such as how to grow crops, hunt, preserve food), and some range of *institutional practices* (such as local markets, or foreign trade, or some sort of money). These are simple facts whose complex ramifications will occupy us later. Here we need stress only that institutions, natural resources, and technology are parts of an economy. In short, all societies structure the provisioning of material goods and services to sustain physical and social life. An economy consists of a society's institutional rules and practices which organize people, natural resources, and technology to provide (produce, acquire, and distribute) those goods and services in repetitive fashion. Like language and the family, some form of economy is a "functional requisite" of all human societies. And, like language and the family, the economy too takes on varying *forms* and *functions*. The Soviet, the American, and the Trobriand economies do have things in common because all people and all societies have things in common.

FUNDAMENTAL CONCEPTS

Section 1 gave us a bird's eye view of the study of economics; Section 2 gives us a worm's eye view. Now that we have a general idea of the large-scale problems that economics tries to clarify, we must turn our attention to the means by which economics undertakes its ambitious task. The purpose of Section 2 is to introduce you to these ideas, which we will be using throughout the rest of our work.

Important Note: Many of the ideas in Section 2 will be taught again in the text. You don't have to master the whole section now. In the workbook pages that follow, we will point out those things that you should learn firmly at this time, and we will also reassure you about things that will be explained again, in greater detail, later on.

Economic Behavior and Nature

3

LEARNING OBJECTIVES

Economics is a study of the interaction of man and nature, as man tries to solve the economic problem.

In this chapter we learn about two great generalizations on which economic analysis rests:

1. The "laws" of economic behavior

2. The "laws of nature's resistance.

You should come away from this chapter with a clear idea of economic man — a rational, competitive, creative maximizer — and of nature's constraints, expressed in diminishing returns, increasing cost, and returns to scale.

What is this first close look at economics really about? What should you get from this chapter? The answer can be put very succinctly: *economics is the study of what happens when economic man contends with a resistant nature.*

BEHAVIOR

What is "economic man"? He is a convenient abstraction that enables us to describe the way we assume most individuals *behave* in a market society. We assume that individuals are:

1. Maximizers of utilities.
2. Minimizers of disutilities.
3. Competitive.
4. Rational.

We further assume that individuals have:

5. Limitless wants for things-in-general.
6. Limited wants for particular things.

How would we translate these assumptions into everyday language? We would say that:

1. Men and women are acquisitive.
2. They tend to dislike most work.
3. They will outbid one another.
4. They choose the means best suited to reach their objectives.
5. They want "more."
6. They get less and less additional pleasure out of successive additions to any given source of pleasure.

NATURE

Now what about nature? Here we find three "laws":

1. The law of diminishing returns.
2. The law of increasing cost.
3. The law of economies of scale.

How do we translate these into English?

1. As we add more and more of any one kind of input — more labor, more land, more capital — to a fixed amount of other inputs, the amount of additional output eventually tends to decrease.
2. As we shift all inputs — land *and* labor *and* capital — from one use to another, the amount of additional output will eventually decrease.
3. Generally speaking, we can make things more efficiently after we reach a certain size of operation.

Note: All these behavioral assumptions and laws of production will be gone into later very carefully. Here it is enough to get the idea. You don't yet have to master the concepts in detail.

An Elementary Quiz on Elementary Ideas

You should now be able to answer these questions:

1. If you have a choice between a five-dollar bill and a ten-dollar bill, your choice of the ten-dollar bill shows you are a _____ .

2. If you prefer to dig ditches for only five hours instead of ten hours for the same total pay, it shows you are a _____ .
3. If you get what you want by paying more or taking less than the next person, you are _____ .
4. If you give up income today to acquire an education in the hope of making more money tomorrow, your choice is _____ .
5. If you never seem to have enough income, it is because your wants are _____ .
6. If you do not want a second refrigerator, or a second copy of a book you already have, it is because your wants for particular goods are _____ .

The answers are obvious: you are a *maximizer* of income; a *minimizer* of disutilities; *competitive;* a *rational* chooser; a person of *unlimited wants;* and someone whose utilities for any one good or service are *satiable.*

Note: These ideas seem elementary. They are. But they are indispensable for economic analysis. This is because they enable us to picture economic man as behaving in a predictable way.

Some More Basic Questions

Now for some questions about nature.

1. If you add more and more workers to a farm, output will not increase as rapidly as the work force. This is because the law of _____ is at work, along with the workers.
2. If you put more and more farms to raising wheat, after a while the output of wheat will not rise as fast as the additional farms because the law of _____ is in the way.
3. If you want to go into the cattle business, you will have trouble doing so in your back yard because of the small _____ of your operations.

Diminishing returns, increasing cost, and *scale* are the obvious answers.

CONSTRAINTS

These properties of nature are called *constraints*. They mean that man cannot maximize as he wishes, but only as nature allows. The farmer who wants to get rich cannot feed America from his farm alone because the law of diminishing returns won't let him. The hungry nation that wants to feed itself by using all its land, labor, and capital for wheat (or beef or whatever) will find that wheat costs a fortune when it is raised on ground and with labor and equipment not suited for it. The man who wants to make his fortune by building a better mouse-trap had better consider what size operation he will need if he is to undersell his competitors.

There are two important constraints in addition to those imposed by nature. Our *budget* (income and wealth) is a constraint. We may not be able to build a profitable mousetrap factor if we do not have the money. *Institutions* are also constraints. We are not allowed to maximize our incomes by stealing. We are not allowed to make our mousetraps by seizing another man's factory. We are not allowed to avoid our budget constraint by printing money. There are dozens of such institutional constraints. Most laws are constraints. Many customs are.

These ideas are also elementary. But they are equally indispensable for economic analysis. This is because they depict the economic process in terms of men seeking to maximize in a constraining environment. This is the single big idea of this chapter, the one you should learn solidly. Here is some help toward mastering that idea.

Problem 1.

We have a dish in which bacteria multiply. We begin with one cell, which divides each second. At the end of ten seconds how many bacteria are there; What is the maximizing force at work? Suppose there is only enough nutrient in the dish to support a colony of 100 bacteria. What would then be the constraint?

Problem 2.

A ball is attached to a long rubber band and dropped from a building. What force causes the behavior of the ball? If you were a physicist and knew the length and properties of the rubber band, could you predict where the ball would be (more or less) each second? At the end of an hour, when the ball was quietly dangling at the end of the rubber band, what would be the maximizing force still acting on the ball? What would be the constraint?

Problem 3.

Consider the flight of a cannon ball, shown below. What is the behavioral force? The constraints? (There are more than one!)

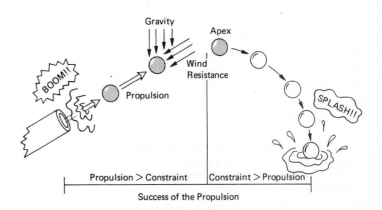

Problem 4.

Let the maximizing force be the assumptions about economic behavior, and the constraints be the laws of production. We will forget about budgets and institutions for the moment. You live in a two-dimensional graph-world, shown below, and you want as much as you can get of two kinds of goods, A and B.

Now follow the graphs, left to right. Assume there were no laws of production. You would push out in all directions, acquiring unlimited amounts of A and B. Next, introduce the laws of production, resisting economic effort, like coiled springs. We now arrive at an equilibrium between force and resistance, the production possibility curve. It is a picture of the best you can do, given the obstacles you face. (The production possibility "frontier" can be moved out, but that is a story for later).

Notice something about this last diagram. If we had enough information, we could predict

gravity or population growth. If men did not seek more, there would be no force pushing against nature.

3. The solution would also not be predictable if nature (and institutions and budgets) didn't offer calculable resistances. If we had no laws of diminishing returns, increasing cost, scale, or any budgets or institutions, men could have as much as they wanted.

How about those other things in the chapter? Demand curves? Supply curves? Wait. You will learn about them in the next chapter.

TEST YOURSELF

_ 1. Economies of scale means
   a. you can always produce more cheaply if you produce more.
   b. big production operations are always cheaper than small ones.

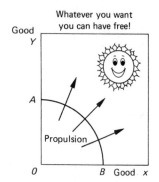
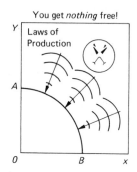
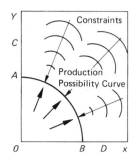

where the production possibility curve would lie. We would have to know how richly endowed nature was, how easily accessible were its riches, what skills and techniques were at your disposal. Of course this is much easier said than done. But think about this:

1. In principle, the solution to the economic problem is no different from that of solving the outcome of any known force pitted against a known resistance.

2. The solution could not be predictable if we didn't have a maximizing force similar to

   c. nature imposes constraints on the costs of different sized productive processes.

_ 2. Diminishing utility means
   a. you get less output as you use more input.
   b. people seek to minimize disutility.
   c. you get less satisfaction from having more and more of a commodity.

_ 3. Increasing cost states that
   a. "you can't grow all the world's food in a flower pot."
   b. "milk will cost more and more if you turn the whole nation into a dairy."

c. "you can't make all the nation's cars in one factory, even with all the nation's workers."

_ 4. Diminishing returns means

    a. more and more of input A gives you less and less of output X.

    b. more and more of inputs A and B give you less and less of output X.

c. a decrease in scale diminishes the output of X.

_ 5. Economics is a predictive science because

    a. behavior is presumed to be maximizing.

    b. we have knowledge about constraints.

    c. both of the above are true.

Answers: 1. c; 2. c; 3. b; 4. a; 5. c.

PRACTICE WITH GRAPHS

1. On the graph to the right draw a curve showing diminishing returns.

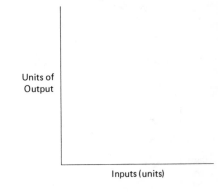

Units of Output

Inputs (units)

2. On the graph draw a production possibility curve for two goods, *X* and *Y*. Indicate on the graph:

maximum output of *X* (mark this x′)

maximum output of *Y* (mark this y′)

Some maximum combination of *X* and *Y* that you *can* produce. Mark this *a*.

Some combination of *X* and *Y* that you can't produce, even though you could produce either *X* or *Y*. Mark this *b*.

Some combination that is beyond all hope of production, either for *X* and *Y* together or separately. Mark this *z*.

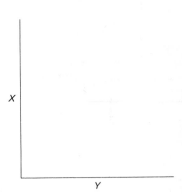

X

Y

3. Draw a curve that shows the typical effect of increasing scale on costs per unit.

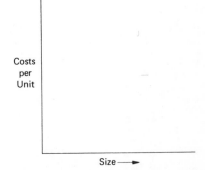

Costs per Unit

Size ⟶

Answers on next page.

Answers:

1.

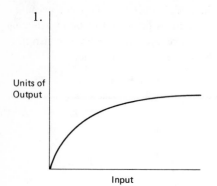

2.

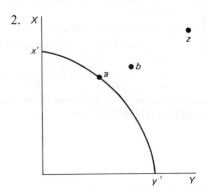

3.

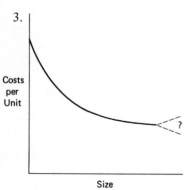

The Market
Mechanism

4

Supply and demand is the most important
single analytical tool of economics. The interplay
of supply and demand is the concept by which
we are able to understand many problems in
both micro and macroeconomics. Fortunately,
the basic concepts are not difficult to understand. But unlike the previous chapter, where it
was sufficient to get the idea, in this chapter you
will really want to master the ideas.

Therefore we begin this chapter by giving you
a reading from another text. Professor Dorfman's
exposition of supply and demand is not different
from ours, but it covers the same ground by
means of another example, and it should rein-
force the material you are already familiar with.
It should be very easy to read and understand,
and we suggest that you go over it thoughtfully
before you turn to the exercises that follow.

SUPPLY AND DEMAND

Robert Dorfman,

Whenever anything worthy of public concern happens to an economy, people tend to furrow their brow knowingly and explain the phenomenon away with the pat phrase, "It's caused by the forces of supply and demand." They are usually right (although most of them can't explain why). Supply and demand most assuredly *are* at the bottom of practically everything that happens in an economy: they determine the quantity of every commodity that is produced, the amount purchased, and the price it commands. But (unfortunately, perhaps) even this time-honored cliché really won't explain any economic incident very fully, because "supply" and "demand," like many other terms, are empty words until we have defined them carefully and have seen how the activities they represent interact. Our present task, therefore – and no task is more important to an understanding of how an economy works – is to do just this.

The most important economic facts about a commodity are the quantity of it produced and the price it commands. These are determined simultaneously (and at this point, not surprisingly, we hope) by the forces of supply and demand. To see how these forces operate, we have to do what may seem a strange thing: turn the relationship around and ask how prices influence the amounts of a commodity that are supplied and demanded. An example will help show why this is necessary, and will also give concrete form to the economic forces we are studying.

Bituminous coal will provide our example. Coal is gathered from more than 7,000 working

(productive) mines—underground mines, strip mines, a few auger mines.[1] The ages of these mines range from those being opened from time to time today, to those that are remarkably ancient; and of course some tap thick veins of coal while others tap thin ones, and some are deep and difficult to work, whereas others are shallow and convenient. Costs of operation vary widely in this industry, as in most others. The result is that whatever the price of coal may be, there will be some mines and parts of mines that can be operated profitably (in the sense that the price will exceed the costs of operation) and some that cannot be. Coal mine operators keep a watchful eye on price trends; they extract coal from the profitable mines and close down the others. Thus the higher the price of coal, the more mines it pays to operate, and the larger the volume of coal that is produced.

These facts can be summarized and made specific by a kind of table called a *supply schedule.*

A supply schedule is a table that shows the amount of a commodity that will be produced per year in response to every possible price.

Table 1 is an example of a supply schedule. According to this table, if the price of coal is $4.50 a ton at the minehead, it will pay to operate mines capable of producing 400 million tons a year. That was essentially the situation in the early 1960s. If the price of coal were to rise to $5 a ton, it would pay to open up additional mines capable of producing 38 million tons a year, for a total of 438 million tons. On the other hand, if the price were to fall to $4.25 a

Reprinted from Robert Dorfman, *Prices and Markets* (Englewood Cliffs, N.J.: Prentice-Hall, Inc., 1967), pp. 11-16.

[1] In an auger mine the ore is extracted by a revolving bit (an auger) that looks like an enormous screw.

TABLE 1. Supply Schedule for Bituminous Coal (Hypothetical data)	
Price ($ per ton)	Volume of Production (Million of tons per year)
6.00	485
5.75	475
5.50	462
5.25	450
5.00	438
4.75	422
4.50	400
4.25	378
4.00	350
.	.
.	.

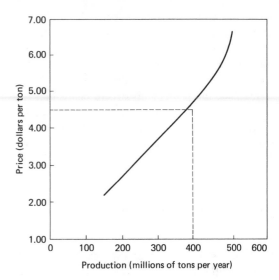

FIGURE 1. A typical supply curve. Larger amounts are offered at higher prices.

ton, some mines that operated at $4.50 a ton would become unprofitable, and output would fall by 22 million tons. Such a table, in short, summarizes the responses of an industry to changes in the price of its product. A good many considerations lie behind such a curve, and we shall consider them in the next chapters. But for the purposes of price determination, the significant data about an industry are contained in its supply schedule.

The same facts can be displayed more vividly by a graph known as a *supply curve.*

A supply curve is a graph of a supply schedule, showing the amount of a commodity that will be produced per year in response to every possible price.

The supply curve corresponding to the data in Table 1 is shown in Figure 1. In this graph, possible prices of coal are marked along the vertical axis and possible volumes of production along the horizontal axis. Each price-quantity pair listed in the supply schedule is plotted on the graph. For example, the dashed lines indicate that a price of $4.50 will elicit a supply of 400 million tons a year. The gaps remaining on the graph when the data in the supply schedule have been plotted are then filled in by a smooth curve.

The supply curve vividly presents some features of the supply schedule that are not easily seen in a table. In this case, for example, the supply makes it clear that when high volumes of output are reached, it becomes increasingly expensive to increase production still further. This is shown by the increasing steepness of the curve, so that larger and larger increases in price are required to induce successive increments of, say, 10 million tons after output has reached about 450 million. At this production level some very poor mines must be brought into the picture and each successive increase in output requires resort to significantly poorer ones. According to the graph, outputs of above 500 million tons a year are almost prohibitively expensive to obtain.[2]

The supply curve drawn for the coal industry is typical of those pertaining to many industries. In agriculture and manufacturing, as well as in mining, costs of production are different in different establishments. Even within a single factory or farm, after an efficient level of output has been attained, increases in production can be coaxed out only by resorting to poorer land,

[2]Warning: these are hypothetical data. In fact, 630 million tons were mined in 1947, the industry's peak year.

older machines, overtime work, and the like, all of which increase costs of operation. An industry will not increase its output from any going level unless the price rises enough to make the more costly production worthwhile. Conversely, if the price falls, the plants and parts of plants that are most expensive to operate will go out of production, and output will fall. This behavior will generate a supply curve similar to the one we have drawn for coal.

THE EFFECTS OF PRICE ON DEMAND

You know from your own experience that you are more careful in using things that cost more. Everyone is lavish with water; few are lavish with champagne. This suggests that the effect of price on consumption or demand is just the opposite from what it is on supply: the higher the price of a commodity, the less that will be consumed. This is true, and for a variety of reasons.

Consider coal again. Very little is used nowadays by private households. Electric utilities are the largest consumers, and steel plants are next, followed by a variety of other industries. When the price of coal rises, these different types of users react in ways that differ in detail but lead always to the same result: the reduced use of coal. To get a good idea of the reactions that take place when the price of coal rises, we need look no farther than the most important users, the electric utilities. A power company will meet an increase in coal prices by taking one or more of three different measures. It may operate some "convertible" power plants, stations whose boilers can be switched from coal-burning to oil-burning with little trouble. If so, it will switch them from coal use to oil use when coal becomes expensive and back again when coal becomes more economical. Second, every power company of any size has a variety of stations, some coal-fired, some oil-fired, some gas-fired, some

hydroelectric. It will shift its load when fuel prices change, generating a smaller proportion of its power in coal-burning stations when the price of coal increases. Third, power companies are constantly replacing, modernizing, and expanding their plants. They will design the new equipment to use coal or gas or nuclear fuel depending on which fuel they expect to be cheapest — a judgment that is strongly influenced by the current price of coal. When coal prices are high, new equipment is designed to use other fuels, and the coal industry loses customers for a long time in the future. In a variety of ways, then, power companies can and do cut back on the use of coal when its price is high.

But that is not the end of it. An increase in the price of coal raises the generating costs of utilities that use coal and therefore the price of the power they sell. Higher electricity prices naturally influence the decisions made by electro-power users. For example, when a homeowner is deciding whether to buy an electric dryer, a gas dryer, or a new clothes line, his decision will be affected by the price of power which, we have seen, reflects the price of coal. There is a chain of influence that extends to the ultimate consumers: higher coal prices mean higher electricity prices, higher electricity prices mean less use of electricity, less use of electricity means less use of coal by coal-burning power companies.

These are just some of the responses of an economy to an increase in the price of coal. The details are unimportant except to call to mind the variety of ways in which an increase in the price of a commodity discourages its use. The response of consumers to a price change may be prompt or slow — in the case of coal it tends to be slow because of the vast amount of equipment that is tied to particular sources of energy — but its direction is universal: the higher the price, the smaller the use.

In strict analogy with what we found when studying supply, the effects of price changes on demand can be expressed in a *demand schedule*.

A demand schedule is a table that shows the amount of a commodity that will be consumed per year at each possible price.

Table 2, a demand schedule for coal, illustrates this concept. According to these data, 400 million tons a year would be consumed at a price of $4.50 a ton. If the price were to rise to $5.00 a ton, consumption would fall to an annual rate of 352 million tons. This decline would not occur overnight; we have already seen that some of the most important responses to a change in the price of coal are slowed down to the pace of power-plant renovation. But if the price of coal rises to a new level, consumption will sag gradually as both coal users and the customers of coal users react, until the new, lower level is reached.

Just as in the case of supply, the data in the demand schedule can be presented most vividly in the form of a demand curve. A demand curve is a graph of a demand schedule, showing the amount of a commodity that will be consumed per year at each possible price.

Figure 2 displays the data of Table 2 in the form of a demand curve. It is interpreted just as the supply curve was.

SUPPLY AND DEMAND IN THE MARKET

The supply and demand schedules contain all the data that determine the price of the commodity and the quantity that will be produced and consumed. They express both the wishes of consumers (how much they are willing to pay for different amounts of the commodity) and the capabilities of producers (how much they can produce profitably at different selling prices). These data are brought together in the market — that is, in the dealings of the people who buy and sell the commodity; the supply and demand schedules show just how this happens. And if we plot the supply and demand curves on a single graph we can easily compare the amounts supplied and demanded at every price. This is done in Figure 3.

TABLE 2. Demand Schedule for Bituminous Coal (Hypothetical data)

Price ($ per ton)	Level of Consumption (Million of tons per year)
6.00	284
5.75	300
5.50	314
5.25	335
5.00	352
4.75	375
4.50	400
4.25	428
4.00	453
3.75	485
3.50	520
.	.
.	.

FIGURE 2. A typical demand curve showing how the quantity consumed declines when the price increases.

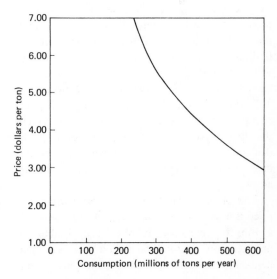

Consumption (millions of tons per year)

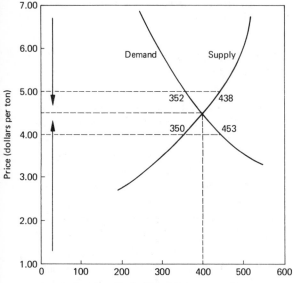

Suppose, to begin with, that the price of coal is $5 a ton. The supply curve shows that it will be profitable at that price to operate coal mines with an aggregate capacity of 438 million tons a year, but the demand curve shows that consumers will desire only 352 million tons at that price. With producers offering more coal than consumers are willing to buy, the price will have to give way. The supply schedule shows that producers of 422 million tons can operate profitably at a price of $4.75. Some of these, finding it impossible to sell their coal at $5 a ton, will offer it at a lower price, and the mines that were finding customers will have to follow suit. This, indeed, will be true for any producer charging a price above $4.50, the price at which the two curves cross, because supply exceeds demand at those prices. The downward pressure on prices is indicated by the downward-pointing arrow.

The pressures are just the opposite when the price is below the crossing point. At a price of $4 a ton, for example, it will be profitable to produce only 350 million tons a year, although demand will be some 100 million tons a year

greater. In this case, dealers' inventories will be drawn down, and some users will find their orders delayed or refused. Many users will be willing to pay more than the going price if necessary to obtain delivery; the demand schedule shows that consumers of 428 million tons are willing to pay $4.25 a ton. The price will therefore tend to rise. and this increase will in turn elicit stepped-up production. All this is suggested by the upward-pointing arrow in the range of prices below $4.50 a ton.

For prices below $4.50 a ton, each small increase in prices narrows the gap between demand and supply by simultaneously snuffing out some demand and calling forth some new supply. As the number of unsatisfied orders diminishes, the upward pressure on the price relaxes, until finally, at the crossing point, demand and supply are in balance. The same is true in the range of prices above the crossing point. Here each decline in the price stimulates some new demand and simultaneously drives out of production some of the barely profitable mines. The pressure of overproduction is gradually reduced until the crossing point is reached. But at the crossing point, all is in balance. Production is neatly meshed with consumption. The mines that can be operated profitably at that price produce just the amount that consumers want to use at that price. There is neither upward nor downward pressure on price. This, accordingly, is called the *equilibrium point;* when it has been attained the market is said to be in equilibrium.

The equilibrium price of a commodity is the price at which the amounts demanded and supplied are equal. The equilibrium quantity is the level of demand and supply corresponding to that price.

... When the price is $4.50 a ton, each consumer can buy the amount that he wishes, and each producer can sell all the coal that he can produce profitably. At no other price is this true.

Since the equilibrium price and quantity are graphically shown by the point at which the supply and demand curves cross, the demand curve-supply curve diagrams neatly synopsize the "forces of supply and demand." The conditions of supply and demand determine the shapes and positions of the two curves, and the curves themselves determine whether there will be an upward or downward pressure on prices, or neither, and what the equilibrium price and quantity will be.

Exercises on Supply and Demand

You should now be ready to do work with supply and demand curves. Let's begin by making sure that you understand the meaning of the words "supply" and "demand." Try these questions:

T F

1. By "supply" we mean the quantity sold. — —
2. "Demand" means our willingness to buy the quantity supplied. — —
3. Supply and demand curves are graphical depictions of market behavior. — —
4. In order to know our demand for a commodity we have to know our potential purchases at different prices. — —
5. Supply and demand schedules show relationships between prices and quantities and also between quantities and prices. — —
6. A normal demand schedule shows that we are both willing and able to buy larger quantities as the price falls. — —
7. A normal supply schedule shows that we are both willing and able to supply larger quantities as the price falls. — —
8. An equilibrium price is the price at which the supply and demand schedules are equal. — —
9. As prices change, quantities offered and sought change. — —
10. Only at equilibrium prices will the quantity demanded equal that quantity supplied. — —

Answers: 1.F; 2.F; 3.T; 4.T;
5.T; 6.T; 7.F; 8.F; 9.T; 10.T.

If you got any of these wrong it was probably because you forgot:

1. Demand and supply are both schedules. They show relationships of prices and quantities (or quantities and prices) over a range of both prices and quantities.
2. At equilibrium, the *quantities* offered or bought are the same. But the *schedules* are not the same. "Supply and demand" are not equal: quantities demanded and supplied are equal.

FROM INDIVIDUAL TO COLLECTIVE DEMAND AND SUPPLY

We learn about supply and demand by studying the behavior of individuals. But usually we apply supply and demand in markets where numerous individuals concert their buying power or their supplies. Going from individual to market demand or supply curves is easy enough, but it is useful to go through the actual process of constructing a market curve, either for supply or demand. Let's use supply.

Below we give partial information on supply curves for three individual sellers *A, B,* and *C,* and partial information for total (market) supply for the three together.

Begin by filling in the blanks:

Price	Quantity Supplied			Market Supply
	A	B	C	
$1	2	4	6	—
2	—	5	7	15
3	6	—	10	23

(Note that each seller offers more as price rises from $1 to $3, but that their individual supply curves differ. There are many possible reasons: perhaps C is a lower-cost producer. Perhaps he is more eager to sell because he needs cash. It doesn't matter for our purposes.)

Now it will help if you graph the information above on the ruled graph below. Follow these steps:

1. Label the axes and insert numbers for price and quantity. (Remember price is vertical axis, quantity the horzontal one.)
2. Put a dot for each price-quantity relation for Seller A. Helpful hint: Because quantity is considered to be dependent on price, it is good to develop the habit of first looking at price, then at the related quantity. Thus go up the price axis to $1, and across the supply axis to two units, and put in your first dot.
3. Connect the three dots for *A,* to get *A's* supply curve.
4. Do the same for *B* and *C.*
5. Fill in the market supply curve.

GRAPHING SUPPLY AND DEMAND

Now let us work out an actual equilibrium price. We start with the data below, giving us market supply and demand schedules, for some commodity:

Price	Quantity Demanded	Quantity Supplied
$1	10	0
2	9	1
3	8	2
4	7	3
5	6	5
6	5	6
7	4	7
8	3	8
9	2	9
10	1	10

Before we graph, let's look at the schedule. At a price of $3 what is the quantity demanded? _____ Supplied? _____ Are they equal? Which is larger, the quantity demanded or supplied? Is this because the price is above or below an equilibrium price? To make sure you understand the interplay of the two schedules, ask yourself the same questions with respect to a price of $8. These questions are easy, but do them for the sake of practice.

Next: is there an equilibrium price? Look at the relationships of quantities demanded and supplied at $5, then at $6. At $5 which is larger, quantity demanded or supplied? at $6? This suggests that the equilibrium price must lie *between* a price of $5 and $6.

Now let's graph the schedules and see if this is so.

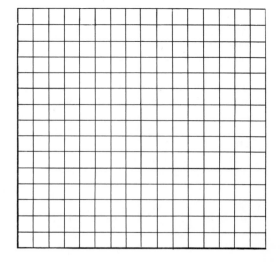

Follow these steps once again;

1. Label the axes and put in the appropriate price and quantity numbers.
2. Plot the demand points and draw a demand curve. Remember: go from the price axis out to the appropriate quantity.
3. Plot the supply points and draw a supply curve.
4. At which quantity (as far as you can tell from the graph) does the quantity supplied equal the quantity demanded?
5. At what price are quantities supplied and demanded equal?

THE MARKET PROCESS

All that is very easy. Now here is a more difficult but essential point to master. Take some price above the equilibrium price, say $8. What is the quantity supplied here?_____The quantity demanded?_____Will suppliers be able to sell the goods they have brought to market?

What will sellers do with the units they have brought and cannot sell at $8? Can you see from the graph that there are many such sellers *who are willing and able to sell their goods for much less than $8?* Can you understand how competition will begin to bring prices down?

Now look at another nonequilibrium price, say $3. What will be the volume of goods sellers are able and willing to offer at that price? _____ What will be the quantity of goods buyers are willing and able to buy? _____ *Can you see that*

many buyers are both willing and able to pay more than $3? What will unsatisfied buyers do to try to get goods? Can you see how competition will bring prices up toward equilibrium?

Now here is the last and most important point of all. Look at the equilibrium price of $5.50. Answer these questions thoughtfully:

1. Are there buyers who will be unsatisfied – that is, unable to enter the market – at this price?____ (yes/no)

   The answer – *and this is important* – is *yes*. All the buyers who can't afford to pay $5.50 are unsatisfied. But none of them is able to enter the market at a price above $5.50.

2. Are there any unsatisfied sellers at $5.50?____ (yes/no)

3. Are they able to enter the market at a price *below* $5.50? ____ (yes/no)

4. Can they affect the equilibrium price just because they are unsatisifed?_____(yes/no)

   The answers are: 1. yes; 2. yes; 3. no; 4. no.

We will come back to this rationing process of the market in Chapter 8. But already you should be able to see the central idea.

A market establishes equilibrium prices through competition among unsatisfied buyers and unsatisfied sellers. Above or below equilibrium prices, these unsatisfied buyers or sellers can enter the market and will move prices upward or downward toward equilibrium. At the equilibrium price, unsatisifed buyers and sellers can no longer enter the market. The price therefore no longer moves.

The Tools of Economic Analysis

5

Here are seven important items that belong in every economist's kit of tools. Some you will learn in a flash; others will take some thought and work. They are
1. The idea of ceteris paribus
2. An understanding of functional relationships
3. A definition of identities
4. A definition of tautologies

5. Schedules
6. Graphs
7. Equations.

All these tools will help you think clearly and systematically and will help you avoid fallacies. At the end of the exercise ask yourself if you understand these seven objectives.

In the first chapter of Section 2, we suggested that it was enough to get the idea, rather than to learn all the material. With the last chapter, getting the idea was not enough. You should now be very familiar with the concept of how a market works. In this chapter we introduce you to various tools of the trade that you should also master now. None of them is difficult, at least as we use them here: equations can, of course, be terribly difficult, but not the *meaning* of equations, which is all we ask you to know.

Here, then, is a review of things you should understand *thoroughly,* in order to have at your disposal the analytical techniques that we will use in later chapters.

CETERIS PARIBUS

Ceteris paribus means "other things being equal." It refers to the indispensable technique of holding everything constant, except the particular elements in which you are interested. There are complex statistical means of doing this, but for our purposes all we need is a little imagination.

Example

Sales of a local newspaper at 15¢ are 25,000 per day. Last year, at a price of 10¢ the paper sold 50,000 per day. Is this just a case of the quantity demanded decreasing as price increases?

The answer depends on what we have and what we have not taken into account. From our bare description we cannot tell whether: (1) there was now another newspaper competing with the first; (2) incomes had changed in the community; (3) the newspaper had changed its editorial policy; (4) people's views (tastes) had changed; or (5) some other part of the "ceteris" of the economic environment was not "paribus."

In real life, it must be clear, it is often impossible to know that a condition of ceteris paribus exists. *The main lesson of ceteris paribus is therefore to make us very cautious about declaring that a given change in one variable is wholly the effect of a change in another.*

Ceteris paribus is an absolutely essential assumption if we wish to trace the effect of one element on another, such as the effect of price on quantities demanded or supplied. But do not forget that it is exceedingly difficult, or even impossible, to be sure that ceteris paribus conditions exist in the real world when we go to test our theories with observation.

FUNCTIONAL RELATIONSHIPS

Economic analysis bases its analytical and especially its predictive powers on functional relationships. Assuming that we have *ceteris paribus,* we predict that a rise in prices will result in a fall in quantity demanded and a rise in quantity supplied because there are functional relationships between demand and supply behavior on the one hand, and prices on the other.

Functional relationships express cause-effect relationships. A more careful statement might be that they express relationships in which a change in one variable is regularly associated with a change in another.

QUIZ

Which *one* of the following is a functional relationship? Place a check beside it.

— 1. When you whistle, your dog comes.
— 2. When steel prices rise, auto prices rise.
— 3. When mortages become cheaper, building increases.
— 4. When you add more of one factor to given amounts of others, after a time you get diminishing returns.
— 5. Costs tend to decline as scale increases.
— 6. As population rises, so does demand.
— 7. As quantities supplied rise, prices fall.
— 8. As prices fall, quantities supplied rise.
— 9. If the quantity supplied rises, the quantity demanded falls.

The answer is that all are functional relations except the last. There is no causal relation between changes in the quantity supplied and that demanded. It is true that if prices rise, Q_s will rise and Q_d will fall. But here we have *two* functional relationships, Q_s and price, and Q_d and price. The mere fact that Q_s has risen does not affect Q_d: if grocers offer more bread at various prices, there is no causal link that will affect your ability and willingness to buy bread.

IDENTITIES

When we wish to express a functional relationship mathematically we say that "x is a function of y" or simply "$x = f(y)$." But when we want to define x as being the same thing as y, we say that "x is identical to y" or that $x \equiv y$." Note that $x \equiv y$ means that x and y will be identical for all values of x and y. Functional relationships imply that x and y will *not* always be equal, except at certain values for x and y.

Quiz

Here are some statements. Put a check next to the identities:

_ 1. Income equals receipts.

_ 2. Purchases equal sales.

_ 3. Quantity supplied equals quantity demanded.

_ 4. 2 + 2 equals 4.

_ 5. 2 + x equals 4.

_ 6. Total receipts equal the quantity sold times the price at which it is sold.

_ 7. Total purchases equal quantity bought times price paid.

_ 8. Total receipts equal total expenditures.

_ 9. Q_d equals some function of price.

_10. Q_d equals some function of income.

Answers: Numbers 1, 2, 4, 6, 7, 8, are all identities. This is because they are definitions: income is the same thing as receipts, and no matter how high or low your receipts, they will constitute your income. Purchases are always the same thing as sales, looked at from the buyer's point of view instead of the seller's. 2 + 2 is defined as 4. Receipts are *identical with* the quantity sold times the price; the same for purchases as the quantity bought times price. Total receipts must be *identical* with total expenditures because you cannot have a receipt unless someone has made an expenditure.

On the other hand, quantity supplied is not identical with quantity demanded, as a quick look at a supply and demand diagram shows: they are only equal at equilibrium prices. 2 + x = 4 is not an identity because it is only true when $x = 2$. Q_d is not an identity with price, but varies with prices, and so does Qd and income.

TAUTOLOGIES

Tautologies resemble functional relationships, but they are different in an important way. *A tautology is a statement that may or may not be false, but that cannot be* proven *false.* Consider the following statements:

1. The more money you have, the more you will spend.
2. The more money you have, the richer you are.
3. The more money you have, the more utilities you have.

Which is a functional relationship, which an identity, and which a tautology?

Obviously the first statement is a functional relationship. If S is spending and M is money, we are saying that $S = f(M)$. This describes the way we may (or may not) behave. The second is an identity. The meaning of the word "rich" is having money. It is a description that has nothing to do with behavior. If W is wealth and M is money, we can write $W \equiv M$. The third statement is a tautology. There is no way of measuring utilities. We assume that money brings "utilities," but there is no proof that is the case. We might ask a person who has made money if he or she is conscious of having more utilities than before, but even if the answer were negative, we could find some way of explaining that the utilities were there even if the rich person was not aware of them!

Because tautologies are inherently unprovable in empirical terms, what use are they? The answer is that they express feelings or beliefs that help us think systematically about problems, even though those feelings or beliefs cannot be tested. Take that enormously useful idea we call "cause and effect." If you have taken courses in philosophy, you will remember that there is no proof of a cause. We simply use the word to express an idea. Moreover we use it tautologically, by calling a cause whatever it is that produces an effect.

Words like "utility" play a similar role in economics. They escape detection, measurement, or "proof." But they are enormously valuable in giving us a means of thinking systematically about how people behave (maximizing utility), and from these unprovable assumptions we derive interesting and testable propositions about the real world.

SCHEDULES, GRAPHS, EQUATIONS

We have had considerable experience already with schedules and graphs, and we will not review these essential tools of the trade here. But a word or two about equations may be useful.

Equations are mathematical expressions that are the equivalent of sentences. They say something. Specifically, they say that there is a relationship between variables, such that changes in one variable (the independent variable) will produce changes in another variable (the dependent variable) in the manner that the equation describes.

All the equations you will use in introductory economics are linear equations, or equations that describe straight-line "curves." Of course, nonlinear equations exist — every time we have a real curve we have a nonlinear equation — but we will not encounter the equations for these curves in this text.

Most students of economics have had elementary algebra, so that straight-line equations, such as $Q_d = a - b(P)$, do not mystify them. Those who would like a quick review of some of the characteristics of straight-line equations, might like to look at the appropriate material in Section 7, Quantitative Methods, of the text.

FALLACIES

The last item in this review is the troublesome subject of fallacies, troublesome because it is not possible to give a sure guide for avoiding fallacies. Fallacies arise from imprecise thinking, and we are all prone to imprecise thought at one time or another.

The most important fallacy in economics is the fallacy of composition. This is a fallacy that arises when we take a statement that is perfectly true with regard to an individual case and apply it to a large group of individuals. The reason the fallacy exists is that when we study the individual case we ignore very small side effects that can be very large when we become interested in the outcome of cases involving large numbers of individuals. Suppose we argue that because one farmer can increase his planting and thereby augment his sales and his income, all farmers should be able to do the same. Here is a clear example of ignoring a small side effect — the impact of output on prices. This is perfectly all right, so long as we focus attention on *one* farmer. But it is not all right when we widen the focus of attention to *all* farmers. The effect on price of one farmer increasing his planting is negligible. But what will be the effect on price if all farmers increase their sales? Obviously, it will fall. Can we then predict confidently that incomes will be higher for all? Not if prices fall faster than output rises. Thus what is good for one may not necessarily be good for all.

Fallacies of composition often arise when we carelessly reason or argue by analogy. We will find many examples of such fallacies of composition in both micro and macro analysis. Learn the principle now so that you will be quick to recognize it when it comes up later. Which of these are examples of this fallacy?

1. What is good for one is necessarily good for all.
2. Sound economic policy for a family is necessarily sound economic policy for all families.
3. If one town can gain business by cutting taxes, all can gain business by doing likewise.
4. Paying low wages makes money for one business, and therefore paying low wages should make money for all businesses.

Answers: *All* are examples of the fallacy of composition. Remember, however, that not all examples of composition are fallacies. If honesty is the best policy for one, it is also the best policy for all. Why? Because there are no hidden individual side effects in honest dealings that can become massed central effects when we aggregate all dealings.

Can you classify the following?

	Good for the individual, not for society	Good for the individual and for society
Using a tax loophole	——	——
Health	——	——
Making money	——	——
Being efficient	——	——

It's easy to decide about the tax loophole and health. Are there clear-cut answers about making money and being efficient? Really not. It rather depends on *how* we make money and what impact our efficiency has on others. The fact that many activities are ambiguous, with regard to their side effects, is one reason why the fallacy of composition is so commonly encountered.

Some Basic Problems

6

LEARNING OBJECTIVES

This is really a chapter to make you think *critically* about things you have already learned. It points out three main problems.
1. How secure is our knowledge of economic facts?

2. How deceptive are some economic definitions?
3. What are the problems that we face in making economics relevant to the real world?

This chapter does not lend itself to review so much as to reflection. Thus we have appended a reading that highlights some of the difficulties of economics and advises against the dangers of swallowing it whole. Nevertheless, there are a few matters that could be profitably stressed. Let us attend to them first.

DATA

No need to review the problem. Here is a case in point: one would think that the easiest datum to collect would be something you could easily measure, such as land area or people. What then is the area of the United States today, and what

was it in 1950? Questions: (1) How do you count
Alaska and Hawaii in 1950, before they became
states? (2) Do you include the areas of U.S.
territories such as the Virgin Islands, the Canal
Zone, Guam, and so on? (3) What do you do
about Puerto Rico? (4) How do you estimate
erosion? (5) Do you include off-shore territory as
part of the United States? If not, how do we
justify keeping other nation's ships out of these
waters?

Population? What about U.S. citizens residing
abroad? What about U.S. citizens traveling
abroad when the census was taken? Ships' crews
at sea? Visitors from other countries present in
the United States during a census? Permanent
residents in the United States who are not
citizens?

AGGREGATION

Wheat seems like a nice homogeneous commodity. In fact there are two varieties of wheat
that sell at very different prices. To get even
more specific, here is the description of what
"iron ore" means to a trader who wants a
particular kind of ore delivered on his contract:

. . . $4.60 per gross long ton of 2,240 pounds
of Mesaba Bessemer ore containing exactly 51.5
percent of iron and 0.045 percent of phosphorus,
with specified premiums for ore with a higher
iron content or a lower phosphorus content and
with specified discounts for ore with a lower iron
content or a higher phosphorus content; samples
of be drawn and analyzed on a dry basis by a
specified chemist at Cleveland, the cost being
divided equally between seller and buyer. . . .

These two examples should convince you
that economics is a discipline where scrupulous
care must be exercised in gathering and interpreting data. This is not a matter that can be
taught in detail. Everyone has to discover the
problems for himself by making a few egregious
statistical mistakes.

The other problems discussed in Chapter
6 – problems such as the predictive reliability of
economics or its relation to value judgments –
cannot be taught very easily by means of
problems or drills. It might help, however, to
read the following short essay, written as a
Foreword for a collection of articles called *Is
Economics Relevant?* As you will see, it covers
many questions raised by the text and may give
you some added insight into the problems of
economic analysis.

IS ECONOMICS RELEVANT?

Robert L. Heilbroner

There is a word that makes professors of
economics wince these days. The word is *relevance.* There was a time, not so many years ago,
when I could teach an introductory class the

From *Is Economics Relevant?*, by Robert L. Heilbroner and Arthur Ford, eds. (Pacific Palisades, Cal.:
Goodyear Publishing Company, 1971), pp. ix–xix.

mysteries of diminishing marginal utility, explaining why the man in the Sahara desert would
not be willing to pay as much for the third pint
of water as for the second, confident that when
the hands went up it would be because someone
wasn't convinced that he shouldn't pay more,
because his *total* utility was greater. Now when
the hands go up, I know what the question is

going to be: "That's clear enough, Professor, but we don't see how it's relevant."

Is it relevant? It is certainly easy enough to understand why it does not seem so. What has diminishing marginal utility to do with giant corporations, the military-industrial complex, inflation, ghetto life? Isn't time spent on the study of marginal utility simply time diverted from the consideration of real issues, such as these? Worse, isn't the very act of taking seriously a figment like "diminishing marginal utility" apt to cultivate an ivory-tower frame of mind that will no longer wish to come to grips with the brute problems of the real world?

I think these are the kinds of misgivings that first come to the surface when economics students begin to ask questions about the discipline they are learning, rather than merely swallowing it down like so much medicine. Yet I do not think that these initial objections count for very much. As a rule, the aspect of economics that upsets those who begin to study it is its abstractness, its seeming removal from life, but any instructor worth his salt can reassure his students that this abstract quality is a strength and not a weakness if we are to study large-scale questions, and that the "unreality" of many economic conceptions conceals a sharp cutting edge.

Thus, for example, the rationale for progressive taxation hinges on nothing less than the belief that successive dollars of income, like successive pints of water in the Sahara, yield ever smaller increments of enjoyment to its recipients. In the same way, an ivory-tower idea such as pure competition, which every first-year student regards as utterly irrelevant, suddenly turns up as the indispensable starting point for an understanding of Marx's model of capitalism! . . .

Indeed, by the time an overly zealous instructor is through, the danger is that the shoe will be on the other foot, and that the class will have been persuaded that the charge of "irrelevance" is nothing but the ill-considered objections of

those who have not yet mastered the subject. But if he proceeds this far, it is now the instructor who risks becoming irrelevant. For if the initial objections to the abstractions of economics tend to be wide of the mark, this is very far from saying that the feelings of unease aroused by the study of economics have no validity. What the freshman student wants from economics – and hopefully what he will continue to want when he has become an instructor – is a heightened ability to understand, and if possible to control, important aspects of the social system in which he lives. Long after he has accepted the need for the abstract character of economic thought, the student (and his instructor, too) may still feel that economics ignores the most pressing issues of society, or that it gives unsatisfactory answers to them. At this point, the charge of "irrelevance" is no longer an objection that can be easily overcome, but a serious challenge to the validity of the discipline itself.

Is economics a penetrative and reliable guide to the nature of society? Of course it can be. But in this essay I shall concentrate on the other side of the coin: on why economics frequently does not ask the kinds of questions that would most clearly illumine society, or why it gets unsatisfactory answers to some of the questions it does ask, or why it often fails to offer us the historic or philosophic guidance we seek from it.

THE IRRELEVANCE OF ECONOMISTS

Let me begin this analysis of the failures of economics by taking up a touchy issue, but one that cannot be sidestepped. This is the fact that the "irrelevance" that most disturbs many students is the unwillingness of academic economists to ask disturbing or unpleasant questions with regard to the social order, and in particular to avoid social criticism that is radical in intent. Economics thus appears to many students not as a genuinely objective science that sheds its illumination on the good and bad aspects of

society alike, but as a kind of high-level apol-
ogetics that tends to illumine only those issues
for which economics has an "answer," and to
overlook those for which it has none.

I think one should admit that, on the whole,
this criticism is fairly taken. Many textbooks are
bland in tone and pussyfoot around thorny
questions. Moreover, students who have gone
beyond the textbooks into the professional
journals know that this blandness is by no means
confined to the delicate atmosphere of the
classroom, but extends into the dialogue that the
profession holds with itself. With exceptions to
which we will return, it is simply a fact that most
of the things that economists write about are
not matters of burning social importance, and
that the prevailing tone in which they do write
about social questions tends to be one of a
sympathetic conservatism rather than of indignant radicalism.

Why are most economists so conservative in
their outlook? Professor Stigler, one of the
best-known exponents of the conservative economic philosophy, has contended that it is the
result of the training that economists undergo, a
training that disabuses them of heady notions
with respect to the changes that socialism (or
some other form of institutional rearrangement)
could bring and that persuades them of the
propriety of the market system.

It is probably true that a study of economics
does tend to make one wary of sweeping
statements and unconsidered jumps, as does the
study of almost anything; but I am not wholly
convinced by Stigler's argument that conservatism is somehow more *intelligent* than radicalism.
I would rather raise another, less elegant, possibility as to why economists are predominantly
conservative in their outlooks. This is because
economists tend to be located in the upper
echelons of the pyramid of incomes and thus
tend to share, consciously or otherwise, the
conserving attitude that is characteristic of top
echelons in all societies. I do not mean that

economists are the spineless servants of the very
rich. But in 1967 the average income of associate
professors of economics (the middle group of
academic rankings) was $14,000 and the average
income of a "superior" full professor was
$21,000. That was sufficient to place associate
professors in the top 10 percent of income
receivers in the country, and superior full professors in the top 2 percent. I do not see why it
should be doubted that economists, like all
groups, take on the values and standards of the
socioeconomic milieu in which they live.

Yet, what is generally true of the group as a
whole is certainly not true of each and every
member of it. If, as both Professor Stigler and I
believe, the economics profession is marked by a
general conservatism of views, there are still
economists enough, including some very eminent
ones, who do not share the prevailing attitude.
Hence, it is not the discipline of economics,
diminishing marginal utility and all, that can be
held responsible for its lack of relevance, if we
mean by this its frequently observed failure to
direct its attention to important social issues.
The fault lies rather with the reluctance of many
of its practitioners to use their economic skills
for purposes that may be intellectually uncomfortable, or politically risky, or simply out-of-
step with their colleagues. To that extent, the
irrelevance of which students complain lies not
within the discipline of economics but within
that of sociology, and the cure for the problem
lies in the determination of these students to put
their own skills to good use when they take the
places of their former instructors.

THE LIMITATIONS OF ECONOMICS

But there is a second, and perhaps deeper,
meaning to the charge that economics is "irrelevant." It is that the results produced by the
application of conventional economics too often
have no usefulness — that the answers that economics gives to the problems to which it does

address itself are frequently untrustworthy as guides to social policy.

This is a charge that, as we shall shortly see, contains what I believe to be an important core of truth. Yet, before we examine the limits beyond which economic reasoning cannot be relied upon, it is important to establish the things that economics can do and the extent to which it can be put to practical use.

The dividing line, as I see it, that separates what economics can do from what it cannot, lies between the usefulness of economics in explaining the structural characteristics of a market economy, and its relative uselessness in predicting how a market economy will behave in a given instance. To put it differently, economics is extremely relevant when we want to know how the economy is constructed, so that we can trace the numerous possible connections between one part and another; but usually "irrelevant" (by which I mean unreliable) if we want to know exactly which of these connections will be triggered off by a particular economic stimulus.

We shall consider in a moment the reasons for this predictive failing of economics. But at this juncture, while we are still concerned with the positive, relevant aspects of conventional economic thought, it is important to emphasize the enormous contribution that the structural insights of economics offer us. Perhaps only someone who can remember the intellectual confusion of the Great Depression, or the sense of heretical shock that greeted President Kennedy's proposal to spur economic growth by deliberately incurring a federal budgetary deficit, can fully appreciate the gain that has been won by the gradual clarification of the macrostructure of the economy.

Microeconomics is not far behind, moreover, in claiming for itself a similar relevance. As with macroeconomics, microeconomics is also a poor guide for prediction. But without its general structural concepts – its ideas of demand and supply, of short and long run, of elasticity and

inelasticity, of marginal and average costs and revenues and products – the operations of a market system would be virtually impossible to conceive, much less to control. Since all economic systems, socialism included, depend to some extent on the operation of a market mechanism, the linkages revealed by microeconomic analysis are indispensable for the understanding of all modern industrial systems. Whether it is to determine the best way to alleviate poverty, or to curb pollution, or to distribute scarce resources, or to judge the incidence of a tax, or to gauge the effects of raising the price in a nationalized industry, it is to the apparatus of microeconomics with its criss-crossed lines and its bowl-shaped curves, that we must turn if we are to think clearly about the consequences of our actions.

There are, however, very important limits on the extent of the reasoning power of economics, and it is to these limits that I will now turn.

I have already indicated one of the limits – the poor capabilities of economics as a predictive science. One reason for this, with which we are all familiar, is the inability of the discipline to handle more than a limited number of variables at one time. Economics is forced to approach the complexity of real-life situations exactly as we do in the classroom, on a *ceteris paribus* – other things being equal – basis. But the one-thing-at-a-time approach often breaks down hopelessly when we try to apply it to the world. Economics calculates its predictions as if the disturbance it studies were the only stone dropped in a pond; whereas in fact, of course, the surface of the pond is covered with the expanding concentric waves of a hundred disturbances. It is hardly surprising that the patterns of the disturbance in which we are interested become confused with or indistinguishable from those of other disturbances, and that our predictions lose their sharpness accordingly.

There is, however, a deeper reason for the unreliability of economic prediction than this.

It is that the entire predictive capability of macro and micro-theory rests on a highly simplified set of assumptions with regard to economic activity itself. These assumptions tell us that human beings constantly try to maximize their receipts (or to minimize their expenditures) as the paramount "behavior directives" in the course of their daily lives. To the extent that firms or factors or consumers do not obey these assumptions – that is, to the extent that they do not constantly strive to move to the frontiers of their production possibilities or their indifference maps – economics loses virtually all of its ability to predict the effects of stimuli on the economic system. In that case, for example, we can no longer state with certainty that a rise in price will result in a fall in the quantity demanded and an increase in the quantity supplied, for both of these classical behavior patterns are nothing but maximization in action.

Do we actually maximize? The concept itself is full of ambiguities. Maximize what, over what period of time? If we define maximization to mean "psychic income" or "satisfactions," then the concept loses its predictive power because *any* course of action may be said to lead to maximum "well-being," since we have no objective measure of whether that well-being is really maximized or not. On the other hand, if we define maximization to mean something specific, such as cash income, then we encounter a problem with regard to predictions over any period of time but the shortest run. A giant corporation, consciously trying to maximize its income over a period of ten years, may rationally decide to undertake any number of actions – raising prices, lowering them, increasing or decreasing its current investment – depending on how it interprets the future. In this case, maximization may accurately enough describe the state of mind of the management, but it is of little use in foretelling exactly what management will do.

It is because of these difficulties that economics is much better at describing the *consequences* of various paths that corporations or

consumers may follow, than in predicting exactly which they will in fact elect to take. But there is a still more troublesome limit to its power of prediction. For even if we could define maximization in such a clear-cut way that we knew precisely what course of action it would enjoin, economic theory still finds itself stymied before the awkward fact that maximization can lead to different – indeed, contradictory – behavior in different expectational settings.

Ordinarily, as we have just said, a factor or a firm will try to maximize its income by selling more of a commodity when its price goes up and less when its price goes down. But what if the rise in price leads us to believe that prices will continue to rise in the future? In that case, the road to maximization lies in a different direction, namely in holding back on our offerings today so that they can be sold at a better price tomorrow, or in buying more today before the price goes up further. In a word, when expectations tell us that an observed change in price will continue in the same direction, then the rational pursuit of maximum income bids us to behave in exactly the contrary fashion to that which we do "normally."

If this abnormal kind of economic behavior were limited to occasional periods of extreme crisis, we might relegate it to a footnote. But unfortunately, precisely this kind of behavior is all too normal, whenever the economy is moving from one prevailing psychology, whether boom or bust, to another. Then, typically, markets become unstable just because expectations change, and the predictive capabilities of economics diminish accordingly. That is why even the most sophisticated econometric models of the economy do well only as long as the basic direction of economic movement remains the same, but fail badly in telling us the one thing we want to know; that is, when that basic direction itself will change.

Thus, one endemic shortcoming of economic reasoning is its inability to alert us to the timing of economic events. But there is a second quite different limitation to economic theory that interferes with its predictive capability from another angle. It is that economic reasoning is unable to connect changes in the economic variables with changes in the political and social spheres of social activity. As a result, economics makes its predictions as if the stimuli and constraints of the market were the only forces impinging on the activities of men, ignoring entirely the social and political and psychological consequences of economic action. To put the matter differently, conventional economics deals with the economy as if it were only a mechanism for allocating goods and services, and overlooks the fact that the economy is also a mechanism for allocating privilege and power.

As a result, economic predictions often fail because they do not anticipate the "feedbacks" of noneconomic activity. Typically, for instance, economic theory will project a growth path by calculating the effects of labor and capital inputs, and so on, in this way arriving at a course of economic output in the future. But the trouble with these projections is that economic theory does not take into account the noneconomic changes that the growth process itself may initiate. Economics does not, for example, connect the trajectory of growth with social frictions to which the growth process may give rise, or with political resistances that may be encountered if growth brings a shift in income as between regions or social groups. Nor does it ask whether a growing level of income may alter our life-styles or our working habits in such a way as to change our labor inputs. In a word, economic theory gives us a picture of change from which the political or sociological elements have been rigorously excluded, although it is just these factors that are often all-important in determining the ultimate results of economic change itself.

This restricted scope of economic vision serves to limit the relevance of economic theorizing even more severely than its inability to handle the vagaries of economic behavior. Indeed, here

is where the freshman's unease about the "abstractness" of economics comes home with a vengeance. But at this level of analysis the student's objections are not so easily brushed aside. No one denies that abstraction is an essential precondition for a social science if it is to reduce the complexity of the real world to manageable proportions. But we can now see that the sharper and clearer the abstract model we create, the less "interdisciplinary" that model tends to be. Thus we learn how to handle the idea of a "firm," but only by blotting out the political and sociological attributes of real corporations; or we invent the very convenient fiction of a "factor of production," but only at the cost of losing sight of the existence of individuals who are also voters and members of social classes.

The fault, however, is not just that of a failure of nerve on the part of economists. *The essential problem is that we do not know the nature of these subtle linkages between the economic mechanism and the political and social spheres of activity.* What we lack, in a word, is a unifying theory of social change in which the distinctions of "economics" and "sociology" and "political science" would yield to a new "holistic" science of society. The discovery of such a new integrating model or paradigm would be the greatest triumph of social science in our time, but at the moment no such paradigm exists. As a result, we must admit to a profound limitation to economic analysis for which no solution is now in sight.

THE RELEVANCE OF ECONOMIC PHILOSOPHY

These considerations bring us to the last meaning that we can attach to the word *relevance* — the possibility of using economics as a guide for social philosophy, in the sense of helping us to understand the direction in which our social system is headed, or still more important, the direction in which it should head.

In the light of the severe limitations that we have put upon the predictive power of economics, can we really look to economics as a reliable guide for the future? The answer is necessarily disconcerting. We cannot. At best, an economist who postulates a rationale for the historic setting of our time or who projects the shape of society into the future is engaged in no more than a kind of controlled speculation. ... [T] hese speculations can be both eloquent and plausible.... But it would be wrong to pretend that even at their most convincing such speculations attain the status of genuine scientific effort, at least in the meaning that economics usually arrogates to that word.

This is an important matter to which we shall revert at the very conclusion of this essay. But meanwhile, for students who have read the works of Smith, Ricardo, Mill, or Marx, this must seem like a serious retreat for economics. For surely the great classical writers did not regard their large-scale economic philosophies as mere "controlled speculations." In their hands economics seemed capable of presenting a perspective on the present and the future in full accord with the scientific canons of their day. Why, then, were they able to create economic philosophies of greater power than we can?

From the vantage point of contemporary history, we can discern two attributes of classical economic thought from which this extraordinary self-assurance emanates. One of these, which is frequently overlooked, is the strong feeling of social destination that infuses all the classical writers. Smith, Ricardo, Malthus, Mill, and above all Marx, firmly believed that they knew the direction in which society was heading, and moreover they strongly approved of that destination as being in the best interests of mankind. Thus, economics became for them not alone an objective explanation of the "laws of motion" of their respective economic societies, but also an instrument to assist the evolution of those societies in the various directions in which they wished them to hurry.

A second common attribute of their thought was their frank willingness to discuss their societies from the point of view of class composition and conflict. In place of the neutral "factors of production" with which modern theory deals, the classical writers spoke openly of a contest of landlords, workers, and capitalists, so that their theories of distribution (which were intimately intertwined with their theories of growth) were also guides to major political and social tensions within their societies. And whereas the outcome of the struggle among the classes was differently diagnosed by each writer, according to his differing assessments and assumptions regarding resources, demographic behavior, technology, and the psychology of the social classes, in every instance his pursuit of the logic of economic interaction led him directly to an associated drama of political and social change.

In our own day, both these underlying premises of classical reasoning have lost much of their erstwhile force. The blows of 20th-century history, devastating for the prospects of liberal capitalism and orthodox socialism alike, have largely obscured the vista of welcome historic destination that unified and fortified so much of classical thought. Today the great majority of social scientists, economists included, stand before the realities of 20th-century technology, bureaucracy, nationalism, and militarism with a sense of genuine perplexity, or even despair, that blurs the vision of even the boldest of them.

Then, too, the increased complexity and growing modest affluence of Western society have equally undermined the second of the premises of classical analysis — that the dynamics of social change could be directly predicted from the clash of social classes. In our day, the once decisive clash of classes has given way to the cohesion of a "mass society" in which the sources of social conflict take on wholly new forms, such as the conflict between generations. As a result, even the most fully worked-out philosophy of historic change and social evolution — the imposing structure of Marxism — finds itself in need of rethinking its traditional views in the light of present-day realities.

Against these vast historic changes, it is hardly surprising that economics has lost the self-assurance of a former age. The problem of constructing a plausible model of social change is much more difficult in our day than in a simpler age, for all the reasons we have disucssed in the previous section as well as in this one. Yet it is one thing to take cognizance of the difficulties of a task, and another to abandon it. Rarely has there been a period of history as much in need of illumination as our own, and however partial or uncertain, the controlled speculations of economic thought, meshed as best they can be with political and sociological analysis, still constitute the best response that we can make to our human situation.

Perhaps in the end, the answer to this impasse of the social sciences lies in a new appraisal of the relevance of *science* itself. When we said before that economics could offer no foresight that could be given the name "scientific," we may have inadvertently opened the direction in which to seek the new paradigm of social unity that we need. The word "scientific," as we commonly use it, refers today to a rigorous model of a mathematical kind from which all considerations of social values have been carefully excluded. In the great question of human destination, however, values must surely occupy a central place: the future is meaningful because it offers us choice. Perhaps, then, the very aim of economic philosophy as a "scientific" guide to the future must give way to economic philosophy as a consciously value-laden guide — a guide that uses the enormous powers of scientific analysis, not to predict the future, but to assist society in reaching the goals that it has elected to pursue. In such a basic reorientation of the discipline, economics would become the handmaiden of politics, advising us of the institutional and behavioral and technical conditions necessary to achieve a destination that society has chosen through its political processes. Such a far-reaching suggestion takes us well beyond the confines of this essay, although not, I am glad to say, beyond the confines of what may ultimately be most relevant for economic thought.

TEST ON FUNDAMENTAL CONCEPTS
(Chapters 3, 4, 5, 6)

— 1. The economic behavior of man is described as being

    a. maximizing.

    b. subject to diminishing marginal utility.

    c. rational.

    d. competitive.

    e. all the above.

    f. all above except b.

— 2. The laws of nature are called

    a. diminishing returns

    b. constraints

    c. environmental conditions

    d. production possibility curves

— 3. Economic activity can be described as

    a maximizing subject to constraints

    b. maximizing subject to competition

    c. maximizing without constraints

    d. maximizing rationally

— 4. Demand means

    a. the amount we buy

    b. the amount we are willing to buy

    c. the relation between price and quantity bought

    d. a schedule of prices

— 5. Supply means

    a. the amount we are willing and able to sell at different prices

    b. the amount we actually sell at equilibrium prices

    c. the amount we seek to sell at market prices

    d. the schedule of sales prices

_ 6. At an equilibrium price

    a. market demand equals supply.

    b. market sales equal purchases.

    c. supply and demand balance.

    d. quantities supplied and demanded are equal

_ 7. At prices above equilibrium

    a. the market clears.

    b. there are more unsatisfied sellers than buyers.

    c. there are more unsatisfied buyers than sellers.

    d. both buyers and sellers are equally unsatisfied.

_ 8. Prices move toward equilibrium because

    a. competition pushes them there.

    b. supply and demand push them there.

    c. the market fails to clear.

    d. the laws of production push them there.

_ 9. When prices rise

    a. buyers normally buy less.

    b. the quantity supplied normally falls.

    c. the demand curve slopes upward.

    d. all the above.

    e. all but b.

_10. Prices are signals because

    a. competition makes them so.

    b. they tell buyers and sellers how to maximize.

    c. they lead to equilibrium.

    d. they fluctuate.

_11. Functional relationships

    a. relates changes in one variable to another.

    b. are the same as identities.

    c. always involve two independent variables.

    d. cannot be expressed in equations.

_12. "Purchases equal sales" is an example of a(n)

    a. tautology.

    b. equation.

    c. identity.

    d. functional relationship.

_13. A tautology is

    a. a meaningless statement.

b. a statement that cannot be proven.

c. a statement that can be shown to be false.

d. an identity.

_14. This diagram could be

    a. a demand curve.

    b. a supply curve.

    c. either of the above.

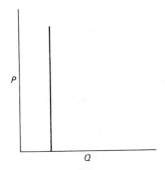

_15. Identities are

    a. always tautologies.

    b. sometimes useful.

    c. functional equations.

    d. all the above.

_16. The following diagram shows

    a. supply greater than demand.

    b. quantities supplied greater than quantities demanded.

    c. that purchases are greater than sales.

    d. an equilibrium position.

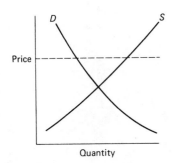

_17. Economic prediction depends on
   a. stable behavior patterns.
   b. supply equal to demand.
   c. markets clearing.
   d. equilibrium prices.
_18. Using economic theory to gain a desired end is called using it
   a. positively.
   b. predictively.
   c. normatively.
   d. functionally.
_19. Expectations are important in economics because
   a. they make people act irrationally.
   b. they change rational behavior.
   c. they lessen maximization.
   d. they prevent maximization.
_20. When supply equals demand it means
   a. that we can't tell what prices will be.
   b. that prices are at equilibrium.
   c. that sellers and buyers are equally willing and able to buy at equilibrium.
   d. that competition has cleared the market.

MICROECONOMICS: ANATOMY OF A MARKET SYSTEM

A BEFORE-AND-AFTER TEST
ON MICROECONOMICS

Here is a short true-false test that you might enjoy taking *before* you've studied any microeconomics. There are no trick questions, no need to possess a special vocabulary or to have mastered complicated analyses. These questions just pose problems that you will meet in everyday life, and give you a chance to see how well you can answer them before you've studied economics.

That's the before part. On page 156 in this guide you will find the same test, to be taken *after* you have completed the course. So when you've finished, enter your score on the bottom of page 157.

Put a check under T (True), F (False), or ? (Don't Know).

T F ?

1. Suppose that a necessity, like medicine, sells for $10 a bottle and that a luxury, such as perfume, also sells for $10 a bottle. If the prices of both commodities are cut by 10 percent, we would expect the sales of the necessary good – the medicine – to grow much faster than the luxury.

— — —

2. If a price ceiling is put on a desired commodity, such as apartment rentals, a shortage usually results.

— — —

3. One important difference between monopolistic and competitive firms is that monopolies try to make as much money as they can, whereas competitive firms do not strive after maximum profits.

— — —

4. The law of supply and demand means that in the end high prices tend to come down, and low prices tend to go up.

— — —

5. The advantage of a market is that it avoids allocating goods because it allows people to buy and sell freely.

— — —

6. Because a sales tax is levied on retail goods, it is entirely borne by the retail buyers.

— — —

7. Taxes on effluents, such as smoke, are a poor way to curb pollution (because the polluter can go on making smoke even if he has to pay a tax).

— — —

8. If we have a choice of buying two different goods with a limited budget, we will always make the most rational choice if we buy the good whose price is lower.

— — —

9. Antitrust laws aim to discourage monopolies. One main reason they are difficult to administer is because it is hard to define a monopoly.

— — —

10. What we mean by "wage discrimination" is that women are paid less than men because their productivity is less.

— — —

11. An entrepreneur in a competitive firm has no say over the prices he pays or the prices he charges.

— — —

12. If the price of a commodity, such as margarine, goes up, it is likely that the price of a similar commodity, such as butter, will also go up.

— — —

13. Industries with a few large sellers, such as the auto industry, are usually marked with severe price competition.

— — —

14. If one farmer can increase his receipts by cutting his price, it stands to reason that all farmers can do the same.

— — —

15. The distribution of income is more equal than the distribution of wealth.

— — —

16. An economist would claim that profit-making is a way of minimizing waste.

— — —

17 The prices of most goods reflect the intensity of demand for them.

— — —

18. When supply and demand have worked themselves out, the resulting price can be described as a just or fair price.

— — —

19. If a commodity is not abundantly found in nature, it tends to sell at a high price.

— — —

20. One of the benefits of the market system is that it is an administratively convenient rationing mechanism.

— — —

Score yourself by subtracting five points for each mistake and three points for each "Don't know." Don't forget to enter your score on the bottom line on page 157, after "Score Before."

Answers:

1. F	8. F	15. T
2. T	9. T	16. T
3. F	10. F	17. F
4. F	11. T	18. F
5. F	12. T	19. F
6. F	13. F	20. T
7. F	14. F	

Introduction to the Microeconomy

7

LEARNING OBJECTIVES

This is a short and simple chapter. Two main ideas should be mastered in it:
1. A clear definition of microeconomics,

2. A precise understanding of the circular flow.

With this short chapter we start our study of microeconomics, a study that will take us through Chapter 18. In these introductory pages there are only two things to learn, both simple, both important.

The first is the meaning of microeconomics. *Microeconomics is an approach to economic analysis that concentrates on the actions of firms and households (or individuals).* It is more concerned with the composition and distribution of output than with its total. Microeconomics asks: what? and to whom? Macroeconomics asks: how much altogether?

The second important idea in this chapter is *the circular flow.* This gives us a picture of market society as a system — of how thousands or hundreds of thousands of markets are linked together into a unified mechanism. It is really important to understand this circular flow; a good way to be sure that you do understand it is to fill in the following:

1. Notice that the household is divided in two by a dotted line. This is because the household has two economic functions. What are they? Indicate them in the two sections of the square.

2. In one of its functions the household is active in the goods market. Here it is the active force behind the —————— (demand/supply) curve. Draw an arrow that connects the appropriate half of the household square to

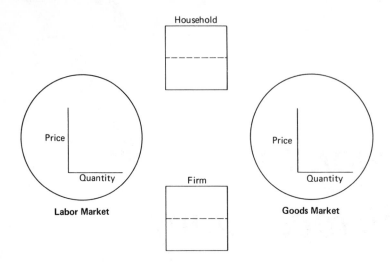

the goods market, and draw in the _____ (demand/supply) curve to which it gives rise.

3. The household in its second function is also active in the second great market – the market for factors of production. Here, it is a _____ (seller/buyer) of its own services. With an arrow connect the appropriate half of the household square to the factor market and draw in the _____ (supply/demand) curve to which it gives rise.

4. The firm also has two functions. Indicate these in their respective places.

5. The firm is also active in each market. In the goods market it is the force behind the_____ curve; in the factor market behind the _____ curve. Draw in the appropriate arrows, from the correct portions of the firm's box.

Now check your finished diagram with page 84 in the text. If yours is not correct, do it again. You should be able to do this perfectly, and you should explain to yourself how the two institutions and two markets form one unified system.

Prices and Allocation

This chapter is one of the most important among those on the first main subject in microeconomics, the investigation of how markets work. It brings us to the subject of *rationing*, distributing scarce outputs among claimants. First we are going to consider how markets ration goods, then how prices enable households to ration their own purchasing power so as to maximize their well being.

MARKETS AND RATIONING

The schedules on the next page show the quantities of goods that will be demanded and supplied at differing prices. Fill in column 4 and then plot columns 2 and 3 on the graph. The most important thing to notice is this: at every price except the equilibrium price there is an excess of quantities demanded over quantities supplied, or vice versa.

PRICES AND RATIONING OF SUPPLY

Now let us suppose that the price is $80. The quantity demanded is _____. The quantity supplied is _____. The excess of _____ (supply/demand) over _____ (supply/demand) is _____.

1	2	3	4
			Excess of Quantities Demanded over Quantities Supplied (+) or of Quantities Supplied over
Price	Quantities Demanded	Quantities Supplied	Quantities Demanded (–)
$100	0	100	–100
90	5	80	– 75
80	10	50	
70	20	20	
60	50	5	
50	100	0	+100

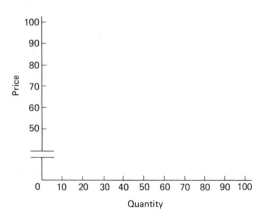

You can determine the answers either from the schedule or the graph. At $80, 50 units are offered, 10 are bid for. There is an excess of supply (more accurately of *quantities supplied)* of 40 units.

Question: who among the various sellers will be able to sell the 10 units for which there is a demand? Answer: *if there were no market, we could not tell.* Perhaps the sellers with the most political influence. Perhaps those who were just lucky. (You can't answer that the 10 lucky ones

would be those who provided something extra, such as the best service, because in that case the sellers wouldn't be offering *exactly* the same commodity!)

But now suppose there is a market. At a price of $80 there will be a great many sellers whose reservation prices are less than $80. A reservation price is the lowest price at which a seller is willing and able to enter the market. On the graph below, draw a ring around the portion of the supply curve in which sellers' reservation prices are below market prices. Draw a second ring around the sellers whose reservation prices are above the market price. At the market price which group is rationed out of business?

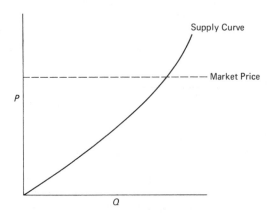

DEMAND RATIONING

Now back to our original supply and demand diagram. Suppose the market price was $60. Quantities supplied at that price are _____ ; quantities demanded _____. There is an excess of _____ (demand/supply) of _____ units.

No doubt your answer shows that there is an excess of quantity demanded of 45 units: 50 units demanded, but only 5 supplied. Question: who, among the buyers, will be allowed to acquire these 5 units? Once again, suppose there were no market, no competition. Suppose the commodity in question is rental apartments. The line of applicants will be much longer than the small group who finally sign leases. Who gets the 5 apartments; those at the head of the line? those who can prove their need? those who are related to the renters?

Now we once again activate the market. There are many demanders whose reservation prices are much higher than the going market price of $60. Don't forget: a demander's reservation price is the highest price he is willing and able to pay. In the graph below, indicate with two rings those whose reservation prices are *above* the market price.

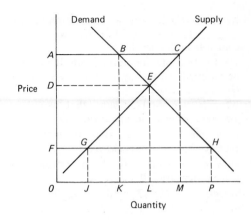

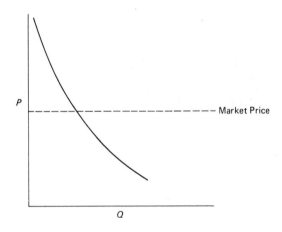

Put another ring around the group whose reservation price is below the market price. These demanders will be rationed out of the market at that price. Draw in a lower market price and notice how the number rationed out changes: larger or smaller? How about at a higher price?

RATIONING AT EQUILIBRIUM PRICES

Now go to the diagram below, where for simplicity's sake we omit numbers. Fill in the following blanks:

1. The equilibrium quantity is _____ .
2. At the equilibrium price, buyers and sellers to the _____ (right/left) of quantity *OL* are rationed out of the market.
3. At price *OA*, quantity supplied is _____ .
4. At price *OA*, quantity demanded is _____ .
5. At price *OA* there is an excess _____ (supply/demand) equal to _____ .
6. At price *OF*, quantity demanded is _____ .
7. At price *OF* quantity supplied is _____ .
8. At price *OF* there is a _____ (surplus/ shortage) of _____ .
9. Price *OA* is _____ (above/below) the reservation prices of most sellers located to the right of point *J*.
10. Price *OA* is _____ (above/below) the reservation prices of most buyers located to the right of point *J*.
11. At the equilibrium price *OD* there _____ (are/are not) unsatisfied buyers.
12. If there are any, they are located to the _____ (right/left) of point *L*.
13. At the equilibrium price there _____ (are/are not) unsatisfied sellers. Their reservation prices are _____ (above/below) the equilibrium price.
14. At price *OF* there is an excess of quantities _____ over quantities _____ .
15. This is called a _____ (shortage/ surplus).

16. At price *OF* sellers whose reservation price is _____ (above/below) *OF* will be excluded from the market.

17. What is the total amount of output that will be rationed among buyers and sellers at price *OD?* _____

18. What is the total amount that would be available for distribution at price *OA?* _____

19. How much of this amount would be rationed by price? _____

20. How much would have to be rationed by some other means? _____

Answers: 1. *OL;* 2. right; 3. *OM;* 4. *OK;* 5. supply, *BC = KM;* 6. *OP;* 7. *OJ;* 8. shortage, *GH = JP;* 9. above; 10. above; 11. are; 12. right; 13. are, above; 14. demanded, supplied; 15. shortage; 16. above; 17. *OL = DE;* 18. *OM = AC;* 19. *AB = OK;* 20. *BC = KM.*

The analyses of shortage and surplus are extremely helpful in grasping many economic problems. Try your hand at the problems below:

1. When the government sets a minimum wage that is above the equilibrium wage, this will create a _____ (shortage/surplus) of would-be workers. Show this on the diagram below. Show with dotted lines how great this surplus will be.

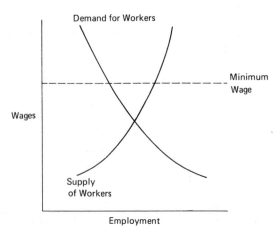

2. If government action keeps the price of dollars too high on international money markets, the result is a _____ (shortage/surplus) of dollars. Show that on the graph below, again using dotted lines to show the difference.

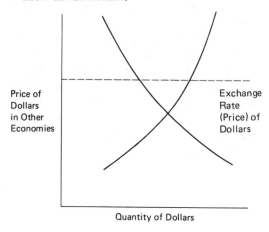

3. When prices are set below equilibrium prices, there will be a _____ (shortage/surplus) of the controlled good. Graph that.

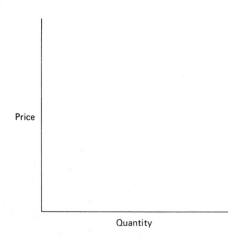

ALLOCATING INCOME

Now we are going to turn to the second main idea of this chapter. It is that the price mechanism allows us to allocate (ration) income in such a way as to maximize consumers' and producers' surpluses.

SURPLUSES AND SURPLUSES

The surpluses we are now talking about are not the same as the physical surpluses we just discussed, when quantities supplied were greater than quantities demanded. The surpluses we are going to maximize are the differences between reservation prices and market prices.

Consumers' and Producers' Surpluses

We have seen that markets ration output to those sellers who can offer goods and services *below* the going prices; markets simultaneously ration goods and services to householders who can offer to pay *more* than market price.

The following figure simply generalizes the lesson we have already learned on page 92 in the text (see figure 8-1 there). At the equilibrium price, all consumers whose reservation prices are higher than *OA* will be satisfied. Everyone enjoys some surplus except for the last buyer, who pays his full reservation price to buy the goods. The triangle of consumers' surplus measures the amount that consumers would have paid if we could have charged each buyer as much as he had been willing and able to pay. Many of us would pay more than the actual price for many commodities if we had to.

Producers' surpluses are the other side of the coin. All producers who are able to enter the market make producers' surpluses, except the last one (the marginal producer) who can just meet the market price with his reservation price. Because reservation prices of sellers should reflect their efficiency or natural advantages — the most efficient seller selling cheapest *if he has to* — the market has also confined economic activity to those who are best qualified to be producers.

Questions:

1. If your income were such that you could only enter the market at price *OA*, would you enjoy a consumers' surplus?

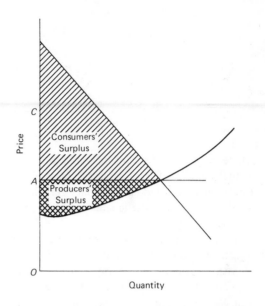

2. If your income allowed you to enter the market at price *OC*, show the size of your surplus.
3. If the price were *OC*, how large would the producers' surplus be? Show this by shading in the area.

Remember: Consumers' surplus reflects the initial distribution of income. With a different initial distribution, the outcome would be different. Remember too that the remarkable allocatory powers of the market are only just or fair to the extent that we think the initial distribution of income is just or fair. We will come back to this very important problem at the end of our study of microeconomics.

Maximizing Individual Surplus

The last item in our review completes our understanding of how prices allow us to make rational calculations as to how to spend our income. How *do* we decide how to spend our limited income — the income that is our budget constraint? We all know the answer intuitively. We decide at any moment to spend it on

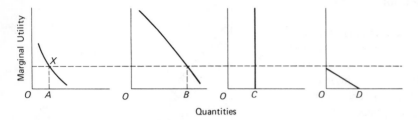

whatever we need or want or would most enjoy at that moment. That is, we try to maximize our total utility by spending our money for whatever goods would make the greatest addition to our well-being at the moment.

Look at the graph above. It shows the marginal utilities of Goods *A, B, C,* and *D* at a particular moment. Different goods can give us different amounts of satisfaction as circumstances change (consider the marginal utility schedule of a trip to the dentist before and after you develop a toothache). In the graph, Good *A* gives us much less *total* utility than Good *B*; Good *C* is a good that gives zero *additional* utility once we have acquired *OC* worth; Good *D* obviously ranks very low.

Suppose we had unlimited income. How much of each good would we buy? The answer in each case is that we would keep on buying the good until it no longer gave us any more marginal utility. We would buy whatever quantity of each good is represented by the length of the quantity axis from the origin to the point where the marginal utility curve intersected it.

Budget Constraints

Once we introduce a budget constraint, we cannot buy indefinitely large quantities of everything. Suppose our budget constraint is such that the next unit of Good *A* would give us an amount of satisfaction represented by the vertical distance between the dotted line and the base of the diagram, *OX* in the first graph. How much of Good *B* do we buy? Obviously amount *OB*, where the marginal satisfaction of the last unit

of *B* is the same as for Good *A*. How much of Good *C?* As we can see, we will buy quantity *OC.* Good *D?* None at all. The marginal utility of even one unit of this good isn't as great as that of various quantities of Goods *A, B,* and *C.*

In the following figure, notice that the total utility of Good *B* is larger than the total utility of Good *A*. In the diagram, we assume that we have very little money (a tight budget constraint) shown by the dotted line *L*. We will buy quantity *OQ* of Good *B* and none of Good *A*.

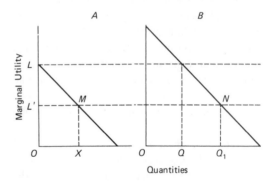

Now our budget constraint eases to *L'*. We have more money. We buy OQ_1 of Good *B* and *OX* of Good *A*. We still get much more total utility from Good B than from Good *A*. But we would get less utility from our total budget if we did not now buy some of Good *A*. How do we know? Because the addition to our pleasures from *OX* of Good *A* is *MX*. This is greater than the addition to our pleasures beyond point Q_1 of Good *B*.

Have you ever made a purchase and then walked away feeling "That was a foolish thing to buy"? You had just bought too much of Good B, instead of some other good such as A.

Prices

How do we know how to allocate our incomes among goods so that their marginal utilities will be equal? By comparing our marginal utilities with prices. Prices do not change our marginal utilities; they give us something to measure them against. Suppose that Good B is meat and Good A is spinach. The graph shows that we like meat more than spinach, and this will be true whether meat is cheap or dear. But the amount of meat that we will buy depends on how expensive it is compared to spinach. As we go on buying meat, the marginal utility of additional amounts of meat will fall. Eventually we will prefer spending our next dollar on spinach. When do we switch? When the marginal utility of another dollar's worth of meat has fallen to equal that of the first dollar's worth of spinach.

How much meat will we have bought? That depends on how much we had to pay for it. In the end we want to balance meat and spinach so that:

$$\frac{\text{marginal utility of meat}}{\text{price of meat}} = \frac{\text{marginal utility of spinach}}{\text{price of spinach}}$$

Let's give an arbitrary value of 10 to the marginal utility of meat and 2 to that of spinach. Suppose that meat costs $2 per pound and that spinach costs 20¢ per pound. Then:

$\dfrac{10}{\$2}$ will have to be compared with $\dfrac{2}{\$.20}$

We will be getting 5 units of utility *per dollar* spent on meat ($10 \div \$2$), 10 units of utility *per dollar* spent on spinach ($2 \div 20$). We will buy spinach.

Remember, as we buy spinach (or meat), its marginal utility will change even though its price

won't change. Therefore as we buy more and more of whatever item gives us the most utility per dollar, we will be getting less and less marginal utility from that good. As we go on buying spinach, its marginal utility will fall. When it reaches 1, we will be getting only 5 units of marginal utility ($1 \div \$.20$) for that spinach. This is the same as our marginal utility per dollar spent on meat. Our next purchase will give us equal satisfaction, whether spent for meat or spinach.

Remember:

1. Because we have budget constraints, we must decide how much of each good to buy.
2. As we continue to buy goods, their *MU* falls.
3. We will be best off when we get the same *MU* for each dollar spent on any good.
4. There, we will maximize our well being by allocating our income so that *MU* of Good A in proportion to its price equals *MU* for Good B in proportion to its price.
5. In shorthand: $\dfrac{MU_A}{P_A} = \dfrac{MU_B}{P_B}$

Let's see if you understand this: T F

1. By marginal utility we mean the satisfaction gained from the *last unit* of the good.   __ __
2. As we add more and more of a good, *total* utility falls.   __ __
3. We try to spend our incomes so that the *total utility* of all things we buy is equal.   __ __
4. If the marginal utility of X is greater than that of Y, our next purchase should be Y.   __ __
5. If we had no budget constraints, we would acquire goods until the marginal utilities of *all* goods were zero.   __ __
6. If we had no budget constraint, total utilities would be zero.   __ __
7. If $MU_A/P_A = MU_B/P_B$, we are spending too much on A.   __ __
8. Prices tell us what utilities goods will give us.   __ __
9. Prices tell us how much of any good to buy, given our own knowledge of each good's utilities.   __ __

                                                    T F

10. The marginal utility of a good can
    change.   — —   _ 3. The equi-marginal rule allows us to maxi-
                                                                 mize total well being because
    Answers:
                                                                 a. no good will yield a positive consumers'
    1. T   5. T   8. F   surplus.
    2. F   6. F   9. T   b. no good will yield more total utility
    3. F   7. F   10. T   than any other.
    4. F   c. a dollar spent on acquiring more of any
                                                                    good will bring us the same additional
                                                                    satisfaction.

TEST YOURSELF   _ 4. A budget constraint

                                                                 a. determines the total we can spend.
_ 1. The equi-marginal rule means that
                                                                 b. affects our marginal utility or consumer
     a. we spend the same amount on two   surplus schedules.
        goods selling at the same price.
                                                                 c. is necessary for the equi-marginal rule to
     b. we try to maximize the total satisfac-   apply if we seek maximum satisfaction.
        tions of two goods.
                                                                 d. is all the above.
     c. we maximize our total utilities by trying
        to equalize the marginal utilities of all
        goods.
_ 2. If we follow the equi-marginal rule   *Answers:*

     a. total utilities of all goods will be equal.   1. c   3. c   4. a
     b. total utilities from all goods will be   2. b
        maximized.

c. total expenditure will be the same for
   each good.

The Market in Movement

9

LEARNING OBJECTIVES

In this chapter we learn how economists use supply and demand curves to explain changes in price. Here is what you should keep foremost in mind:
1. *Shifts in Demand*
   a. How does a *shift* in demand (or supply) differ from a movement along a demand (or supply) curve?
   b. How do shifting curves affect prices?
2. *Elasticity*
   a. What is the meaning of elasticity?
   b. What is the role played by elasticities in the determination of price?

Chapter 9 is interesting; watching demand and supply curves shift is much closer to reality than thinking about the effects of price changes on quantities demanded and supplied. We shall see in our next chapter that it can lead to some surprisingly enlightening results.

Two big ideas should be learned in this chapter. The first is the effect of shifting curves, rather than movement along curves. The second

is a clear understanding of elasticity — the name that describes the shape of curves.

SHIFTING CURVES

What does it mean to shift along a curve? What does it mean when a curve itself shifts? The difference is fundamental and should be learned once and for all. *You shift along curves when you are considering the effect of price alone. You shift the curves themselves when you are not considering the effect of price but of other influences on demand and supply.*

1. Examples: "The demand for butter has increased" means that at the _____ (same/higher) price, we will buy _____ (the same/a larger) quantity of butter.

2. "The quantity of butter demanded has fallen" means that at _____ (the same/a higher) price for butter, our purchases of butter have _____ (increased/remained the same/fallen).

You should be certain that your answers read: (1) same . . . a larger; and (2) the same . . . fallen. In the first case the demand curve has shifted to the right; in the second, we have moved along the curve. We will show this in the graphs below:

Graph I

1. Label the axes and draw a demand curve.
2. Indicate a market price and note the quantity of butter demanded (mark this *ox*).
3. Show an increase in demand with a dashed line.
4. Show the increased quantity of butter demanded (*ox'*).

Graph II

1. Label axes and draw in a demand curve.
2. Indicate a market price and note quantity of butter demanded (mark this *oy*).
3. Show a rise in price with a dotted line.
4. Indicate the new quantity of butter demanded (*oy'*).

Check your diagrams with these below.

I

II

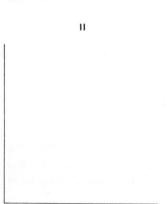

I

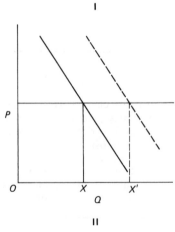

II

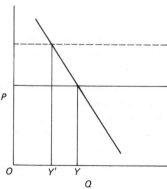

Now do the following exercises:

1. Show a *decrease* in supply with a dashed line.

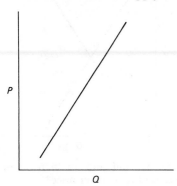

2. Show the change in quantity supplied (oy') at new price p'.

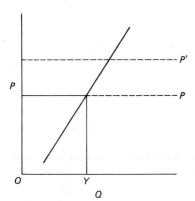

3. Show an *increase* in both demand and supply that will result in a higher price. Use dotted lines.

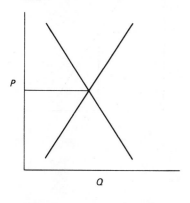

4. Show a *decrease* in demand and an *increase* in supply that will result in a lower price. Use dotted lines.

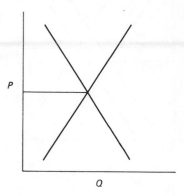

Check with the graphs below.

1.

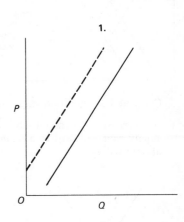

2.

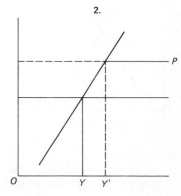

3.

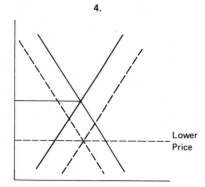

4.

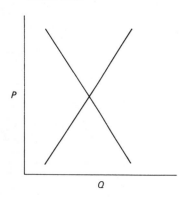

Can you draw the following:

1. A decrease in demand and an increase in supply that will lead to a *higher* price? Think about this!

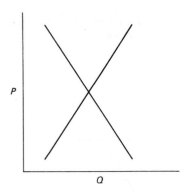

2. An increase in demand and a decrease in supply that will lead to a higher price?

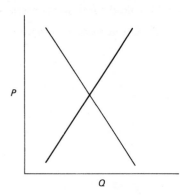

3. An increase in demand and an increase in supply that will lead to a higher price?

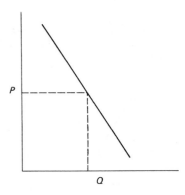

4. An increase in quantity demanded at the same price? Think!

Answers:

1. Impossible;

2.

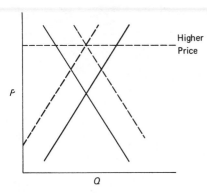

3.

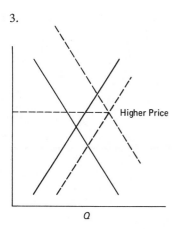

4. Impossible.

One last set of exercises:

1. You cannot have an increase in price if both supply and demand fall.

2. You cannot have an unchanged price if both supply and demand rise.

3. You cannot have a fall in price if demand rises and supply falls.

4. You cannot have an increase in the quantity supplied, unless the price changes.

__ __

__ __

__ __

__ __

Answers: 1. F; 2. F; 3. T; 4. T

An important point in this chapter is that the effect of a shift in supply or demand curves will bring different price and quantity effects, depending on the shape of the curve. In the graphs below, draw in the following:

Graph (a) A very inelastic supply curve. Now move demand to the right, D'D'.

Graph (b) A very elastic supply curve. Now move demand to the right by the same amount.

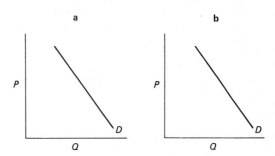

Which has the greater effect on price? On quantity?

Answers:

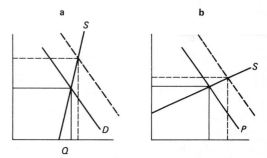

On the answers above, indicate as OX the original quantity supplied in both cases, and OX' the new quantity supplied. Which is larger? Mark the original and the new prices OA and OA'. Which is higher?

Now answer the following:

1. With a given supply curve, the effect on price of a shift in demand will be larger if the supply curve is _____ (elastic, inelastic).

2. With a given demand curve, the effect on quantity of a shift in supply will be larger if the demand curve is ＿＿＿＿＿(elastic/inelastic).

3. With a totally inelastic S curve, the effect on price of a fall in demand will be ＿＿＿＿ (zero/large).

4. With a totally elastic S curve, the effect on quantity will be ＿＿＿＿ (zero/small/large) if demand shifts to the right.

5. With a totally elastic D curve, a shift in S will exert its effect wholly on   (P/Q).

6. With a totally inelastic D curve and a totally elastic S curve, a shift in D will exert its effect wholly on ＿＿(P/Q).

Check your answers by matching each of the above with the appropriate diagram below.

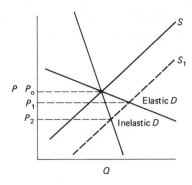

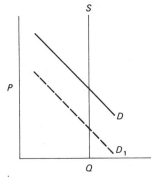

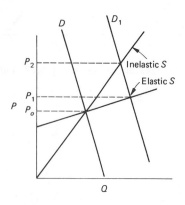

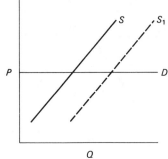

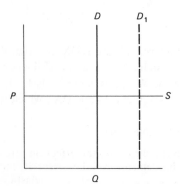

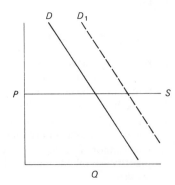

ELASTICITIES

The word elasticity describes the shapes of curves. *But curves only describe in a highly abstract fashion our behavior on the market.* By an elastic curve we mean one that shows a very sensitive response to changes in price. Note that the word elasticity refers to the shape of a *given* curve, not to any changes in its position.

Special note: This refers to price elasticity — the sensitivity of our willingness and ability to buy or sell at various prices. We can also speak of income elasticity — the response of our willingness and ability to buy at the same price with a change in income. Income elasticities are every bit as important as price elasticities, but in this exercise we will be dealing only with price elasticities.

There are three things to learn about elasticities: (1) what causes our differing sensitivities to price change? (2) how do we measure them? (3) what effect do they have on expenditures or receipts? Let us take up these problems in turn.

1. ELASTICITIES DEPEND ON SUBSTITUTES.

If our response to a price rise is to decrease greatly the quantities demanded, this must mean that we shift away from the higher-priced good to something else almost as good. *Goods with close substitutes therefore have higher elasticities of demand than goods with few substitutes.* But it follows that the good in question must also *be* a substitute for many other commodities. As its price falls, the quantity demanded therefore increases sharply.

Elasticity of supply does not depend on substitutes but on the ease with which we can increase production at higher prices. Here time plays a very important role. In the long run, supply curves tend to be much more elastic than in the short run. Compare the elasticities of

supply of cut flowers today, tomorrow, new week, next year. Graph them.

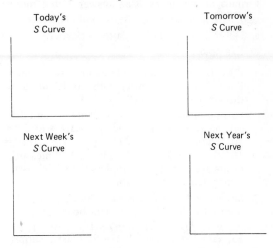

Important Note: The prices of substitutes move in the same direction as the prices of the original good. If the price of beef rises, people switch to lamb, and lamb prices rise. As the price of lamb rises, people switch to chicken, and poultry prices rise. We will see this effect at work in our next chapter.

2. MEASURING ELASTICITIES

Learn this formula:

$$\frac{\Delta Q/Q}{\Delta P/P}$$

What does it mean? The sign "Δ" means "change in." It is pronounced "delta." Therefore, $\Delta Q/Q$ means the change in quantity demanded or supplied divided by the *original* quantity demanded or supplied (or the percentage change in quantity demanded or supplied). In the same way, $\Delta P/P$ means the percentage change in price. Therefore, the formula relates the percentage change in quantity to the percentage change in price. We put a minus sign in front of it because the change in quantity goes down as prices go up. Thus the formula always gives us an answer with a minus sign. The minus sign in the formula corrects this and gives us a positive measure of elasticity.

Examples:

1. Price is $10, quantity demanded is 18 units. Price doubles, quantity falls to 12 units. Is this an elastic demand?

   Putting numbers into our formula (and forgetting about minuses) we get: $\Delta Q = 6$; $\Delta P = 10$. Therefore $6/18$ ($\Delta Q \div Q$) = $1/3$. $\Delta P/P = 10/10 = 1$. $1/3 \div 1 = 1/3$. We call all measurements of elasticity that are less than 1 inelastic. Hence demand is inelastic.

2. Supply is 100, price is $10. Price rises to $15, supply to 200. Elastic or inelastic supply?

   Answer: $\Delta Q = 100$; $\Delta Q/Q = 100/100 = 1$. ΔP 5. $\Delta P/P = 1/2$. $1/ \ 1/2 = 2$. Elastic supply.

3. Price is $10; $Q_d = 10$. Price rises to $15. What Q_d will give unit elasticity?

   Answer: We need the same percentage change in numerator and denominator. The change in the denominator = $\Delta P/P$, or $5/10 = 1/2$. What $\Delta Q/Q$ will also equal $1/2$? Obviously, $5/10$. Therefore, ΔQ must be -5.

These are so easy we won't even give the answers.

Note: Elasticities vary along straight-line curves. The best way to prove this to yourself is to work out the following examples.

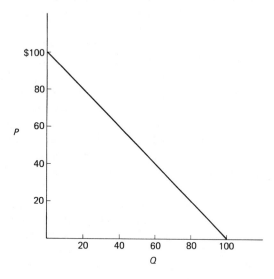

MORE PRACTICE

You should be able to fill in the following:

1. If the percentage rise in quantity is equal to the percentage fall in price, demand is _____ (elastic, inelastic, unit elastic).

2. If the percentage fall in price is 5 percent and the rise in quantity supplied is 7 percent, the supply curve is _____ (elastic/unit elastic/inelastic).

3. An inelastic demand curve means that the substitutes for the commodity are _____ (many/few).

4. An inelastic demand curve means that the percentage change in _____ is _____ (greater/less) than the percentage quantity in _____.

1. Draw in a price line at $80. What is the quantity demanded at this price? _____

2. Drop price to $60. What is ΔP? What is the new Q? What is ΔQ? _____

3. What is the price elasticity of demand over this range? Remember the formula: $\Delta Q/Q \div \Delta P/P$. _____

4. Draw in another price line at $40. What is the Q_d _____?

5. Drop price to $20. What is the new Q_d? What is ΔQ? _____

6. What is the price elasticity over the price range $40–$20? _____

7. Now figure backwards. What is the Q_d when price is $20? _____.

8. What is Q_d when price *rises* to $40? _____

9. Is the elasticity the same going down as going up? _____

10. If not, why not? _____

Only the last question needs explanation. Don't forget that you are figuring percentage price changes and percentage quantity changes. In the first case (going down) your original number for price is larger in proportion to the price change than in the second case: When you go from $40 to $20, the change ($\Delta P$) is $20. This is a 50 percent change compared with a base of $40, but a 100 percent change compared with a base of $20. The same reasoning applies to changes in supply.

Note: If we took smaller and smaller ranges in price, the effect of going up or down would also get smaller. If we examine elasticity at one point, it is the same going either way.

3. EFFECTS OF ELASTICITY

We do not study elasticities just to draw diagrams. We study them because they tell us about changes that we can expect in the marketplace when prices move. When demand is inelastic, for example, quantities demanded do not change much compared to prices. This is very good for a businessman who raises his price. But suppose a businessman cuts his price. Does he want the quantity demanded to increase greatly or little? Greatly, of course. Therefore he hopes that his demand curve will be elastic if he cuts price and inelastic if he raises price.

Consider the consumer. If his demand curve is inelastic and the price of a commodity goes up, his quantity demanded will not fall percentagewise as much as the price rises. Therefore the total amount he will spend on the commodity will increase. Contrariwise, if his demand is elastic, he will spend less on the commodity. Why? Because he will have switched to substitutes.

To drive home this central idea, construct a schedule that will show an inelastic demand as

price falls. We have helped a little. You can fill in the gaps.

Price	Quantity Demanded	Total Expenditure
$100	100	$10,000
90	105	
80	——	8,800
70	——	——
60	——	——
50	——	——

Does your total expenditure column constantly decrease? If not, you haven't constructed an inelastic demand schedule. Go back and try again. Now construct a schedule for an elastic demand. You can fill in all the figures to suit yourself. Remember one condition. The column showing total expenditure must increase steadily as price falls.

Price	Quantity Demanded	Total Expenditure
$100	100	$10,000
90	——	——
80	——	——
70	——	——
60	——	——

Can you construct a demand schedule of unit elasticity? It's not as hard as you think. Steps:

1. Set up a price schedule.
2. Set up a total expenditure schedule that remains constant.
3. Divide price into expenditure to get quantity demanded at each price.

Try it. Then plot it on a set of axes.

Finally, test your understanding of elasticities on the following exercise. The figure shows the supply curves of two industries facing different demand curves. Suppose a union has just won an equal wage increase in both industries.

Show the new supply curve with a dotted line in both left- and right-hand portions of the diagram.

B

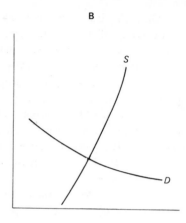

A

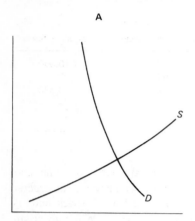

better able to pass along the wage increase in the form of higher prices?[1]

Now indicate the change in sales in Industry A and in Industry B. What will be the effect on price of both industries? Which industry will be

[1] Industry A passes much more of the wage increase along than Industry B.

10

The Microeconomics of Farming

LEARNING OBJECTIVES

Here is economic analysis put to work. Set these objectives for yourself:
1. Be sure you understand how expectations can alter the outcome of the normal supply/demand interaction.

2. Test your understanding of supply and demand as an analytical tool in elucidating the movements of prices in the real world — in this case, agricultural prices.

There is an interesting reading for this chapter, but there is one analytical point that we should spend a few minutes reviewing. Actually the point occurred at the end of the last chapter, but it found clear-cut application in connection with the workings of agricultural markets. This is the role of expectations in affecting the outcome of market prices.

EXPECTATIONS AND BEHAVIOR

Behind a great deal of economic analysis lie those laws of behavior which we have already mentioned. One of them states that as prices fall, we are willing and able to buy a larger quantity. The fact that we are *able* to buy more reflects the fact that our budget constraint loosens as prices fall: we are richer, with a given budget, when we can buy things more cheaply.

But will we necessarily be willing to buy more goods at lower prices? Not if our expectations lead us to believe that prices will be still lower tomorrow. In that case we will hold off until tomorrow. The fall in prices will result in a smaller, not a larger, quantity demanded.

The same perverse reaction holds in the case of supply. The normal law of behavior governing supply says that we will offer more if prices go up. But this will not be true if we expect the price to go still higher. Then we will hold back, waiting for those higher prices to materialize. Meanwhile, our actual offerings will fall, not rise.

TEST YOURSELF

— 1. If prices fall, and we expect them to fall further,
   a. buyers rush in.
   b. buyers hold back.
   c. sellers rush in.
   d. sellers hold back.
   e. a and b.
   f. a and c.
   g. b and c.
   h. b and d.

— 2. If prices rise, and we do not expect them to rise further,
   a. a new equilibrium price will be established.
   b. prices will fall.
   c. supply will rise.

— 3. If prices rise, sellers will offer more
   a. if they expect prices to continue rising.
   b. if they expect prices to level off.
   c. if they expect buyers to rush in.

— 4. Normal supply and demand behavior
   a. assumes that buyers and sellers expect prices to continue to change in the direction they are moving.

   b. assumes that price changes will have no effect on demand or supply curves.
   c. assumes that demand and supply curves shift as prices change.

— 5. For a buyer to hold back if prices fall and are expected to fall more
   a. is rational maximizing behavior.
   b. is irrational behavior.
   c. is maximizing but irrational.
   d. is rational but not maximizing.

— 6. An orderly market assumes that changes in prices
   a. affect the positions of curves.
   b. only induce movements along curves.
   c. affect one curve only.

— 7. So-called cobweb markets reflect
   a. irrational behavior.
   b. time lags in adjustment.
   c. shifts in S or D curves.
   d. b and c.

— 8. Perverse market behavior reflects
   a. irrationality.
   b. imperfect knowledge.
   c. expectations.
   d. controlled markets.

— 9. Normal expectations for buyers or sellers result in
   a. perverse markets.
   b. cobwebs.
   c. laws of supply and demand.

—10. Expectations of further price changes
   a. move you along D and S curves.
   b. move D and S curves.
   c. cause cobwebs.

Answers:

1. g	5. a	8. c
2. a	6. b	9. c
3. b	7. b	10. b.
4. b		

DOWN ON THE FARM . . .
AND BACK TO THE FACTS

Q. *When is a farm* **not** *a farm?*
A. *Surprisingly often.*

Shirley H. Rhine

A staff researcher at The Conference Board presents some
surprising facts on what the contemporary American farm
(and farmer) is – and is not.

About half of the total income of farm operators (after deduction of production expenses) comes from nonagricultural sources. This rather curious phenomenon reflects to a large extent the dependence of small, low-output farms on nonfarm sources (primarily earnings from nonfarm employment) for the great bulk of their income. For farm-operator households with sales of farm products of less than $5,000, income of nonfarm origin in 1971 constituted four-fifths of their total income, compared with three-tenths for farm-operator households with sales of $5,000 and over.

In 1971 farms with less than $5,000 in sales numbered 1,481,000, or fully half of the 2,876,000 number of farms. Not only do the operators* of these small units depend on nonagricultural sources for the overwhelming share

From Shirley H. Rhine, "Down on the Farm . . . and Back to the Facts," The Conference Board *Record* (May 1973). © The Conference Board, Inc.

*A farm operator, as defined by the Bureau of the Census, "is a person who operates a farm, either doing the work himself or directly supervising the work. He may be the owner, a member of the owner's household, a salaried manager, or a tenant, renter, or share-cropper. . . . In the case of a partnership, only one partner is counted as an operator . . . the number of farm operators is the same as the number of farms." The farm operator may or may not live on the farm.

of their livelihood, but these low-output farms contribute only nominally to total farm output.

These observations seem to beg the question, "what is a farm?" or, alternatively, "when is a farm *not* a farm?" The official definition of the Census of Agriculture qualifies as farms places of 10 acres or more whose sales of agricultural products during the year amounted to, or normally would amount to, at least $50; or places of fewer than 10 acres whose sales of agricultural products amount to, or normally would amount to, at least $250. So broadly defined, it is little wonder that a substantial share of places designated as farms in fact do very little farming.

It is appropriate to note that in the 1970 Census of Population, only 1,426,000 persons were classified as "farmers or farm managers," i.e., farm operators. Is this figure a more realistic count of farms than the Department of Agriculture's estimate of 2,924,000 for 1970?

The number of farms is a crucial statistic since it is used in the computation of all sorts of averages, e.g., average cash receipts from farming, average net income per farm, average government payments, etc., which have an important impact on farm policy and public attitudes toward the farm sector. Except for off-farm income, the inclusion of the 1,481,000 low-output units in the count of farms naturally yields much lower per farm averages than if they were excluded. It is quite evident that the question "what is a farm?" is of considerable consequence.

RELYING ON NONFARM INCOME

Off-farm income as a percentage of total income of farm-operator families rose from 42% in 1960 to 53% in 1971. Approximately four-fifths of the off-farm income represents earnings of operators and their families for work performed outside their farms (68% from wages and salaries from off-farm jobs and 11% from non-farm business and professional income, according to 1965 estimates); the remaining one-fifth is mainly from interest, dividends, rents from real estate, unemployment compensation, pensions, welfare payments, Social Security payments, and veterans' benefits.

Since a small portion of the wages and salaries consists of earnings of operators and their families for work performed on other people's farms, "off-farm" is not quite synonymous with "nonfarm." However, it is estimated that about 95% of the off-farm income is of nonfarm origin. Converting the off-farm income to a nonfarm estimate shows that farm-operator families received approximately 50% of their total income outside of agriculture in 1971, compared with some 40% in 1960. The farm sector is obviously approaching the paradoxical position of receiving the bulk of its income from non-agricultural sources.

On the average, some three-fourths of off-farm income from all sources is contributed by the operator himself and the remaining fourth by other members of the family. And about three-fifths of total off-farm income consists of earnings for work done by the operator himself outside the farm.

It is not surprising, then, that the mounting importance of off-farm income is accompanied by a rising percentage of operators who work

outside their farms. This trend reflects the increasing share of all farm operators who work off their farms *200 or more days;* the proportion of farmers who work off-farm from one to 199 days a year showed relatively little change during the past three decades (Chart 1).

AT WORK OFF THE FARM

It is also not surprising to find that the smaller the volume of his sales, the more likely it is that the operator will work outside of his farm. To wit, in 1969 some 73% of the operators of farms with less than $2,500 in sales worked off their farms and the proportion declines with each successively higher sales class to only 27% of the operators of farms with sales of $40,000 and over. Moreover, the lower the receipts from farm marketings, the more likely it is that the farm operator will work off his farm for *200 or more days* annually. . . .

The majority of farmers with sales of less than $2,500 have full-time nonfarm jobs, i.e., they work off-farm for at least 200 days.* Their "farms" are in the main rural residences on which they do a bit of farming (usually as a hobby), enough to qualify as a farm by the Census of Agriculture. Those operators with sales

*Of the nearly one million farms with sales of less than $2,500 in 1969, some 58% were part-time farms, i.e., they had operators who were less than 65 years old and worked off the farm at least 100 days during the year (over four-fifths of these part-time farmers worked off their farms 200 or more days); another 23% were part-retirement farms, i.e.: the operators were at least 65 years old regardless of how much time they worked off the farm (some 14% of these farmers worked off-farm 200 or more days); the remaining 19% of the farms had operators who were less than 65 years old and worked off the farm less than 100 days. The latter, on the average, receive far less income from nonfarm sources than the part-time farmers and even somewhat less, on the average, than part-time retirement farmers. Hence, this group of farm-operator households tends to have the lowest income (from all sources) per farm and most of the families in this group are likely to be among the rural poor.

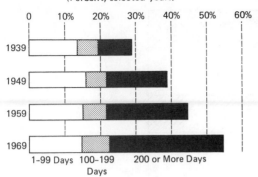

CHART 1. Farm operators working off-farm.
(Percent, selected years)

1-99 Days 100-199 200 or More Days
Days

Source: U.S. Bureau of the Census.

of less than $2,500 who devote the bulk of their time to farming are largely subsistence farmers and any off-farm work they perform is probably out of necessity to supplement their inadequate farm revenues. Among operators with sales of agricultural products of $2,500 to $4,999 there is a substantial minority who have full-time nonfarm employment. . . . However, for many of the farmers in the $2,500 to $4,999 sales group, income from farming probably constitutes the primary source of livelihood and nonfarm work supplies supplementary revenues.

The higher the sales of farm products and therefore the higher the net income from farming is likely to be, the less urgent it becomes for the farmer to supplement his agricultural income with off-farm work. The larger operations tend to require the full-time attention of the operator, generally leaving him little or no time for working off his farm. Hence, a much smaller proportion of farmers who operate farms in the higher sales classes work off their farms 200 or more days.

FEWER THAN HALF PRODUCE 95%

Ranking the farms by size of output shows that a small proportion at the top produces the major proportion of the output. In 1971 farms

with sales of agricultural products of $40,000 and over constituted barely 9% of the farms, but accounted for 60% of the cash receipts from farming. Conversely, the least prosperous farms, those with sales of less than $2,500, represented 37% of the farms but only 2% of the output. Another 14% of the farms, those with sales between $2,500 and $4,999, accounted for only 3% of output (Chart 2). While these two groups of low-production units account for fully half of the number of farm enterprises, they produce just 5% of the products.

Not only do farms with sales of less than $5,000 contribute minimally to the nation's farm output, but they derive only a small fraction of their income from their farms. For example, in 1971 average realized net income from farming on farms with sales of less than $2,500 was $1,039, while off-farm income averaged $8,479. For farms with sales of $2,500 to $4,999, average realized net income per farm was $1,993, while off-farm income averaged $5,743. Hence, money from *off-farm* sources amounted to 89% of total income for those farms with sales of less than $2,500, and 74% for those with sales of $2,500 to $4,999.

The greater the income from farming, the less dependent the farmer is likely to be on off-farm income. However, even those farmers who in 1971 had sales of agricultural products of $40,000 and over, averaging $33,736 per farm in total income (income from all sources minus farm production expenses), derived 19% of their income from off-farm sources. . . .

NOMINAL FARM INCOME FOR 1½ MILLION FARMERS

In view of the immense importance of off-farm income to many operator families, principally to those with low returns from farming, income from farm operations alone is scarcely a measure of how well off they are. For example, average off-farm income of farms with less than $2,500 in sales is not only *relatively* larger than

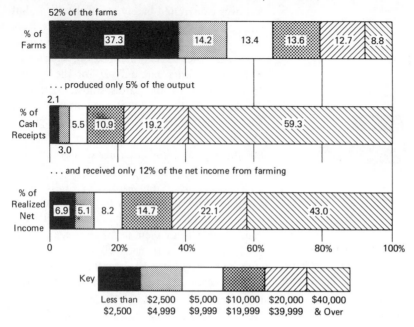

CHART 2. Farm output and income, 1971. (Shares by sales class)

52% of the farms

% of Farms | 37.3 | 14.2 | 13.4 | 13.6 | 12.7 | 8.8

... produced only 5% of the output

2.1

% of Cash Receipts | 5.5 | 10.9 | 19.2 | 59.3

3.0

... and received only 12% of the net income from farming

% of Realized Net Income | 6.9 | 5.1 | 8.2 | 14.7 | 22.1 | 43.0

0   20%   40%   60%   80%   100%

Key

Less than $2,500 | $2,500 $4,999 | $5,000 $9,999 | $10,000 $19,999 | $20,000 $39,999 | $40,000 & Over

Source: U.S. Department of Agriculture.

the more prosperous farms but is substantially larger even in absolute amount. For these very low output farms, total income from all sources in 1971 averaged $9,518, considerably greater than the average income for farms with sales of $2,500 to $9,999 and even approaching the $9,702 for farms with sales of $10,000 to $19,999. . . .

Moreover, the major share of net realized income from farming for farms with less than $5,000 in sales is in the form of nonmoney income. For farms with less than $2,500 in sales, after subtracting nonmoney income and direct government payments from realized net farm income, there is actually a *deficit* of $226. For farms with sales of $2,500 to $4,999, net realized income from farming after deducting nonmoney income and government payments amounts to merely $499 per farm. . . . Hence, the income received from sales of farm products

after subtracting production expenses is either negative or nominal for most of the farms with less than $5,000 in sales.

IT'S STILL THE FAMILY FARM

In the three decades since 1940 the number of farms has dwindled from 6,350,000 to 2,876,000, while the average size of farms has grown from 175 acres to 390 acres. Despite this trend toward larger units, farming continues to be primarily a family business. Approximately 95% of the farms today are family farms. (This is the proportion found in 1949, 1959 and 1964, according to estimates made by the Department of Agriculture from census data of those years. While information on number of family farms is not yet available from the 1969 Census of Agriculture, there is no reason to believe that any sizable shift has occurred in recent years.)

Since the 5% of total farms that are not family farms are predominantly large-scale operations, they account for a disproportionately large share of farm output, some 35% in 1964.

In 1964 not only were virtually all farms with sales of less than $20,000 family farms, but so were the majority of agricultural units with sales of $20,000 to $99,999. Furthermore, a significant portion of the largest, those with sales of at least $100,000, were also family farms (Chart 3).

Technological advances have made possible enormous gains in farm productivity. Farm output per manhour in 1972 was three-and-a-half times what it was in 1950. Through the growth of labor-saving practices, such as more efficient machinery and equipment and the increased availability of agriservices through the marketplace, many relatively large farms are run solely by the farm family with little or no hired help.

The rate of decline (60%) in the number of family farm workers (operators and unpaid family workers) from 1940 to 1972 was of a similar magnitude to the decline (57%) in number of hired farm workers and to the decline (55%) in number of farms. Consequently, recent ratios of these three are relatively unchanged from 1940. For example, in 1972, 26% of the farm labor force (4,392,000) were hired workers; in 1940 they were 24% of the 10,979,000 total. Also, in 1972 there were .4 hired workers per farm, or 4 for every 10 farms, about the same as in 1940.

CHART 3. Number of family farms, 1964. (Percent of total farms in each sales class)

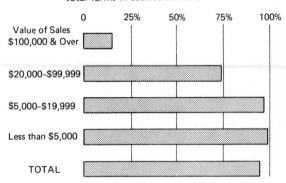

Source: U.S. Department of Agriculture; U.S. Bureau of Census.

Corporate farming has made significant inroads in terms of volume of business, accounting for 14% of total sales of agricultural products in 1969. However, the number of corporate farms is still relatively tiny, constituting only 0.7% of total, i.e., seven out of 1,000 farms in 1969. Moreover, the overwhelming majority of the latter were closely held corporations, i.e., owned by a relatively small number of individuals and many of these were family owned and managed. Over nine-tenths of the corporate farms had 10 or fewer shareholders in 1969. Many of the partnerships and even some of the corporations are also family farms, i.e., the operator and his family work the farm with less than 1.5 man-years of hired labor during the year.

TEST ON SUPPLY AND DEMAND
(CHAPTERS 7, 8, 9, 10)

__ 1. The circular flow relates
   a. two markets and two institutions.
   b. supply and demand in the factor market.
   c. firms and markets.
   d. householders and markets.

__ 2. In the circular flow the firm is
   a. a buyer in the goods market.
   b. a seller in the goods market.
   c. a buyer in the factor market.
   d. a seller in the factor market.
   e. a and b.
   f. b and c.

__ 3. Markets ration by
   a. excluding buyers whose reservation prices are too low.
   b. excluding buyers whose reservation prices are too high.
   c. excluding inefficient sellers.
   d. a and b.
   e. a and c.
   f. b and c.

__ 4. At an equilibrium price
   a. there are no unsatisfied buyers and sellers.
   b. no unsatisfied buyers or sellers can enter the market.
   c. supply equals demand.
   d. supply schedules equal demand schedules.

__ 5. A shortage means that
   a. prices are above reservation prices.
   b. equilibrium prices are above market prices.
   c. market prices are below equilibrium prices.
   d. prices are fluctuating.

— 6. Surpluses result when
   a. supply curves shift to the left.
   b. demand curves shift to the left.
   c. supply and demand curves intersect below market prices.
   d. supply and demand curves intersect above market prices.

— 7. A consumers' surplus means that
   a. you can buy a good for less than your reservation price.
   b. you can buy a good for less than its equilibrium price.
   c. you can buy a good because your demand curve has shifted.
   d. you have too much of a good.

— 8. With a rational allocation of income
   a. we distribute our purchases so that $MU_a/P_a = MU_x/P_x$.
   b. we spend all income on the good with the largest utility.
   c. the total utility of all goods is equal.
   d. we get rid of consumers' surplus.

— 9. A budget constraint
   a. limits the amount we can buy.
   b. limits the amount we can spend.
   c. prevents us from buying goods until the marginal utilities are zero.
   d. does all the above.

—10. A change in price, ceteris paribus,
   a. changes quantity demanded.
   b. changes demand.
   c. shifts demand curves.
   d. a and b.

—11. An increase in demand means that
   a. at same price we buy more.
   b. at higher price we buy less.
   c. we shift along our demand curve.
   d. we shift along a supply curve.

—12. An increase in demand coupled with a decrease in supply
   a. must raise prices.
   b. must lower prices.
   c. leads to same prices.
   d. means you can't tell about the effects.

—13. An increase in demand coupled with an increase in supply
   a. leads to lower prices.
   b. leads to higher prices.
   c. means you can't tell about the effects.
   d. leads to disequilibrium prices.

_14. If Good A has closer substitutes than Good B
  a. demand for A is more elastic than B.
  b. demand for B is more elastic than A.
  c. demand for A is less elastic than B.
  d. demand for B is less elastic than A.
  e. a and d.
  f. b and c.

_15. An inelastic demand means that $\Delta Q/Q \div \Delta P/P$ is
  a. less than 1.
  b. greater than 1.
  c. equal to 1.
  d. Something you can't tell about without actual figures.

_16. A businessman would like the elasticity of demand for his product to be
  a. elastic upward, inelastic downward.
  b. elastic in both directions.
  c. inelastic in both directions.
  d. inelastic upward, elastic downward.

_17. A totally elastic supply curve means that an increase in demand will result in
  a. large changes in prices.
  b. changes only in Q_s.
  c. no changes in Q_s.
  d. small change in Q_s.

_18. A totally inelastic demand curve means that a decrease in supply will
  a. raise price.
  b. lower Q_d.
  c. a and b.
  d. decrease Q_d at same price.
  e. cause none of above.

_19. If price raises induce expectations of further price raises
  a. we get a cobweb.
  b. buyers will hold back.
  c. sellers will rush in.
  d. none of above.

_20. Normal market behavior assumes
  a. no expectations.
  b. expectations that price changes will continue.
  c. expectations that price changes will not change D and S curves.
  d. expectations that price changes will affect D and S curves.

Operating a Competitive Firm

11

LEARNING OBJECTIVES

In this chapter we begin the study of production, focusing on how the competitive firm works. Central to the chapter are these ideas that you should learn:
1. The meaning of economic profit
2. The operation of the law of variable proportions (also called the law of diminishing returns)

3. The idea of maximizing profit by equating returns to factors at the margin.

This is an easy chapter to get the idea of, but not an easy chapter to master in detail. Work it through slowly and carefully, taking your time, and making sure that your answers are correct.

This chapter shifts the focus away from the market for goods to a crucial institution in a market society, the firm. We are going to investigate how the firm works in a market system, first in a competitive milieu, later in a more realistic monopolistic one.

TWO NEW TERMS

There is a small amount of vocabulary to learn in this chapter and a very important analytical principal, *the law of diminishing returns* (or variable proportions). Let us take up vocabulary first. Two new terms are added to our lexicon. The first is *entrepreneur*. The entrepreneur is the active organizer and director of the business enterprise. He is not necessarily its owner. His input is organization know-how, and he is rewarded for this by wages of management, which may be very high indeed.

This brings us to the second term, *economic profit*. The stress here is on economic. Profit in the everyday sense includes a number of returns that the economist groups under costs of production, such as interest on capital or land rents. *Economic* profit is a residual left over after the firm has paid out all costs, including wages of management and interest. We will see that these economic profits, which belong to the owner of the business, are short-lived under competition but that they play a vital role in guiding the entrepreneur to make maximizing decisions.

THE ENTREPRENEUR AT WORK

What does the entrepreneur do in a competitive firm? He tries to maximize economic profit. Unlike the entrepreneur in a monopolistic firm he is not able to do so by making special bargains in the factor market or by selling his goods through advertising campaigns and the like. Our entrepreneur — whom we can think of as a farmer or the operator of a small enterprise making a very standard product, such as nails, thread, machined parts, and so on — has only one means of seeking a profit. *He must buy the right amounts of the various factors of production and combine them in such a way as to produce as inexpensively as possible for any given level of output.*

THE LAW OF
VARIABLE PROPORTIONS

Now we come to the heart of the chapter. Suppose our entrepreneur has determined the minimum amounts of factors he needs to open shop, and suppose that he has borrowed (or has himself risked) the funds to begin operations. His next question is how much of each factor to add to that basic minimum. And here is where diminishing returns enters.

The law of variable proportions (or diminishing returns) describes what happens to output as we add more and more of one factor, holding fixed the amounts we use of the others.

It shows us that, typically, output rises more rapidly at first than the amount of the factor we add. This is a stage called increasing returns. Thereafter output continues to rise but more slowly than the additional inputs of the factor. This is the stage of diminishing returns. Finally output actually falls, the stage of negative returns.

Note that the law depicts the results of altering the inputs of *one* factor only. If we added two or more factors, we could not claim that there was a functional relationship between one factor and output. There would be no way of knowing whether changes in outputs were the result of adding one factor or another, or of both combined.

Note also that this is a law whose results follow from the constraints of nature, not from behavior. Behind the law of variable proportions is the fact that some combinations of factors are physically or chemically more productive than others. To go back to the example of growing food in a flower pot, if we used only one unit of capital — one single seed — we would be wasting the chemical powers of much of the soil that would never touch the seed. As we added seeds, we would make better and better use of the chemical powers of the soil. But after a certain point, we would be pouring more seed into the pot than could be nourished by the soil. The output from that point on would fall.

THE LAW AT WORK

In the table on page 80 we see the principle at work. Here we show the changes in output as we add workers to a simple production process, such as that in Adam Smith's pin factory.

Our table shows what happens to *total output* as we add manpower. It also gives us a chance to understand the relationship between marginal output and average output to total output and to each other. Can you answer the following?

No. of Men	Total Output	Marginal Output	Average Output
1	100	100	100
2	300	200	150
3	550	250	183
4	780	230	195
5	980	200	196
6	1160	180	193
7	1310	150	187
8	1430	120	178

1430

1. What is the marginal product of the fourth man? It is the total output of all four men less the total output of three men. Fill in this marginal output.

2. What is the average output of four men? It is the total output of all four men, divided by four. Fill in this average output.

3. Now figure the marginal and average outputs of the fifth, sixth, seventh, and eighth man.

4. Add up all the marginal outputs. The answer should be exactly the same as total output. Why is this? Because each marginal figure is the *addition* to output when we add one man. Total output is the sum of all these additions.

5. If you added the average outputs, would that also equal total output? No, it would not. Each average output applies only to that level of output. It makes no more sense to add these average outputs than it would to add the column of total outputs. Only the column of marginal outputs can be added.

6. Note what happens to marginal product and average product. Do they both rise at first? Do they both eventually fall?

7. Which declines first, marginal or average product? The table shows the answer. Now think: could the average product fall if the marginal product were rising or unchanged? If you understand this question, you have really grasped the relation of marginal and average. Suppose that average product did fall. Would this not mean that total output *per man* was falling? But how could output per man (average output) fall, unless the output of the marginal added man were falling? Suppose three men produced 300 bushels of grain, and that after the addition of a fourth man, output was still 300

bushels. Average output has fallen from 100 bushels (300 ÷ 3) to 75 (300 ÷ 4). This must mean that the fourth (marginal) man added zero to output.

8. At what level of manpower does diminishing marginal productivity set in? The answer is with the fourth man (in our table above). Why? Because marginal output with three-men is _____, and with four men is

_____ .

9. Does average productivity necessarily fall when marginal productivity falls? Look again at the table. When the fourth man is hired, we have just seen that marginal productivity drops. What happens to average productivity? With three men, average output was _____ . With four men it is

_____ .

10. How can average output be rising if marginal output is falling? Here is another important point to grasp. Even though marginal output is now declining, it is still higher than average output. In our table, the fourth man adds _____ to output. The average output of three men is _____ . Thus even though the marginal output of the fourth man is lower than the marginal output of the third man, it still pulls up the average performance of the four men compared with the average performance of the three.

11. On the graph below, plot the marginal, average, and total curves. Now show that marginal output can be falling, even though average output is still rising.

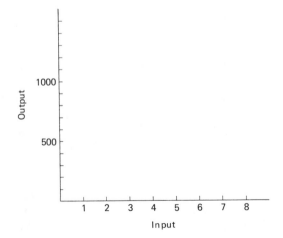

12. When marginal output hits the horizontal axis, does total output come to a peak? Why?

FROM DIMINISHING RETURNS TO MARGINAL REVENUE PRODUCT

Diminishing returns is a physical phenomenon. Our entrepreneur, however, has to go by economic data. Therefore, he has to convert the changing flow of physical output into economic terms by multiplying the value of output by its selling price. For example, if the selling price of each unit in our table is $30, then the entrepreneur can speak of the marginal revenue product of the first man as $3,000 (100 units × $30), the marginal revenue product of the second man as $6,000, and so on.

This now enables him to make an economic judgment as to how many units of a factor to hire. The judgment is easy but fundamental, and you should know it:

A factor is hired as long as its marginal revenue is larger than its marginal cost.

If we go back to our original table, we can now see how the entrepreneur figures his costs and revenues. Let's suppose that each worker costs $5,400 per year. Can you complete the table below? Work carefully; it is not difficult, and it is worth the trouble to do it once.

How many men should our entrepreneur hire? There are three ways of telling, all actually the same:

1. Compare marginal cost and marginal revenue product. Hire men until their cost is greater than their revenue product. This means we will hire ___5___ men.
2. Look at marginal profit per man. Go on hiring as long as a man brings in *some* marginal profit. This means we will hire ___5___ men. (Can you see that this is exactly the same as the first method? Marginal profit *is* marginal revenue product minus marginal cost.)
3. Keep an eye on total profits and go on hiring men as long as total profits are rising. This will mean we hire ___5___ men. Can you see why this answer is also the same as 1 and 2 above? As long as each man is bringing in some marginal profit, total profit must be rising. Look at what happens with man Number 6. His marginal cost is exactly equal to his marginal revenue product. Therefore, his marginal profit is zero. Therefore, also, there is no addition to total profit. From an entrepreneur's standpoint, it is pointless to hire him. (See the table at the bottom of this page.)
4. Explain why it would not be rational or maximizing to hire man number seven.

MIXING FACTORS

We have discovered the means by which the entrepreneur can decide how much of *one* factor

No. of Men	Marginal Cost per Man	Marginal Product	Marginal Revenue Product (@ $30 per unit)	Marginal Profit per Man (Marginal Revenue less Marginal Cost)	Total Profit = total Revenue less total cost
1	$5,400	100	$3,000	−$2,400	−$2,400
2	5,400	200	6,000	+ 600	− 1,800
3	5,400	250	7500	+2100	+ 300
4	5,400	230	6900	+1500	1800
⑤	5,400	200	6000	+600	2400
6	5,400	180	5400	0	2400
7	5,400	150	4500	−900	1500
8	5,400	120	3600	−1800	− 300

Marginal Revenue per Man (Marginal Output x $30)	Marginal Profit per Man (Marg. Revenue minus Marg. Cost)	Total Profit
$3,000	$-2,400	$-2,400
6,000	600	-1,800
7,500	2,100	300
6,900	1,500	1,800
6,000	600	2,400
5,400	0	2,400
4,500	-900	1,500
3,600	-1,800	-300

Factor	Marginal Cost	Marginal Revenue Product
labor	$6,000 per man	$13,000
land	$ 400 per acre	1,000
capital	$ 750 per machine	1,500

How do we figure the best buy? By comparing how many dollars of revenue we get back for each dollar of marginal cost. In the example above:

If a man costs $6,000 and brings in $13,000, then a dollar spent on labor will return $13,000 ÷ $6,000 or $2.16+.

If an acre costs $400 and brings in $1,000, then a dollar spent on land will return $1,000 ÷ _____, or $2.50.

If a machine costs $750 and brings in $1,500, then a dollar spent on capital will return _____ ÷ _____, or $ _2.00_ .

Now compare the three returns:
Per dollar of expenditure we get back $2.16 on labor, 2.50 on land, and 2.00 on capital.

Obviously we buy land.

to buy. But we have not yet determined which among all the factors he should first hire.

The answer is again simple. Our entrepreneur compares the marginal profit to be had from all the factors. For each in turn he compares marginal cost and marginal revenue product, and he buys the factor whose return is greatest.

Suppose he faced the following choice:

Factor	Marginal Cost	Marginal Product in Units
labor	$5,000 per man	1,000
land	$1,000 per acre	250
capital	$ 500 per machine	400

1. What is the cost of one unit of output for labor? The answer is 1,000 units ÷ $5,000 or $.20 per unit.
2. What is the cost of one unit of output from land? The answer is 250 units ÷ $1,000 or $ _____ per unit.
3. What is the cost of one unit of output from capital? The answer is _____ units ÷ $_____ or $.80 per unit.
4. Which of the three factors is the best buy for the money – that is, which gives a unit of additional output for the least cost?

Comparing Marginal Profits

We can perform the same operation in terms of marginal revenue products instead of physical units. Look at the table below, where we use new figures for variety's sake.

The Effect of Buying a Factor

How much land will we will hire? That depends on two things:

1. What will happen to the marginal product of land, as we add more and more of it. If the marginal product falls – if we are well into the stage of diminishing returns – we will experience a corresponding fall in the marginal revenue product of land.

2. As our entrepreneur hires more and more land, we can assume that other entrepreneurs in his competitive industry are doing likewise. The price of land will rise. As the price of land rises, its marginal cost rises, and the profitability of land falls.

THE EQUI-MARGINAL RULE

As the profitability of land falls – either because its price rises, or because its marginal revenue product falls, or both – land will cease to be the best buy. Our entrepreneur will then hire more of the next most profitable factor.

Again, this will raise its price, either because all entrepreneurs are bidding for it or because its marginal productivity (and therefore marginal revenue product) is falling.

By following these steps, our entrepreneur is following the equi-marginal rule:

1. *He is bidding for factors according to their marginal profitability, thereby equalizing that marginal return.*
2. *He continues to bid for factors until there is no longer any marginal profit to be had from any of them. All marginal factor profits are zero.*

Do you see that this equi-marginal rule is exactly the same as that for the consumer trying to maximize his surplus? Both consumer and entrepreneur look to the margin when deciding what to buy. And both buy as long as there is any profit (or consumer's surplus) to be had at the margin.

This is a long chapter, and you should review your understanding by taking the following quiz:

Quiz

T F

1. An entrepreneur is not always a capitalist. T _
2. A capitalist is always an entrepreneur. _ F
3. Economic profit includes interest on capital. _ F
4. Economic profit does not include interest cost. T _
5. The entrepreneur's main task in a competitive firm is to organize production by hiring the right amounts of various factors. T _
6. The law of variable proportions tells us that as we combine two or more factors, output first rises faster than combined factors, then eventually falls. T F
7. The law of diminishing returns applies to only one factor at a time. T _
8. Increasing returns refers to the fact that as we begin hiring a factor, we

typically experience proportionately larger increases in output. T _
9. Diminishing returns is a physical, not a behavioral, constraint. T _
10. Suppose that we have the following schedule:

No. of Machines	Total Output	Marginal Output	Average Output
1	100	—	—
2	400	—	—
3	600	—	—

From this, we can deduce the marginal and average figures. T _
11. Marginal output for the third machine is less than for the second. T _
12. Average output for the three machines is higher than for two. F _
13. Diminishing returns has already set in with three machines. T _
14. Diminishing returns means that average output is falling. _ F
15. If we know only the marginal outputs gained by adding a factor, we can deduce the total and average outputs. _ T
16. If we know only the average outputs, we can deduce the total and marginal outputs. T _
17. If each unit of output is sold for $10, the marginal revenue product of the third machine is $6,000. F _
18. The marginal revenue product of the second machine is $3,000. T _
19. Suppose each machine cost $3,000. The loss if you hired one machine would be $2,000. T _
20. If you hired two machines, total cost would be larger than total revenue. T _
21. If you hired a third machine, its marginal revenue product would be less than marginal cost. _ _
22. In the example above you would be best off hiring no machines. _ _

T F

23. If the cost fell to $1,500 it would now pay to hire the first machine.

24. The second machine still yields no net profit.   — —

25. If you hired three machines, you would make $1,500 profit.   — —

26. If you hired machines, it would mean that you could not get a higher return on your cost from labor or land.   — —

27. Because of diminishing returns, machines will return less and less profit as you go on hiring them.   — —

28. You will hire any factor as long as its marginal revenue product is greater than its marginal cost.   — —

29. As one entrepreneur bids for a factor, his additional demand for that factor causes its price to rise.   — —

T F

30. Profits will rise as long as we hire any factors whose marginal revenue product exceeds its marginal cost, by however small an amount.   — —

Answers:

1. T	11. T	21. T
2. F	12. F	22. T
3. F	13. T	23. F
4. T	14. F	24. F
5. T	15. T	25. T
6. F	16. T	26. T
7. T	17. F	27. T
8. T	18. T	28. T
9. T	19. T	29. F
10. T	20. T	30. T

The Competitive Firm in Action

12

LEARNING OBJECTIVES

Here is the conclusion of our study of the competitive firm. Once again, slow and careful work will be needed. When you are done, ask yourself:
1. Do you understand the idea of costs and revenues per unit of output?
2. Do you clearly see the difference between variable and fixed costs per unit?

3. Do you see why unit costs and revenue curves have their typical shapes?
4. Can you draw a diagram of a competitive firm making a profit?
5. Can you explain the competitive forces that tend to eliminate these profits?
6. Can you diagram the competitive firm in equilibrium with no profit?

This chapter will require a lot of pencil work, but when you have finished it, you should have a full understanding of how the competitive firm works. So take time to answer all the questions. There isn't a difficult step along the way — just a good many steps.

In our last chapter we explained how we chose an amount of factor *input* that maximized profits. Now we are going to use that information as the entrepreneur uses it — to determine how much *output* a firm should make to maximize its profits.

REVENUE AND COSTS PER UNIT

In figuring the most profitable output for the firm, we usually convert our total costs or total revenue into costs or revenue *per unit*. We do so by dividing total costs and total revenues by total output. The reason we do so is simply that it is much easier to work on a unit cost basis. We could work on a total cost basis, and we would, of course, get exactly the same answers if we did so.

Thus we are going to talk about costs and revenues per unit of output, not – as before – per unit of input. As we will see, going over from input to output is not difficult. It is the way we usually think in business terms: "How much will another unit of output cost me? How much will it bring in?"

FIXED VS. VARIABLE COSTS

We begin with a differentiation between two kinds of costs per unit of output – fixed and variable. What distinguishes the two? Not, as many students think, the physical attributes of capital or land contrasted with labor. The difference is the legal or contractual basis on which we hire factors. Rent (the payment for land) is usually fixed because we sign rent contracts of some duration; overhead is similarly fixed. Interest, the payment for capital, is also often a fixed cost. So too depreciation, the cost of using capital, is fixed because we own the asset and cannot fire it the way we can fire labor. Notice that a computer you own is a fixed cost because you have to maintain it whether you use it or not; a computer you hire by the day or week is a variable cost!

FIXED COSTS PER UNIT

First and simplest in our new calculations is to determine what happens to fixed costs as output increases. The answer is self-evident. Fixed costs per unit decline. This follows from the logic of

the case. If the fixed costs – the rent, the real estate taxes, the depreciation, the interest, and so on – of a plant are $5 per day and the plant produces 1 unit of output, fixed costs per unit must be $\_\_\_\_\_$. If output rises to 10 units, fixed costs per unit must decline to $\_\_\_\_$. Suppose that F_{total} stands for total fixed costs, O for output and F_{unit} for fixed cost per unit. What is the formula that relates these terms?$_____$. [1]

VARIABLE COSTS

More interesting is what happens to variable costs. Don't forget that by "variable" we mean the costs of those inputs we can easily add or dispense with in production. It does not just mean any costs per unit that vary. Fixed costs per unit also vary!

In the following table we assume that labor is the only variable cost, and let us put a price of $9 per day on labor. Begin by filling in the blanks of this table. See the table below and the following instructions.

1. First figure out the marginal output per man. This is just the same as in our last chapter. Marginal output is derived by calculating the change in output after we have added a man. We find it by looking at the change in the column of total output. Here we see the familiar law of diminishing returns at work.

2. Total variable cost is simple: it is the variable cost per unit ($9) times the number of units.

[1] Answer: $F_{unit} = \dfrac{F_{total}}{O}$

Number of Men	Total Output (units)	Marginal Output per Man	Total Variable Cost	Average Variable Cost per Unit
1	1	1	$ 9.00	$9.00
2	6	5	18.00	3.00
3	15	—	27.00	—
4	22	—	—	—
5	27	—	—	—
6	30	—	—	—
7	32	—	—	—
8	33	—	—	—

3. Average variable cost per unit is *total variable cost divided by the total number of units.*

4. After you have filled in the table, check your results with the answer table on p. 89.

TOTAL COSTS PER UNIT

Now for the last operation on the cost side. We want to add fixed costs per unit to variable costs. We will assume that fixed costs per day are $5. Fill in the blanks in the table at the foot of the page. You have all the information you need except average fixed costs per unit. Obviously this is total fixed cost ÷ output. The last column is nothing but the sum of the preceding two.

divide the change in total cost per unit by the change in total output (not by the change in the number of men). Can you complete the table below? The instructions may help.

In the table below, we find marginal cost in three steps: (1) we find the *change* in total cost – for example, $23.00 - $14.00 = $9.00; (2) we find the *change* in total output: 6 units - 1 = 5 units; and (3) we divide the first number by the second: $9.00 ÷ 5 = $1.80.

Number of Men	Total Output	Total Fixed Cost	Average Fixed Cost per Unit	Average Variable Cost per Unit	Average Total Cost per Unit
1	1	$5.00	$5.00	$9.00	$14.00
2	6	5.00	.83	3.00	3.83
3	15	5.00	.33	1.80	2.13
4	22	—	—	—	—
5	27	—	—	—	—
6	30	—	—	—	—
7	32	—	—	—	—
8	33	—	—	—	—

MARGINAL COSTS PER UNIT

You can now derive the important item of cost that you still lack – *marginal cost*. Remember, we are not figuring marginal cost per man, but marginal cost *per unit*. Thus we will have to

Total Output	Total Cost (Total Fixed Cost + Total Variable Cost)	Marginal Cost per Unit (Change in Total Cost ÷ Change in Total Output)
1	$14.00	$14.00
6	23.00	1.80
15	32.00	1.00
22	—	—
27	—	—
30	—	—
32	—	—
33	—	—

Note: This is not really an accurate measure of the marginal cost of the sixth or the fifteenth item of output, but of all the items *between* the first and the sixth, or *between* the sixth and the fifteenth. But it is the simplest way to do the basic arithmetic, and it gives us the cost curves we want.

COST CURVES

The next step is to transfer the information from schedules to a graph. Using the following graph, put in dots to mark the information you have about *marginal costs* and *average cost per unit*. Then join the dots with a freehand curve. Work slowly, being sure that each dot joins the proper pair of units and costs. Label the curves *MC* and *AC* respectively. If you are not sure about your graph, you might take a quick look at the graph below (try not to, since it will clue you into the next step). Notice that your marginal cost curve cuts your average cost curve at its lowest point.

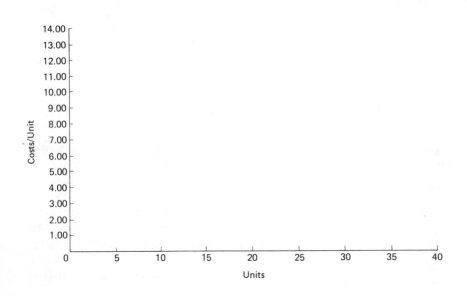

REVENUES

Now we have half the information that a profit-maximizing entrepreneur needs. Revenue is still missing from the picture. Let us assume that the selling price for your product is $3. This price is your total revenue ÷ output, or your average revenue per unit of output. Because you are a small firm in a large market — one wheat farmer among many — the price will remain the same, regardless of how large your output is. Therefore each additional unit will sell at $3, adding that much to your total revenue. *Both average revenue and marginal revenue are the same.*

On your graph draw in the marginal revenue (or average revenue) "curve." Where it touches the cost axis, mark the point *C.* Mark the curve *MR.*

Now remember the rule about your most profitable level of output. It will be where *marginal cost equals marginal revenue.* Mark this point *X,* and connect *X* with the output axis, marking an *A* where it intersects the axis. Next, mark with a *B* the point where the *AX* line cuts the average cost curve. Now connect B with a straight line to the cost axis, marking that point *Y.*

Now check your graph with the figure:

Table of Answers

Number of Men	Total Output	Total Fixed Cost	Fixed Cost per Unit	Total Variable Cost	Average Variable Cost per Unit	Total Cost	Average Total Cost per Unit	Price or Average Revenue per Unit	Marginal Revenue per Unit	Total Revenue
1	1	$5.00	$5.00	$ 9.00	$9.00	$14.00	$14.00	$3.00	$3.00	$ 3.00
2	6	5.00	.83	18.00	3.00	23.00	3.83	3.00	3.00	18.00
3	15	5.00	.33	27.00	1.80	32.00	2.13	3.00	3.00	45.00
4	22	5.00	.23	36.00	1.64	41.00	1.86	3.00	3.00	66.00
5	27	5.00	.19	45.00	1.66	50.00	1.85	3.00	3.00	81.00
6	30	5.00	.17	54.00	1.80	59.00	1.97	3.00	3.00	90.00
7	32	5.00	.16	63.00	1.97	68.00	2.13	3.00	3.00	96.00
8	33	5.00	.15	72.00	2.18	77.00	2.33	3.00	3.00	99.00

REVENUES, COSTS, PROFITS

Now is the time to go from geometry to understanding. Can you answer these questions:

1. At a price of *OC*, what is your most profitable output? ————

2. At the most profitable output *OA*, what is your average cost per unit? ————

3. At an output of *OA*, what is your selling price per unit? ————

4. At output *OA*, what is your profit per unit? ————

5. If your profit per unit is the amount *CY* (or *BX*) what is your total volume of profits? It is *CY* times output ————, or the rectangle ————.

6. Total profits should be equal to total revenue minus total costs. What is the rectangle of total revenue on the graph ————? The rectangle of total costs? ———— The difference is the rectangle *CXBY*, isn't it?

7. At a selling price of $3 is your firm in equilibrium? Can you show on the graph that selling either more than, or less than quantity *OA* would bring in less profit? Can you tell this just from looking at the *MR* and *MC* curves or do you need any other information?

8. What would be an equilibrium volume of output if price rose to $4? (Don't bother about the numbers! Just show it with a dotted line.)

FROM FIRM TO INDUSTRY

We have reached an equilibrium for the firm, but if you remember the chapter, it is not an equilibrium for the industry. This is because other firms will move into the industry. This *may* raise the prices of factors of production and thereby shift cost curves up; and it will *surely* increase the volume of supply in the industry and

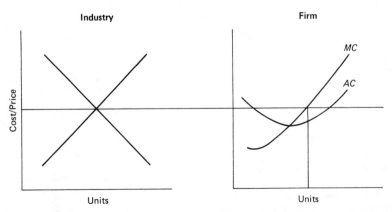

push prices down. In the diagrams on page 89 we show how a price for the product is set in the industry market and then "taken" by the firm. *Now draw in a new supply curve as firms move into the industry.* Show with a dotted line how price falls in the industry market, lowering the selling price that our firm can get.

What would be the result if the influx of firms moved the supply curve for the industry so far to the right that the price dropped *below* the average cost curve for our firm? How would it minimize its losses? Can you explain how the output of the firm will be determined by the shape of its marginal cost curve? If its marginal cost curve determines *output,* what does its average cost curve determine? If in doubt, look back at the previous diagram.[2]

FINAL EQUILIBRIUM

Last, we assume that a price has been reached that just allows the least efficient firm in the industry to stay alive. Indicate in the next diagram what the equilibrium position of this firm looks like, following the steps below. Remember, at equilibrium there must be four equalities:

$$P = MR = MC = AC$$

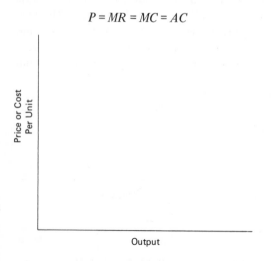

1. Draw in and label the *MR* curve. Is this the same as the average revenue curve? Is it determined by price?
2. Draw in the *AC* curve. What must be the relation of the *AC* curve and the *MR* curve in equilibrium?
3. Draw in the *MC* curve. Where does it cut the *AC* curve? What is its relation to *MR*?

Your diagram should look like this.

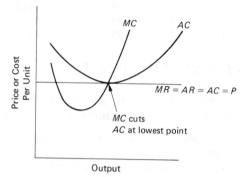

Now suppose that your firm is not the marginal one, but a firm that enjoys special cost advantages, perhaps of location, or entrepreneurial skill. In the figure below we have drawn an "intramarginal" firm. Show its profits in a shaded rectangle.

Remember: (1) output will be where *MC* = *MR;* (2) profit will be the difference between revenue and average cost of that output. If in doubt, check back to your previous diagram above.

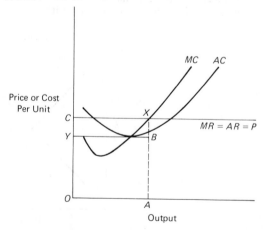

SCALE

Now suppose that demand grows for your product and you decide to rebuild your plant on a larger and more efficient scale. Draw a series of average cost curves that depict economies of scale. Will the "envelope" curve that encloses this series eventually level out?

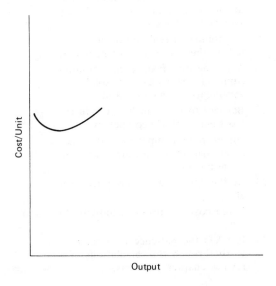

Note: If it doesn't, it would mean that a large enough plant could produce at zero cost!

More important, *why* do we encounter the phenomenon of scale? The answer is *not* "diminishing returns" because all factors, not just one, are being added. It is *not* "increasing cost," because we are not concerned with nonhomogeneous factors — that is, using factors less and less suitable to the firm. *The effects of scale result, in the main, from the fact of indivisibilities.* Indivisibilities in turn refer to minimum amounts of one factor (usually capital) that must be assembled to attain certain engineering objectives. Up to a certain point, as we assemble larger amounts of capital, it becomes possible to increase the division of labor, or to utilize certain physical or chemical processes, that are not within reach at smaller sizes of operation. The assembly line is a good example of this.

Beyond a certain size, further economies of scale disappear (an assembly line ten miles long would probably be more subject to breakdown than one a half-mile long). Thereafter the "scale" effect within a plant ceases or gives rise to increasing costs of management. Note: this applies to a single plant — not a firm that expands by building a second plant.

COMPETITION

We have almost finished this lengthy review, but there remains one very important point to be summarized. These are the conditions for the state of "pure" competition that sets the stage for the actions of the firm.

There are three such conditions and you should learn them:

1. **Large numbers of marketers.** *The market must be large enough so that no firm, by its own actions, can affect the prices it pays for factors or the price of the product it sells.*
2. **Ease of entry and exit.** *Firms must not be blocked from entering a profitable industry by patents, by the huge scale of operations required, and so on. They must also be able to leave the industry if prices are below average cost. This last requirement is difficult to obtain in the short run.*
3. **Nondifferentiated products.** *Firms must sell goods that are indistinguishable from each other, such as pins, wheat, thread, and so on. The reason is that nondifferentiated products ensure that firms must compete by* **price** *only. We will look into the effects of differentiating products in our next chapter.*

A Review Quiz

We have covered a great deal of ground. See if you have mastered the material by taking the quiz below.

T F

1. Fixed costs apply to immovable objects only, such as buildings.
2. Fixed costs per unit fall continuously as output increases. — —
3. Average variable costs vary because of the law of variable proportions. — —
4. Average total cost minus average variable cost equals average fixed cost.
5. Average variable cost can be rising even though marginal cost is falling. — —
6. When average output per unit of input reaches a maximum, average variable cost per unit of output reaches a minimum.
7. The marginal unit cost curve cuts the average unit cost curve at the lowest cost per unit. — —
8. If you have marginal cost data per unit for a factor's inputs, you can compute total cost and average cost per unit. — —
9. The demand curve for a single competitive firm is perfectly inelastic. — —
10. When a single competitive firm expands beyond the equilibrium output, its cost of unit production rises. — —
11. Rising unit costs of production for a competitive firm are always the result of rising costs of inputs. — —
12. At equilibrium, the entrepreneur of a competitive firm tries to set marginal costs equal to average cost. — —
13. For a competitive firm, marginal revenue equals price. — —
14. If marginal cost is above marginal revenue at normal levels of output, the firm should contract output. — —
15. If marginal cost is above marginal

T F

revenue, and marginal cost is decreasing, the output should be increased. — —
16. The "four-way" equilibrium reads: $P=MR=MC=AC$. — —
17. If profits are being earned in a competitive industry, output in that industry will rise because the firms in it will increase output. — —
18. In the short run a firm should shut down as soon as price falls below average variable cost. — —
19. Economies of scale mean that costs fall as the size of output increases. — —
20. A competitive firm reaches equilibrium in the short run solely by varying its volume of output. — —
21. Barriers to entry make an industry less than perfectly competitive. — —
22. Under pure competition, the marginal firm in an industry earns no economic profit. — —
23. In the long run all costs are variable. — —
24. Fixed cost is a result of indivisibilities. — —
25. It takes the patience of a saint to work through the calculations of a review chapter like this. — —

Answers:

1. F	10. T	18. F
2. T	11. F	19. T
3. T	12. F	20. T
4. T	13. T	21. T
5. F	14. T	22. T
6. T	15. T	23. T
7. T	16. T	24. F
8. T	17. F	25. T
9. F		

Monopolies and Oligopolies

13

LEARNING OBJECTIVES

The key concept in the study of monopoly, oligopoly, or monopolistic competition is the sloping demand curve. Be sure you understand how a sloping demand curve gives rise to a marginal revenue curve that is different from the marginal revenue curve faced by a competitive firm. Thereafter focus on three points:

1. What is the equilibrium position of a monopoly?
2. What is the tactical problem of an oligopoly?
3. How does a monopolistically competitive firm differ from a purely competitive one?

There is one crucial difference between the competitive firm and the oligopolistic or monopolistic one. *It is the shape of the demand curve that each faces.* The competitive firm faces a horizontal demand curve; the noncompetitive firm faces a sloping curve. All the rest follows from this.

MARGINAL REVENUE

Why is the slope of the demand curve all-important? Because the demand curve is the average revenue curve for any firm, competitive or monopolistic. Any point on the demand curve indicates the quantity sold and the price per unit (equal to average price). Therefore total revenue always equals quantity times price. When the average revenue curve is flat, as it is with competitive firms, each additional unit is sold at the same price as the preceding unit, and marginal revenue is always the same as average revenue. *This means — cost considerations aside — that a competitive firm always wants to sell as much as possible.* Indeed, the only reason a competitive firm does not sell an "infinite" quantity is because its cost curve makes this impossible. As we have seen, at some point its *MC* curve rises above its *MR* curve. Beyond that point it loses money if it increases output.

Now consider the monopoly. Its average revenue curve slopes downward. This is because the firm is the only seller on the market and *therefore has the same demand curve as the competitive industry.* To sell each additional unit, the monopoly must cut its price. But this lower price applies to *all* units it sells. Therefore, its revenue is not simply determined by its output multiplied by a fixed price, but its output multiplied by a *changing* price. The marginal revenue of the monopoly is therefore not the same as its average revenue. Hence a wholly new consideration enters into its calculations — namely, how large a volume of output is most profitable to sell, not only with regard to cost, but also with regard to revenue.

AN EXERCISE IN MARGINAL REVENUES

Let us work out this important principle. The following table gives you the data from which a monopolist could figure his total, marginal, and average revenues. Use the following questions as a guide.

Price	Units Demanded	Total Revenue	Marginal Revenue	Average Revenue
$10.00	3	$30.00	—	$10.00
9.50	4	38.00	$8.00	9.50
9.00	5	45.00	7.00	9.00
8.50	6	51.00	6.00	—
8.00	7	—	—	—
7.50	8			
7.00	9			
6.50	10			
6.00	11			
5.50	12			

1. Fill in the total revenue column. Total revenue is derived by multiplying_____by _____.

2. From total revenue it is simple to derive marginal revenue. It is the difference between total revenue at one level and at the next. If total revenue at a price of $8 is $56, marginal revenue is the difference between $56 and $51, or $____.

3. Average revenue is the total revenue divided by the _____ . Therefore it is the same as the _____ .

4. Why does marginal revenue fall as sales rise? The answer is that the larger number of units is not multiplied by the same price, but by a _____ price.

5. Which would be more beneficial for a monopolist that was lowering its price, an elastic or an inelastic demand curve? Think: if demand is elastic, a given increase in sales can be achieved with a _____ (smaller/larger) cut in price than if demand were inelastic. Therefore marginal revenue would be _____ (larger/smaller).

6. Would a monopoly also want demand to be elastic if it were forced to raise its price?

GRAPHING EQUILIBRIUM

Now graph the average and marginal revenue curves from your table in Figure 13-1. Draw in an average and marginal cost curve, wherever you wish. Will these curves have the same general shape as with a competitive firm? Why? Now carefully follow these steps:

1. What will the most profitable output be? Remember the rule — expand output until marginal _____ is equal to marginal _____ . Locate the point on your graph, and mark it *x*. Be sure it is where the marginal cost curve cuts the *marginal* revenue curve, not the average revenue curve (that's a common mistake to make).

2. From this intersection of *MC* and *MR*, drop a line to the output axis to show the quantity that the monopolist will produce. Call this output *OY*. Does this tell you some informa-

FIGURE 13–1

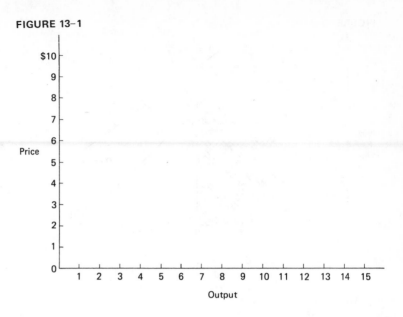

tion that will be useful later in figuring his profits? (Hint: your line will cut the monopolist's average cost curve. Mark this point *Z*, and *Z'* on the price axis.

3. From the intersection of *MR* and *MC*, extend your line up to the price curve. Mark this *A*, and *A'* on the price axis. How do you know that this will be the price at which your output is sold? Answer: because the price curve (or the average revenue curve) is the _____ curve.

4. From the intersection of your output line with the demand curve, draw a horizontal line to the price axis. This should now show you total receipts. Total receipts will be price (average revenue) times output. Lightly shade in this area of total receipts. It will be quantity _____ times price _____.

5. Now calculate your total costs. This will be _____ (average/marginal) costs times output. Be sure you get the right one. Indicate the total cost area by slightly heavier shading. It will be quantity _____ times cost _____.

6. Finally, profit. It is the difference between total _____ and total _____. It is therefore the portion of the total revenue rectangle that has not been heavily shaded, or quantity _____ times profit _____. It can also be defined as the profit

per unit times output. Profit *per unit* is the difference between _____ per unit and _____ per unit. It is _____ .

Now check your diagram with Figure 13–2.

THE KINKED DEMAND CURVE

The oligopolist faces a different kind of demand curve from that of the monopolist. He does not sell to the entire market, but must share it with his oligopolistic competitors. Suppose you were an oligopolist seller, selling output *OX* at price *OA* as shown in Figure 13–3.

Suppose that you wanted to raise prices. If your competitors also raised their prices, all would be fine. You and your competitors together would lose some sales (the amount depending on the elasticity of demand for the product of your industry) but your *share* should remain the same. But suppose that your competitors did not raise prices. There is a strong likelihood that buyers of the product would switch from your high-priced product to theirs. Draw in a demand curve for your product under these conditions.

FIGURE 13-2

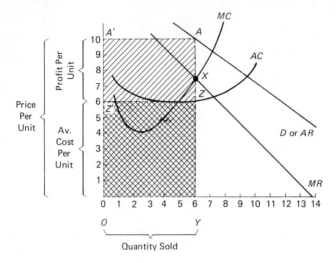

Quantity Sold

Now suppose you cut prices and your competitors did not. You might then "steal away" a lot of their business. But if your competitors matched your price cuts with similar cuts, your total sales would increase only to the extent that those of the industry increased. Draw in a demand curve under these assumptions. This is the famous "kinked" oligopoly demand curve.

FIGURE 13-3

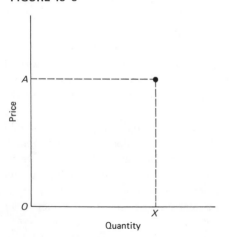

MONOPOLISTIC COMPETITION

A third very important case involves competition among many firms that compete by differentiating their products. If your product is differentiated by design, "style," or even just by trade name, you can expect to keep *some* customers even if you raise your price. Consider the case of the following commodities, all of which have many substitutes.

toothbrushes
soap
picture wire
lamp cord
typewriting paper
carbon paper
light bulbs

Can you think of a brand name or other aspect of product differentiation that would entice you to buy one particular manufacturer's product even if you knew that his prices were, say, 10 percent higher than those of extremely similar brands?

In the graph shown in Figure 13-4 we show an average and marginal revenue curve for a firm in a monopolistically competitive market. Note that

FIGURE 13–4

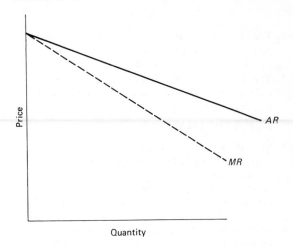

it is downward sloping, as is the demand curve for a monopoly.

Now draw in marginal and average cost curves, as you have in the previous case. Indicate the following:

1. Optimum output. This will be where the _____ curve intersects the _____ curve.
2. Selling price and total revenue at that output.
3. Total cost at that output.
4. Total profit at that output.

Your answers should look exactly like the former exercise on monopoly. What, then, is the

difference? It is that there is easy entry into this industry, unlike the case with monopoly. The result of more firms entering the field will be to divide the sales of the industry among more sellers. The demand curve of each will move to the left. Show this by drawing a series of *AR* curves (you can omit the *MR* curves because the graph gets too complicated). The graph in Figure 13–5 shows the final equilibrium position.

Is it in equilibrium? Does *AC* = *AR*? Can any more firms enter the industry? (That is, does this "typical" firm make any economic profits?)

Show in Figure 13–5:

FIGURE 13–5

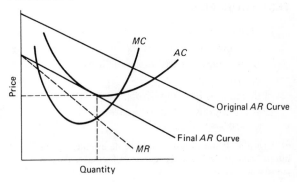

1. The loss in output due to monopolistic competition. What would output be under conditions of pure competition?
2. The increase in price due to monopolistic competition. What would price be under pure competition?[1]

Points to Remember:

1. The difference between monopoly, oligopolistic, or monopolistic competition, and pure competition *is not the result of different motives.* All entrepreneurs are presumed to be rational profit maximizers. It is the result of an altered market structure, which permits firms to exercise strategies. Firms under pure competition are *price-takers;* firms in imperfect competition (including monopoly, which is the least "perfect" competition of all) can alter prices, within limits. They are *price-searchers.*
2. The introduction of price-searching brings a new dimension to competition — by differentiating its product, a price-searching firm can affect the shape and position of the demand curve. This brings *selling costs* as a new category of cost.
3. Even pure monopolies do not have limitless ability to manipulate price. They are constrained by the demand curve, which in turn is established by the presence of substitutes.
4. The idea of "maximizing" loses its clear-cut meaning when firms can plan strategies that seek to maximize profits over *long periods of time.*
5. Oligopolies seek to maintain high prices by tacit collusion, by price leadership, or other means of concerting industry action.

TEST YOURSELF

_ 1. Market structure essentially refers to
   a. number of competitors.
   b. geographic distribution of firms.
   c. size of firms.
   d. motives of competitors.
_ 2. A monopolist seeks to equate
   a. *MR* and *MC.*

[1]*Answer: P* and output would be determined by the intersection of *MC* and *AC* curves. Of course, the *AR* curve would be flat.

   b. *MR* and *AC.*
   c. price and *AC.*
   d. *MR* and *AR.*
_ 3. A monopolist's *MR* curve is
   a. horizontal.
   b. below *AR* curve.
   c. below *AC* curve.
   d. indeterminate.
_ 4. A monopolist's demand curve is
   a. the same as the demand curve of an industry.
   b. subject to influence by seller.
   c. affected by substitutes.
   d. all of the above.
   e. all of the above except c.
_ 5. An oligopolist's strategy is
   a. unaffected by behavior of other oligopolists.
   b. revenue, not profit-maximizing.
   c. similar to that of the monopolist.
   d. all of the above.
   e. none of the above.
_ 6. Monopoly output is
   a. less than that of a competitive firm.
   b. more than that of a competitive firm.
   c. same as that of a competitive firm but sold at higher price.
_ 7. Monopolistic profits reflect
   a. inability of firms to enter industry.
   b. inelastic demand curve.
   c. lower cost curves than that of competitive firm.
   d. ability to equate *MR* with price.
_ 8. A "kinked" demand curve is the result of
   a. selling costs.
   b. inelastic demand above selling price, elastic demand below.
   c. ability to influence demand by advertising.
   d. response by other oligopolists.
_ 9. Imperfect competition yields an outcome in which
   a. all economic profits are competed away.
   b. less than competitive output is attained.
   c. $P = AC = MR = MC.$

_10. Equilibrium of the firm in all market struc-
tures requires that.
   a. $MR = MC$
   b. $MR = P$
   c. $MC = P$
   d. $MC = AC$
   e. all of the above be true.

Answers:

1. a   3. b   5. e
2. a   4. d   6. a

7. a   9. b   10. a
8. d

Readings

Here are a few readings to round out your study of monopoly and oligopoly. In the excerpts that follow, you will have a chance to look into the question of large-scale enterprise from many points of view: its legal organization, the problems of defining an industry, the controversial question of oil.

WHAT IS AN INDUSTRY?

Richard Caves

We have seen that it is not a simple matter to define a monopoly. Professor Caves, a specialist in industrial organization, discusses the related problem of defining an industry and describing its structure.

We defined an industry as the sellers of a particular product, one side of the market in which buyers and sellers arrange their transactions. This simple notion corresponds to the way we speak of industries in everyday life. We need only to identify the product and find out who sells it. For instance, before World War II the Aluminum Company of America was the sole producer of aluminum ingots within the United States. American tariff walls kept out most imports, and other metals were not suitable substitutes for aluminum. Buyers in the market wanted aluminum, not some other metal; and Alcoa was the "industry" from which they could buy it. The description of this market and

From Richard Caves, *American Industry: Structure, Conduct, and Performance,* 2nd ed. (Englewood Cliffs, N.J.: Prentice-Hall, Inc., 1967), pp. 6-9.

industry poses no problem. Likewise, the many persons who wish on any particular day to buy or sell common shares of the American Telephone & Telegraph Co. all make their offers through a single center, the New York Stock Exchange. Again, the market and its participants are easy to identify.

THE PROBLEM OF INDUSTRY BOUNDARIES

Just counting the heads of buyers and sellers participating in a product market does not, however, solve all the problems associated with labeling its sellers as a separate industry. Economic theory tells us that all participants in a market should be highly sensitive to changes in the terms of transactions offered by the other participants. And they should *not* be sensitive to such moves by outsiders located in other markets. The industries which we identify for discussion in the real world ought to satisfy this requirement. Herein arises the problem of *industry boundaries* — boundaries between products, boundaries in space, and even boundaries in time.

For instance, as aluminum has grown more important among the key basic metals used in the modern economy, it has found itself in close rivalry with steel and other metals for more and more uses. Nowadays, a major price change in either the steel or the aluminum industry stirs some talk about a possible change in the other. Yet these parallel changes do not always occur, and many minor developments can happen in either industry without clearly affecting the other. That is to say, the buyers in the aluminum market are *very* sensitive to the price offers made by the aluminum industry, but they are also *somewhat* sensitive to the price offers made by other metals producers. Where should the industry boundary be drawn — around the sellers of aluminum or around the sellers of "basic metals"? That is the problem of industry boundaries.

A problem of industry boundaries can arise because sellers can shift from one group of buyers to another, as in the case just mentioned in which some metals buyers could shift between aluminum sellers and steel sellers. Producers weaving cotton fiber into cloth might easily be able to shift their looms to the weaving of linen or other fibers. In this case, the cotton-weavers would be somewhat sensitive to developments in the linen industry. Should the industry boundary fall between cotton-weavers and linen-weavers or around the "weaving industry"?

Any attempt to classify all firms in the economy according to separate industries obviously runs into thousands of boundary problems like these. Settling each one must be a matter of judgment. Drawing the boundaries too widely lumps together producers who are somewhat insensitive to one another's actions. Drawing

them too narrowly places in separate industries firms which are actually quite sensitive to one another's actions. Published statistics for the United States and other major industrial countries usually give you a choice, identifying both a small number of widely defined industries and also a number of narrowly defined groups within each large industry. By fiddling with these statistics, one can usually draw a personally satisfactory boundary among groups of sellers. These statistics perform less well for the buyers' side of the market, however, and they often define industries catering to buyers who are also quite sensitive to offers being made by other industries.

The other major problem of industry boundaries arises for products which are sold in regional markets. Consider the case of beer, a product which consists — let us face it — mostly of water. Its transportation costs thus are quite high relative to the sale value of the product. In the United States a number of brands are advertised and sold nationally, but in every area they compete against a different group of "local brands," which typically sell at a lower price and often hold a large share of the local market. Should we consider breweries a national industry, or a group of interrelated regional industries? The problem calls for the same kind of judgment that is required in drawing the line between closely related products. The issue of local markets gets even more troublesome when we consider retail trade. People seldom go to the next city to shop, so the only question would seem to be whether we consider only the local shopping center, or the whole urban area. But what about the existence of Sears, Roebuck & Co.?

DESCRIBING THE STRUCTURE OF AN INDUSTRY

Besides applying judgment to fix the location of industry boundaries between similar products, we need a method of describing the different industry structures found within these boundaries. Economic theory provides a set of categories or market models which offer valuable guidance, but they fail to go the whole distance. You have learned that "monopoly" implies a single seller and "pure competition" a very large number of sellers within the relevant markets. "Monopolistic competition," like pure competition, depends on a very large number of sellers occupying the market, even though each of them has some touches of individuality. Oligopoly, usually defined as "few" sellers occupying the market, covers everything else. If "few" includes all markets lying between "one" and "many," it surely has a large territory to itself.

Be that as it may, these concepts need some modification before they can guide us in forming a description of the industries and markets in the American economy. For instance, an oligopoly of 3 sellers may behave very differently from one of 20 firms — unless, of course, 3 of the latter 20 have almost the whole market to themselves, with their 17 rivals subsisting on the fringe. We need a measurement tool which takes account of both the *number* and *size distribution* of firms in a market, yet presents the result in a form simple enough that it is easy to interpret. The most widely used device is the *concentration ratio.* To compute a concentration ratio, you rank firms in order of size, starting from the largest in the industry. (Size is usually measured in terms of either sales or employees.) Then, starting from the top of the list, you add up the percentages for the top *x* firms. Published statistics usually give concentration ratios for the largest 4, largest 8, and sometimes the largest 20 firms in an industry. The concentration ratio for a monopoly would, of course, be 100 percent; the ratio for the largest 4 firms in a competitive industry would have to be very small, perhaps 5 or 10 percent. The ratio for an oligopoly would lie between these limits. . . .

Another important qualification for interpreting concentration ratios is the role of foreign trade. A single seller monopolizing the entire domestic market is a very different thing from a single domestic producer holding half of domestic sales in competition with imports. Concentration ratios, however, are calculated on the basis of sales by domestic producers only, and so the statistics will show the same concentration in both cases. For most products, imports hold a relatively small share of the United States market. Disregarding them causes less trouble than if we were studying a country such as Denmark or Italy, where imports bulk much larger in the domestic market. Nonetheless, even a small market share held by importers can make a big difference, as was shown by the "compact car revolution" spurred by imported automobiles.

Two industries, A and B, both with 80 percent of their sales controlled by the largest 4 firms, might still differ in important ways. Industry A could embrace as few as five firms; if each of them held just 20 percent of the

FIGURE 1. Possible differences in number and size distribution of firms between industries with identical concentration ratios.

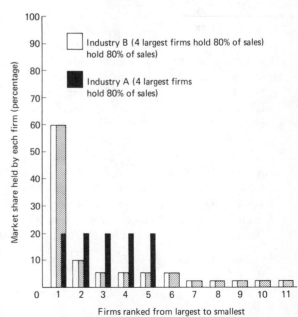

Firms ranked from largest to smallest

industry's sales, then the "largest 4" would account for 80 percent. Industry B might have a very large number of firms accounting for the remaining 20 percent of sales. Likewise, the biggest firms might have a differing degree of dominance. The largest single firm in industry A might have as little as 20 percent of total sales; the leader in industry B might control as much as 50 or 60 percent. [Figure 1] gives an example of how different these industries might look. Despite these problems, the concentration ratios for different industries usually give a fairly accurate picture of where they stand comparatively in the spectrum running from pure competition to "pure" monopoly. This is because, as a matter of fact, most industries have some large and some small firms in them. One Gulliver surrounded by a crowd of Lilliputians (industry B) is uncommon; so is a clump of equally giant Brobdingnagians (industry A). Still, it is [often] hard to answer the question: Which industry is more concentrated?

THE CASE AGAINST BIG OIL

Brit Hume

A Washington-based investigative reporter for ABC News describes the background to the oil crisis of 1973. Here is a background study before *the Arab oil embargo that will add depth to the analysis of the oil industry given in the text.*

In September, 1972, supplies of home heating oil in the United States were dangerously low and stocks of crude oil, from which heating oil is refined, had fallen to their lowest level since World War II. A serious fuel shortage seemed inevitable as winter approached. President Nixon authorized the petroleum industry to import more foreign crude oil. It was the second time in five months he had increased the allowable imports of foreign oil, which had been under tight government restriction since 1959. A few weeks later, in a speech to the National Petroleum Council, Gen. George Lincoln, head of the White House Office of Emergency Preparedness,

From *The New York Times Sunday Magazine* (December 9, 1973). © 1973 by The New York Times Company. Reprinted by permission.

which had charge of oil imports, strongly urged industry leaders to crank up their refineries to full capacity to head off a heating-fuel crisis. Simultaneously, the Interior Department sent telegrams to the major oil refineries urging them to do the same.

The response of the major oil companies, which control most of the nation's fuel production from the wellhead to the retail dealer, was to import only one-third of the additional crude oil the President had authorized and to run most of the refineries below capacity for the rest of the year. "This," concluded a staff study made for the Senate Permanent Investigations Subcommittee, "was the beginning of the first peacetime petroleum shortage in the United States."

The petroleum industry in the United States is dominated by 18 large firms which are, in the language of economists, "vertically integrated." This means that they operate in all phases of the oil business — exploration and production, transportation, refining, distribution and marketing. These 18 generally are known as the "majors," although the term is used more and more often to refer to the top 10 oil companies. The majors produce about 70 percent of the domestic crude oil, control some 80 percent of the refinery capacity and market about 72 percent of the gasoline sold in this country.*

The largest of the majors also dominate the production of natural gas in the United States and have made heavy investments in the coal industry in recent years. Despite this heavy concentration of a relatively small number of companies in all phases of domestic fossil-fuel production, the major oil companies vigorously resist any suggestions that they are not fully competitive. Nevertheless, they cooperate rather than compete in a wide variety of ways. It is common for several oil companies, for example, to submit joint bids on multimillion-dollar leases of government-owned oil reserves and to pool resources for joint exploration ventures seeking crude deposits. Most of the huge pipelines, which are the principal form of transportation in the oil business, are jointly owned by several companies. Major firms often engage in exchange agreements where one will supply the other's markets — for gasoline, for example — in one area where it lacks facilities in exchange for a similar favor in a different region. Reciprocal processing agreements among major firms are also frequent (one company will refine another's crude oil in one place in exchange for having its own crude processed in another).

*The 18 leading oil companies, as measured by total assets, are: Exxon, Texaco, Gulf, Mobil, Standard of California, Standard of Indiana (American), Shell, Tenneco, Atlantic Richfield, Phillips, Continental, Sun, Union Pacific, Union Oil, Cities Service, Getty, Standard of Ohio and Marathon.

Perhaps the most obvious clue to the state of competition in the oil industry is its national advertising. The majors spend heavily to gain recognition for their brand names, promote product ingredients and advertise giveaways. Instead of bargains on gas and oil, the consumer hears about Tony the Tiger, Platformate, free drinking glasses and National Football League trading cards, Sunoco station owners who "can be very friendly" and Texaco stations where "you can trust your car to the man who wears the star." In contrast, the independents advertise little. Their stations are typically low-overhead, self-service operations which offer almost none of the mechanical services and auto supplies, such as tires and batteries, available at the majors' outlets. They stick to high-volume sales of gas and oil at prices below those at major stations. And although their share of the market was growing rapidly in the early part of this decade, the independents were still at a disadvantage.

A principal reason: They are not vertically integrated. Independent refineries have had to rely on the majors for a large part of their crude oil. And independent marketers must turn to other independents or to the majors to obtain refined products. What's more, the oil depletion allowance has encouraged the majors to push all their profits into crude-oil production where a large portion could be deducted. To do this, the majors kept crude prices as high as they could and cut profit margins on their refining and marketing operations to the minimum. For them, this generally involved only bookkeeping transactions since they were selling their crude to their own refineries and their refined products to their own marketers, or engaging in reciprocal arrangements with other majors to achieve the same results. But for the independent refiner, high crude-oil prices usually represented a real additional cost. And since it was necessary for independent refiners to show a profit on refining, prices for their finished products tended to be pushed upward still more. This left the independent marketer in an even more difficult position. Nevertheless, the independents were resourceful and innovative and they found ways to cut costs and prices and gain ground on the majors steadily through 1970. After that, though, things began to change rapidly.

Although there could be no doubt that demand for oil products would continue to boom in the early nineteen-seventies, the majors decided not to increase their refinery capacity significantly. An efficient refinery costs about $250 million to build and this has generally meant that only the majors have been able to afford new ones in the past 20 years. The majors' spokesmen have insisted that uncertainty about Government policy on oil imports and environmentalist objections to new plant construction were the main reasons behind the failure to expand refinery capacity. Whatever the reason there was no uncertainty about the result it would have. By early 1971, Oil and Gas Journal, the most authoritative of the industry's trade publications, reported that the nation might be on the way toward a shortage of refinery capacity. The American Petroleum Institute, the industry's voice in Washington, predicted that the shortage would come before 1975. The Interior Department's Office of Oil and Gas published a study containing a similar forecast and declaring that existing refineries would have to be run full tilt to keep up with demand.

In August, 1971, President Nixon imposed wage and price controls. Gasoline prices were frozen at seasonal highs and heating-oil prices at off-season lows. Gasoline was always more profitable to produce, but the freeze made it more so and created a strong disincentive to the production of heating oil. The freeze was lifted in November, but oil prices were not decontrolled. In February, 1972, the Cost of Living Council refused to grant the industry a price increase for either crude oil or gasoline and heating oil. For the first six months of 1972, profits fell almost 5

percent, although sales were up by an even greater amount.

In early 1972, industry journals were reporting that crude-oil production in both Texas and Louisiana, the two biggest oil states, was declining. While this was apparently true,* it is difficult to know whether it was caused by an actual decline in reserves or by the industry's failure to produce as much as it could. There are at least some indications the larger companies might have been deliberately slowing production. The Texas Railroad Commission requires the oil companies that do business in the state, which includes nearly all the larger firms, to report "desired" levels of crude-oil stocks, nationwide.

The commission's records show that the 10 largest of the oil companies reporting (all of them majors) "desired" smaller stocks of crude oil to feed most of their refineries in 1972 than they had had in 1971, even though demand for petroleum products had risen about 7 percent. Their actual crude-oil stocks were also less than they had been the year before. The commission's records show that the drop in "desired" levels was reported only by those top 10 oil companies, with the next 15 reporting increases in their desired levels. But since the top 10 account for about three-quarters of the oil production among the top 25 that report to the Texas commission, it averaged out to an over-all drop in the "desired" stocks of crude.

Moreover, an investigation by the Federal Trade Commission has turned up evidence that the natural-gas reserves *reported* by the nation's oil and gas companies are smaller that the *actual* reserves. "From the documents received," James Halverson, chief of the FTC's Competition Bureau, told a Senate subcommittee, "it appears that there has been serious underreporting of proved natural-gas reserves." The natural-gas sit-

*There are virtually no independent statistics on the activities of the oil industry. State and Federal agencies rely on data furnished by the oil companies themselves.

uation is important for two reasons. One is that the major oil companies are also the major gas-producing companies. The other is that a shortage — or a seeming shortage — of one kind of fuel places added pressure on the others.

Besides indicating a desire for smaller crude oil stocks last year, the major petroleum firms also kept the bulk of their refinery capacity below maximum output for most of the year. In the first four months of 1972, according to their reports to the Texas Railroad Commission, the top 10 firms actually kept their refineries running below the level of the same period of 1971. As a result, supplies of gasoline and heating oil dropped below their levels of a year before. Refinery runs were sharply increased in the next five months, largely to head off a summer gasoline shortage. But this meant that heating fuel was scarce by fall. And, as was mentioned earlier, when the government appealed for full use of increased import allowances and maximum refinery output to avoid a winter heating oil crisis, the major companies did not comply. When the crunch came, they accelerated refinery operations to take up the heating oil slack, but this, naturally, got them behind in gasoline production. So that shortages of gasoline in the summer of 1973 became inevitable. Industry spokesmen point out that, despite less than maximum refinery operations for much of last year, overall fuel production increased over the previous two years. But, as both industry and government projections had indicated, demand was increasing too fast for anything but maximum output to fill the need.

Meanwhile, a number of the majors were continuing the process, begun some years before, of shutting down marketing units in certain areas, apparently to withdraw from their least profitable operation. Industry spokesmen insist they were merely liquidating "uneconomic" operations. But to some students of the oil business, it looked suspiciously as if the big oil companies were carving up the domestic market to share among themselves. A Federal Trade Commission report on the industry completed last summer explained it this way: "All the majors can increase their regional market concentration simultaneously by pulling out of markets where their share is lower than their national average and selling their operations to those majors who remain. This strategy will work, however, only if the majors can retain or expand their regional market shares. To do so, they must prevent the further entry and expansion of independent marketers. Ultimately, the only way to contain or reduce the independents' market shares is through monopoly power at the refining or crude pipeline stages."

In fact, since the onset of the shortages, the majors have increasingly been telling independent refiners and marketers they could not supply them with either crude oil or refined products because they needed all they had for their own operations. Independent refiners have been forced to operate well below their normal capacity. The impact on independent marketers has been devastating. Hundreds of independent gasoline stations have shut down because of a lack of supply. Many that stayed open were forced to raise prices, wiping out their competitive edge. And the majors increasingly opened up so-called "fighting brand" stations which emulate the high-volume, low-overhead, discount approach pioneered by the independents.

· · ·

The pesky independent companies have been gravely weakened. And the majors' sagging profit picture of the late nineteen-sixties and early seventies has taken a dramatic turn for the better. Exxon, the nation's leading energy company, has seen its profits rise more than 80 percent in the third quarter of [1973] over the same period in 1972, the worst of the industry's recent lean years.

[In 1973] none of the top five oil companies

reported third-quarter profit increases of less than 50 percent over 1972. Gulf, the third-leading oil producer, said its profits were up 91 percent from the third quarter of 1972.

There are some who believe the major oil companies conspired to bring about these results. Indeed, the Federal Trade Commission, as a result of the previously mentioned study of the industry finished last summer, has filed a huge antitrust case against the top eight oil companies accusing them of collusion to monopolize the industry.

The FTC's central allegation is that the eight oil majors have "maintained and reinforced a noncompetitive market structure in the refining of crude oil into petroleum products." They have done this, the FTC charges, by — among other things — "pursuing a common cause of action to abuse and exploit the means of gathering and transporting crude oil to refineries ... participating in restrictive or exclusionary transfers of ownership of crude oil among themselves and with other petroleum companies ... using their vertical integration to keep profits at the crude level artificially high and profits at the refining level artificially low ... accommodating the needs and goals of each other in the production, supply and transportation of crude oil to the exclusion or detriment of independent refiners." The commission also charges that similar practices have given the eight firms "monopoly power" over the marketing of petroleum products. The industry has vigorously denied the charges. The case will take years to litigate.

The Problems of
Big Business

14

Here is a series of readings that focuses on the problems discussed in Chapter Fourteen. We begin with a brief look at the statistics of bigness. The figures at the top of the next page show the top twenty-five industrial corporations, ranked by size. (Note that they omit nonindustrial firms such as banks, insurance companies, or utilities such as the giant of giants, AT&T.) The figures also show the ranking of these companies in pre-

vious years. Notice the rise of the oil group over the decades. To what do you attribute this? The dashes in the earlier columns indicate companies that used to be among the top twenty-five, but that have now declined below the peak. Do you think reliable conclusions could be drawn from this table as to the rate of turnover of the top businesses in America?

Rank							Company	Total Assets (in Millions of Dollars) 1973
1919	1929	1935	1948	1958	1968	1973		
2	2	1	1	1	1	1	Exxon	21,558
5	3	3	2	2	2	2	General Motors	18,273
15	9	11	6	6	4	3	Texaco	12,032
7	6	6	10	7	3	4	Ford Motor Co.	11,634
—*	—	—	—	18	7	5	IBM	10,792
20	15	12	7	4	5	6	Gulf Oil	9,324
9	7	4	5	5	6	7	Mobil Oil	9,216
—	—	—	—	30	15	8	ITT	8,617
27	10	10	11	10	10	9	Standard Oil (Calif.)	8,084
11	11	13	9	11	11	10	General Electric	7,401
1	1	2	3	3	8	11	U.S. Steel	6,570
34	4	5	4	9	12	12	Standard Oil (Indiana)	6,186
—	45	33	25	19	13	13	Chrysler	5,497
—	13	15	21	13	14	14	Shell Oil	5,171
—	—	—	—	—	16	15	Tenneco	4,838
—	—	50	34	41	25	16	Atlantic Richfield	4,629
—	—	—	14	20	21	17	Western Electric	4,309
18	12	9	8	8	17	18	Dupont	4,283
30	28	32	17	17	31	19	Westinghouse	3,843
—	—	49	33	34	23	20	Eastman Kodak	3,757
26	24	22	15	14	18	21	Union Carbide	3,718
6	5	7	12	12	19	22	Bethlehem Steel	3,645
49	32	35	32	26	26	23	Goodyear Tire and Rubber	3,476
—	—	—	—	29	29	24	Dow Chemical	3,312
—	—	44	22	15	20	25	Phillips Petroleum	3,269

*The company did not exist at the time.

ATTENTION MONOPOLISTS:
SENATOR HART IS WATCHING

David Schwartzman

Here is the first of three readings on What to Do About Big Business. Should we "bust up" the largest companies? Professor Schwartzman, an expert on industrial structures, says No, and tells why not.

For years economists have complained about the ineffectiveness of the antitrust laws in dealing

From *Challenge* (September/October, 1973).

with entrenched monopoly. Now they seem to have won political support in the form of a bill that one of their number might have written — and probably did. Introduced a year ago by

Senator Philip Hart, chairman of the Senate Subcommittee on Antitrust and Monopoly, the appropriately named Industrial Reorganization Act would result in the dissolution of IBM, General Motors, General Electric, U.S. Steel and many other leading companies in "concentrated industries."

The proposed law is consistent with the standard argument that economists constantly repeat in textbooks and journals: that a high concentration ratio signifies monopoly power regardless of the behavior of the companies which possess it and that to destroy that monopoly power it is necessary to break up the leading firms in concentrated industries. If the bill is passed, it would no longer be necessary to demonstrate overt collusion, predatory behavior or monopolistic intent to find a violation of the antitrust laws. The test would be economists' criteria of monopoly power: high profit rates, high concentration ratios and the absence of price competition.

According to the bill's provisions, monopoly power will be presumed to exist under the three sets of circumstances: (1) if an industry's concentration ratio (the proportion of sales accounted for by the four largest firms) exceeds 50 percent; (2) if the companies within an industry have not competed in price for three years; and (3) if a firms's rate of profit has exceeded 15 percent for five consecutive years. Any one of these three criteria would be sufficient to establish a violation. Although other evidence could be introduced, the burden of proof would be on the defendant, which could avoid dissolution by showing that patents legitimized the monopoly or that a breakup would result in the loss of significant economies of scale.

The bill would also create an Industrial Reorganization Commission and an Industrial Reorganization Court to investigate and judge possible monopoly situations. It also calls for investigation of seven industries regardless of whether the basic criteria have been met. Those named in the Hart Bill are: chemicals and drugs,

electrical machinery and equipment, electronic computing and communications equipment, energy, iron and steel, motor vehicles, and non-ferrous metals. Together they account for about 40 percent of manufacturing output.

Economists may be tempted to rejoice at their new-found influence, but further thought should give rise to some misgivings. For despite their well-scrubbed academic credentials, the proposed criteria of monopoly power are highly uncertain. In addition, there is simply no basis for the judgment that the performance of concentrated industries warrants drastic reorganization — particularly since such reorganizations carry substantial risks of reduced efficiency. Unfortunately the economic case for the Hart Bill rests on unverified theory concerning the effects of concentration and on an exaggerated estimate of society's loss due to monopoly.

THE ECONOMIC ISSUES

Economists are very much the disciples of Adam Smith the philosopher, rather than social scientists observing behavior. The economic theory of oligopoly consists largely of inference from a few plausible assumptions about business motivations. Not until recent years has there been any attempt to quantify the social loss that economists assumed to be the bitter fruit of monopoly.

Proponents of the Hart Bill have cited one such estimate — that of F. M. Scherer, who places the welfare loss attributable to monopolistic pricing at an appalling $60 billion a year. And to put the economic issues in clearest perspective, it is useful to examine the components of this loss: the "deadweight loss," losses through technical inefficiency and losses through excessive selling costs.

The concept of "deadweight loss" is an extension of the traditional economic argument that competition leads to optimum resource allocation. More specifically, it refers to the increase in total social utility that it is assumed would result from changing oligopolistic industries into something more nearly resembling the competitive model of classical economics. According to theory, oligopolistic firms maintain high prices by restricting output, and a reorganization to enforce competition would therefore generate an increase in output for the affected industries. Since these industries must draw additional resources away from competitive industries in which they are currently employed, the net increase will not be as large for the economy as a whole as for the oligopolistic industries themselves. But Scherer estimates that it would still be a substantial $10 billion a year.

Scherer's estimate is ten times larger than an earlier calculation by Arnold Harberger, which put the deadweight loss at a comparatively modest 0.1 percent of GNP, and represents, according to Scherer, a correction for various technical errors.

TECHNICALLY INEFFICIENT

In any event, most of Scherer's $60 billion monopoly loss comes not from a misallocation of resources, but from sloppy management. His premise is that, lacking the spur of competition, oligopolistic firms don't make the most of their opportunities. Or, as Adam Smith put it two centuries ago, monopoly "is a great enemy to good management."

Scherer estimates that society's tab for such "technical inefficiency" amounts to some 3.7 percent of GNP — roughly $30 billion to $40 billion a year. He admits that this number is essentially arbitrary but holds that it is well grounded in both economic theory and common sense. Economists find it difficult to visualize managers who are inefficient under conditions of vigorous competition or who don't relax a bit under the shelter of monopoly profits.

Despite its plausibility, age, and general acceptance, the theoretical argument lacks validity. For inefficient firms can operate in competitive industries if competitors are equally or less

efficient. The picture of the driven manager of the competitive firm is a romantic generalization. Instances of inefficiency in industries containing many sellers (the technical definition of a "competitive industry") are plentiful. For example, an investigation of British industries in the 1950s indicated that they were substantially less efficient than their U.S. counterparts. Despite a similar basic technology, British plants were not handling materials, equipment or space as well as they might — as demonstrated by the experience in U.S. plants.

The picture of the relaxed monopolist is no more realistic. Managers of monopolistic as well as competitive firms are rewarded not only for high levels of profits but also, through stock options and the like, for increases in profits. There is thus a constant pressure to increase efficiency to offset other changes which tend to reduce profits. In addition, monopoly profits are not so large as to afford much of a shelter. For monopolistic industries as a group, the rate of return on net worth after taxes is unlikely to exceed that of other industries by more than 5 percentage points. This is perhaps a large enough margin to reward investors who get in on the ground floor in some monopolistic venture, but it provides a very thin cushion indeed for managers who are tempted to relax. The excess profits are equivalent to no more than 2 percent of total costs.

In individual cases, of course, the profits may be large. But even then, managers are not insulated from declines in profits resulting from a cutback in demand, faulty forecasts, increases in wages, or any of the other things that can result in a decline in profits. And whether a firm is monopolistic or not, when its profits fall, the price of its stock reacts accordingly, and managers begin to feel the heat from shareholders and directors.

Far from supporting the notion that an attack on big business will enhance efficiency, logic and evidence point in the opposite direction: breaking up large companies in concentrated industries is likely to decrease their efficiency. Where there are large differences in efficiency, those firms which are superior capture a larger share of the market and the industry automatically becomes more concentrated. This hypothesis is at least partly confirmed by a study by Harold Demetz which showed that profits in concentrated industries were positively correlated with the size of the firm. If the high profits of the leaders had been due only to monopoly power, the profits of small firms would have been just as high. At the very least, there is some ground for skepticism about the general view of economists that economies of scale are not sufficiently large to justify the present size of large business organizations. Certainly there is no evidence to support the view that breaking them up will add the equivalent of a year's growth to the nation's GNP.

HARD SELLING

Consistent with the economists' traditional hostility toward advertising, Scherer puts a $10-billion tag on the welfare loss due to excessive selling costs. Advertising is, to be sure, vulnerable to attack as deceptive and wasteful; and I perhaps risk a cynical response by suggesting that it may also be informative. Yet Phillip Nelson reasons persuasively that for advertising to be effective, brands must be remembered favorably. The biggest advertisers are thus not those with the greatest effrontery but, on the contrary, those whose products generally offer the best value for the money. The actual amount of advertising may exceed the socially desirable amount, but it is not a total waste, since it does provide consumers with some useful information. Scherer's estimate of society's loss through monopoly is here, as elsewhere, wide of the mark.

An argument can also be made that Senator Hart has the wrong targets in his sights. Reflecting a desire to simplify and expedite antitrust proceedings, his proposal is to fragment the leading firms in industries in which the concentration ratio exceeds 50 percent. True, the bill invites defendants to demonstrate that they do not possess monopoly power and places no limit on the kind of evidence they may use. But because all evidence in this area is ambiguous, this shift in the burden of proof is tantamount to finding them guilty. Indeed, Hart's measure goes well beyond the recommendation of economists, who are generally reluctant to depend on the concentration ratio, but would use it in combination with other factors, such as the character of competition in an industry or its profit rate.

Hart's blanket condemnation of an absence of price competition is likewise questionable. It is not certain that price competition is socially superior to product competition, since the latter may accelerate the rate of product improvement and of the growth of technology in general. In drugs, computers, industrial machinery, farm equipment and consumer durables, success depends on new products and, in some cases, the quality of ancillary services.

Moreover, price competition may be unattainable without substantial increases in costs that we are unprepared to assume. The bill would require "substantial" price competition for a period of three consecutive years between two or more firms. But this would probably require fragmenting the leading firms into parts so small that a price reduction by any one of them would not be regarded as so great a threat that the others would retaliate. The insistence on price competition reflects the appeal of simple theory over ambiguous reality.

It has long been one of the staples of standard industrial organization that persistently high profits are a sure sign of monopoly power – a standard doctrine which stems from the theory that in the long run all competitive firms will earn no more than a normal rate of return. Estimates of the normal rate usually rely on the average rate of return of manufacturing, after some adjustment for risk. The inference is that if a firm enjoys for long a rate of profit in excess of the norm, it must be reaping the fruits of monopoly.

The inference, however, is wrong. Competitive firms can earn a rate of return persistently over the average if they have special advantages — particularly advantages that are not traceable to any particular agent of production. The organization may be good; employee morale may be maintained at a high level; the executives may get along together particularly well. Such "advantages" cannot be purchased by other firms or easily duplicated, and the high rate of return can continue indefinitely.

With majestic simplicity, the Hart Bill would dissolve those firms which earn over 15 percent on net worth after taxes in five consecutive years. Looking back through the data for the five years ending in 1971, these firms would be put on the chopping block: IBM, Xerox, Procter & Gamble, Eastman Kodak, Philip Morris, Coca-Cola, U.S. Industries, Amerada-Hess, Kellogg, Heublein, Champion Spark Plug, AMP, Avon, Minnesota Mining and Manufacturing, and American Home Products. This collection of names itself suggests that high profits are more an indication of efficiency than monopoly. IBM's skill is attested to by the low profits of firms which are in the same industry. Lever Brothers has not been able to equal P & G's merchandising success, and its profits show it. Kellogg does considerably better than General Mills, which is by no means a dwarf.

IS THERE AN ALTERNATIVE?

Monopoly power probably does exist in the American economy, and it should be the object of public policy to uncover and excise it. But the present state of knowledge does not give us simple rules to locate that power. Evidence of a high degree of concentration, high profits, and the absence of price competition is insufficient, either singly or together. Industrial organization economists notwithstanding, the legal tradition of attempting to establish monopolistic intent on the part of sellers has a great deal of merit. It is difficult to discover intent, but it is also doubtful whether monopolistic power has been obtained unless the intent is unmistakable. The Hart Bill represents an overly simplified view of the problem that is both alarmist and misdirected.

The measures of monopoly power which economists use do not, in fact, reveal where monopolies really operate in the American economy. In particular, they do not reach the collusive agreements which exist in certain professions and which have traditionally been tolerated — and even enforced — by state laws. The Justice Department has recently become interested in developing antitrust suits aimed at increasing competition among real estate agents and lawyers. The Securities & Exchange Commission has moved to promote price competition among stockbrokers. Cases might also be brought against artificial restrictions by unions on entry into the building trades or against analogous professional requirements imposed by state law. These instances of monopoly power are not exposed by measures of concentration or of profit rates and are thus not affected by the Hart Bill. But they represent the hard core of monopoly in the U.S. economy.

THE CASE FOR SOCIAL OWNERSHIP

Michael Harrington

What should be done about big business? America's best-known democratic socialist explains why the gradual nationalization of large-scale enterprise offers the best solution.

Even if society would socialize more and more investment, consciously planning the allocation of resources for cities, transportation, and human care, that in itself would not change the prevailing order. For the control of the means of production and of wealth is not simply economic power; it is political power as well. If over a long period of time private ownership of huge corporations were to coexist with planned social investments, the corporate rich, be they managers or owners, would come to dominate the new, supposedly democratic institutions. Socialists cannot abandon their insistence on social ownership.

Paradoxically, I will base the case for social ownership on the same economic trend – the separation of ownership and control under contemporary capitalism – which was cited by many socialists in the sixties as a reason for giving up the traditional position on the nationalization of industry.

For the continental socialists who revised their basic programs in the late fifties and early sixties, this development made the classic case for nationalization seem irrelevant. Now that rational, plan-oriented managers have taken over from individualistic capitalists, they argued, it is no longer necessary to change the title to property. For the socialists in control of the

From Michael Harrington, *Socialism in America.* © 1970 by *Dissent.*

government will follow full-employment policies that will yield a growing fund for social spending and, in any case, the corporate executives will see that it is to their interest to observe the broad priorities established by the state. I would argue that this very trend of separating ownership and control increasingly demonstrates the functionless character of the legal title to property and suggests a very practical, unapocalyptic method of doing away with it.

It was a distinguished conservative who most clearly drew the socialist conclusions from this economic tendency. Frederick A. Hayek has said,

So long as the management is supposed to serve the interests of the stockholders it is reasonable to leave the control of its actions to the stockholders. But if the management is supposed to serve wider public interest, it becomes a logical consequence of this conception that the appointed representatives of the public interests should control the management.

There are two reasons why I believe this straightforward proposal of socialization is to be preferred to the European social democratic notion of the state programming a market economy with social goals. First, the recent experience of the continental social democrats confirms the tendency of the corporations to try to dominate, rather than obey, the government that is supposed to control them. Second, it is now possible to have a relatively painless transition to social ownership if socialists will only learn how to give direction to the underlying trends of the coporate economy.

"Euthanasia for Rentiers":
A Modest Proposal

Social ownership now seems easier to achieve if socialists will encourage the "euthanasia of the rentiers." The Swedish socialists bring an ingenious contribution to this area. They propose to socialize the functions of property while leaving the title to it temporarily undisturbed. In this way socialization will be part of a historic process rather than a sudden and drastic leap to new forms of property.

We tend to reify private property into something indivisible, so that one either owns or does not own. But in the case of the means of production (and they, not personal property, are what is of concern to socialists), one can think of private property as conferring series of functional and divisible rights. In the class theory of laissez faire, ownership allowed a man to utilize existing fixed capital resources; to determine investment policy; to deploy the labor force; to set wage levels; to distribute profits; to retain profits; and so on. This model has, of course, already been modified: wage levels are fixed through collective bargaining agreements overseen and encouraged by the state; tax policies can provide incentives for internal financing or for distributing profits; etc. Now a much more profound and conscious socialization is required of more of the functions of property. Taking property as, in A. A. Berle's phrase, a "packet of permissions," what is proposed is not a sudden, wholesale takeover by the state but a process that progressively abolishes all these private permissions and that substitutes domocratic decisions for them.

For example, private investment decisions must be socialized. The right to locate or relocate a plant in a given area can no longer be considered a private matter. For in order to engage in regional planning and to aid in the construction of new cities and towns, the geography of employment has to be publicly determined. A strict system of licensing the permission to build a factory could work toward this end. (The Attlee government initiated some measures of this type, and various Italian governments have tried to use such techniques to promote the development of the South.)

Technology also has to be monitored. The decision to build a supersonic transport has so many consequences (noise, air traffic congestion, airport construction) that even if it were not a government-subsidized project, the public interest would have to be asserted. There is a need, as a National Academy of Science panel pointed out, for "technological forecasting." One cannot trust these matters, as the *Wall Street Journal* put it in a telling anticapitalist phrase, to the "mindless market."

Putting a Limit on Profit

Profit is another function of property that must be subjected to social control. In 1967, the Council of Economic Advisers — hardly an anticapitalist agency — noted that government direction of the economy had smoothed out the cycle of boom and bust and therefore removed a great deal of the risk in the marketplace. Under such conditions, the Council argued, business should be prepared to take a lower rate of return. But in point of fact, American corporations chafed under the voluntary controls of the Kennedy-Johnson administrations even though their profits rose by 78.7 percent between 1960 and 1970, and their cash flow (profits plus depreciation) was up by 85 percent in the same period. When Richard Nixon came into office, he abandoned all efforts to persuade industry and labor to obey guidelines in price-and-wage policy. Whereupon, the London *Economist* reported, the steel industry increased its prices in 12 months by 7 percent — as contrasted to a 6 percent rise in the previous 10 years.

Government, we must conclude, cannot leave profit policy to the "conscience" of the corporations. It can use an array of techniques to socialize this important area of economic life: price-and-wage controls in an inflationary period; a requirement that big companies open up their books and justify any increase in prices before an independent board; the use of vigorous tax policy (more on this shortly). However this be done, the fundamental purpose of the reform is clear enough. The society cannot afford to leave to private decision the pricing of basic goods — or how the huge annual increments in wealth are to be distributed.

There are other structural changes that could socialize some of the functions of property. The voting rights of all speculative, short-term shareholders could be abolished. (This would make it clear that many of the transactions on the stock market are nothing but a socially-approved form of gambling — and an enormous waste of resources and energy.) It has been proposed that the government give itself the right to act as if it were a majority stockholder in all major industries, but without taking legal title. In this scheme, the corporation would be left to its own devices as long as it conformed to the national plan and did not irresponsibly impose social costs upon the country. When its private egotism led to antisocial behavior, the government would intervene in the same way major shareholders confront poor management. The state would not assume permanent control but see to it that the direction of corporate policy was changed so as to observe the proper social priorities.

In France in 1970, the Radical party under the urging of Jean-Jacques Servan-Schreiber adopted a policy "to abolish the hereditary transmission of property in the means of production." In effect, Servan-Schreiber advocated a confiscatory tax on the stock holdings of very wealthy individuals. There have been debates on how effective such measures would be, yet the principle is both clear and excellent. A quite similar idea was proposed by Douglas Jay of the British Labour party, which would make a government investment bank the recipient of the stock paid as death duty.

Taken individually, none of these changes would basically transform the power relations within capitalist society. But if they were part of a comprehensive policy which sought to limit progressively the rights of property in the means of production, they could encourage and direct the "euthanasia of the rentiers." The gradualism of this strategy is not derived from any abstract principle but from the actual experience of socialist governments over half a century — as well as from a sense of what may be acceptable to the American people. In the United States (and in all the advanced capitalist countries, for that matter) there is neither political support nor administrative feasibility for the sudden decisive nationalization of an entire economy. In any case, a socialist movement could take the opportunity provided by such a process to promote as much diversity as possible within the forms of social property.

TEST ON THE FIRM
(CHAPTERS 11, 12, 13, and 14)

_ 1. Economic profit is
   a. a residual after all factors have been paid in full.
   b. a residual minus interest costs.
   c. interest plus rent.

_ 2. The law of diminishing returns shows how
   a. output varies as we vary all inputs.
   b. output varies as we vary one input.
   c. output varies as we increase size.

_ 3. Total output is always
   a. the sum of marginal outputs.
   b. average output multiplied by price.
   c. both of the above.

_ 4. Marginal output per factor unit
   a. cannot fall until average output falls.
   b. can fall before average output falls.
   c. can rise, although average output falls.

_ 5. Marginal revenue product is
   a. average output times price.
   b. marginal physical product times prices.
   c. total revenue minus total cost.

_ 6. The equi-marginal rule for hiring states:
   a. We hire the factor whose total product is greatest.
   b. We hire the factor whose marginal revenue product is greatest.
   c. We hire all factors until their marginal revenue products equal their marginal costs.
   d. a and b
   e. b and c

117

_ 7. Optimum output is determined by the relation of

    a. *AC* and *MC.*

    b. *AR* and *AC.*

    c. *MR* and *MC.*

_ 8. Profit is determined by the relation of

    a. *AC* and *MC.*

    b. *AR* and *AC.*

    c. *MR* and *MC.*

_ 9. A competitive *firm* is in equilibrium if:

    a. $MR = MC.$

    b. $AR = MC.$

    c. $MR = P.$

_10. A competitive *industry* is in equilibrium if its marginal firm has

    a. AR equal to AC.

    b. MR equal to MC.

    c. a and b.

_11. Economies of scale result from

    a. diminishing returns.

    b. increasing cost.

    c. technological considerations.

_12. Fixed costs apply to

    a. any factor that cannot be fired.

    b. land and capital.

    c. any large costs.

_13. The supply curve of the firm is given by its

    a. average cost curve.

    b. total cost curve.

    c. marginal cost curve.

_14. Monopolistic competition results in

    a. higher than competitive prices.

    b. less than competitive output.

    c. product differentiation.

    d. all of the above.

_15. A sloping demand curves means that

    a. *MR* will lie above *MC.*

    b. *MR* will lie below *AR.*

    c. *MR* will lie on *AR.*

_16. A monopolistic firm
   a. acts exactly like a competitive firm in establishing optimum output.
   b. acts differently from a competitive firm in establishing optimum output.
   c. cannot be compared with a competitive firm.
_17. An oligopoly is necessarily
   a. a large firm.
   b. a firm whose actions must take into account competitors' reactions.
   c. a firm with high profits.
_18. Competitive market structures depend on
   a. ease of entry and exit.
   b. differentiated products.
   c. nonmonopolistic motives.
_19. The marginal firm in a competitive industry
   a. makes no economic profit.
   b. makes no return on capital.
   c. may make intramarginal profit.
_20. The entrepreneurial function in a competitive firm is to
   a. establish optimum price.
   b. establish optimum revenue.
   c. establish optimum output.

REVIEW TEST ON THE FIRM
(CHAPTERS 11, 12, 13, and 14)

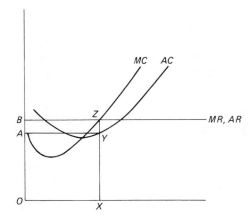

— 1. The graph above pictures a competitive firm because
   a. *MR* is horizontal.
   b. *MC* is horizontal.
   c. *MR* = *MC.*

— 2. The *firm* is in equilibrium because it finds
   a. *MR* = *AR.*
   b. *MR* = *MC.*
   c. *MR* = *AC.*

— 3. Output is determined in the eyes of the firm by the intersection of
   a. *MR* and *XZ.*
   b. *MC* and *AR.*
   c. *MR* and *MC.*

_ 4. Profit per unit equals
   a. *OA.*
   b. *XY.*
   c. *AY.*
   d. *ZY.*

_ 5. Total revenue equals
   a. *OBZX.*
   b. *OAYZ.*
   c. *ABZY.*

_ 6. Total cost equals
   a. *ABZY.*
   b. *OBZX.*
   c. *OAYX.*

_ 7. Total profit equals
   a. *OBZY – BAZY.*
   b. *OAYX – ABZY.*
   c. *OBZX – OAYX.*

_ 8. The industry is not in equilibrium because
   a. $MC \neq AC.$
   b. $AC \neq AR.$
   c. $MC = MR.$

_ 9. In equilibrium
   a. *AB* will tend to disappear.
   b. *OA* will tend to fall.
   c. *OX* will tend to shrink.

_10. The supply curve of the firm is determined by
   a. *MC.*
   b. *MR.*
   c. *AC.*

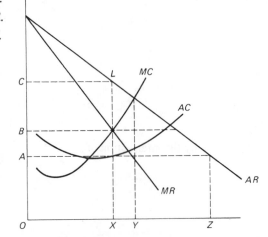

_11. This monopoly is in equilibrium because

    a. *MC = AC.*

    b. *MR = MC.*

    c. *AC = MR.*

_12. Its equilibrium output is shown by

    a. *OX.*

    b. *OY.*

    c. *OZ.*

_13. Selling price to maximize profit is shown by

    a. *OC.*

    b. *OB.*

    c. *OA.*

_14. Profit per unit at equilibrium equals

    a. *OB – OA.*

    b. *OC – OB.*

    c. *OC – OA.*

    d. *OA.*

_15. Total revenue is indicated by the prices and quantities

    a. *C* and *X.*

    b. *B* and *X.*

    c. *A* and *Y.*

    d. *A* and *Z.*

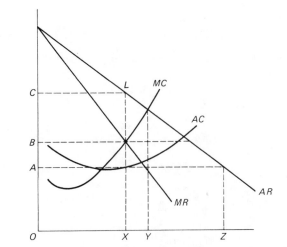

_16. Total costs equal

    a. *OX × OA.*

    b. *OX × OB.*

    c. *OX × OC.*

    d. *OY × OC.*

_17. This firm in monopolistic competition is in equilibrium because

    a. *MC = AC.*

    b. *MR = MC.*

    c. *MR = AR.*

_18. Total receipts are
    a. $OB \times XY$.
    b. $OC \times OX$.
    c. $OA \times OX$.
    d. $OA \times OY$.

_19. Total profit is
    a. $(OB \times OX) - (OB \times OY)$
    b. $(OB \times OY) - (OA \times OX)$
    c. $(OC \times OX) - (OX \times OA)$

_20. The marginal cost curve cuts the average cost curve at its lowest point under conditions of
    a. competition only.
    b. monopoly only.
    c. oligopoly only.
    d. all of the above.

Economics and

the Environment

15

LEARNING OBJECTIVES

The problem of negative externalities is a complicated one. In our text we learn about the three main ways in which we deal with them:
_ regulation
_ taxation
_ subsidy

You should know the advantages and disadvantages of these methods. But you should also be eager to apply your knowledge to the real world. This is the purpose of these readings.

SIDE EFFECTS OF RESOURCE USE

Ralph Turvey

*In this back-up lesson for our chapter on the environment
we are not going to review the lessons of the text. Instead,
let us see how these lessons can be translated into policy.
Ralph Turvey, an English economist known for his work on
environmental problems, gives us a close analysis of the
ways pollution can be minimized. He shows that
economic principles must be supplemented by a test of
fairness before any one can be advocated as the best
means of attaining a desired end.*

Many of the problems with which this [chapter] is concerned involve some sort of failure of the market mechanism as it now functions. The failure arises because decisions concerning the use of natural resources do not always take into account all the effects of that use. The neglected or side effects on the quality of the environment can, however, be very important, and thus need examination.

My purpose here is not to list and evaluate such side effects. It is the more limited one of analyzing their nature and introducing the various possible ways of coping with them. Economists have thought about all this and have produced an extensive and fairly technical literature on the subject. I have endeavored to distill from it the main ideas that are relevant to this volume and to present them in practical terms. Although I shall try to minimize the amount of jargon, I had better begin by stating that the technical terms used include "side-use effects," "spillovers," "externalities" or "external economies and diseconomies." These can be roughly and generally defined as the impacts of the activities of house-

From Henry Jarrett, ed., *Environmental Quality in a Growing Economy* (Washington, D.C.: Resources for the Future, 1971).

holds, public agencies, or enterprises upon the activities of other households, public agencies, or enterprises which are exerted otherwise than through the market. They are, in other words, relationships other than those between buyer and seller.

To make this notion clearer it is best to proceed directly to the examples that I shall use. All seven of them are significant in practice. But it is important to note that they are used only as illustrations and that I do not pretend to deal fully with any of them.

Fisheries constitute the first example. In some kinds of fisheries, once a certain intensity of fishing is reached, the stock of fish is reduced with the result that fishing is made more difficult and costly. This means that each fisherman, by taking fish, is adding to the costs of all the other fishermen. What is more, not only the scale of activity, as measured by the weight of fish caught, but also its nature is relevant, since (in a trawl fishery) the mesh size of the nets used also affects the stock. An increase in mesh size, by raising the minimum size of fish caught, would in some fisheries ultimately result in an increase in the stock, so making fishing easier. Thus by using a smaller mesh instead of a larger one, each fisherman is raising the costs of all the other fishermen.

In this example the impact of each fisherman's activity upon that of others is reciprocal. This feature is shared with the next two examples while, as we shall see, this is not the case with the last four of our seven examples, where the impact of one activity upon another is unidirectional.

The second example consists of traffic congestion on roads or in an urban street network. Once traffic flow exceeds a certain level, vehicles (and pedestrians) get in each other's way and slow down the traffic flow. Thus any one vehicle affects other vehicles by increasing the time spent and the fuel used in the journeys which those other vehicles are making. The relationship is reciprocal because the presence of each vehicle adds to the costs of all the others.

The same is true of the third example: wells which all tap a common source of water. Each well deprives other wells of some water, either by reducing their rate of flow or by bringing nearer the day when their yield diminishes.

Reciprocality is not the only common feature of these three examples. They are also alike in that, usually at least, a large number of households or enterprises are involved: hundreds of fishermen, thousands of vehicles, and dozens of wells. These two features are not logically connected, of course, but just happen to be common to these three examples.

My other cases are unidirectional. The fourth is the adverse effect upon households living round an airport of the noise of jets landing and taking off; the fifth is river pollution by the discharge of industrial effluents, and the sixth is the destruction of visual amenity involved in placing overhead power transmission lines in areas of scenic beauty.

Seventh, and last, is cattle poisoning by the emission of fluorine in the smoke from brickworks. Fluorosis causes cows' teeth to mottle and wear faster than normal. Their bones grow deformed and brittle and may break. The consequence is that milk yields and the values of the animals drop considerably; cows may even have to be slaughtered.

We can now use our examples to show that where side effects – externalities – are involved in resource use, the market mechanism, i.e., buyer-seller relationships, alone may not produce the best possible allocation of resources. Some additional mechanism may produce a better allocation of resources by causing households or firms to alter the scales or the nature of their activities.

This is rather a general statement, so I must use my examples to show what it means. But there is another general statement to make first: the right word is "may" not "will." We should never aim to get rid of absolutely all external effects of one activity upon another, since the net gain from doing so would be negative. A world with no traffic congestion at all, never any noise, no overhead power lines, and not a trace of smoke is a nice thought, but irrelevant to action. Thus the question is not one of abolishing adverse unfavorable effects, but is one of reducing them in some cases where investigation shows that on balance such a reduction is worthwhile.

Let us now list the main activity adjustments that are possible in the seven examples. First, fishing. Here a reduction in the amount of fishing effort and an increase in mesh size will first lower the catch and then raise it and/or make possible a further reduction in the amount of fishing effort. Thus there is an initial loss, in that fewer fish are caught, followed by a continuing gain, in that the catch will rise more or fall less than the number of boats and men engaged in the fishery. In either case, cost per ton of fish caught will end up lower than it was to start with.

Second, roads. A reduction in the number of vehicles would reduce the time and running costs incurred in the journeys of the remaining vehicles. Similarly, a reduction in the amount of on-street parking is a nuisance for the drivers who wish to park but will benefit moving traffic (and pedestrians).

Third, wells. If fewer wells were drilled, drilling costs would be saved while the off-take of water would be reduced less.

Fourth, aircraft noise. In unidirectional cases, such as this, there is usually scope for both the creator of the adverse external effect and the sufferer from it to adjust the scale and the nature of their activity. Thus airlines can reduce the number of night jet take-offs, modify engines to reduce noise, and alter the speed and angle of ascent — all at a cost. The households around the airport, on the other hand, can install sound-proofing or move.

Fifth, the emission of effluent into rivers. The enterprise or sewerage authority can treat the effluent before discharging it and possibly install storage facilities in order to reduce the rate of discharge at times when the river is low. In some cases an enterprise can also alter its production process in order to reduce the noxiousness of its effluent or it can even shift its location. Those enterprises or public authorities downstream can also spend money on treating the polluted river water in order to reduce the adverse consequences of the pollution and households can move.

Sixth, power lines. These can be sited differently or put underground.

Seventh, brickworks. Smoke filtering is possible and so is a change of location — two very expensive alternatives. Farmers, on the other hand, can shift from dairy farming to poultry or arable farming.

This review of the examples shows that there are frequently several possible ways in which the nature or scale of activities can be modified in order to reduce the adverse consequences of external effects. In most actual cases, therefore, the problem is a multidimensional one: who should do what how much?

An economic criterion can be used in answering this question. It is simply that the present value of the monetary measure of all gains from modifying activities less the present value of the monetary measure of all losses from these modifications be maximized. Unfortunately, this test is rarely sufficient in itself to provide an answer, and often cannot be applied in practice.

Nobody is going to quarrel with this criterion as a principle; it is like being against sin! But it is able to give an answer only when all gains and all losses can be satisfactorily measured and expressed in terms of a common denominator, dollars. Gains and losses occurring at different times are rendered comparable by using a discount rate which expresses one's evaluation of futurity to turn them into their equivalent gains and losses at a common reference date. Given satisfactory measurement, given expression in dollar terms, and given an agreed discount rate, to apply the criterion is to choose the best.

The beauty of this criterion, in the eyes of some conomists, is that whenever its application indicates that some course of action is desirable — gains exceed losses — the gainers can fully compensate the losers and still remain better off. Thus nobody loses on balance and at least some of the parties end up better off. What can be fairer than that?

The answer is that payment of compensation by gainers to losers is not always considered fair, so that even if it were always practicable it would not always be done. Yet the idea which lies at the root of the criterion (namely, that a course of action can be regarded unequivocally as desirable if it makes some people better off and nobody worse off) requires that compensation actually be paid.

The brickworks example can be used to illustrate this, if we take it that all that matters are brick costs and farming costs and sales, all of them measurable in monetary terms. Suppose (though it is probably not true at present) that application of the criterion showed the best course of action to be cleansing brickwork smoke. This would mean that the gain to farmers from an improvement in the health of any cows they keep would exceed the cost to the brickworks of cleansing the smoke, so that farmers could fully compensate the brickworks and yet remain net gainers. My point is that many people would not regard it as fair to make the farmers compensate the brickworks; on the contrary, they would claim that fairness requires the brickworks to meet the cost of cleansing the smoke since the brickworks is responsible for the damage.

Let us accept this judgment. Then the introduction of smoke cleansing will not make some people better off and nobody worse off; instead it will harm the brickworks and benefit the farmers. Thus, in deciding whether or not the smoke ought to be cleansed, we are not just comparing total gains with total losses; we are also deciding whether or not it is fair to impose a loss on the brickworks.

What this example shows, then, is that even when all gains and losses can be measured and rendered comparable by expressing them in dollar terms, the economic criterion taken by itself is not always sufficient for choosing the right course of action. Considerations of fairness may also be relevant. In a democratic country this means that the problem may have a political aspect.

When some of the gains and losses cannot be expressed in dollar terms, the choice of the right course of action always has a political aspect, for it always involves judgments about fairness as well as mere calculation. The airport example illustrates this. The cost to airlines of reducing noise and the cost to householders of sound-proofing their dwellings can no doubt be calculated in monetary terms. But the gain to householders from a reduction in noise cannot.* Hence deciding what measures, if any, should be taken involves:

*Asking people how much they would pay to obtain a given reduction in noise and comparing the prices of similar houses near and remote from the airport are both impracticable.

Ascertaining the cheapest way of achieving various reductions in noise levels;
Choosing the reduction to aim at;
Deciding who should bear the cost;

and the two latter issues, which are interdependent, both involve judgments of fairness or what I am here calling political considerations.

All this goes to show, then, that who should do what how much is often a question which cannot be decided on a purely technical basis by an economic calculation. Political considerations — judgments of what is equitable – are also required. This is the message for economists and technologists. On the other hand, there also is a message for administrators and politicians; namely, that even though an economic calculation of gains and losses is often not sufficient to reach a well-based decision, it is nearly always an essential preliminary.

We are now ready to go on to discuss possible mechansims for dealing with external effects. Since these, by definition, are relationships which are not coordinated by the market mechanism, it is a truism to say that these mechanisms are either nonmarket ones or that they involve the creation of a market where none existed before, i.e., the creation of rights which can be bought and sold. These are like the classical alternatives of status or contract.

Regulation is the mechanism of most general appeal, at least to noneconomists. It is easy to find examples:

Specification of a minimum mesh size to be used in a fishery.

Prohibition of parking at certain times in certain streets.

Confining the use of water from wells to certain purposes.

Limitation of the number of night take-offs by jet planes.

Requiring that effluents be treated before discharge into a river.

Forbidding the erection of overhead power lines in areas of natural beauty.

Prohibition of brickworks in certain areas (zoning).

It is scarcely necessary to say that regulation of one sort or another is often the most appropriate way of dealing with external effects. What does need saying, however, is that this is not always true: sometimes the cure is worse than the disease and sometimes other mechanisms of control are better. I do not believe that any general classification can be provided to tell us what is best in any particular case; on the contrary, I think that each case must be examined in some detail. My task is therefore to show by example what alternatives there are and to indicate the circumstances under which they may be feasible.

The first alternative involves creating a contract between the parties. If B carries on an activity which damages A, A can offer to pay B some money in consideration of his reducing the scale or changing the nature of his activity in order to diminish or abolish the damage. Such a bargain will be mutually advantageous when the economic criterion discussed above is fulfilled. If some alteration of B's activity costs B less than it profits A, the latter can afford to pay B enough to meet these costs. Thus suppose that an expenditure of $1,000 by B is worth $1,500 to A. Then if A pays B anything between $1,001 and $1,499, B will gain something between one dollar and $499 and A will gain between $499 and one dollar.

When the point is put in these abstract terms it invites the response that this sort of bargaining is open to blackmailers. Might not B be tempted to bother A solely in order to turn a dishonest penny by getting A to pay him to stop? The answer is, of course, that the parties must act within a legal framework of rights and obligations which determines their bargaining positions. The law of nuisance is particularly relevant here, both because it is an important part of this framework and because it provides a second alternative to the sort of regulations listed above; namely, the award of injunctions by the courts.

Nuisances, in the legal sense, are acts not warranted by law (or failure to discharge legal duties) which obstruct, inconvenience, or damage the public or which, when concerned with the use or occupation of land, damage another person in connection with his occupation or use of land. This latter category constitutes private nuisance and it is only here that a private individual has a right to legal action and may claim damages or an injunction. Whether an act constitutes a nuisance is a matter either of common law or of statute; thus the Public Health Acts specify a number of statutory nuisances where legal proceedings are initiated by public authorities. It is important to note that some acts which would otherwise be wrongful may be authorized by statute. Thus actions for nuisance arising from civil aircraft are prohibited.

The law of nuisance may, however, apply to another of our examples. Certain farmers are taking legal proceedings with the object of obtaining redress for the loss and damage which their farms have suffered due to fluorine. (They are not seeking an injunction; in the case of brickworks because it is not practicable to eliminate the fluorine from the emissions.) An alternative method which has actually been used in one or two cases is for the manufacturer to purchase an affected farm on such terms as to avoid claims in respect of fluorine pollution.

Leaving aside the technical point, yet to be resolved, as to whether damage can be proved to the satisfaction of the courts, this case shows that if the farmers have a right, their bargaining position will be improved. An alternative to payment of damages is a private contract which avoids claims for damages. In this particular case it appears that the cost (to brickworks) of ceasing to emit fluorine exceeds the cost (to farmers) imposed by its continued emission. Thus the economic criterion suggests that the right thing is for the emission to continue, whether or not the farmers have a right against the brickworks. If they do not have such a right, they bear the cost. If they do, the brickworks bears the cost either in the form of damages awarded by the courts or by payment made under a contract. Thus the absence or existence of the right on the part of the farmers does not affect the allocation of resources between activities but only the distribution of the gains and losses between the parties. The law of nuisance is thus only relevant to the fairness of what happens.

.   .   .

Fishery regulation, street congestion and the use of water from wells are all examples in which economists have urged that a properly designed tax would be superior to any form of regulation. Actually, some combination of both is probably required. Thus, in the case of fish, it can be shown that a tax on catch should be accompanied by regulation of mesh size if the present value of gains minus losses is to be maximized.

The external diseconomies in these three examples are reciprocal. Reflection suggests that this is because all three involve what economists call a common property resource. This is a resource required in production which is significantly limited in availability but whose use is nonetheless free. In the three examples this resource is, respectively, the fish stock, the street system, and the underground water. An increase in the catch, the number of journeys undertaken, and the amount of water abstracted lowers the fish stock, increases street congestion, and reduces water reserves. This raises the costs of all fishermen, all drivers, and all water users by making fish more difficult to catch, slowing down traffic, and lowering the water table. But this effect of an increase in the use of the common property resource by one user is not felt by him; it is felt by his fellows. Thus the social cost of any given increase in the catch, vehicle-miles, or gallons exceeds the private cost

of such an increase to the one who provides it. By using up more of the common property resource he leaves less of it for his fellows; this is a cost but it is a social cost only and not a private cost as well because he does not pay for its use. Putting a price on the use of the common property resource, however, could raise private cost to equality with social cost and put an end to the wasteful and excessively intensive use of the common property resource. It is wastefully used because it is free to the user but significantly scarce; it is treated like air but is really like good agricultural land.

This last paragraph aims to set out the essentials of the matter, not to provide a rigorous demonstration. It suffices here to point out that agricultural land would be wastefully exploited if farmers could use it without buying or renting it — as indeed happens sometimes with common land. Thus the proceeds to be got from a properly designed tax on catch, urban road journeys, or water abstraction constitute the rent which society as a whole could obtain from better utilization of its common property resource.

Urban roads differ from the other two examples in that the amount available is entirely within the control of man. But this does not affect the present issue which is to make the best use of the roads we have at any particular point of time. It should by now be obvious that gasoline taxes paid in respect of a vehicle, being only very loosely related to its utilization in congested conditions, do relatively little to optimize road usage. What is needed are charges for road use which are closely related to the amount of use made of congested roads at times of congestion. Modern technology has made possible several ways of achieving this.

A tax may also be the best method of dealing with unidirectional external diseconomies when the numbers of people or firms concerned is so large that only collective action is possible. On the other hand, it may not be the best method. Writers of economic textbooks like to use the example of smoke nuisance, but none has explained how a smoke tax could in practice be levied or has discussed how its rate should vary with the height of the chimney or the composition of the smoke, though both are relevant to the amount of damage caused. . . .

This completes our review. The main points which I have made are that each case must be considered on its merits and that these should be set out in economic terms as far as possible. Administrators should consider alternatives to direct regulation, economists should not exaggerate the applicability of tax devices, and both should remember that, in a democratic country, questions of fairness require legal or political decisions.

The Market for
Factors of Production

16

LEARNING OBJECTIVES

Here we begin three chapters on income distribution. In Chapter 16 we focus on the marginal productivity theory of factor earnings. After you have finished this chapter and this exercise, you should be able to do three things:

1. Explain how the wages of labor, the rent of land, and the interest on capital are determined in a market system.

2. Differentiate between real rent and quasi-rent.

3. Explain why marginal revenue products should equal factor prices in a competitive market.

In this chapter we study what is known as the *marginal productivity theory of distribution,* a theory widely used to explain how factor prices are determined. In our next chapter we will criticize the theory, but you can't criticize something without knowing it thoroughly.

DEMAND AND SUPPLY FOR FACTORS

Factor prices interest us because they are the key to income distribution. The price of labor is

wages; the price of capital, interest; that of land, rent. Hence the object of our inquiry will be to discover how wages, rent, and interest are determined in the market where factor services are bought and sold.

The demand side offers nothing new to be grasped. We buy factor services for two reasons: (1) because we want to enjoy these services directly, as when we buy medical care, or the land on which to build a house, or borrow money for a vacation; and (2) because we want

133

to use the services of land, labor, and capital in production. The latter case is called *derived demand:* it is a demand for factors "derived" from the demand for the goods into which factor services will enter.

Here one point is crucial to understand: *Derived demand for factors depends on the marginal revenue product that the use of the factor will bring.* Remember that an entrepreneur will buy more units of any factor as long as its marginal revenue product is less than the marginal cost of that factor.

FACTOR COSTS

But what will be the marginal cost of a factor? For the individual entrepreneur, it is simply a "given." But for all entrepreneurs who are in the competitive market for a given factor, it will be the price that is determined by the interplay of supply and demand for that factor. In Figure 16-1 we show the cost of wages for one firm, and determination of that cost in the labor market.

We have seen that the demand curve for all labor will be the marginal revenue product of labor for that industry. But what about the supply curve? That is what we must learn in this chapter.

SUPPLY CURVES

Let us take the case of labor first. Here we distinguish between the curious "backward-bending" supply curve of labor for one individual, and the positively-sloped curve of labor for the market as a whole.

Why does the curve of labor supply bend backward? The answer involves *the interplay of utility and disutility.* As wages rise, the utility of an hour's work increases. An individual will make more money for each hour of work, and will be tempted to increase his sum of utilities by working more hours. But work also involves disutilities. These also rise with added hours of work. Moreover, the *marginal* utility of added income should be falling because the marginal utility of any good or services declines, and the *marginal disutility* of work should be rising.

We can picture the process in Figure 16-2. *OA* represents the original *marginal* (not total) utility of a given wage per hour: note that it falls as we work more hours. *OB* represents the marginal utility or disutility of labor. Note that the *initial* hour of work is positively enjoyable, but that additional hours become less so, and soon give rise to disutilities (after point *X*). We will work *OY* hours, where the marginal disutility of work (*YL*) just balances the marginal utility of the income from work (*YZ*).

FIGURE 16-1

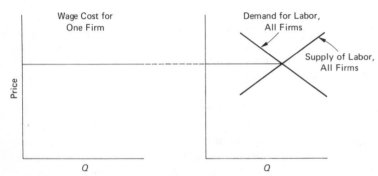

FIGURE 16-2

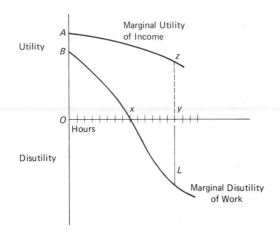

FIGURE 16-3

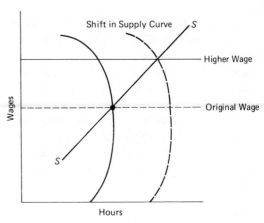

When we speak of a backward-bending curve, we speak of hours beyond the point OY, where marginal disutility is greater than marginal utility. Take a carpenter who works 50 hours a week, and whose pay rises from $5 an hour to $10. If he works 60 hours a week at the higher rate, he could earn $600. But he may well prefer to work only 40 hours, lifting his income to $400, and "trading off" $200 of foregone income for the utilities of 10 hours per week of added leisure.

Collectively, however we can think of the labor supply curve as positively sloping, at least in the short run. The rise in pay from $5 to $10 may well result in fewer hours per week worked by the existing labor force of carpenters, but it is likely to tempt workers from other occupations into carpentering. In Figure 16-3 we can see how a rise in wage rates will reduce the supply of hours offered by the existing number of workers, but cause an influx of new participants into the labor force, causing the total supply (SS) to increase.

LAND AND CAPITAL

The supply curves of land and capital resemble each other some ways, and are different in others. This means that land and capital *owners*

behave differently, or are affected by different constraints. The main resemblance between the two supply functions is that the supply of total land and total capital is fixed at any moment. However, we can slowly add to land, and more quickly add to space only by adding labor and capital to land; whereas we constantly add to capital by *saving*. Saving is thus the behavioral function that affects capital: it is price-inelastic, although income-responsive. There really is no behavioral counterpart to saving as regards land.

However, it is important to recognize that both land or space and saving are highly responsive to changes in the price paid for *their use in different employments*. Although the supply curve of land and of savings is price-inelastic as a whole, the supply curve of land and of saving for any one use shows a quick response to changes in price. Review the diagrams at the top of the page to be sure you understand the difference.

SUPPLY AND DEMAND

Let us put these supply and demand curves together, before going on into quasi rents and capitalization. The essential point to understand is that the supply curves of land, labor, and capital determine the quantity of each factor service that will be forthcoming at any price for that factor. *Whatever the quantity, the price that the entrepreneur will pay will be determined by the marginal revenue product curve. Thus in all cases, the wage or rent or interest paid will be equal to the marginal revenue product of the factor.*

Figure 16-4 shows a variety of curves. Which curve shows the supply of labor of an individual? Which could be the supply curve for total land or total saving? For land or saving for a particular use? Label these.

FIGURE 16-4

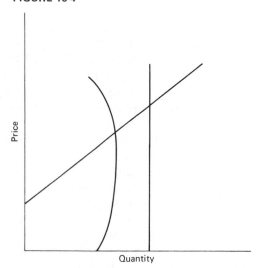

Now draw in an imaginary marginal revenue product curve for each factor. Show that the wage, or rent, or interest, will be equal to the marginal revenue product of that quantity of the factor. Now put in a new dotted supply curve for each factor, and mark the *new* levels of wage, interest, and rent. Will this also be equal to their marginal revenue product?

MARGINAL PRODUCTIVITY

This is the framework for the marginal productivity theory of income distribution. Be sure you understand these questions:

1. What determines the shape of the *MRP* curve? You might review by filling in the following table:

Quantity of Factor	Total Output (Units)	Marginal Physical Product	Total Revenue @ $10 per unit	Marginal Revenue Product
1	10	10	$100	$100
2	18	—	180	—
3	23	5	—	$ 50

2. What is the *MRP* of the second unit of the factor?

3. Does this marginal revenue product fall because of a change in selling price, or because of a change in physical productivity? The change in productivity is called the law of
_____ .

4. What will be the earnings of the second unit of the factor if the employer hires it?

5. Can we tell from the information above if the entrepreneur will hire it? (Hint: do we know the marginal cost of the factor?)

6. Suppose the factor costs $50 per unit. How many units will be hired? $49 per unit? Can you see that a factor, in pure competition, will be paid as much as it brings into the firm as added revenue?

7. Suppose (this is a new problem) that the 100th unit of Factor A brings in $10 to a firm and that the 10th unit of Factor B brings in $15. How much will Factor A be paid? Factor B? Suppose Factor A is labor. The wage rate will be $10, and the number of men employed 100. What will the payroll be? If Factor B is land, the rent of the 10th acre (or 10th unit of floor space) will be $15. How much will the landlord get for renting all ten acres (or units of floor space).

8. In the case above a unit of land gets paid one and one-half times the price of a "unit" of labor. This must mean that its marginal revenue product is also one and one-half times as large. What proportion does the marginal *physical* product of land bear to that of labor?

9. Suppose that the marginal physical productivities changed, and that the last unit of labor now yielded 10 units of output and the last unit of land (acre, or floor space)

also yielded 10 units of output. If each unit of output sold for $1, what is the *MRP* of labor? Of land? What will be the wage of labor? The rent of the last acre?

10. Complete the following equational description of the marginal productivity theory of distribution:

$$\frac{\text{Marginal Product of Factor A}}{\text{Price of Factor B}} =$$

11. Can you turn the formula around:

$$\frac{\text{Marginal Product of Factor A}}{\text{Marginal Product of Factor B}} = \frac{\text{Price of}}{\text{Price of}}$$

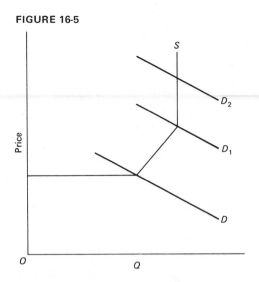

FIGURE 16-5

QUASI RENTS

Quasi rents (also called Economic Rents) are a very important element in income distribution. First let us understand their essential difference from rent. *Rent is the supply price of land.* If we do not pay rent, we do not enjoy the services of land. Therefore, rent is a cost that determines prices.

Quasi rents are not supply prices but scarcity prices. If we do not pay quasi rents, we do not lose any factor supply. They are purely returns to scarcity. Therefore they do not determine prices, but are determined by prices. The higher are prices, the higher will be quasi rents. See if you can fill in Figure 16-5.

Let us suppose that this shows the supply (*S*) of arable land. If demand is shown by *D*, what will be the supply of land offered for rent? Show what this will be by a dotted line, and mark *X* where it touches the quantity axis. What will be the rent per acre? (Indicate with letter *A* on the vertical axis.) If the price drops below *OA*, will there be any land offered for rent? Will this rent be part of the cost of production of crops?

Now suppose that demand climbs to D_1. What will be the supply of land offered? Mark this *OY*. At what rent? (Mark the rent *OB*.) Will the

farmers who *formerly* supplied quantity *OX* be getting quasi rents? Will each new landlord who is tempted into the market also get a quasi rent? Think! A landlord who was situated just to the right of point *X* did *not* offer his land at price *OA*. As rents rise, will quasi rents be earned by more and more landlords? At rent *OB*, is there *any* landlord who does not earn quasi rents?

Now demand jumps to D_2. What will be the level of rents? (Mark this *OC*.) Will *all* landlords now earn quasi rents? Will they *only* earn quasi rents, or will their earnings be a mixture of real rent and quasi rent? If you could tax away the amount $OY \times BC$ would you reduce the supply of land at all? If you taxed away amount $OY \times AC$, would the supply of land be reduced? By how much? If you taxed away $OC \times OY$ what would happen to the supply of land?

CAPITALIZATION

Now suppose that you owned some land which yielded a rent of $1,000, and suppose that this $1,000 just tempted you to rent the land rather than keeping it for your own use. Would you be making rent or quasi rent?

If the going rate of interest were 10 percent, what would be the price at which you could sell your land? The answer is some sum that would give you $1,000 at 10 percent. Obviously, this is $10,000. We call this process *capitalization*. We capitalize an asset by dividing its return by the rate of interest (or by a rate of return appropriate to the opportunity cost of money put to that use).

If the rate of interest fell to 5 percent, what value would your land have? Can you explain how a *fall* in interest rates causes a *rise* in the capitalized values of assets? The answer is found by asking how large a capital sum you need to give you as much income as you formerly got from the factor service.

Suppose that prices rose and that your rental income rose to $2,000. Are you now making quasi rents as well as rent? What is the capitalized value of your land now at 10 percent? At 5 percent? Suppose you sell your land at the latter capitalization figure. The buyer will have paid $40,000 ($40,000 × .05 = $2,000). He will continue to enjoy a return from the land of $2,000, but he has a new cost – the opportunity cost of 5 percent on his $40,000. Therefore his return on the land is no more than the interest on its capital cost. He has bought an income of $2,000 for a capital outlay of $40,000. He has no quasi rents at all.

How about yourself as seller? You now have a capital sum of $40,000. If the rate of interest is 5 percent, you can expect an income of $2,000. Will it be a quasi rent? Can you see how the process of capitalization has removed quasi rents by converting them into interest costs?

Last point: quasi rents are clearly monopoly returns that contribute nothing to output. But remember, all prices, including monopoly prices, serve an allocatory function. If quasi rents exist, a factor must be in "short supply." If we could remove quasi rents by price controls, we would

have land whose *MRP* was $2,000 selling at $1,000. The quantity demanded would be much larger than the quantity supplied. How would we allocate that land to those users who could put its productivity to greatest advantage? Can you see how quasi rents accomplish this end?

TEST YOURSELF

We have done a lot of explaining: now see whether you can do the explaining. Answer these questions and then grade yourself by the answers below.

— 1. Derived demand refers to
    a. entrepreneurs' demand for factors.
    b. demand for goods and services.
    c. demand for personal services derived from factors.

— 2. The backward-bending supply curve represents
    a. a preference for work over income.
    b. preference for leisure over income.
    c. diminishing marginal utility of work.

— 3. The supply curve of land is
    a. price-elastic for particular uses.
    b. price-inelastic in total.
    c. both of the above.

— 4. The supply curve of capital is
    a. price-elastic.
    b. price-inelastic.
    c. backward bending.

— 5. Capitalization is the process by which we
    a. estimate the earnings of factors.
    b. estimate the *MRP* of factors.
    c. estimate the asset value of factors.

— 6. If land rents at $1,000 and the rate of interest is 10 percent, the capitalized value of the land is
    a. $10,000.
    b. $1,000.
    c. 10 percent.

T F

_ 7. To capitalize an asset we
  a. multiply yield times earnings.
  b. multiply yield times rate of interest.
  c. divide factor earnings by interest rate.

_ 8. Rent, as the supply price of land, is
  a. determined by the *MRP* of land.
  b. independent of the *MRP* of land.
  c. the same as quasi rent on land.

_ 9. Capitalized values vary with
  a. interest rates.
  b. quasi rents.
  c. selling prices.

_10. Quasi rents
  a. induce owners of factors to increase supply.
  b. have no effect on supply.
  c. may or may not affect supply.

_11. Quasi rents can accrue to
  a. labor.
  b. land.
  c. all factors.

_12. Quasi rents
  a. help allocate factors.
  b. play no useful function.
  c. interfere with supply.

_13. Marginal productivity theory says that
  a. factor earnings are equal to factor disutility.
  b. factor earnings are equal to marginal revenue products.
  c. factor earnings are proportional to factor costs.

True-False Questions: T F

14. A backward-bending labor supply curve means that the utility of income is greater than the disutility of labor.   _ _

15. The supply curve of capital is nor-

mally highly responsive to interest rates.   _ _

16. Quasi rents disappear when we capitalize an enterprise that yields them.   _ _

17. If the interest rate is 5 percent, the capitalized value of land that rents for $1,000 is $20,000.   _ _

18. If the interest rate falls, the capitalized value of an asset rises.   _ _

19. Quasi rents are the marginal revenue product of scarce factors.   _ _

20. Quasi rents are determined by prices.   _ _

21. If the price of a product falls and its supply decreases, this shows that no quasi rents were earned before the price fall.   _ _

22. The higher the rate of interest, the lower the capitalized value of an asset.   _ _

23. In perfect competition, wage earnings will be proportional to factor productivities, and equal to factor *MRPs*.   _ _

24. Quasi rents are determined by prices but also determine costs.   _ _

25. Quasi rents play no useful role in inducing output.   _ _

Answers

1. a	10. b	19. T	
2. b	11. c	20. T	
3. c.	12. a	21. F	
4. b	13. b	22. T	
5. c	14. F	23. T	
6. a	15. F	24. T	
7. c	16. T	25. T	
8. a	17. T		
9. a	18. T		

Problems in the Distribution of Income

17

LEARNING OBJECTIVES

Is income distributed in the way that marginal productivity theory suggests? These facts and figures, and this brilliant reading, show that this is not so.

What is your learning objective here? It is simply to gain a familiarity with some very important facts.

SOME FACTS AND SOMETHING FOR YOU TO FIGURE

Discrimination is not, of course, limited to racial discrimination. The two graphs below give you an idea of the income disparities existing between men and women. Look carefully at the graphs; some questions relating to them follow.

Here are some exercises to acquaint you still further with the facts. Your answers do not have to be precise — rough approximations will do.

1. According to Graph 1, at about what age does a male college graduate earn his maximum income? _____ What is this income? _____ Answer the same questions for a female college graduate: _____ ; _____ .

2. At age 24, what is a woman college graduate's average income? _____ A man's? _____

3. Between ages 24 and 60, by what percentage does a woman college graduate's income increase, on the average? _____ By what percentage does a male graduate's income rise from age 24 to 51? _____

140

DOLLARS¹ (RATIO SCALE)

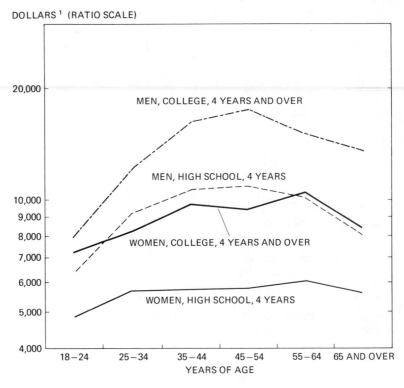

*Median income of full-time, year-round workers, 1971.
Source: Department of Commerce.

4. Over the full earning lifetime of a female high school (but not college) graduate, what is the approximate *average* income? _____ . For a female college graduate? _____For a male non-college graduate? _____ For a male college graduate? _____

5. If you compare the curves for male non-college and female college graduates, do you think there are factors other than education that influence annual incomes? What do you think some of these influences might be?

6. Turning now to Graph 2, in 1968 what percent of white families with male heads were below the low income level?____ Black families? _____ What about white families with female heads? _____ Black families with female heads? _____

7. Answer the same questions for the year 1970:

White familes, male heads   _____
  "   female heads _____
Black families, male heads _____
  "   female heads _____

8. Between 1968 and 1970, which of the six groups represented in the three sections of Graph 2 actually lost ground, in terms of the percentage of that group falling below the low income level? _____

Answers:

1. Men, age 50, $18,000; women, age 60, $11,000 (approx.)

2. Women, $7,500; men, $10,000

141

GRAPH 2. Percent of Families below the Low-Income Level.

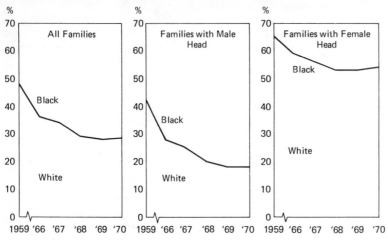

Source: Bureau of the Census.

3. Women's percent increase, 33%+; mens, 80%
4. Female high school, $5,500 approx.; female college, $9,000 approx.; male high school $9,000 approx.; male college, $12,000 approx.
5. Life-styles? Biases against women? Women's role as mother? Union discrimination?
6. White families, male head 6%; female head, 25%

   Black families, male head 20%; female head, 53%
7. White families, male head 6%; female head, 25%
   Black families, male head 19%; female head, 55%
8. Only black families with female heads (from 53 to 55 percent)

SOME FACTS TO BE EXPLAINED

Jan Pen

A PARADE OF DWARFS
(AND A FEW GIANTS)

In this section we are concerned with a first impression. For this purpose we shall organize a parade in which everyone takes part who gets money. We could give all the marchers a sign to hold stating his or her pay, but it is more

Abridged from Jan Pen, *Income Distribution* (New York: Praeger Publishers, 1971), pp. 48–59.

spectacular if we make everyone's size proportionate to his income. To achieve that we call in Procrustes, a cruel host whose custom it was to adapt the height of his guests to the size of the bed in the guest room. We shall ask him to stretch or to contract every income recipient in such a way that his height corresponds to his income. The average income recipient gets the average height. Anyone who earns more than average becomes taller; anyone who earns less than average shrinks (let's hope that the proportions of the victims, and their health, remain intact). The average income is computed by adding all incomes together and dividing by the number of income recipients. Taxes are not deducted ... but social benefit, family allowances, pensions, etc., are thrown in. We can therefore see by looking at people what they earn.

It is worth mentioning that in this procedure we consider individual incomes. We ignore wealth, and we concern ourselves with *individual* remuneration. This is not the most decisive criterion of prosperity; usually family incomes are more important. We shall presently come across tiny women, but before we pity them we must bear in mind that perhaps they have a husband who is also earning, so that the wife merely supplements the family income. And young girls are as a rule reduced to pygmies without being bowed down by that; they live with their parents and earn plenty of pocket money. (Unfortunately, other young girls must live on their wages and rent expensive rooms, and some women have to support families and really ought to earn more and not less than men.) Old people are sometimes small without this troubling them overly; but fathers of large families who have been stretched to more than average height by Procrustes may be financially pinched to a considerable degree. The smallest of all are schoolchildren and students, who work for money for a few months a year; on an annual basis that income is minuscule, but that does not affect their enjoyment of life. These restrictions disappear from sight in our approach. We observe only tall and short human beings. Before passing judgment on their prosperity we ought to know more about them, but we are not attempting that.

The procession is now forming up; just as when a school marches in from the playground, the smallest ones are in the van. The parade moves on at uniform speed in such a way that it is past in one hour, which means that the

marchers are going to have to move in double-quick time. They *flash* past. You and I, two persons of average height,* watch the strange spectacle. What do we see?

In the first seconds a remarkable thing already happens. If we have superhuman powers of observation (and why shouldn't we confer them upon ourselves?) we see a number of people of negative height passing. On closer inspection they prove to be businessmen who have suffered losses and whose capital is reduced. They are not necessarily short people. In fact, right in the front we spot a few very tall men, with their feet on the ground and their heads deep in the earth. The first one may be as tall as ten yards – he must be rich to indulge in that kind of thing. It's an unhealthy way of carrying on, and most of them don't keep it up long. This vanguard is not so small in number either; we live in a rough world, where many are attracted by the successes of private enterprise which, however, pass them by. A third to half of all retail businesses close down within two years of their start – and all this mortality is not without losses.

After this tragi-comic opening we see tiny gnomes pass by, the size of a matchstick, a cigarette. We think we see among them housewives who have worked a short time for some money and so have not got anything like an annual income, schoolboys with a paper round and once again a few entrepreneurs who didn't make it (though without their having applied for National Assistance). It takes perhaps five minutes for them to pass. We should bear in mind that those who have no income and don't want one either – children, nonworking housewives – are not taking part in the parade at all.

Suddenly we see an increase by leaps and bounds. The people passing by are still very small ones – about three feet – but they are noticeably taller than their predecessors. They form a heterogeneous group; they include some young people, especially girls who work regularly in

*I'm just assuming. I can hardly know your income; mine is far above the Dutch average.

factories, but above all people who are not in paid employment: very many old-age pensioners without other means of support, some divorced women without alimony, people with a physical handicap. Among them are owners of shops doing poor trade. They supply the smooth transitions. And we see artists – they may include geniuses, but the public does not understand their work and the market does not reward their capacities. Unemployed persons also belong to this heterogeneous company, but only in so far as they received a low wage while they were working (otherwise they would be coming later). Some members of this group receive National Assistance. It takes them at least five or six minutes to pass by.

After them – the parade has been going on for about ten minutes – come the ordinary workers about whom there is nothing out of the ordinary except that they are in the lowest-paid jobs. Dustmen, Underground ticket collectors, some miners. The unskilled clerks march in front of the unskilled manual workers. Precisely among these lower-paid categories each group applies the principle of ladies first – particularly in Britain equal pay is far from being a reality. We now also see large numbers of coloured persons. These groups take time to pass; we have ample opportunity to observe them at our leisure. It takes almost fifteen minutes before the passing marchers reach a height of substantially more than four feet. For you and me this is a disturbing sight; fifteen minutes is a long time to keep seeing small people pass by who barely reach to our midriff. More than a third of them are women, dwarf-like human beings. In embarrassment we avert our gaze and look in the direction of the approaching parade to catch sight at long last of normal people.

But a new surprise awaits us here. *We keep on seeing dwarfs.* Of course they gradually become a little taller, but it's a slow process. They include masses of workers, just ordinary people with not inconsiderable technical knowledge, but shorties.

After we have waited another ten minutes small people approach who reach to our collar-bones. We see skilled industrial workers, people with considerable training. Office workers, respectable persons so to say. We know that the parade will last an hour, and perhaps we expected that after half-an-hour we would be able to look the marchers straight in the eye, but that is not so. We are still looking down on the tops of their heads, and even in the distance we do not yet see any obvious improvement. The height is growing with tantalizing slowness, and forty-five minutes have gone by before we see people of our own size arriving. To be somewhat more exact: about twelve minutes before the end the average income recipients pass by.

We are of course interested as to who they are. Now, they prove to include teachers, executive-class civil servants, clerical workers, older N.C.O.'s, grown grey in the services. Of course we also encounter shopkeepers, together with sales representatives and insurance agents (a number of *them* do not come along until later). This group also includes people in overalls and rubber boots and with callouses on their hands; they are a number of foremen, superintendents and technicians, and a few farmers.

After the average income recipients have passed, the scene changes rather quickly. The marchers' height grows; six minutes later we see the arrival of the top ten percent, a group that will turn up again repeatedly in the following pages. The first to arrive are around six feet six inches, but to our surprise we see that they are still people with modest jobs. Headmasters, Assistant Principals and Principals. (Our parade is being held in Britain; in other countries the exact order is sometimes a little different, but the picture is the same.) University graduates, but most of them are very young. Small contractors who lend a hand themselves. Seamen too. And once again farmers; in Britain their income is higher than the national average (in this respect this country differs from the United States and from all countries of Continental Europe!). Again office staff, department heads, but certainly not yet genuine top executives. They are people who had never thought that they belonged to the top ten percent.

In the last few minutes giants suddenly loom up. A lawyer, not exceptionally successful: eighteen feet tall. A colonel, also of much the same height. Engineers who work for nationalized industries. The first doctors come into sight, seven to eight yards, the first accountants. There is still one minute to go, and now we see towering fellows. University professors, nine yards, senior officers of large concerns, ten yards, a Permanent Secretary thirteen yards tall, and an even taller High Court judge; a few accountants, eye surgeons and surgeons of twenty yards or more. This category also includes managers of nationalized concerns; the Chairman of the National Coal Board is likewise a good twenty yards.

During the last seconds the scene is dominated by colossal figures: people like tower flats. Most of them prove to be businessmen, managers of large firms and holders of many directorships, and also film stars and a few members of the Royal Family. There prove to be towers and towers, and we cannot describe them all. To mention a few examples of persons whose salaries have been published: we note, with due respect, Prince Philip, sixty yards (too short to play polo), and the senior managing director of Shell, David Barran, who measures more than twice as much.

Now these giants are still people with salaries (the interest on their wealth makes them still taller – how much so we do not know), and the yard is still a practical measure of their height. But the rear of the parade is brought up by a few participants who are measured in miles. Indeed, they are figures whose height we cannot even estimate: their heads disappear into the clouds and probably they themselves do not even know how tall they are. Most of them are men of

venerable age, but they also include women; these are as a rule younger, and we even think that we can see a few babies and adolescents. (Their ranks include Tom Jones; nearly a mile high.) These super-rich people are almost all heirs, and the tallest of them have managed to multiply their inheritance. The last man, whose back we can still see long after the parade has passed by, is John Paul Getty (though as a rule we have not invited American guests, Getty lives for much of his time in Britain and is an Oxford B.A.). At the time of writing he is almost 80 years old and made his money in oil. Few know what he earns (perhaps nobody does); his fortune is estimated at 1,000 to 1,500 million dollars. His height is inconceivable: at least ten miles, and perhaps twice as much.

Suddenly the parade is gone – the income recipients disappear from sight and leave the spectators behind them with mixed feelings. We have watched a dramatic spectacle, full of unexpected scenes.* It is worthwhile summarizing a few of our impressions.

(a) A striking fact is that we have to wait so long for the average income recipient. The reason lies in the fact that a number of colossal people are bringing up the rear. Not only do they attract the attention of the spectator so much, but they also raise the average; it shifts to well above the great mass of income recipients. For that reason by far the greater part of the parade consists of small men and women, not to say dwarfs. If we were to exclude from the parade those who bring

*Honesty compels me to admit that I have intensified the effect because spectators usually pay attention not only to height but also to width of shoulders, size of chest and volume. In our case they should not do so, because a person's volume increases with the third power of his height. You and I must therefore consider only the distance between soles and crown, and ignore the frightening effect of volume. If you think that we are asking too much of our capacity for abstraction, we ought to ask Procrustes *not* to leave the proportions intact; a thirteen-yard general then acquires a very weedy figure, and the gnomes look like soup plates. Getty becomes as thin as gossamer, relatively speaking.

up the rear, say during the last minute, the average height – that is to say your height and mine – would drop considerably. Those remaining in the parade would not become any taller as a result, but the impression would be removed that we have organized a parade of dwarfs. After just over half-an-hour we would already be able to look the marchers in the eye. People desirous of assessing income distribution should bear such things in mind.

Incidentally we could also have brought the height of the participants closer to the average if we had considered family income instead of individual incomes. That would have removed many women and young people from the procession; their husbands and fathers would have grown taller and many dwarfs would have risen to almost average height. The marchers of the first five minutes would almost all have remained at home. The parade would have been less colourful and less dramatic. A few giants might have grown still taller: wealthy people who have set fortunes aside for their wives and children.

(b) The end of the parade makes a shattering impression. The marchers' height increases with incredible speed in the last minutes, and above all *within* the last minute. It therefore makes a great deal of difference whether we watch the marchers of the last minute (the top 1.7%) or whether we consider those of the last seconds. There is not just a great difference in height: the last minute starts with six yards or so, and the last second we see people of five to ten miles; but there is also difference in the nature of income. A member of the top 1.7% need not necessarily be fabulously rich. He may be wealthy, but this fortune is not essential. His top income may consist in a salary: a senior civil servant, a professor, a manager. It may also be a professional income, earned with the hands: the surgeon. These people have such generous incomes that they can save. This of course breeds wealth, and we consequently see that the top 1% almost always have some wealth in reserve. But this is

not a *sine qua non* for their high incomes – the interest is nice to have, but this "private income" is not essential to their position in the parade.

That is where they differ from the participants of the last seconds. They may also have salaries, but at the same time they are immensely rich. In their case the salary is often subordinate. Their main income consists of interest and profit (these two components of personal income cannot always be sharply distinguished from one another. Their source is different, and consequently we shall at all times keep profit and interest apart in this book. But when the dividend reaches the income recipient it sometimes begins to look like interest). The top fortunes are not only a welcome supplementation to income from work – the capital is the essential basis of the economic position of the financial giants. Their wealth is not always invested in a wide portfolio of shares – it is often deliberately invested in their own firms, in which they have a say. Considerable misunderstanding occurs through confusion of these two groups – the last minute and the last seconds – though it is of course true that there are smooth transitions between them. The top 1% (and even the top 10%!) are too often identified with the very wealthy capitalists. The latter group is tiny.

The question is how these enormous fortunes are accumulated. The answer is a straightforward one: the source is always formed by profits. You can save a modest little capital from a salary, and so become well-to-do, but if you really want to build up a huge fortune you cannot leave it at that. (It is of course easier to inherit the money, but that passes over the manner in which the testator came by the money.) Savings from wage and salary may form a springboard, but ultimately the aspiring Croesus will have to rely on the rewards of entrepreneurship. The best thing is to have the disposal of a good, brand-new product (with the necessary patents) and to start producing it with drive. You might come a financial cropper, but you might bring it off. The survivors cross a threshold after which their profits accumulate, and so the lucky ones join the rear ranks of our parade.

The process of getting rich sometimes goes faster than you might think. It does not always take generations; the list of the enormously wealthy is growing. The theory that it is impossible to become colossally wealthy nowadays and that the big fortunes are at least a generation old is unrealistic. A well-known example in support of the contrary is that of Dr. Edwin H. Land, who invented the sixty-second camera in the Forties. At first the public did not see much in it, but took a second look and found this way of photography attractive after all. Incidentally, Dr. Land has many other optical inventions to his name. In 1968 he was Number 4 on Fortune's list of the Super-Rich, that is to say behind J. Paul Getty (oil), Howard Hughes (aircraft, among other things) and H. L. Hunt (oil), but ahead of the old families like the Duponts, the Fords, the Mellons, and the Rockefellers. Land's fortune is estimated at $500 to 1,000 million. Chester Carlson is another example of an inventor (Xerography; he started as a lawyer!); he is said to be worth $150 to 200 million. According to *Fortune* there were 153 people in the United States with a net worth of above $100 million in 1968 (including wealth held by spouses, minor children, trusts, and foundations). A third of these 153 were not yet really wealthy ten years before. Of course the big heirs with the familiar names are still to be found on the list of 153. They have been displaced from top position by the *nouveaux riches,* but they're keeping their end up very nicely.

(c) The head of the procession naturally also deserves closer attention. We must make a distinction between the part-time workers and casual earners on the side on the one hand and the shocking social emergency cases on the other. Recently more has become known about the latter group. . . . This group is of importance to social policy (minimum wages, social security,

tax exemption limit, negative income tax). Some are inclined to make this very group the principal objective of distribution policy, and I heartily agree. In my opinion they form a more urgent problem than the very rich.

(d) Also of interest is the great difference in predictability and determinateness of the incomes. People are marching in our parade whose earnings we know within narrow limits. That applies to all wage-earners whose incomes are laid down in collective agreements, to civil servants, to many other salary-earners: a good 80% of the population. But the fact that someone is called a rentier or capitalist (depending on the observer's preference) tells us nothing at all about his place in income structure. He may scrape together a small income from interest, just enough to supplement his pension slightly; he may also belong at the end of the procession. We already know much more about him if he tells us how great his wealth is — then his income can be predicted within certain limits.

But this predictability does not apply to profits. The man who lives on profit may pop up anywhere in the procession. Even further information on the size of a person's business is no criterion of his income. Firstly because there are flourishing and highly profitable small businesses that place their owners in the last minute of the parade, and there are large firms that make a loss. In the second place because the distribution of a firm's profit may differ so greatly. Three brothers may each pocket one-third of the profit made by the family business, but that may also be arranged quite differently. The very large firm has again a wider variation in its arrangements: shareholders, top executives and staff may share in the profit in accordance with different criteria. And then there are profits whose volume it is difficult to estimate. If a wealthy shipowner wants to know how much he earns and how that income is made up, he has to ask his accountant. We, as inquisitive outsiders, certainly cannot find out. It is profit that often escapes our understanding and at the same time creates the tremendous inequality.

(e) Our procession has the attractive property that we can see and recognize the participants. We saw men with boots on and dirty hands, respectable gentlemen with briefcases, striking figures and ordinary ones. We saw with our own eyes the richest man in the world. We saw great numbers of very small women, an appalling sight. The other side to this dramatic effect is that our procession is an imaginary one. It is not the custom to organize such shows, and they would in any case meet with opposition from the participants, if only because of the preliminary treatment by Procrustes.

In a highly watered-down form we can achieve something similar by a graph that hurts no-one.... On the horizontal axis of this graph (Figure 1) minutes are plotted, and on the vertical the height of the income recipients. The curve illustrates the dwarf-like nature of most people; the average is indicated by the arrow. The recognizability of the individuals has now disappeared. Nor does the graph lend itself to accurate reading-off, because the right-hand part

rises so steeply that small inequalities in the drawing lead to great difference in income. The last millimetre comprises, on a reduced scale, a top manager of a good 100 yards and the super-rich capitalist of 10 miles. The vertical axis ought in fact to be well over two hundred yards long. Is this perhaps why the graph does not appear in the books?

And yet this drawing suggests one of the most striking properties of income structure: the huge inequality illustrated by the right-hand part of the curve. Other drawings conceal this property....

The Lorenz curve, yet another technique, shows us the same facts through yet other eyes, so that yet other properties strike us. This illustrates my argument that income distribution (and even the narrower subject of *personal* income distribution) has many different faces. It depends on the temperament, the intellectual structure and the political preference of the reader which face he recognizes best. If I may speak for myself, I am rather struck by the presentation in this section. The inequality that emerges from it colours my view of the problem.

FIGURE 1. A Parade

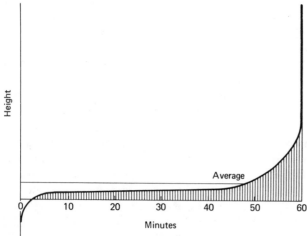

18

Changing the
Distribution of Income

LEARNING OBJECTIVES

The chapter on changing income distribution is not easy to summarize. We have decided to emphasize one very important idea in it — the idea of the *value judgments* implicit in all efforts to change income distribution. Two points to remember:

1. Values are difficult or impossible to separate from economic analysis. Your task is to learn to recognize them.
2. Equity and efficiency are both values. Many difficult problems in income distribution arise from their conflicting demands.

TAXES, POVERTY, AND EQUALITY

Irving Kristol

A conservative critic examines our income distribution and argues that it is less unfair than appears at first sight. Are there value judgments in his critique?

It was not so long ago — in 1958, to be exact — that John Kenneth Galbraith could casually observe, in the course of analyzing *The Affluent Society,* that "few things are more evident in modern social history than the decline of interest in inequality as an economic issue."

From "The Public Interest," No. 37 (Fall 1974), pp. 3–28.

Obviously, times have changed, though in what way or for what reason it is not at all clear. The question of inequality is now widely regarded as an urgent one, expecially in connection with our present system of taxation, which many hold responsible for a distribution of income deemed to be flagrantly unequal and hence inequitable. No one has a kind word to say for our tax structure; everyone appears utterly convinced that it is in a miserable condition and that drastic surgery is as necessary as it is desirable.

In this atmosphere of feverish discontent, meaningless rhetoric and misleading statistics flourish. They are so common that most of us simply nod at them, in some kind of vague assent or toleration: The urge to scrutinize has withered away. Thus, the *New Republic's* eminent columnist, TRB, could calmly inform his readers (on June 22, 1974) that "wealth at the rate of $10 billion annually is now flowing from the lowest three-fifths of America's income groups to the richest one-fifth." That *sounds* precise and authoritative enough — only, if one stops to think, one is prompted to wonder what this "flowing" means and just how it is happening. It cannot mean what it seems to mean: that the distribution of income in this country is all of a sudden becoming more radically unequal, to the benefit of the very rich, than it had been. Such a statement would simply be false, and no reputable economist, of whatever political persuasion, has sanctioned it. Presumably, TRB had some more arcane bit of economic intelligence in mind. Or perhaps he was merely giving an extremely loose interpretation of something he read, somewhere. But what is absolutely certain is that the readers of the *New Republic* are not going to bother him with demands for an explanation. On this subject, they — like most of us — are credulous to the point of numbness.

The fact is that the partisan use of statistics, in the modern world, seems to have outdistanced the ability of even well-informed and educated citizens to cope with them. Thus, one reads that the top 20 per cent of families, which receive a little over 40 per cent of total income, now pay 50 per cent of total taxes, and the top five per cent, which receive 16 per cent of total income, pay 25 per cent of total taxes. This statistic is accurate and conveys the impression that our present tax system distributes the tax burden rather fairly. One also reads that the top 20 per cent pay in taxes about the same proportion (33 per cent) of their income as the lowest 20 per cent. This statistic, too, is accurate in its own way and, while not contradicting the first, conveys a quite opposite impression. One can do quite marvellous things with statistics, and the sad truth is that most of us are utterly defenseless against their inherent persuasive power.

Similarly, one can make (many do make) much of the fact — and it is a kind of fact — that families with annual incomes below $2,000 pay 50 per cent of their income in taxes. That sounds horrendous — until one is made aware of the complications lurking in the background. To begin with, we are not talking about *income* tax, from which these families are exempt. Nor are we even talking about such familiar "regressive" taxes as the sales tax, which obviously cannot amount to 50 per cent of expenditure. (Among such low-income families, expenditure can be assumed to be identical with income.) No, we are talking about payments which most of us do not regard as "taxes" at all — e.g., that portion of our rent which represents the landlord's real estate tax. And it further helps to put this statistic in perspective if we realize (a) that in most cases this income is not *earned* income but represents tax-free (of income tax, that is) transfer payments from the government in the first place (welfare, social security, unemployment insurance, etc.); and (b) that not all of these families with incomes below $2,000 a year are really poor — a 24-year old married graduate student, who earns $1,800 as a research assistant or teaching assistant, and who also receives financial support from his and his wife's parents, or who borrows on the basis of his (or her) future earning prospects, is not so much terribly poor as very young. Now, none of these qualifications should be taken to imply that we do not have a problem of poverty in the United States. They do suggest, however, that mixing up the problem of poverty with the problem of tax equity is not very enlightening, though the political and rhetorical advantages of such confusion are evident enough.

As with income distribution, so with the distribution of wealth. TRB, in the aforementioned column, declared indignantly that "fewer than one per cent of the people currently own over 50 per cent of the corporate stock in the country." And, from other recent and reputable publications one can cull similar statistics: that two per cent of individual stockholders own about two thirds of all stock held by individuals, or that the top one per cent of adult American wealth holders own roughly 25 per cent of all personal property and personal financial assets. Now, there is no doubt that wealth is unequally distributed in the United States — but it is also certain that wealth is not nearly so concentrated as those statistics would lead the casual reader to think. The phrase "corporate stock" brings to mind the stock of General Motors or IBM — one is not likely to think of all those thousands of small or tiny businesses where stock is owned mainly by an individual founder or members of his family, and where the value of the stock may be modest or even negligible. Who owns what proportion of "the total corporate stock" tells you far less than it seems to. Similarly, the percentage of "all stock owned by individuals" slides around the fact that a significant percentage (35 per cent is a common estimate) of the stock of the larger corporations is owned by institutions — pension and profit-sharing funds, mutual insurance companies, mutual funds — which are surrogates for individuals who, in their own name, own no stock at all.[1] In other words *the mode of stock ownership by less wealthy people is collective rather than individual,* so that statistics on individual stock ownership exaggerate the degree of concentration. And much the same thing is true for "personal financial assets": For most working-class and middle-class people, *impersonal ownership* of financial assets is more important than personal ownership. These assets are mainly in their pension plans — and also, of course, in social security and medicare (the equivalent of an annuity and a medical insurance policy, respectively), which are not counted as "assets" at all but which, if capitalized and included in the statistics, would significantly reduce the degree of inequality in the ownership of "wealth." We have gone to great pains to create a "welfare state," but our statistics on the distribution of wealth utterly ignore the existence of the institutions of the welfare state, and of the claims upon the nation's wealth which these institutions "own."

To repeat, the ownership of wealth in the United States is unequally distributed — somewhat more unequally than income, most economists estimate. But those isolated and scary statistics — all technically correct — which convey the notion that this country is "owned" by a tiny oligarchy of rich people are the stuff of paranoid fantasies, not of economic or social reality.

THE "FACTS" AND THE "TRUTH"

The basic facts about the distribution of income in the United States over the past

[1] Thus, the Sears Roebuck pension and savings fund owns 20 per cent of all outstanding shares of the company. The value of the common stock owned by all pension and savings funds amounts to about 15 per cent of the total market value of all shares of all companies listed on the New York Stock Exchange. The assets of these funds are growing at the rate of 14 per cent a year — i.e., they will quadruple by 1985. "Social ownership" of the "means of production" is proceeding faster than anyone realizes — only not in ways that either socialists or capitalists anticipated.

decades are well known, and are set forth in the following table, constructed by the Council of Economic Advisers in February 1974:

	1947	1972
Bottom 20% of population received	5.1% of total income	5.4%
Top 20% of population received	43.3% of total income	41.4%
Top 5% of population received	17.5% of total income	15.9%

Over the past 25 years, there has been a slight shift of (pre-tax) income away from the very rich to the middling ranks — not, in any significant degree, to the poor. That is what the statistics show. They also show, beyond question, a substantial and persistent degree of inequality in the distribution of income. So far, so uncontroversial. However, as is almost always the case, the statistical "facts" may as easily obscure as reveal the "truth" of the matter.

To begin with, there is always the question of the subjective impression created by objective statistics. In this case, especially, there is the way most of us react to any statistics concerning "the top five per cent" or "the top 20 per cent" of the income-receiving population. It is in the nature of a democratic, affluent society that quite well-to-do people never do *feel* as well-off as they statistically are. Later on, it will be suggested why this is so; but, for the moment, it suffices to say that most people, when they think of "the top five per cent" or the "top 20 per cent," promptly have visions of the Great Gatsby, or the Rockefellers, or at least the executives of major corporations. It comes as a great shock to them to discover they may very well, without knowing it, be thinking of themselves. The "top five per cent" consists of all households with incomes over $30,000 a year. The "top 20 per cent" consists of all households with incomes over $20,000 a year. Most of these "rich" people are people who, in the ordinary

course of events, are regarded as "middle-class" — our doctor, our dentist, our lawyer, our accountant, our children's professors, perhaps ourselves. This confusion of socio-economic perspectives creates a special problem for politicians, who start out with the idea of "taxing the rich" and end up with a "middle-class tax rebellion" on their hands.

But there really is much more to it than that. These objective statistics are not only easily misread — they are also, *objectively,* very misleading. They grossly exaggerate the degree of income inequality in the first place, because, like all such cross-sectional statistical pictures snapped at a moment in time, they overlook a very significant human and social phenomenon: age, and the relation of age to income.

Young people earn less than mature adults in the prime of their working lives. Old people, over 65, earn less than younger adults in the prime of their working lives. We all know this and take it to be perfectly natural and proper and inevitable. *But the table cited above, like most such tables on the distribution of income, does not "know" this.*

Just how important the question of age is in determining the distribution of income may be seen from a look at the 25 per cent of all households that earn less than $5,000 annually. In 10 per cent of these households, the head is under 25 years of age. In 46 per cent, the head is over 65. Only 22 per cent of these households have more than two people. The conclusion is inescapable that the conventional cross-sectional "picture" of income distribution in the United States significantly overstates the degree of income inequality.[2]

[2]Presumably the same is true for the distribution of wealth. The London *Economist* (June 22, 1974), after estimating that 10 per cent of Britain's population owns 40 per cent of all personal wealth, reckons that since "the old are bound to have larger savings than the young because they have been longer at it . . . the age distribution of the population alone accounts for the concentration of 30 per cent of wealth in so few hands."

Moreover, once we are alerted to the importance of age in affecting the distribution of income, we become aware of some odd and paradoxical connections between demography and the distribution of income. Thus the postwar baby boom, by increasing the proportion of young workers, is clearly making the distribution of income today at least slightly more unequal than would otherwise be the case. The same is true for the postwar boom in higher education: It has increased the number of households consisting of married graduate students (including medical students, law students, etc.) who have (temporarily) lower incomes than if they were working at full-time jobs — and who can expect to have much better than average incomes eventually.

Social policies further complicate the relationship between age and income. More generous social security payments to the aged encourages them to retire from full-time (and better-paid) work at an earlier age. Medicare for the aged increases (one hopes) their longevity, which is good for the people but bad (in terms of equality) for the income distribution curve. It is facts such as these which make it so senseless to demand, as many of our egalitarians are now doing that no "person" or "household" should have an income of less than 60 per cent of the national median. The categories of "person" and "household," which disregard age and specific circumstance, are just too vague for any serious discussion of the "fairness" of income distribution.

Lester Thurow, in his analysis of income inequality in *The Public Interest* (No. 31, Spring 1973), does take age partially into account. He points out that the top 14.5 per cent of adult, white, fully-employed males earn 28 per cent of total earnings for this group. And he suggests that this fairly modest degree of inequality — modest in view of the differences in occupation, from doorman to surgeon — serve as an appropriate goal for a redistribution of income among the population as a whole. To which one may say: (a) Since men have to be young before they become adult, and become old after passing through their prime, it is not obvious that *this* pattern of income distribution among adult males should or can serve as a model for the population as a whole at any single point in time; and (b) Thurow's own statistics do not distinguish between the younger man beginning his career and the mature man at the height of his earning power, so the degree of inequality among white, fully-employed, adult males is certainly even less — perhaps substantially less — than he estimates.

So where does all this leave us? Well, it leaves us with the distinct impression that the "truth" about income distribution in the United States is far more complex and confusing than the "facts," as ordinarily presented, would imply. That incomes are unequal, is clear enough. That they are less unequal than indignant critics assert, is certain. Is the inequality that does exist too large? That question admits of no easy answer. Christopher Jencks, in his study, *Inequality,* reports: "The average white child born into the most privileged fifth of white American familes could look forward to an annual income 75 per cent greater than the average child born into the least privileged fifth of white families."[3] He also reports that income differences between brothers who have been raised in the same home are almost as great as the difference between any two individuals chosen at random. Jencks, who is a socialist, was frankly surprised to discover so little inequality — though, as an absolute egalitarian, he still thinks it is too much. Others will be immensely reassured to find that traditional "equality of opportunity" still works so well. Obviously, the issue of how much inequality is

[3]The inclusion of black children would certainly worsen the statistics. But the issue here is not the inequalities suffered by blacks, which are real enough and beyond dispute, but the extent of inequality throughout American society as a whole.

consistent with a "fair" distribution of income in a democracy is anything but a simple matter of arithmetic.

OF TAXES AND "LOOPHOLES"

So far we have been talking about pre-tax incomes. What is the effect of our tax system upon the distribution of income? The question is easy to ask, much less easy to answer. Not only do we have a very complex system of taxation, so that its impact is diffused in ways very difficult to trace or measure, but we also have a complex economic and social system, and the interaction of these two complexities is such as to defeat the capabilities of the most powerful computer. Take the apparently simple matter of defining "income." In a welfare state, much of our tax monies – in fact, 20 per cent of our gross national product – goes to the support of services and grants which are not ordinarily counted as "income," but which are intended to function as income supplements. Here again, a good portion of the "income" of the less well-to-do, and most especially of the poor, is *impersonal income:* subsidized housing, food stamps, medicaid, free legal services, scholarships for poor students, etc., etc. There is little doubt that when the effects of such expenditures and "transfer payments" are taken into account, the post-tax distribution of income in the United States is less unequal than the pre-tax distribution.[4]

Most of the controversy over our tax system concerns itself with the progressive income tax, and expresses the disappointments of those who expected this tax to be more redistributive than it is. Indeed, among some such people the disappointment is so keen that they declare the progressive income tax to be one huge fraud, in that there is nothing progressive about it. This is patently false. As Roger Freeman has shown, the only class for which the income tax is not progressive is the middle class – i.e., those earning $7,000 to $20,000 a year. This class has 60 per cent of the nation's adjusted gross income, but bears only 54 per cent of the income tax liability. In contrast, those over $20,000 have 21 per cent of adjusted gross incomes but bear 36 per cent of total tax liability.[5]

But why, then does the progressive income tax not result in an obvious and substantial redistribution of income? The explanation is manifold: (1) To begin with and as has already been mentioned, much of the redistribution that does occur takes the form of services and subsidies on the part of the state which do not show up in conventional income statistics. (2) To some degree, the progressive character of the income tax is counterbalanced by the non-progressive character of other taxes (e.g., the sales tax and the social security tax). (3) Most important, the expectations about the redistributive consequences of the progressive income tax were unrealistic in the first place; there just are not enough "rich" people, and their share of the national income is just not large enough, for the progressive income tax to have massive results by way of redistribution.

[4]The effects of the welfare state, in its totality, upon income redistribution are exceedingly difficult to calculate – there are so many different programs, in cash and kind, with so many different consequences for people in different circumstances. Robert J. Lampman has made the most sophisticated analysis, and his findings are as follows:

Some 20 per cent of the American population have an "original income" – i.e., before social security, unemployment insurance, welfare, or any other transfers in cash or kind – which puts them below the official poverty line. Their total "original income" represents three per cent of national income. As a result of transfers in cash and kind (e.g., food stamps, low-cost housing, medicare and medicaid, etc.), this 20 per cent of the population increases its share of the national income from three per cent to nine per cent. As a result of cash transfers alone, about one third of these people are taken out of poverty.

Obviously, we have not abolished poverty in the United States. Equally obviously, we have made substantial progress in that direction. Recent increases in social security will undoubtedly make these statistics look even better.

[5]See Roger A. Freeman, *Tax Loopholes: the Legend and the Reality,* an AEI-Hoover Institution study (May 1973).

It would be nice, from the point of view of egalitarians, if our income structure resembled an inverted pyramid, in which a slice from the top yielded a visible dividend for everyone else. But, in actuality, our income structure is diamond-shaped; a slice from the very top yields a barely visible dividend for everyone else — and, if you start slicing further down, you quickly find that you are taxing large numbers of people who do not think of themselves as "rich" and who will tell their elected representatives, in no uncertain terms, that their tax burden is heavy enough already. Senator McGovern discovered this fact of economic life when he proposed his "demo-grant" scheme (a $1,000 tax credit per person), to be financed by tax reforms that would affect "the rich." In its final version, this scheme required that 35 per cent of the American population pay more taxes than they do now. That is a "minority," true; but it is evidently far too large a minority for a politician to trifle with.

But what about all those "loopholes" which permit the wealthy to evade their share of the tax burden — the sort of thing that Philip M. Stern writes about in his much-discussed book, *The Rape of the Taxpayer: Why You Pay More While the Rich Pay Less,* or that Michael Harring-ton has in mind when he declares (*Saturday Review,* October 21, 1972): "The unconscion-able fact is that the Internal Revenue Code is a perverse welfare system that hands out $77 billion a year, primarily to the rich"?

Alas, this vast and passionate literature about how the rich maneuver without cost through our tax system tells us more about the prevalence of egalitarian passions in our democracy than about our tax system.[6] This $77 billion figure is derived from a Brookings study by Joseph Pechman, which showed — in the course of proposing a simplified recasting of our tax system — that *all* tax exemptions and allowances total $77 billion dollars.[7] Repeat: *all* tax exemptions and allow-ances, for everyone. Mr. Pechman never said — a serious scholar, he never would say — that these deductions and allowances benefit the rich ex-clusively. He never even said that they benefit the rich "primarily." It is others who made that intellectual leap from bare statistics to gaudy indictment.

As a matter of fact, if all these exemptions and allowances were repealed, some 55 per cent of that $77 billion dollars would be derived from families earning under $25,000 a year. In addi-tion, some 10 million families who earn less than $10,000 a year, and who now pay no tax because of these exemptions and allowances, would be added to the tax rolls. So there is no question at all of any total repeal of these "loopholes" — which include (it is worth a reminder) such things as personal exemptions, deductions for all dependents, the tax-exempt status of social

[6] It also tells us something about the uses of political demagoguery in a democracy. Back in 1969, Joseph Barr, a former Democratic Representative with a keen eye for a headline, became acting Secretary of the Treasury for 31 days. In that period, he caused a sensation by announcing, two days before leaving office, that 155 taxpayers with an adjustable gross income of $200,000 or more had paid no income tax in 1967. He offered no explanation, but merely created the impres-sion that some ghastly inequity in our tax system made this possible. Subsequently, the matter was analyzed by Roger Freeman and others, and it was revealed that Barr either didn't understand the tax laws or wished deliber-ately to mislead. Thus, the incomes he was talking about were "adjusted gross incomes," not "net in-comes" — i.e., not income after costs that might have been incurred in earning that income. (For example, he counted the income received from investing a large sum of borrowed money but not the interest that had to be paid on that loan.) The failure to make this distinction explains why 55 out of the 155 paid no taxes. The other hundred are explained by the fact that they earned their money abroad and paid foreign taxes on it (sometimes larger than the American tax they might have paid), or because they made a generous charitable gift (e.g., to a university or a museum) larger than their income for that year, or because they had tax-loss carry-forwards from previous financial disasters. It is worth noting that there are some 15,000 people at the above-$200,000 income level, and they paid taxes in 1967 at a rate of 44 percent on adjusted gross income. Nevertheless, Barr made his point: Most Americans are now convinced that it is easy for the very rich to pay no taxes at all.

[7] For a brilliant and definitive discussion of this whole topic, see Professor Boris I. Bittker's article, "Income Tax 'Loopholes' and Political Rhetoric," in the *Michigan Law Review,* Vol. 71 (May 1973).

security, unemployment insurance, workmen's compensation, veteran's disability benefits, various tax privileges for the blind and the handicapped, all charitable deductions, and all sorts of other exemptions and allowances in the tax laws that no one thinks of as "loopholes."

The real issue raised by Pechman and others is whether a portion of this $77 billion — $10 to $15 billion dollars is the figure most often arrived at — which mainly does benefit the well-to-do, can be "captured" by tax reform. The "loopholes" which such a tax reform would be directed at include (a) taxation of capital gains at special, lower rates; (b) the tax-free status of interest on municipal and state bonds; (c) the "depletion allowance" for oil and other extractive industries; (d) the exclusion of unrealized capital gains from income tax on death of the taxpayer; (e) the tax-deductibility of interest on home mortgages; and, depending on who is composing the list, a few other miscellaneous items.

One thing can promptly be said about any such agenda for tax reform: It will certainly end up "recapturing" far less than $15 billion, or anything like it. The trouble is that the easy and obviously desirable reforms (e.g., ending depletion allowances or taxing unrealized capital gains in death) raise only a little money (a billion dollars or so in the case of depletion allowances) or a relatively modest sum (perhaps $3 to $4 billion in the case of taxing capital gains at death). In contrast, the reforms that might raise more substantial sums will either never be enacted by Congress or will be enacted in such a way as to fall short of this goal: Congress is not about to affront American homeowners by ending the tax-deductibility of interest payments on their mortgages; nor is it likely to tangle with the nation's governors and mayors by ending the tax-exempt status of state and municipal bonds; nor is it going to tax more heavily the capital gains realized by middle-class homeowners or small businessmen. Congress might fiddle around with these issues so as to squeeze out a little extra revenue from the more affluent beneficiaries, but we should then be talking about, say, $6-$8 billion in extra revenue.

The really interesting question about these and other "loopholes" is not how much extra tax money can be squeezed back through them — several billion dollars probably can, which would certainly be useful but which would have only a slight effect on the federal budget, and no noticeable effect on the post-tax distribution of income. The more interesting question is how they ever came to be regarded as "loopholes" at all. By far the most important feature of the discussion of this whole matter is not the numbers and the details, but rather the way in which the question itself has come to be defined. It is a way suggestive of implications for our understanding of the role of taxation in a democratic and liberal society with a "mixed economy."

THE BEFORE-AND-AFTER TEST AGAIN

Here is the before-and-after test you took "before," many chapters ago. We presume you've forgotten the answers by now, but you should have your first score at the bottom of the next page. Try it again: five points off for each error, three points off for each "don't know."

You *should* do a lot better than the first time. We wish we could offer you your money back if you're not satisfied, but our publisher won't allow that. Instead let us take a chance and congratulate you on how much you've learned.

Put a check under T (True), F (False), or ? (Don't Know).

	T	F	?
1. Suppose that a necessity, like medicine, sells for $10 a bottle. If the prices of both commodities are cut by 10 percent, we would expect the sales of the necessary good – the medicine – to grow much faster than the luxury.	—	—	—
2. If a price ceiling is put on a desired commodity, such as apartment rentals, a shortage usually results.	—	—	—
3. One important difference between monopolistic and competitive firms is that monopolies try to make as much money as they can, whereas competitive firms do not strive after maximum profits.	—	—	—
4. The law of supply and demand means that in the end high prices tend to come down, and low prices tend to go up.	—	—	—
5. The advantage of a market is that it avoids allocating goods because it allows people to buy and sell freely.	—	—	—
6. Because a sales tax is levied on retail goods, it is therefore entirely borne by the retail buyers.	—	—	—
7. Taxes on effluents, such as smoke, are a poor way to curb pollution (because the polluter can go on making smoke even if he has to pay a tax.)	—	—	—
8. If we have a choice of buying two different goods with a limited budget, we will always make the most rational choice if we buy the good whose price is lower.	—	—	—
9. Antitrust laws aim to discourage monopolies. One main reason they are difficult to administer is that monopolies are hard to define.	—	—	—
10. What we mean by "wage discrimination," as in the case of women, is that they are paid less than men because their productivity is less.	—	—	—
11. An entrepreneur in a competitive firm has no say over the prices he pays or the prices he charges.	—	—	—
12. If the price of a commodity, such as margarine, goes up, it is likely that the price of a similar commodity, such as butter, will also go up.	—	—	—
13. Industries with a few large sellers, such as the auto industry, are usually marked with severe price competition.	—	—	—
14. If one farmer can increase his receipts by cutting his price, it stands to reason that all farmers can do the same.	—	—	—
15. The distribution of income is more equal than the distribution of wealth.	—	—	—
16. An economist would claim that profit-making is a way of minimizing waste.	—	—	—
17. The prices of most goods reflect the intensity of demand for them.	—	—	—

18. When supply and demand have worked themselves out, the resulting price can be described as a "just" or "fair" price.

— — —

19. If a commodity is not abundantly found in nature, it tends to sell at a high price.

— — —

20. One of the benefits of the market system is that it is an administratively convenient rationing mechanism.

— — —

Score yourself by subtracting 5 points for each mistake and 3 points for each "Don't know."

Answers:

1. F	8. F	15. T
2. T	9. T	16. T
3. F	10. F	17. F
4. F	11. T	18. F
5. F	12. T	19. F
6. F	13. F	20. T
7. F	14. F	

Score ____

Score before ____

PROSPERITY AND RECESSION– THE ECONOMICS OF THE MACRO SYSTEM

A BEFORE-AND-AFTER TEST
ON MACROECONOMICS

Having just completed a before-and-after test in microeconomics, are you game for another? Here is a set of questions which, as before, call for no special knowledge of vocabulary or techniques. Of course you know they are designed to discover your misconceptions, so you will be looking for all the angles. But try to answer the questions in a straightforward way. Then, as in the previous exam, enter your score on the bottom of page 306, where you can eventually compare it with your test results after finishing macro.

Put a check under T (True), F (False) or ? (Don't Know).   T F ?

1. The amount of money in the economy increases when people draw money out of their checking accounts.   — — —

2. Inflation is a "zero-sum" game — a process in which there must be as much gain as there is loss.   — — —

3. One of the most effective remedies for recession is to encourage people to consume more.   — — —

4. A main cause for recession is that not enough incomes are paid out to buy back the output of the economy.   — — —

5. One of the principal sources of economic growth is the increase in skills and knowledge.   — — —

6. It is unsafe for the government to run up a huge deficit for the same reason that it is unsafe for a family to incur a huge debt.   — — —

7. The more rapidly we spend money, the more money there is.   — — —

8. The main purpose of the Federal Reserve System is to safeguard the nation's currency.   — — —

9. Inflation in the United States since World War II has been less severe than in Europe.   — — —

10. A national debt, owed by a country's citizens, can safely be of any size, since we owe it to ourselves.   — — —

11. Banks can actually create new money by loans.   — — —

12. It is possible for employment and unemployment both to increase at the same time.   — — —

13. An economy that is no longer growing will also be an economy that is no longer polluting the environment.   — — —

14. The main purpose of gold is to provide a national backing for currency.   — — —

15. Gross national product is a measure of national well being.   — — —

16. As a result of consumer credit, the households of the nation spend more than their total annual incomes.   — — —

17. When we buy stock on a stock exchange, our purchase usually helps a company finance its expansion.   — — —

18. The chief argument against an unbalanced government budget is that the government can't spend money it doesn't have.   — — —

19. More spending is the way out of a recession.   — — —

20. An economy at full employment will have less inflation than an economy in which there is unemployment.   — — —

Answers:

1. F	8. F	15. F
2. T	9. T	16. F
3. F	10. T	17. F
4. F	11. T	18. F
5. T	12. T	19. T
6. F	13. F	20. F
7. F	14. F	

As before, score −5 for wrong answer, −3 for "don't know." Enter score on p. 306.

19

Wealth and Output

LEARNING OBJECTIVES

The main purpose of this first chapter in macroeconomics is to introduce you to some basic concepts. Here are three things you should know:
1. The meaning of stock, flow, capital, investment, depreciation.
2. The exact definition of gross national product.
3. The basic nature of the circular flow of GNP.

With this chapter we change the lens in our camera and examine the economy from a new perspective. It is no longer the output of a single firm, or the level of prices in an individual market, or the quantity of factors employed in an enterprise or industry that interests us. It is *total* output, *all* prices (the price level), *total* employment. This new perspective is what distinguishes macroeconomics from microeconomics.

WEALTH, STOCKS, AND FLOWS

Our approach introduces us first to the macro concept of our stock of national wealth. Note the word *stock*. Economics frequently distinguishes between stocks and *flows,* and here is a good place to get the distinction clear. A stock is an aggregate quantity of a good or a resource. It exists in its entirety at a moment in time. A flow is an activity that adds to or diminishes a stock. Because it is an activity, we measure it per unit of time.

In Figure 19-1 we show a stock-flow relationship.

In our illustration the outflow is smaller than the inflow. Therefore the stock should increase. If we reverse the arrows the stock would decrease.

FIGURE 19-1

Which of the following are stocks? Which are flows?

Item	Stock	Flow
1 Wealth	–	–
2 Investment	–	–
3 Disinvestment	–	–
4 Population	–	–
5 Births	–	–
6 Deaths	–	–
7 Capital	–	–
8 Consumption	–	–
9 Gross National Product	–	–
10 Depreciation	–	–

Answers: (Items 1, 4, and 7 are stocks; the rest flows. We speak of births *per year*, but population at a given date.)

CAPITAL

The most important part of our wealth is capital, the value of all man-made artifacts. Capital is also a stock. The flow that adds to capital is called ⎯⎯⎯⎯⎯⎯ ; and the flow that diminishes it is ⎯⎯⎯⎯⎯⎯ , or ⎯⎯⎯⎯⎯⎯ . (In addition to disinvestment and depreciation, obsolescence also diminishes the value of our capital, but not its physical quantity. An obsolete machine still exists, but has much less economic value.)

Our stock of private capital is represented by a sum of *claims,* such as stocks and bonds and mortgages. In Figure 19-2 can you correctly identify: (1) investment, (2) disinvestment or depreciation, and (3) claims.

Notice that our stock of capital does not include the value of human capital, although the capitalized value of our labor is larger than the

FIGURE 19-2

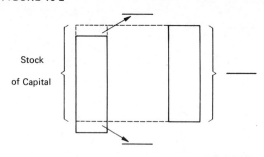

market value of our physical capital. The reason we do not include human capital is that human "assets" are not for sale. A slave society would count the value of its human capital.

PRODUCTION

Wealth, and especially capital, is crucial in determining our flow of output. Thus we can make an easy transition from considering our stocks of wealth to learning about the flow of output (the stream of output per unit time). We call this flow of total output Gross National Product. Here we want to learn two things in particular about that flow:

1. *GNP only includes final output.* It does not add to the value of final output the values of intermediate output that go into the final product. In Figure 19-3 below, note the steadily rising values of intermediate output. What is the value of the final product, bread?⎯⎯⎯⎯⎯ What would be the value

FIGURE 19-3

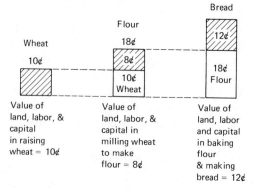

[Note: Value added at each stage is shaded.]

164

if we included wheat and flour *in addition* to bread? _____. *Can you see that in counting bread as part of GNP we include all the "value added" by earlier stages of manufacture?*

2. *There are four final products in GNP.* We have seen that GNP only includes "final" products. What is "final" about a product? The answer is that the product is no longer worked on. It is no longer an intermediate product. It passes into a final use, either as a consumption good or as an export or as a government good or an addition to investment.

   Figure 19–4 is a flow chart showing us a stream of GNP branching into four final products. Can you identify the substreams and fill in the information asked for?

The flow chart enables us to understand the meaning of the identity that you must learn:

$$GNP \equiv C + I + G + X$$

Can you answer these questions:

1. Why is it an identity?
2. Why is gross private domestic investment *gross?* Why is it *private?* Why is it *domestic?*
3. Does *government purchases* distinguish between government consumption and investment?
4. Why is *X net* exports?

Answers: The answers to these questions are important in understanding the definition of GNP. Here they are:

1. GNP is the name for the market value of final output in a given period. We can describe that output in many ways. One way to describe it is to identify its final buyers. These buyers are the household, business, government and "rest of the world." The expenditures they make are abbreviated as *C, G, I,* and *X.* This description holds for all possible levels of GNP. There is nothing "functional" about it. *C, G, I* and *X* are just slices of the GNP pie.

2. Gross private domestic investment is *gross* because it includes replacement investment as well as net investment. It is *private* because it does not include the value of public investment, such as a highway. It is *domestic* because it includes only expenditures on investment made at home.

3. Government purchases does not distinguish between consumption and investment. It includes both public consumption (for example, public school salaries) and public investment, such as the construction of a public building.

4. *X* is "net" exports because it consists of all exports minus all imports. If we imported more than we exported, we would have a negative figure for this sum in our GNP. (We did have such a negative figure in 1972.) This means that part of our annual flow of output consists of goods made abroad. The production available to the nation is larger than that made at home.

FIGURE 19-4

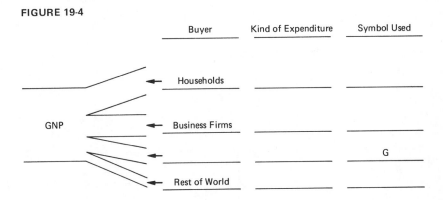

	Buyer	Kind of Expenditure	Symbol Used
GNP	Households		
	Business Firms		
			G
	Rest of World		

THE CIRCULAR FLOW

Now let us return to our flow of GNP and trace what happens to each major branch. In Figure 19-5 we can see that the flows return to replenish our major stocks of capital, human and physical.

Figure 19-6 is a much more complicated chart in which both the consumption and investment flows are broken into public and private components, and in which exports and imports are introduced into the picture. Label the various streams:

private consumption
public consumption
gross private domestic investment
government investment
gross exports
imports

(It doesn't matter which of the two consumption or investment flows you choose to label public: it's the idea that counts.)

FIGURE 19-5

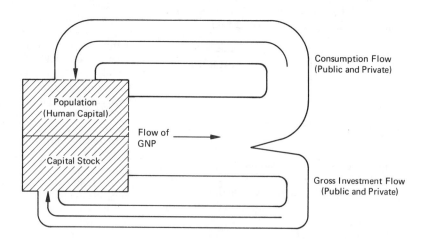

FIGURE 19-6

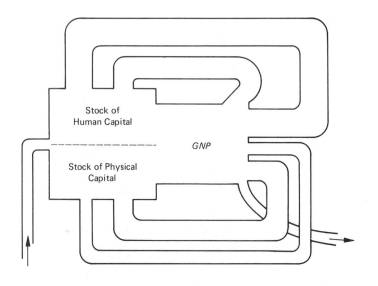

Quiz

To be sure that you understand everything we've covered to here, try this quiz. Put a check under T (True) or F (False).

	T	F
1. Replacement investment adds to the net stock of wealth.	—	—
2. A disinvesting economy has a growing stock of wealth.	—	—
3. Gross investment equals net investment plus replacement investment.	—	—
4. We measure stocks per units of time; flows at a moment in time.	—	—
5. Claims are not an addition to wealth.	—	—
6. Gross national product does not include the value of intermediate outputs.	—	—
7. $C + I \equiv$ GNP $- (G + X)$	—	—
8. The value of final output is the same as the market value of GNP for a given period.	—	—
9. Gross investment minus net investment equals replacement investment.	—	—
10. The circular flow can be used to depict consumption and saving, or public and private uses of output.	—	—
11. Public output can be investment as well as consumption.	—	—
12. In an economy that had no commerce with the rest of the world the formula for GNP would be GNP $\equiv C + I + G$.	—	—
13. The term G includes all government purchases of final output except government investment.	—	—
14. The term I stands for "private net investment."	—	—
15. C is the term used to designate expenditures of households.	—	—

Answers:

1. F	6. F	11. T
2. F	7. T	12. T
3. T	8. T	13. F
4. F	9. T	14. F
5. T	10. T	15. T

CAUTIONS ABOUT GNP

We are not going to review the very important cautions about using GNP as a measure of well being in this review section. There is an interesting reading just ahead that will give you something to think about on that score. But the problem of prices and price indexes is important enough to warrant a small special section of its own. It's optional. Take the quiz if you want. We suggest you do.

Special Quiz on Price Indexes

Below you will find the actual GNP for four recent years. Each of them is in current dollars — that is, in the prices that were current when that GNP was produced. In the next column you will find the actual government price index for GNP, called the GNP Deflator. Notice that its "base" is 1958. This means that the Index for 1958 is 100. The first year in our series, for 1969, shows a GNP Deflator of 128. This means that the price level of GNP was 28 percent higher in 1969 than in 1958.

Year	Current Dollars	GNP Price Deflator (1958 = 100)	GNP in 1958 dollars
1969	930	128	726
1970	977	135	—
1971	1055	142	—
1972	1155	146	—

Now for the quiz. Calculate the value of each year's GNP in 1958 dollars.

We have done the first one for you. Remember, to convert a current dollar value into the dollar value of a given year (such as 1958), you divide the current dollar value by the index (and then multiply by 100). First figure the answer, then check below.

Answers: 1970, 723; 1971, 743; 1972, 791.

1. Did the GNP in 1958 dollars rise or fall from 1969 to1970? How do you explain this?

2. Could you tell the change in real GNP just from the Price Index without any knowledge of current GNP?

3. Assume that between 1975 and 1980 the Price Deflator is unchanged. Could we then tell changes in real GNP directly from changes in current GNP?

Answers:

1. It fell because prices rose proportionally more than the dollar value of output. Real output declined.

2. Of course not. You have to apply the price index to the dollar value of current output.

3. Yes, you could. If there were no price changes, current GNP would be the same as GNP "corrected for price changes." Of course, other warnings would still hold, such as changes in quality, and so on.

WHAT GNP DOESN'T TELL US

A. A. Berle, Jr.

This essay by the late Adolph Berle is somewhat "dated" in terms of the years to which he refers, but it is altogether current with regard to the problem he raises. It is a first-rate discussion of the deceptions of GNP and some good suggestions as to how to remedy them.

It is nice to know that at current estimate the Gross National Product of the United States in 1968 will be above 850 billions of dollars. It would be still nicer to know if the United States will be better or worse off as a result. If better, in what respects? If worse, could not some of this production and effort be steered into providing more useful "goods and services"?

Unfortunately, whether the work was sham or useful, the goods noxious, evanescent, or of permanent value will have no place in the record. Individuals, corporations, or government want, buy, and pay for stuff and work – so it is "product." The labor of the Boston Symphony Orchestra is "product" along with that of the

From *Saturday Review* (August 31, 1968), pp. 10-12.

band in a honky-tonk. The compensated services of a quack fortune teller are "product" just as much as the work of developing Salk vaccine. Restyling automobiles or ice chests by adding tail fins or pink handles adds to "product" just as much as money paid for slum clearance or medical care. They are all "goods" or "services" – the only test is whether someone wanted them badly enough to pay the shot.

This blanket tabulation raises specific complaints against economists and their uncritical aggregated figures and their acceptance of production as "progress." The economists bridle. "We," they reply, "are economists, not priests. Economics deals with satisfaction of human wants by things or services. The want is sufficiently evidenced by the fact that human beings, individually or collectively, paid for them. It is not for us to pass on what people ought to have wanted — that question is for St. Peter. A famous statistic in *America's Needs and Resources* — published by the Twentieth Century Fund in 1955 — was that Americans in 1950 paid $8.1 billion for liquor and $10.5 billion for education. Maybe they ought to have cut out liquor and paid for more education instead — but they didn't, and value judgments are not our job. Get yourself a philosopher for that. We will go on recording what did happen."

What they are saying — and as far as it goes, they are quite right — is that nobody has given economics a mandate to set up a social-value system for the country. Fair enough — but one wonders. Closer thinking suggests that even on their own plane economists could perhaps contribute a little to the subject, although, as will presently appear, we must get ourselves some philosophy, too. One branch of social indicating may not be as far removed from cold economics as it would appear. Another branch is more difficult, though even it may yield to analysis.

Any audit of social result, any system of social indicators, requires solving two sets of problems. First, with all this Gross National Product reflecting payment to satisfy wants, did America get what it paid for? In getting it, did it not also bring into being a flock of unrecorded but offsetting frustrations it did not want? Essentially, this is economic critique. Second — and far more difficult — can a set of values be put forward, roughly expressing the essentials most Americans would agree their society ought to be, and be doing, against which the actual record of what it was and did can be checked? This second critique, as economists rightly contend, is basically philosophical.

As for the economic critique, let us take the existing economic record at face. Work was done, things were created, and both were paid for. The total price paid this year will be around $850

billion. But, unrecorded, not included, and rarely mentioned are some companion results. Undisposed-of junk piles, garbage, waste, air and water pollution come into being. God help us, we can see that all over the country. Unremedied decay of parts of the vast property we call "the United States" is evident in and around most American cities. No one paid for this rot and waste — they are not "product." Factually, these and other undesirable results are clear deductions from or offset items to the alleged Gross National Product we like so well.

The total of these may be called "disproduct." It will be a hard figure to calculate in dollar figures. Recorded as "product" is the amount Americans spent for television sets, stations, and broadcasts. Unrecorded is their companion disproductive effect in the form of violence, vandalism, and crime. Proudly reported as "product" are sums spent for medical care, public health, and disease prevention; unheralded is the counter-item, the "disproduct" of loss and misery as remediable malnutrition and preventable disease ravage poverty areas. Besides our annual calculation of "gross" national product, it is time we had some idea of Gross National Disproduct. Deducting it, we could know what the true, instead of the illusory, annual "net nation product" might be. (Economists use "Net National Product" to mean Gross National Product less consumption of capital — but it is not a true picture.)

There is a difference, it will be noted, between "disproduct" and "cost." Everything made or manufactured, every service rendered by human beings, involves using up materials, if only the food and living necessities of labor. These are "costs." They need not enter into this calculation. Conventional statistics already set up a figure for "capital consumption," and we deduct this from "Gross National Product." That is not what we have in mind here. We are trying to discover whether creation of "Gross National Product" does not also involve frustration of wants as well as their satisfaction. Pollution of air and water are obvious illustrations but there are "disproducts" more difficult to discern, let alone measure.

Scientists are increasing our knowledge of these right along. For example, cigarettes (to which I am addicted) satisfy a widespread want. They also, we are learning, engender a great deal of cancer. Now it is true that at some later time the service rendered in attempting to care for cancer (generated by cigarettes manufactured five years ago) will show up as "product"; so the work of attempted cure or caretaking will later appear as a positive product item. But that item will not be known until later. What we do know without benefit of figures is that against this year's output of tobacco products whose cash value is recorded we have also brought more cancer into being – an unrecorded "disproduct." We know at the end of any year how many more automobiles have been manufactured. We also know that each new car on the road means added injury and accident overall. Carry this process through our whole product list, and the aggregate of "disproduct" items set against the aggregate of production will tell us an immense amount about our progress toward (or retrogression from) social welfare.

Once we learn to calculate disproduct along with product and discover a true "net," as well as a "gross," we shall have our first great "social" indicator. We shall know what the country accomplished.

It could be surprising and disillusioning. It might disclose that while satisfying human wants as indicated by the "gross" figure, in the process we had also violated, blocked, or frustrated many of these same wants and, worse, had done a great deal we did not want to do. Carrying the calculation further, we would probably find (among other things) that while satisfying immediate wants from today's productivity, we had been generating future wants (not to say needs) to repair the damage, waste, and degeneration set up by current production.

Some of today's "gross" product carries with it a mortgage – it sets up brutal defensive requirements that must be met by tomorrow's work and things. Some forms of productivity may prove to generate more decay, damage, or waste annually than their total amount, while neglect of some production may annually place a usurious claim on future years. Failure to maintain cities at acceptable standards is a case in point. It sets up huge but unrecorded claims on the manpower and product of coming decades. It is entirely possible to score annual increases of Gross National Product as we presently figure it – and yet, after reckoning "disproduct," be little better off at the end of any year than at its beginning.

Calculation of "disproduct" is admittedly difficult. If seriously tackled, I think it at least partially possible. At first it would be far indeed from exact. All the same, "disproduct" is a plain fact of life – look out of your window and you can see some. Crude calculation of the probable amounts needed to offset many items of "disproduct" is not insoluble; technicians in some lines have fairly concrete ideas along these lines already. Actuaries compute the "disproduct" resulting from automobile accidents, and your car insurance bill is calculated accordingly. Carry the process through and a crude though probably incomplete item could be developed. Using it, one could judge whether, materially at least, the country had moved forward or backward.

In this first bracket of critique, economists are not required to make value judgements of what is "good or bad." They, with the advice of the technical men in the various sectors, could merely be asked to tackle calculation of "disproduct" as well as of "product."

The second branch of the problem is harder. It raises the question of whether a good deal of Gross National Product should not be steered by social or political action toward creating a more satisfactory civilization. That, of course, requires some elementary assumptions as to what a satisfactory civilization ought to be and do. Can any such assumptions be made?

Constructing enough of a value system to use as critique of a Gross National Product indeed does seem not beyond common-sense possibility. The job does, without question, require setting out some values on which there is sufficient agreement to engage social opinion and, one hopes, social action. Production steered toward realizing these values can be described as "good." Production frustrating or tearing them down can be stigmatized as "bad." Let us try drawing up a list, tentative in the extreme. I think there would probably be considerable agreement that it is "good"; but if not, make a dinner table game of drawing a better one:

1. People are better alive than dead.
2. People are better healthy than sick.
3. People are better off literate than illiterate.
4. People are better off adequately than inadequately housed.
5. People are better off in beautiful than in ugly cities and towns.
6. People are better off if they have opportunity for enjoyment — music, literature, drama, and the arts.
7. Education above the elementary level should be as nearly universal as possible through secondary schools, and higher education as widely diffused as practicable.
8. Development of science and the arts should continue or possibly be expanded.
9. Minimum resources for living should be available to all.
10. Leisure and access to green country should be a human experience available to everyone.

Anyone can add to or change this list if he likes, my point is that at least a minimum set of values can be agreed on. We have done more here than draw up a list of pleasant objectives. We have set up criteria. By applying our list to the actual and recorded output of our Gross National Product, we begin to discern that some of these values are perhaps adequately pursued, some inadequately, some not served at all. Even now, the Gross National Product figure is broken down into many lines. It would have to be split up further or differently for purposes of criticism. The elementary value-system we have projected (or some better edition of it) could provide the basis for critique. It could permit discovery of whether the recorded outturn of our vast hubbub of activity, after subtracting "dis-product" from "product," tended toward producing social results more or less in accord with the objectives implied by our values. If Governor Nelson Rockefeller is right in believing that in a decade the Gross National Product of the United States will be a trillion and a half dollars, it should be possible to steer increasing amounts of it toward realization of this or any similar list of values, and the objectives it suggests.

I am aware that no American value-system can be real except as it express a common divisor of the thinking of 200 million Americans. Only totalitarian police state dictatorships, denying their citizens choice of life and action, can lay down complete and all-inclusive value-systems, force their populations and their production into that mold, and audit the results in terms of their success in doing so. Free societies cannot. They must content themselves with common denomination of basic value judgments on which most of their people have substantial consensus — leaving them free to do as they please in other respects. When a free society attempts to impose value judgments going beyond consensus — as they did when the Prohibition Amendment was adopted in 1919 — it fails. Yet because there is a wide measure of consensus on values, America does move along, does generate its enormous Gross National Product (and let us hope solid Net National Product) precisely because there is substantial agreement on what its people really want.

Also there is probably a high factor of agreement on priorities — that is, on what they want most. There are doubtful areas, of course. I will not risk a guess whether priority would be given to military preparedness over education were a Gallup Poll taken — more expenditures for defense and less for aid to education. But I am clear that both in values and in priorities a large enough measure of agreement does exist so that if we put our minds to it a critique of our outturn performance expressed in Gross National Product can be had.

And we ought not to be stopped or baffled or bogged down because philosophers cannot agree on the nature of the "good," or because scientists cannot predict with certainty the social effects of value judgments carried into action. Wrong guesses about values show up in experience, as happened in the Prohibition experiment. In light of experience, they can be corrected. With even rudimentary social indicators, the current cascade of emotional and sterile invective might be converted into rational dialogue. Constructive use of social-economic forces and even of currents of philosophical thinking might become possible.

I realize, of course, that up to now it has been assumed that social indicators, based on an expressed value-system could not be achieved. Well, only a generation ago scholars assumed nothing could be done to alleviate the impact of assumedly blind economic forces, let alone guide them. We know better today; rudimentary capacity to control and steer these forces already exists; the so-called New Economics increasingly guides their use. Similar thinking and similar

tools can provide material on which social policy can be based. Combined with the economic tools currently being forged, social objectives might be brought out of dreamland into range of practical achievement.

Discussion and debate would inevitably result from comparison of actual operations with desired results. More intense and perhaps more fruitful controversy would be engendered in areas where there were items not appearing in our tentative list of values for lack of sufficient consensus. Protagonists would insist they be included; opponents would object. This could be healthy. It would be ballasted by realization that, were consensus achieved, constructive action could be possible. Any caterwaul that American society is "sick" could be qualified by emerging factual knowledge showing that either the accusation was untrue or, if true, that measures for cure could be taken. The debate might disadvantage some people; for one thing, it might reduce the torrent of boring despair-literature presently drowning the reading public. Possibly even contrasting currents of new Puritanism might emerge perhaps providing a not unpleasant contrast, if not relief.

Knowing where American civilization is going is the first essential to saving it (if it is to be saved) or changing it (if it is to be altered).

The Growth of Output

20

In our chapter we explored the very important problem of long-term growth and its origins. We will not examine that problem further here; we will be discussing it as we move along in the text. But there is one analytical problem that it would be wise to master before we take up various aspects of the growth process. This is an understanding of production possibility curves and their meaning.

PRODUCTION POSSIBILITY CURVES

We have already encountered production possibility curves in Chapter 3 and again in Chapter 11 when we spoke of the law of increasing cost and contrasted it with the law of diminishing returns. Now let us solidify our understanding one last time.

Production possibility curves are ways of representing a fundamental constraint of nature (and human nature) – the constraint of scarcity, or the inability to satisfy all our wants simultaneously. Because nature's resources are too slender, or our appetites too large, or our technical abilities too small, we are constantly forced to make *choices,* satisfying one desire at the expense of another. *Production possibility curves show us the characteristics of this act of choice.*

SCARCITY AND CHOICE

In Figure 20–1 we show two production possibility curves. As you see, the one on the right has a straight-line "frontier," the one on the left a bowed frontier. What is the meaning of these two diagrams?

Note to begin with that both express the fact of scarcity. For both societies point *A* represents a *combination* of goods that cannot be produced. Be sure you understand that both societies *could* produce the amount of goods represented by point *A* on the *X* axis (which we will call

consumption goods), or on the *Y* axis (investment goods) – provided that they cut the production of their other good accordingly. With your pencil show how much consumption goods it would be possible to make if each society chose to make *OA'* of investment. Then show how much investment goods each could make if it chose consumption *OA"*.

Be sure you understand that neither society can combine OA' of investment and OA" of consumption. Each lacks the resources or the technical ability, that is the meaning of the frontier of each curve.

RETURNS TO SPECIALIZATION

Now what about the bowed and the straight line frontiers? Each represents the amount of one good that we have to give up to get a unit of the other good. In Figure 20–2 we show the

FIGURE 20–1

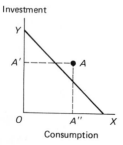

FIGURE 20–2

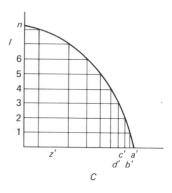

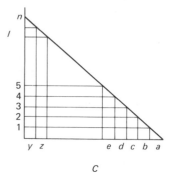

amount of consumption that we have to sacrifice to get 1,2,3 ... n units of investment. Look first at the right-hand diagram. Note that each additional unit of investment costs us exactly the same amount of foregone consumption. (Compare the y and z with a, b, or c.) This means that there are no increasing difficulties in switching into investment the resources devoted to consumption. In technical language, there *are no returns to specialization*. The opportunity cost of the nth unit of investment in terms of foregone units of consumption is exactly the same as the opportunity cost of the first unit of investment.

This is obviously a very unrealistic situation. For many reasons it becomes more and more costly to win additional outputs of one good by shifting resources from other units. There are many reasons for this. Resources may not be homogenous. They are not all equally suited for producing one good: the words land, labor, and capital cover a wide variety of resources, skills, and equipment.

Thus we typically encounter the situation shown in the panel on the left. Notice that as we get our first unit of investment, we only have to reduce consumption by a very small amount (a'). This is because we move into investment the resources and labor that are best suited for that purpose and least well suited for consumption. For a small loss in consumption output we get a large gain in investment output.

But as we continue to add equal amounts of investment output ($2,3 \ldots n$) notice that the successive decreases in consumptions (b', c', $d' \ldots$) get larger and larger. Finally, when we seek to add the last units of investment, we have to sacrifice an enormous amount of consumption (z') to get the same amount for investment that we obtained at the beginning of our process for the tiny sacrifice of a'.

MOVING OUT THE FRONTIER

Production possibility curves make vivid the concept of opportunity cost. They also clarify the idea of growth. Growth consists in moving out the frontier of the p-p curve. We may move out only one "end" of the curve, or we may move out the whole curve. That depends on whether we increase our resources, our skills, or our technologies in ways that affect our generalized ability to produce or only our ability to produce one good (or one kind of goods).

Draw a typical bowed p-p curve. Now show the location of a new p-p curve under the following assumptions:

1. Technological change increases our investment but not our consumption production abilities.
2. An increase in the labor force enables us to produce more of all goods in about the same proportions.
3. Energy shortages bring legislation that preserves our investment capacity but severely limits consumption.

Answers: The answers are easy, and we show them in Figure 20-3.

FIGURE 20-3

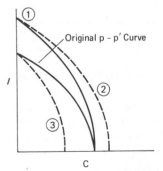

From Growth
to Fluctuations

LEARNING OBJECTIVES

There are two major ideas to be mastered in this chapter. The first is the production function. Remember that:

A production function is a supply curve of GNP, showing how output changes as we change inputs.

The second important idea concerns the business cycle. Our reading tells you something about different types of cycles.

You should bear in mind the typical configuration of a cycle, with its pattern of turning points, contractions, and expansions.

THE PRODUCTION FUNCTION

The principal new analytic issue in this chapter is the aggregate production function, and we shall take a moment to go over this central idea.

We are interested in our macroeconomic studies in examining the forces that give rise to a given level of GNP. We know from our previous chapter that the overall magnitude of *potential* GNP is determined by long-term changes in labor and capital inputs and in the productivities of labor and capital. *Here we want to understand why, in a given short-run period, the economy generates the particular level of GNP that we find.* The very fact of business cycles makes it clear that the level of total output can vary considerably from year to year. It may not exceed the maximum that is available to us from our given supplies and productivities of factors of production, but it can fall far below that level. *The phenomenon of unemployment or unutilized capital means that we are not demanding as*

176

much GNP as we could potentially supply. Our analysis in the coming chapters will help us understand why this is so frequently the case.

In order to understand the reasons for a given level of GNP, we again revert to our powerful concepts of supply and demand. The demand for GNP, as our previous chapters have shown, will stem from the demands of the buyers of GNP — buyers of consumption goods, investment goods, public goods, exports. The motives and patterns of these different demands will be studied one by one in chapters to come.

THE SUPPLY CURVE OF GNP

But these demands must be pitted against supply. *The aggregate production function is a supply curve for GNP* — a representation of the different amounts of total output that could be produced by our existing factor endowments. The aggregate production function is a physical supply curve, corresponding to the supply curve of shoes on a single market. In fact, it is nothing but the summation of a million supply curves in a million markets. We speak here about the *physical* supply because later we will add to this the *cost* of these supplies, to convert physical units into monetary units.

THE AGGREGATE SUPPLY FUNCTION

As Figure 21-1 shows, we could have differently shaped production functions, depending on whether increases in factor inputs would give us proportionately less, equal, or greater increases in output. (Note that we now measure output on the horizontal axis, unlike the case in micro where output is often measured on the vertical axis.)

1. It is important to understand why these production functions have different shapes. Is this because of diminishing returns?
   No, because —————————————————————
   ————————————————————————————————— .

2. Is it because of the law of increasing cost? Again no, because ——————————————————
   ——————— , ——————— .

3. Here we are increasing inputs of *all* factors, by say 1 percent, to make the same array of final outputs, and observing whether these increases in inputs result in a greater, equal, or lesser percentage increase in output. The only phenomenon that could explain such a relationship between increases in all inputs and increases in outputs is ————————————
   ——————————————— .

Answers: 1. We are not adding units of one factor only; 2. We are not shifting from one kind of output to another; 3. Economies or diseconomies of scale.

The phenomenon of economies or diseconomies of scale explains why we can draw a production function that shows increasing returns of output to input when we start at very low levels of employment or utilization, and decreasing returns when we reach "capacity" or full employment and encounter diseconomies of scale. *For ordinary purposes we can think of the*

FIGURE 21-1

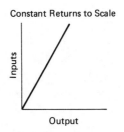

Constant Returns to Scale

Inputs — Output

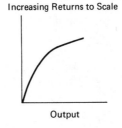

Increasing Returns to Scale

Output

Decreasing Returns to Scale

Output

supply function for the economy as a whole as exhibiting constant returns to scale.

As we know, however, productivity is gradually increasing for all factors. As technology improves, the stock of education per capita increases, and so on. Therefore we should be able to get more output from the same amount of inputs in 1975 than we could have in 1965. We show this by a change in the slope of production function over time, as shown in Figure 21-2. With your pencil indicate the amount of output that would be forthcoming from *OX* amount of all inputs in 1965 and in 1975.

FIGURE 21-2

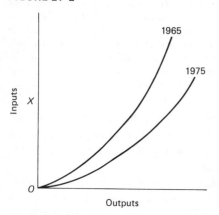

A BRIEF REVIEW

We will come back to the aggregate supply function after we finish studying the demands for GNP. Therefore you should "park" this idea for a few chapters. Fortunately, it is not difficult to understand. Just to be sure, answer these questions:

Put a check under T (True) or F (False). T F

1. The aggregate production function is a term to describe the long run shifts in output.   _ _

2. The degree of employment and the   T F
   utilization of capital account for
   the aggregate production function.   _ _

3. The aggregate production function
   is the summation of physical supply
   curves in all the nation's individual
   activities.   _ _

4. The aggregate production function
   could show constant, increasing, or
   decreasing output as we change the
   level of inputs.   _ _

5. If the production function shows
   increasing outputs as we increase all
   inputs, the reason is that we are
   moving along the portion of the
   production possibility curve that
   gives us increasing returns to specialization.   _ _

6. Diminishing returns has nothing to
   do with the basic idea of a production function.   _ _

7. A straight-line production function
   means that there are no diseconomies or economies of scale as we
   increase all inputs in the short run.   _ _

8. Over time a production function
   will normally show constant returns
   to scale.   _ _

9. For a given short-run period, the
   aggregate production function can
   be considered as a straight line.   _ _

10. The slope of the production func-
    tion shows the percentage increase
    in output associated with a given
    percentage increase in inputs.   _ _

Answers:

1. F	5. F	9. T
2. T	6. T	10. T
3. T	7. T	
4. T	8. F	

BUSINESS CYCLE THEORIES

Howard Sherman

*Here is a brief review of the main types of business cycle
theory. Some of the material covered in this section goes
a bit ahead of the knowledge we have gathered
in our first chapters, but the reading is not
difficult and the thrust of the argument is easy to follow.
Howard Sherman is Associate Professor of Economics at the
University of California, Riverside.*

THE VARIETY OF THEORIES

Until the 1930s the main body of neo-classical economic theory did not try to explain, but instead to explain away, the business cycle. In the first place, it was argued that the amount of unemployment was exaggerated, that there were only partial and frictional fluctuations of production. In the second place, each depression was said to be the last; especially in the twenties they were said to be gone forever — after more than a hundred years of business cycle phenomena.

These attitudes are traceable in the main to the general social outlook of that period, but in part may have resulted from the lack of much theory or interest in the movements of aggregate demand. These economists dealt mainly with demand for particular products based on the subjective utility to individual consumers, which utility must obviously be limited and must begin to decline at the margin after some given quantity is consumed. Thus Robertson[1] asserts: "... it is natural ... that after the brisk demand

[1] D. H. Robertson, *Banking Policy and the Price Level* (New York: Augustus M. Kelley, 1949 edition), p. 10; perhaps it should be mentioned that Robertson is one of the most careful and competent pioneers of business cycle analysis.

From Howard Sherman, *Macrodynamic Economics* (New York: Appleton-Century-Crofts, Inc., 1964).

of the Indian ryot for braziers in 1910, or of the American public for motor cars in 1922–23, the intensity of the desire for these articles should fall away." This approach leads naturally to thinking of the problem as one of absolute overproduction, of "too much" production. When, however, the entire economy is examined rather than each individual product, it becomes clear that the problem in a major depression is not that more is produced than people subjectively desire to consume. On the contrary, there is not nearly enough to fulfill the desires or even minimum health needs; there is only "too much" relative to the objective circumstances of the lack of effective purchasing power.

As long as most economists accepted Say's law, which says that there cannot be a general deficiency of effective demand relative to supply, there were only a few logically possible explanations for the fluctuations of aggregate output. One such explanation is that "external" or noneconomic forces may limit supply or bring sudden demands. For example, sunspots may cause bad weather, and bad weather leads to bad harvests; unions may go on strike; governments may foolishly interfere with production activities; wars may stop the flow of raw materials or bring sudden demands for military production; *et cetera ad infinitum.* Thus, Duesenberry[2] declares: "Major depressions have been produced by a variety of different types of 'shocks,' not by a regular cycle-producing mechanism." Certainly, such shocks as wars and bad weather do affect the economy, but their happenings do not always coincide with the major swings in the economy, some of which occur with no apparent outside shock at that time. Furthermore, we have seen that economies operating with other than private enterprise institutions have reacted quite differently to outside shocks. Therefore, we may at least ask what mechanisms in our economy give rise to cyclical movements as a result of these shocks which occur at random with respect to the business cycle. . . .

One closely related theory concentrates on the reaction of the economy to accidental external shocks. It is observed that enterprises tend to react to changes in the economic situation — for example, rises in demand, by going much farther than necessary in the new direction — for example, excessively increasing supply. Then, to compensate for the excessive movement in one direction, they react excessively in the opposite direction, always swinging beyond the point of "equilibrium" in a sort of "cobweb" pattern woven about that point. This cobweb theory, when applied to the dynamic development of the whole economy, sees it swinging like a pendulum past "equilibrium," always reacting to new random shocks to maintain the length of the swing.[3] This theory has been successfully used to explain the behavior of some individual products. . . .

Another type of explanation emphasizes that accidental dislocations may lead to too much supply in one area while there is not enough in

another area. These writers usually begin with the fact that our industrial economy is very complex and interrelated; and, therefore, that a partial dislocation may spread over the whole economy. For example, a shift in demand from one industry to another may cause unusual profits in one while there are losses in the other. Eventually, adjustment will be made by a shift of capital and labor from the losing to the gaining industry, but in the meantime there may be considerable unemployment. These theories, however, would seem to account only for temporary and partial fluctuations in given industries, not for the general lack of demand in all industries lasting a considerable time.

Another theory which emphasizes one kind of "external" shock is Schumpeter's[4] theory of the impact of technological innovations on the economy. In fact, he explicitly declares that, "The business cycles with which we are concerned . . . are not analogous to the oscillation of an elastic string or membrane . . . which, once set into motion, would but for friction, go on indefinitely . . ." On the contrary, he claims that cycles are not self-generating, but "are due to the intermittent action of the 'force' of innovation . . ."[5] According to this theory, economic expansion begins when an invention is used as an innovation in industry by some one bold entrepreneur, who is then followed by others due to imitation or competition. The boom is brought to an end when the impetus of this innovation expires. It is certainly true that the uneven development of technology combines with entrepreneurial psychology to influence the course of economic events, but we shall have to look further . . . to see whether innovation itself may be determined by economic conditions, though it may then intensify the course of events.

Another type of theory reaffirms Say's law to the extent that aggregate demand cannot

[2] James S. Duesenberry, *Business Cycles and Economic Growth* (New York: McGraw-Hill Book Co., Inc., 1958), p. 11.

[3] See Ragnar Frisch, "Propagation and Impulse Problems," *Essays in Honor of Gustav Cassel* (London: George Allen and Unwin, Ltd., 1933).

[4] Joseph A. Schumpeter, *Business Cycles* (New York: McGraw-Hill Book Co., 1939), p. 175.

[5] *Ibid.*

be deficient for very long. It is argued that it is never rational to hoard money because if it is not used for consumption, it is always most profitable to lend it at interest for further investment. Yet there may be temporary panics with hoarding of money and withholding of credit caused by irrational pessimism. Typical of these "explanations" is the statement that: "The chief cause of the evil is a want of confidence."[6] The defect of these theories lies in the fact that no one has ever demonstrated cycles of optimism and pessimism in businessmen independent of the economic cycle. In fact, the height of optimism is always reached, as in 1929, at the peak of the business cycle. Only *after* economic conditions have objectively worsened are there irrationally large reactions by businessmen, which intensify the economic downturn; or, similarly, may intensify an economic expansion after conditions have objectively improved.

Closely related to the above explanation is the notion that the main fault of the system lies in a banking structure that irrationally brings any industrial expansion to an end. The theory is that the boom is brought about by the expansion of bank credit, but that the bankers cannot or will not continue to expand credit indefinitely at the necessary rate.[7] Certainly, speculative expansion followed by excessive restriction of credit may magnify any disturbance, but banks have generally continued to increase credit rapidly until *after* profit expectations begin to fall. *What must be explained is why these profit expectations change.*

Wesley C. Mitchell was one of the first important and relatively orthodox economists to view business cycle phenomena as other

than accidental or "external" to the economy. (Among the rebels, Karl Marx had long before described the business cycle as an inherent part of capitalist growth, had attacked Say's law, and had foreshadowed elements of every theory that was later to be popular; but he never accomplished the task of synthesizing the diverse elements into a unified cycle theory.) The burden of all Mitchell's works is to show that the business cycle is a self-generating series of "normal" phases of business, each leading into the next under the conditions given by present economic institutions. Although he never reached the comprehensive theory at which he was aiming, his immense empirical research forms the basis for all further scientific investigation of this field.

Until the 1930s however, few economists paid more than lipservice to the facts presented by Mitchell. Those who mentioned these facts at all did so as a special problem beyond the confines of the proper area of economics, which was to describe the process of making minor adjustments by individual firms and individual consumers in a basically stable economy. In the great depression of the thirties that complacency was forever shaken, though it raises its head anew in every expansion period.

The economist whose name is connected with the theoretical "revolution" of the thirties is John Maynard Keynes. Keynes' main contribution was the demolition of Say's law from a sophisticated theoretical viewpoint acceptable to neoclassical economics. He recognized the possibility that the economy as a whole may be in equilibrium at other than full employment — that is, that more or less may be demanded than is supplied at full employment at the present price level. Most of his theory is to be found in some form in earlier, but less orthodox, economists, such as Malthus or Marx. Furthermore, his theory can at best explain a new "equilibrium" position of the economy at less than full employment *after* there has been a once-and-for-all

[6] A. and M. P. Marshall, *The Economics of Industry* (London: Collier-Macmillan, Ltd., 1881), Book III, p. 155.

[7] See, for example, R. G. Hawtrey, "The Trade Cycle," *Readings in Business Cycle Theory* (N.Y.: McGraw-Hill Book Co., Ltd., 1944), pp. 330–50.

change in profit expectations and other variables; he does not explain the origins of disequilibrium and the movements caused by it. Hicks[8] comments that "Keynesian economics, in spite of all that it has done for our understanding of business fluctuations, has beyond doubt left at least one major thing unexplained; and that thing is nothing less than the business cycle itself." Keynes' popularity lay in saying in a striking manner the right thing at the right time — for he not only explained the possibility of depressions and inflations, but also laid down possible solutions for these problems within the bounds of the private enterprise economic system.

Keynes focused attention on the fact that all income derives from either consumers' purchases or purchases for investment purposes. The two principal contenders among modern cycle theories are now usually phrased in terms of the reasons for an upturn and a downturn of these two categories of purchases. On the one side, the theory of "underconsumption"[9] argues that consumption turns downward to cause the end of prosperity because the distribution of income

[8] J. R. Hicks, *The Trade Cycle* (Oxford: Clarendon Press, 1950), p. 1.
[9] See the discussion and works cited in G. Haberler, *Prosperity and Depression,* 4th ed. (Cambridge, Mass.: Harvard University Press, 1960), Chapter 5.

is so concentrated among a few that there is little purchasing power available to most of the population. In this explanation investment declines because the lack of consumer demand causes manufacturers to reduce their own demand for investment goods. This theory is often interpreted, mainly by trade unionists, to mean that higher wages are the cure-all for depressions.

On the other side, the theories of "overinvestment" claim that it is "excessive" investment that precipitates the crisis. They argue that there has been "too much" investment attempted on the basis of the available resources, with a resulting excess demand for labor, machinery, and credit. The problem, they allege, is that not only are the producers' goods industries expanding, but also the consumers' goods demand is rising, so that the latter industrial group is trying to bid factors of production away from the former, with the result that wages, prices of machinery, and interest rates are rising. When costs rise far enough, the rate of profit is lowered and, as a result, investment declines. The recovery begins when costs of production have fallen far enough to again raise the rate of profit. These theories are often interpreted, mainly by managerial personnel, to mean that lower wages are a cure-all for depressions (not to speak of inflations).

TEST ON WEALTH AND OUTPUT (CHAPTERS 19, 20, AND 21)

                                                                            T F

1. Replacement investment adds to the net stock of wealth.   — —

2. Gross investment equals net investment plus replacement.   — —

3. Final goods include the value of intermediate goods.   — —

4. The GNP identity is consumption plus net investment plus government purchases plus net exports.   — —

5. GNP measures the market value of final output during a given period.   — —

6. GNP includes unpaid items such as rent but not other unpaid items such as household work.   — —

7. GNP is a stock, not a flow.   — —

8. A production possibility curve shows us the opportunity costs of goods.   — —

9. A straight line *p-p* curve has constant returns to specialization.   — —

10. A production function relates inputs and outputs.   — —

11. A long-run production function changes its slope because of economies of scale.   — —

12. Changes in real GNP mean changes in the dollar value of final output.   — —

13. A bowed production possibility curve shows variable returns to scale.   — —

14. Participation rates bear the same relation to the labor force as the degree of utilization does to the capital stock.   — —

15. Depreciation is a flow showing the diminution in the value of the stock of capital.

The Demand for Output

22

LEARNING OBJECTIVES

When you have finished this chapter you should know:
1. The *reason* why GNP ≡ GNI.
2. The flow of costs (incomes) into expenditure (demand)

3. The definitions of GNP, NNP, and Y.

Our review aims to give you a step-by-step understanding of the circular flow. Do it very thoughtfully. If you "get it" once, you won't forget it!

This is a very important chapter that you might do well to read more than once. For we are now setting the stage for a discussion of the dynamics of GNP by tracing out the circular flow of payments and receipts in much greater detail than in Chapter Nineteen. Each link in the circular flow should be clearly understood.

THE CIRCULAR FLOW

Why do we use so abstract a conception as the circular flow? The explanation is that there is a common misconception among many who study macroeconomics – that GNP is like a bathtub without a stopper, from which purchasing power is steadily draining. Later we will see that there is indeed a drain in the GNP bathtub called *saving,* but that there is a compensatory faucet called *investment.* The circular flow assumes that the stopper has been put in place and the faucet turned off. There is no net saving or investment. We then want to understand how the purchasing power in the tub can circulate steadily, without affecting the level of GNP as a whole.

185

THE BASIC FLOW

What is the basic flow of purchasing power that we seek to trace? It is the flow from the public to employers (public and private) and from employers back to the public. Let us divide this flow into two parts:

1. *Purchasing power (demand) flows from the public to employers, as the public buys output.*
2. *Employers return this purchasing power to the public in the form of payments to the factors.*

To fix this basic idea in mind, draw arrows connecting the Public, Firms, and Government, in Figure 22-1.

Note that you will have streams going in both directions. One stream will flow from the public to the employers: label it *Demand;* the other from employers to the public: label it *Incomes.*

FIGURE 22-1

Now this presents us with the problem we must solve. Suppose that the public spends $1 trillion on goods and services (public and private), transferring that much purchasing power to employers. How do we know that employers will return the same $1 trillion to the public? And to pursue the question further, suppose that employers *do* return the full $1 trillion to their employees. How do we know that employees will respend the whole $1 trillion, once again returning it to their employers?

The answer is that we do not know that the circular flow will in fact take place so smoothly. It is entirely possible for employers *not* to spend as much as their receipts on the factors of production, or for them to spend more. So too, the public probably will not spend all its incomes; it will save some. So there are many

reasons to picture the real flow of the economy as capable of expansion or contraction, rather than as a smooth, changeless circle of receipt and expenditure. But we have to understand how such a changeless flow is possible if we are to understand thoroughly how the flow can swell or diminish.

COST AND OUTPUT

Let us therefore trace the circular flow in detail. It will be convenient to start inside an imaginary firm that stands for all the employers, private and public, for the nation. Table 22-1 shows a cost summary for our enterprise. *The first exercise is to show that all the costs of the enterprise are paid to one of three sectors: Household, Public, or Business.* Take a moment to prove this to yourself by allocating all costs, adding them up, and seeing that all costs have become incomes or receipts.

There is no trouble allocating Wages, Salaries, Bonuses (they go to *Labor* as wages of management, not to capital), Rent, or Interest (which goes to capital). Social Security and Excise taxes get paid to the public sector (government). But what about Depreciation and Materials? The answer is that both go to the business sector. Let us be sure we understand why.

MATERIALS COSTS

Materials costs represent the items a business has purchased to use in its own production. They are therefore *intermediate goods.* Do you remember the diagram (Figure 19-3) that showed how bread was made from flour and wheat? Let us now in Figure 22-2 work that diagram backward.

Here we see that the cost of bread includes factor costs and taxes (which are paid out to the household sector and to government), plus materials costs for flour. But looking at the flour

TABLE 22–1

Costs		Incomes or Receipts				
		Household Sector				
		Labor	Land	Capital	Public Sector	Business Sector
Wages	$100,000					
Salaries	50,000					
Bonuses	25,000					
Rent	25,000					
Interest	10,000					
Soc. Sec. Taxes	15,000					
Excise Taxes	5,000					
Depreciation	25,000					
Materials	50,000					

FIGURE 22-2

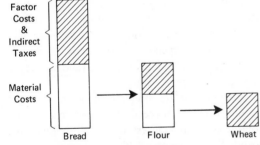

industry we see that it too has paid out factor costs and indirect taxes to households and governments, and that its materials costs (for wheat) were paid to farmers. Looking at the last box we see that the costs of wheat were all paid out to factors or to government.

Therefore all materials costs go to the business sector, but are redistributed within the business sector to households or government. Materials costs become factor costs or receipts of government.

DEPRECIATION

Depreciation also needs a second look. Suppose a firm has machines worth $1 million and that they wear out every ten years. The firm will have to set aside $1 million over ten years to maintain its assets intact. Each year it will "accrue" expenses of $100,000.

But we want to know how this expense becomes income for the business sector. There are two ways. If our firm actually replaces one-tenth of its machines, it will spend $100,000, which will be received by a capital-goods-making firm. But even if our firm does not spend the $100,000, it will have that amount in its cash register because it must have sold its goods at prices that cover depreciation costs. In other words, the cost of depreciation accrues within the firm as part of its receipts, to be spent or not, as it sees fit. *Therefore, the item of depreciation cost is matched by an equivalent receipt by the business sector.*

187

COSTS AND INCOMES

This leads to the first important link in the circular flow. *All costs must become incomes or receipts of one of the three sectors.* Thus there is a basic identity between the cost of total output and the incomes received from total output. The cost of total output is the value of GNP. The incomes received from making that output are GNI (gross national income). Remember this identity:

$$GNP \equiv GNI$$

We can now begin to fill in the bars of the flow chart of a circular flow. In Figure 22-3, match the numbers with the names in the table following it.

FIGURE 22-3

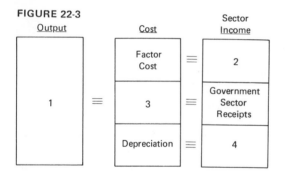

Number	Name
_____	Household sector receipts
_____	GNP
_____	Indirect taxes
_____	Business sector receipts

Can you see from the diagram that GNP is comprised of three different kinds of costs? What are they? (1)_____ ; (2)_____ ____; (3) _____ . Can you see that each cost is *identical* with the receipts of one of three sectors? Show this below:

	Costs	Sectors Receiving this Cost as Income
(1)	_____	_____
(2)	_____	_____
(3)	_____	_____

1. What has happened to materials costs? They have "disappeared" into _____ , _____ , and _____ costs.
2. Why are direct (income) taxes not shown as costs? The answer is that direct taxes are paid by _____ from their incomes.

Answers: 1. *F, T, D;* 2. factors (or businesses).

FROM INCOME TO EXPENDITURE

We have now got halfway around the circular flow. We have shown that all the costs of producing GNP *must* become receipts of households, government agencies, or businesses. Now we have to show that all these receipts can return to the firm.

This requires that the sectors spend their incomes. Here is the critical link in the circular flow and *it is not an identity.* There is no necessary connection between income and expenditure. The sectors could receive their incomes and refuse to spend any of them. If so, the circular flow would break down (and we would have a terrific depression).

But here we are interested in seeing how the circular flow can succeed. And now we see that a condition for its success is that all sectors must spend all their incomes. Figure 22-4 shows how

FIGURE 22-4

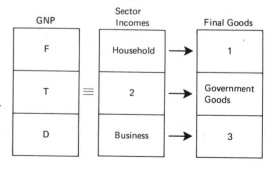

they spend it. Notice that each sector spends its income on a different kind of good, corresponding to the categories of final goods we have already seen in GNP (we are forgetting about exports for the moment).

Fill in these blanks with the proper words from Figure 22–4.

1. _____

2. _____

3. _____

Thus we have seen that *if* each sector spends its income, there will be a demand for consumption, government, and replacement investment goods that is equal to the value of those sectors' incomes. If we now look "inside" the firms making consumption, government, and investment (business) goods (and assume that each kind of good is made by a giant firm) we can see that each giant firm will have received incomes to cover its three items of cost. In the last box, below, we have regrouped all the *F*s, *T*s, and *D*s, and we are back to our original starting point!

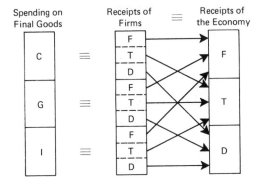

Now let's go back over the circular flow. This is a self-answering quiz:

1. The circular flow shows that purchasing power flows from the public to _____, and back from employers to the _____.

2. The flow from the public to employers is called _____ .

3. The demand (or purchasing power) from the public becomes the _____ of the employer.

4. Therefore the relation between demand or purchasing power and receipts must be an _____ .

5. Another identity describes the relation between the costs of the employer and the _____ of the sectors.

6. These incomes consist of _____ costs that become household income; _____ costs that become receipts of the _____ sector; and _____ costs that are accrued by the business sector.

7. We can sum this up by saying that the costs of GNP are *F* + *T* + *D*. We must remember that *T* only stands for _____ taxes. Direct taxes are not a cost of production, but are paid by _____ and _____ .

8. When factors and business firms pay direct taxes they have already received their _____ .

9. The incomes received by factors, governments, and firms are therefore identical with the costs of output. What is critical in maintaining a circular flow is the act of _____ .

10. Unless expenditure takes place, the circular flow will not continue unbroken. But if each sector does spend its income, the household sector will buy _____ goods; the government sector will buy _____ goods, and the business sector will buy _____ goods.

11. In this case, the expenditures of the three sectors will give rise to a demand for the final types of outputs. Each output will have three kinds of costs, namely _____ , _____ and _____ .

12. Gross national product consists of *C* + *G* + *I* (we continue to leave out exports, *X*, for the moment). But we have just seen that the costs of *C* + *G* + *I* are identical with factor costs, indirect tax costs, and depreciation cost. Therefore we can write an important identity, describing on the left the categories of final output and on the right the costs of that final output:

$$\text{GNP} \equiv C + \underline{} + \underline{} + \underline{} \equiv F + \underline{} + \underline{}.$$

13. We have also seen that all costs become income. Therefore, our identity can also be written to show that all costs become incomes of the sectors (here we use C for the household sector, G for the public sector, D for the business sector). This identity is:

$$GNI \equiv F + \underline{\quad} + \underline{\quad} \equiv C + \underline{\quad} + \underline{\quad} + \underline{\quad} \equiv GNP$$

Did you work your way through? If you had any trouble, think about questions 12 and 13. Question 12 tells us that GNP (the market value of output) is made up of three (really four) kinds of final outputs, and that these final outputs are made up of three kinds of costs, which constitute gross national income. The next question simply turns this around. GNI is made up of three kinds of cost-payments, which arise in the main sectors of the economy in the act of producing GNP.

GNP, NNP, NI

One last easy bit of review. It is to relate Gross National Product with two other definitional concepts, Net National Product and National Income.

Can you label 1 _____ , 2 _____ , and 3 _____?

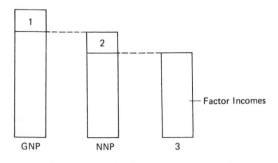

Remember that the reason GNP is "gross" is that it includes replacement investment, not just net investment. In the national income accounts the value of replacement investment is measured by depreciation. Therefore it is depreciation that is

missing from NNP. What is missing from National Income? National income, as the words imply, defines the actual incomes earned by the factors of production. It excludes costs that are added on afterward, namely indirect taxes (and also depreciation).

REVIEW QUIZ

This has been a long chapter with many new terms to learn. Help solidify your understanding by trying this quiz. It should be easy.

1. The three items of cost in GNP are _____ , _____ , and _____ .
2. Factor costs are payments that go to the _____ sector.
3. The sum of all factor costs is a measure of output called _____ .
4. Direct (income) taxes (are/are not) part of the cost of GNP.
5. Indirect taxes and direct taxes are received by the _____ sector.
6. Indirect taxes are part of the cost of GNP. (True/False)
7. Depreciation (is/is not) a cost of production.
8. Factor payments plus indirect taxes are a measure of output called _____ .
9. Depreciation is a cost that is accrued within or paid to the _____ sector.
10. Factor costs, indirect taxes, and depreciation can be larger or smaller than GNP. (True/False) _____
11. Depreciation accruals are typically spent for _____ .
12. All costs are payments to factors. (True/False) _____
13. The household sector receives incomes that correspond to _____ costs.
14. The government sector receives payments that correspond to _____ costs.
15. Depreciation is a cost that becomes a receipt for the _____ .
16. The household sector typically spends its income on _____ .
17. Government spends its income on _____ .
18. Business spends its income on _____ .

19. The sum of spending of the household sector, the business and net export sectors, and the government sector is _____ .
20. We can write the sentence above as GNP ≡ _____.
21. We can also write an identity that shows GNP as a sum of costs: GNP ≡ _____.
22. It follows that a given GNP can be looked at as a sum of costs or a sum of expenditures: GNP ≡ _____ ≡ _____ .

Answers: 1. factor costs, indirect taxes, depreciation (F, T, D); 2. household; 3. national income; 4. are not; 5. government; 6. True; 7. is; 8. net national product, NNP; 9. business; 10. False; 11. replacement investment; 12. False; 13. factor; 14. tax; 15. business; 16. consumption; 17. government goods and services; 18. investment goods; 19. gross national product (GNP); 20. $C + G + I + X$; 21. $F + T + D$; 22. GNP ≡ $C + G + I + X$ ≡ $F + T + D$.

Here is another quiz that you can do in a minute. Put a check under T (True) or F (False).   T F

1. All factor costs enter GNP.   __ __
2. GNP is the sum of all factor costs.   __ __
3. Direct taxes enter GNP as part of its costs.   __ __
4. NNP includes indirect taxes.   __ __
5. National income is figured after direct taxes.   __ __
6. National income includes depreciation.   __ __

7. Replacement investment enters NNP.   T F
   __ __
8. Intermediate costs can be broken down to $F + T + D$.   __ __
9. Costs and expenditures are an identity.   __ __
10. Costs and incomes are an identity.   __ __
11. Incomes and expenditures are an identity.   __ __
12. Expenditures and receipts are an identity.   __ __
13. GNP can be measured in costs or expenditures.   __ __
14. For any given GNP enough incomes are paid out to buy back all output. __ __
15. The crucial link in the circular flow is that between costs and incomes. __ __
16. The crucial link is between incomes and expenditures.   __ __
17. Factor incomes can buy back GNP.   __ __
18. Depreciation is a factor cost.   __ __
19. The circular flow depends on sectors spending all their receipts.   __ __
20. GNP = NNP + NI.   __ __

Answers:

1. T	8. T	15. F
2. F	9. F	16. T
3. F	10. T	17. F
4. T	11. F	18. F
5. F	12. T	19. T
6. F	13. T	20. F
7. F	14. T	

23

Saving and Investment

If you master the central idea of this chapter you will have gone a long way to grasping the most important single idea of macroeconomics. *This is the necessity for the sectors to "co-operate" if we are to avoid a demand gap* (or, as we shall see later, inflation). The principal purpose of this chapter is to explain how demand gaps originate and how they can be offset.

SAVING

Demand gaps come about because the sectors do not spend all their incomes. This brings us immediately to a vitally important macroeco-

nomic term: saving. The meaning of saving is that we do not spend all our income. We can speak of this unspent portion in two ways:

1. It is the *money* we received and did not in turn expend.

2. It is the *resources* we could have used or claimed, but left unused or unclaimed because we did not spend our incomes.

We also speak of gross or net saving. These terms are the exact counterpart to gross or net investment. Gross saving is income we fail to spend (or resources we fail to use) to *maintain* our capital. Net saving is income we refrain from spending on consumption (or their equivalent resources) for the purpose of *adding* to capital.

THE DEMAND GAP

When any sector fails to spend all its income, it fails to complete one link in the circular flow. Our flow chart is simply a way of depicting this circular flow in a way that dramatizes the presence or absence of such a gap. Therefore, it is very useful to learn to draw it correctly. Can you point out the deficiencies in Figure 23-1?

Is the gap in Figure 23-2 in the right place? Is it offset? Note that careless drawing or lack of

understanding has shortened the receipts bar associated with factor costs. Receipts being short of costs is, of course, an impossibility.

Here is another case: what is wrong?

Note that in Figure 23-2 bad drawing has lengthened the receipts bar over costs. Does that make sense in terms of GNP circular flow?

Now look at Figure 23-3.

Is there really a gap in Figure 23-3. What has been left out? _____

What is wrong in Figure 23-4? _____

To emphasize intersectoral relationships, suppose that in one year households decided to save zero, but that the government did not spend all its tax receipts, and therefore performed an act of saving. Where would the demand gap appear in Figure 23-5? Draw in the expenditures blocks to show how it could be offset by business investment, financed out of past business savings.

Answers: In Figure 23-1, there are two errors. The amount of saving received by the business sector is larger than the saving performed by the household sector. In addition, the expenditure of the government is not shown.

In Figure 23-4, the saving made by the household sector is not added to the receipts of the business sector, and no addition to business expenditures (net investment) is depicted to offset the gap.

FIGURE 23-1

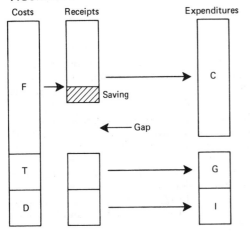

FIGURE 23-2

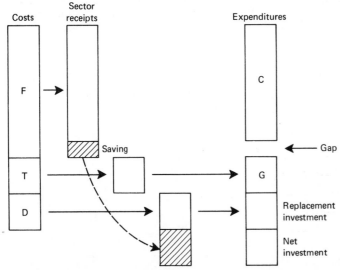

FIGURE 23-3

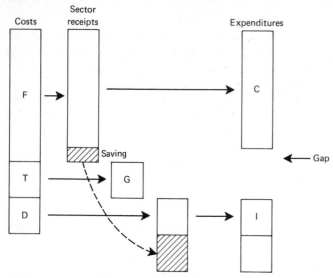

The complete diagram for Figure 23-5 is shown in Figure 23-6.

Remember that the offset process requires an appropriate financial transaction. In the text we list six ways of "transferring" funds to sectors that will perform an offsetting function. Here let us look at four *methods:*

1. *Borrowing.* A sector that will offset the demand gap arising in another sector can borrow the necessary funds. The business sector borrows by issuing bonds. So does the government sector. Could the household sector conceivably offset the saving of, say the

FIGURE 23-4

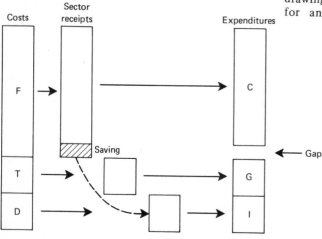

business sector, by borrowing and spending more than its normal income? It could, in theory. Actually the household sector is normally a steady saver.

2. *Issuing equities.* A sector can spend more than its income by attracting savings into partnerships or proprietorships or (usually) into corporate ventures. Note that only the issuance of *new stock* transfers savings into business' hands. When someone buys a stock that has already been issued, he merely transfers savings or capital to another individual.

3. *Dissaving.* All sectors can increase their expenditures, and offset gaps, by dissaving — drawing on past savings. This is rarely done for any sector as a whole, although an

individual corporation often draws on its cash reserves to finance a new investment.

4. *Taxing.* This is a privilege accorded only to governments. We will speak about taxing at some length later when we consider the problems of fiscal policy. But we should note that the taxation of household or business income transfers money to the government, where it can be spent to offset a gap arising elsewhere.

FIGURE 23-5

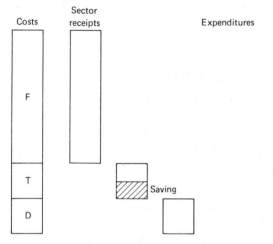

FIGURE 23-6

TRANSFERS AND PROFITS

It is important to be able to graph transfers and the disposition of profits, because this is a good way of making certain that you really understand how these elements enter the circular flow. So let's complete Figure 23-7.

1. First note that we have added profits as an additional item on the initial bar. We must be clear how profits can return to the expenditure stream. There are three ways:

    1. _____
    2. _____
    3. _____

    Show these in the diagram. *Dividends* will constitute an addition to household income. *Taxes* on profits will transfer some of them to the government sector. *Expenditures for new investment from retained earnings* will add to business investment spending. If you're not sure that your flow chart is correct, look at Figure 23-7, page 360 in the text.

2. Next, transfers between the sectors. Here we see visually how income taxes and ordinary transfer payments rearrange the incomes of the sectors but *do not add to aggregate spending power.* Show on your diagram how income taxes shift income from households to government; and how transfer payments, such

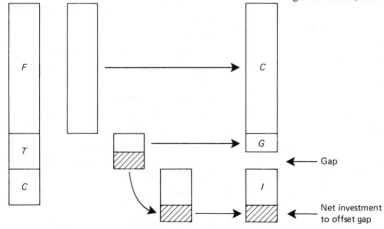

FIGURE 23-7

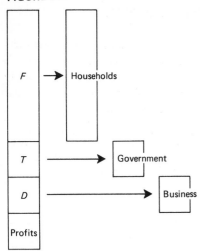

7. Profits must all be returned to households if the circular flow is to be maintained. — —

8. Profits can be spent by households, government, or business. — —

9. A transfer from government to household increases gross national product. — —

10. In order for one sector to offset another, it must borrow, tax, dissave, or issue equities. — —

Answers:

1. T	5. T	8. T
2. T	6. T	9. F
3. F	7. F	10. T
4. F		

as Social Security, transfer it from government to households. The diagram gets complicated: you might check with the text on page 357 to be sure you have it right.

3. Last, *subsidies* from government to business (we have already noted that taxes on business shift spending power from the private to the public sector). Here it is simple to show how subsidies move a portion of the government's spendable income into the hands of business. Show that on your chart, too, once again checking with Figure 23-5 on page 358 in the text.

Here are a few questions to test your grasp of the material. Put a check under T (True) or F (False).   T F

1. Saving is necessary for investment. — —

2. We can have gross saving even without net investment. — —

3. The act of investment frees resources from consumption. — —

4. A demand gap arises when sector receipts are less than the costs of production. — —

5. Demand gaps can arise from business saving as well as household saving. — —

6. The only way a demand gap in one sector can be offset is by the additional expenditure of another sector. — —

TEST YOURSELF

_ 1. If the stock of capital is growing,
   a. dissaving has occurred.
   b. depreciation has increased.
   c. there has been net saving.

_ 2. In a stationary circular flow economy, we know that
   a. all incomes are invested.
   b. all incomes are spent.
   c. net investment is offsetting saving.

_ 3. A demand gap can only arise
   a. when there is gross saving.
   b. when there is net saving.
   c. when saving is not offset by additional expenditure.

_ 4. Subsidies represent
   a. net increases in final expenditure.
   b. transfers from government to private sector.
   c. an offset to saving.

_ 5. Profits will cause a demand gap unless
   a. they are matched by business saving.
   b. they are retained by business.
   c. they are expended by households, government, and business.

_ 6. Income taxes
   a. reduce GNP.
   b. rearrange the receipts of the sectors.
   c. interrupt the circular flow.

196

— 7. One sector can offset the savings of another only if it
    a. increases its own saving.
    b. disinvests.
    c. spends more than its income.

— 8. By gross saving we mean
    a. the saving of the household sector.
    b. the saving of the business sector.
    c. the saving needed to make replacement investment.

— 9. A demand gap could be created by
    a. personal saving.
    b. business saving.
    c. government saving.
    d. all of the above.

—10. The need for offsets to saving arise because
    a. saving results in diminished expenditure.
    b. saving results in investment.
    c. saving reduces the income of the sector that performs saving.

Answers:

1. c	5. c	8. c
2. b	6. b	9. d
3. c	7. c	10. a
4. b		

Consumption Demand

24

LEARNING OBJECTIVES

Two big problems are presented in this chapter. The first is definitional:
1. You should understand precisely how we define GNP, NNP, Y (national income), disposable income, and consumption.

2. The second is analytical:
   You must master the idea of the average and the marginal propensity to consume. When you are done, be sure you know what $C = a + b\ (Y)$ means in terms of behavior.

At the heart of this chapter lies a functional relationship that we will use again and again — the relationship between the incomes received by households and the amounts they spend for consumption. We call this relationship the *propensity to consume,* or sometimes *the consumption function.* In this review chapter, we want to make certain that we understand clearly what these terms mean.

DEFINITIONS

Let us begin by defining much more precisely the income that goes to the household sector. A good way to do this is to work down from the largest income aggregate GNI, stripping away flows that do not go to households and adding transfers that swell the household total.

We know that GNI is the sum of three flows of cost: ___, ___, and ___, that they become the incomes of three sectors: _____ , _____ , and _____ . (We also know that these incomes are identical with the value of output, which consists of four kinds of goods or services ___, ___, ___, and ___.)

To go from GNP to NNP requires us to remove the expenditures that the economy makes for replacement investment. But we can also go from GNI to NNI (net national income) by removing the income from which these replacement expenditures were made. This removes depreciation and leaves us with $F + T$. Now we can easily go from NNI to *NI* (or Y as it is usually written), by taking away the flow of income going to the public sector from indirect taxes. *We are then left with incomes paid only directly to factors.*

In Table 24-1 we see the equivalence of these terms:

TABLE 24-1

Income	*Value of Output*
$GNI \equiv F + T + D \equiv$	$GNP \equiv C + I + G + X$
$NNI \equiv F + T \quad \equiv$	NNP
NI (or Y) $\equiv F \quad \equiv$	NI (or Y)*

Notice that we can't write the value of NNP or Y in terms of $C + G + I + X$. Why? Because there is some F, some T, and some D *within* each term of $C, G, I,$ and X!

Now we have national income as the sum of factor costs. But this is not the total from which households make their savings decisions. This is because the government diminishes these incomes by imposing _____ taxes, and augments them by making _____ payments. After these additions and subtractions, we arrive at _____ , which is the nomenclature for the total that households divide between _____ _____and_____ .

Figure 24-1 will give you all the answers to the questions we have asked.

THE CONSUMPTION FUNCTION

Next, we want to relate the flow that we call saving to disposable personal income (called income, for short). Here there are a few very simple rules to remember:

1. *Income can only be divided between consumption and saving.* This is because we define saving as any income that is not spent.

FIGURE 24-1

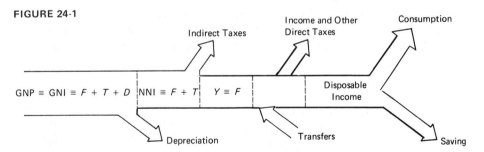

*Economists often write $Y = C + I$, but here I stands for *net* investment, not gross investment as in the GNP definition.

Therefore Y (the symbol for income) $\equiv C + S$. *It follows that $C \equiv Y - S$, and that $S \equiv Y - C$.*

2. *At any level of income, we allocate a certain amount to C and the rest to S.* The ratio of C to Y is called the average propensity to consume (a.p.c.). The ratio of S to Y is called the average propensity to save (a.p.s.). Notice that the two fractions $C/Y + S/Y$ must add up to 1. This is because we define S/Y as the difference between total income and the fraction we spend. The two circle charts in Figure 24-2 should make this relationship clear.

3. *We are also interested in the way in which we divide increases in income between C and S.* We usually save a larger fraction of *increases* in income than of our normal income. The relation between an increase in income and increased consumption is called the marginal propensity to consume, and the relation between increased Y and increased S the marginal propensity to save. We can see this diagramatically in Figure 24-3.

With this information it should be easy to work out the table on page 201.

Now check your answers. In each case, you derived the average propensity to consume by dividing _____ by _____ . For example, the average propensity to consume when income is 100 is 80 ÷ 100 or .8. The average propensity to save is total income divided by_____ . The a.p.c. + a.p.s. must equal unity. If the a.p.c. is .8, then a.p.s. must be___. Check that all your a.p.c.'s add to unity with their a.p.s.'s.

FIGURE 24-2

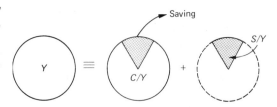

The marginal columns are equally straightforward. To find the marginal propensity to consume (m.p.c.) when we move from an income of 80 to an income of 100, we divide the *increase* in consumption by the *increase* in income. At an income of 80, consumption was 70. At an income of 100, it has increased by___. Income has increased by___. Therefore the m.p.c. is 10 ÷ 20 or .5. The marginal propensity to save (m.p.s.) is the difference between unity and m.p.c., or the complement of m.p.c. If m.p.c. is .77, m.p.s. must be_____ ; and if m.p.s. is .23, m.p.c. must be _____ . Check to make sure that all your m.p.c.'s and m.p.s.'s add to 1.00.

Notice that the average propensity to consume changes, even though the marginal propensity does not. This is because the fraction of saving out of marginal income is larger than the fraction of saving out of total income. The only case in which the m.p.c. and a.p.c. would be the same would be one in which we saved no more out of an increase in income than we did out of all income.

FIGURE 24-3

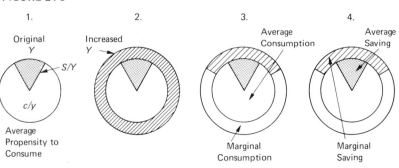

TABLE 24-2

Income	Consumption	Saving	Average Propensity to Consume (C/Y)	Average Propensity to Save (S/Y)	Marginal Propensity to Consume (Change in C ÷ change in Y)	Marginal Propensity to Save (Change in S ÷ Change in Y)
40	50	-10	1.25*	-.25	not calculable	not calculable
60	60	—	1.00	—	10÷20=.5	10÷20=.5
80	70	—	—	—	—	—
100	80	—	—	—	—	—
120	90	—	—	—	—	—

*An a.p.c. of 1.25 means that a household is spending more than it earns by borrowing or spending past savings.

THE CONSUMPTION FUNCTION

Our excercises with the average and marginal propensities to consume have only acquainted us with the meaning of these terms. Now let us be sure we understand the central analytical lesson of this chapter. This is the functional relation of consumption to income.

The most inportant fact about that relation is that income is an independent variable and consumption a dependent variable: *the amount of consumption depends on income.* We write that relationship as follows:

$$C = f(Y).$$

This is a formula you must remember.

However, the letter *"f"* only tells us that there is some kind of regular relationship between our two variables C and Y. What kind? Here empirical tests have described the general nature of the relation in a way that we can write very simply. Let us show it on a chart (Figure 24-4).

THE BOTTOM

In Figure 24-4 we show a possible relation of C and Y — the consumption function. First look at point O, where income is zero. Note that

FIGURE 24-4

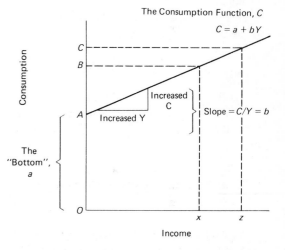

consumption is *not* zero, but is shown by the distance OA. How can consumption be positive if there is no income? The answer is that the society must be dissaving — that is, consuming its past savings. This is a picture of what really happens when a country is devastated by floods or earthquakes. Production stops, and no income is generated for a while. Yet people continue to consume (although often at very low levels) by eating stores of food and using up inventories of goods produced in the past. We call this irreducible minimum of consumption "the bottom." It is a fixed value a of the consumption function (see figure).

THE SLOPE

If consumption remained at level *a,* even though income rose, we would have a horizontal line on our graph. But, of course, consumption rises as our incomes grow. Therefore the consumption function line slopes upward.

What about the slope? As the graph shows, the slope is determined by the ratio between our increased *Y* and our increased *C.* The slope is therefore the diagrammatic depiction of the marginal propensity to consume. As we can see, the slope is constant in our graph.[1] We can describe it as a constant fraction *b.* The slope of the line is therefore *b.*

This enables us to write the equation for a simple consumption function:

$$C = a + bY, \text{ where}$$

a is the "bottom," the irreducible minimum of *C,* and *b* is the marginal propensity to consume, the fraction of additional *Y* that we use for additional *C.*[2]

AVERAGE AND MARGINAL PROPENSITY TO CONSUME

We have described the marginal propensity to consume on our graph; now for the average propensity to consume. Remember this is not the change in *C* divided by the change in *Y,* but *all C* divided by *all Y.* It should now be obvious why the a.p.c. changes even though the m.p.c. is fixed. If we start at point *O,* where income is zero, consumption (*OA*) is larger than *Y.* If we move out along the *Y* axis, we will be adding consumption, as the graph shows. Eventually we reach an income *OX,* where the amount of consumption *OB* is equal to *OX.* Here *C/Y* is unity.

[1] Of course the m.p.c. slope doesn't have to be fixed. It's just simpler that way.
[2] Reminder: There is more on this on p. 374 in the text.

If we move further out to *OZ,* the amount of consumption, *OC,* will be less than *OZ,* so that *C/Y* will be less than 1. The difference between income *OZ* and consumption *OZ* will then be *saving.*

Thus the a.p.c. represents the ratio between total C and total Y at any point along the consumption function. This ratio will change as we move along, although the consumption function does not change.

DYNAMICS OF CONSUMPTION

After these technical matters, there are two broad ideas to bear in mind:

1. *Consumption is largely a passive, rather than an active, economic flow.* There can be short-lived "buying sprees" and periods of exceptionally large saving, but by and large, consumption follows income. As we will see, this has important repercussions for economic policy.

2. *The long-run consumption function shifts upward.* As we have seen, a consumption function of the type *C = a + bY* would lead to a larger and larger *fraction* of income being saved as household incomes increased. This would confront the economy with the need to face demand gaps that were ever larger proportions of income.

    Fortunately this problem is bypassed because the whole consumption function shifts upward over time. One explanation of this is that our saving depends on how *relatively* (not absolutely) rich we are. A $20,000 family will save more today than a $10,000 family. But by the time a $10,000 family has moved into the $20,000 bracket, the $20,000 family will be in the $30,000 or $40,000 bracket. As all families move up the escalator, their *relative* positions remain unaltered. When a $10,000 family doubles its income, it is no longer "rich" by comparison with other families, but only "average." Its savings propensities therefore reflect its "average" position, rather than those of a "rich" family. As we all increase our incomes, we all increase the proportion of consumption spending we make out of any given income.

Quiz

Here is a quiz on the matters we have covered, plus one or two empirical points from the text. See if you get at least eighteen out of twenty questions right. Place a check under T (True) or F (False).

T F

1. Consumption spending can buy back all of GNP if there is no saving. — —
2. $C = a(Y) + b(Y)$. — —
3. $C/Y + S/Y = Y$. — —
4. If the m.p.s. is a constant, so is C/Y. — —
5. Saving is a relatively stable fraction of household income. — —
6. Services are a component of consumption spending. — —
7. The average propensity to save refers to the change in saving divided by the change in income. — —
8. The marginal propensity to save plus the marginal propensity to consume always equals one. — —
9. We call "the bottom" the amount of consumption when $C = Y$. — —
10. $Y = f(C)$. — —
11. Consumption is an independent variable. — —
12. Urging consumers to buy is a useful means of closing a demand gap. — —
13. If Y increases by 20 and C increases by 15, the marginal propensity to *save* is .25. — —
14. Saving plus consumption is an identity with income. — —
15. It is impossible to increase the marginal propensity to consume without also increasing the marginal propensity to save. — —
16. Disposable income is the income consumers have before taxes and transfers. — —
17. The consumption function is another term for the propensity to consume. — —
18. If the average propensity to consume is a constant, so that C/Y never changes, it follows that the marginal propensity to consume must fall as income rises. — —
19. The slope of a consumption function shows the marginal propensity to consume. — —
20. The m.p.s. is the complement of the m.p.c. — —

Answers:

1. F	8. T	15. F
2. F	9. F	16. F
3. T	10. F	17. T
4. F	11. F	18. F
5. T	12. F	19. T
6. T	13. T	20. T
7. F	14. T	

Investment Demand

25 (chapter number graphic)

LEARNING OBJECTIVES

Once again two main ideas are central to this chapter, one definitional, one analytic:
1. The definitional idea: what is real investment, contrasted with our everyday notions of financial investment?
2. The analytic idea: what is the multiplier? How does it work? Why does the size of

the multiplier depend on the leakage fraction?

When you are done, can you write the multiplier formula? You should be sure to know it and understand it.

As in previous chapters, we are not going to review empirical material with you here. This is not to say that it isn't important to know that investment spending consists of four major categories (equipment, business construction, residential housing, and inventories), or that you shouldn't know approximately how large a flow investment is in GNP. But there is little we can add to your understanding by repeating facts

that we presume you have already underlined. Instead, as before, we want to use this review to bring home the important analytical principles in this chapter.

REAL INVESTMENT AND SAVING

The first of these is the crucial difference between *financial investment* – the act we perform when we buy a stock or a bond – and *real investment.* By real investment, as you should know by now, we mean using the factors of production to add to the nation's stock of capital – its plant and equipment, its housing, its inventories.

This act of real storing-up of new capital may or may not be accompanied by an act of financial investment in the everyday sense of buying a bond or a stock: most of the time it is not. But it is always accompanied by an act of *real saving* – that is, by a decision on the part of someone not to use the factors of production to produce consumption goods instead of investment goods. *Real saving is thus the other side of the coin of real investment: it is an identity.*

REAL VS. FINANCIAL INVESTMENT

Not so with financial investment. Most of us think that when we buy a share of AT & T our money goes directly to the company. It does not. It goes to the person who sold us *his* share of AT & T. Perhaps that person was a private investor, perhaps a broker or securities dealer. In either event, our money goes to him, not to the company. It is a swap of assets: we move from money into securities; the seller moves from securities into money.

Then does buying and selling stocks have nothing to do with real investment? There are two answers to this question. (1) *At one time or another, all the securities that are now being traded back and forth were directly issued by companies.* Every share of AT & T (and every other stock or bond) was once sold to the public by the enterprise itself; and at that time the public's money *did* go to the enterprise, usually to finance real investment. Each year many companies still issue *new securities* whose purpose is explicitly to attract savings into the enterprise to finance further growth.

(2) Company managements also watch the prices of their stocks as a kind of index of confidence in their companies. It is easier to issue new securities, or to borrow from banks, or

to persuade a board of directors to undertake an expansion program to be financed out of profits (without a single new share being issued) if the company's shares are "doing well."

THE IMPORTANCE OF INVESTMENT

Why is investment treated with such special attention, when we consider that the flow of gross private domestic investment is smaller than the flow of household or government spending? The reason lies in the high volatility of investment. To a much greater degree than consumption, perhaps even to a greater degree than government, (although that is no longer so certain) investment spending is capable of wide up and down swings.

This is because investment spending is always undertaken in *expectation of profits.* There is nothing about the character of business decisions to invest that has the ironclad necessity of consumption spending. We have seen that households would have to spend money on consumption even if income fell to zero for a short period. There is no such analog for investment. If income fell to zero in a devastated country, businessmen might very well decide to invest nothing for a while, until they had some idea of what the future would bring. Thus it is the *future-orientation* of investment – its linkage with expected profits – that makes it one of the most unpredictable (and therefore independent) variables in the demand equation for GNP.

THE MULTIPLIER

The risk of rapid shifts in investment, whether in inventory or capital equipment, is made much more important because of the *multiplier* mechanism. It is very simple to grasp the idea of the multiplier. It is perhaps more difficult to understand exactly how we determine the size of the multiplying effect. The diagrams in Figure 25-1 explain the problem in a slightly different way

FIGURE 25-1

How the Multiplier Works

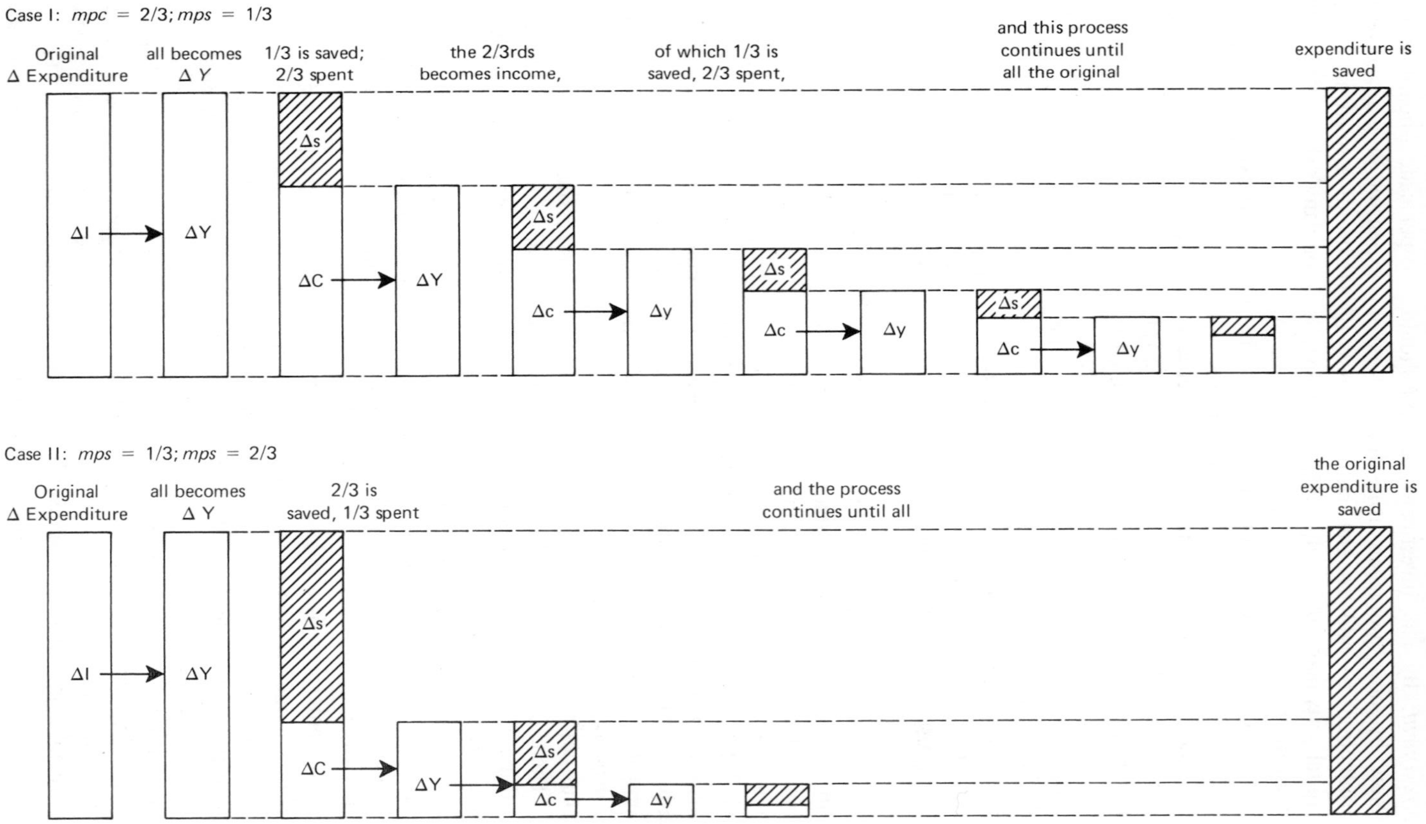

Case I: $mpc = 2/3$; $mps = 1/3$

Case II: $mps = 1/3$; $mps = 2/3$

from that in the text, and should help you master the concept once and for all.

The multiplier results from our "responding" of income. The proportion of income that we spend is indicated by our marginal propensity to consume. That fraction is shown in the white portion of the two different examples shown below. Obviously, the multiplier will be much greater when we spend three-quarters of our income than when we only spend one-third. We will shortly review how large the multiplier will be in each case.

But now let us fasten our attention on the shaded areas that show how much we save. Here the result may be surprising. *Whether our multiplier is large or small, in the end we will end up saving the same amount.* At each "round" we put away some fraction of our added income as savings, and it stands to reason that after enough rounds we will have put it all away. *The effect of the m.p.s. is therefore to determine how many rounds it will take before all income has been saved.* The larger the m.p.s. – the more we save each time – the fewer rounds it will take to absorb all new income into saving as we see in the bottom part of Figure 25-1. The smaller the m.p.s., the more rounds it will take as we see in the upper diagram. This helps us understand why a small m.p.s. gives us a large multiplier; a large m.p.s., a small multiplier.

THE SIZE OF THE MULTIPLIER

Now for the size of the responding fractions. Here it is obvious that the sum of the white ΔY squares in the two cases is not the same. Our task is to understand how we calculate the total in each case. How do we know that the total of the white squares on the upper half of the diagram will be four times the original additional expenditure, whereas the multiplier in the bottom part of the diagram will be only one and one-half times the original increase?

There are two answers to this question. One involves a knowledge of the mathematics of converging series, which we explain in the text. This will explain matters to those who are not daunted by a few exponents (the math is really very easy). For those who prefer to take the matter on faith, the answer is given by our *multiplier formula* which gives us the relation between ΔI, a change in investment, and ΔY, the change in income after all the rounds of respending have taken place.

The formula is:

$$\Delta Y = \frac{1}{\text{mps}} \; \Delta I$$

A few things should be clearly understood about this formula.

1. It holds good for the multiplier effect of *any* increase in spending: ΔG, ΔX, or even ΔC.
2. It is a formula that *disregards time.* In actual fact the initial recipients of a new investment are apt to be the factors of production, whose marginal propensities to consume will probably be quite high. But the next round of recipients – the butchers, bakers, and candlestick makers, who have had their incomes increased by the spending of the first recipients – are likely to be enterprises. Their additional receipts will go into the till, and their marginal propensity to consume is apt to be small. That is why the overall national m.p.c is roughly .5 and not .9+, as it would be if it were the result of household spending decisions only.
3. *Remember that the critical multiplier effect resides entirely in the fraction 1/mps.* The "*mps*" includes all leakages – additions to savings, profits, taxes and imports. All these leakages can return to the circular flow, but none of them returns automatically through the regular rhythm of consumption spending.
4. In calculating the multiplier, never forget that the m.p.s. is a *compound fraction.* It is "one *over mps*," and *mps* is itself a fraction. The most common error is to multiply the increase in expenditure by the *mps,* rather than by its reciprocal (which we get by dividing 1 by the m.p.s.). Go through the

example below and be sure you understand each step:

Given $\Delta I = 10$; mps = 1/3, what will be ΔY?

Steps: $\Delta Y = \Delta I \times 1/\text{mps}$

$$= 10 \times \frac{1}{1/3}$$

$$= 10 \times 3$$

$$= 30$$

Now find the multiplier and solve these for ΔY:

	ΔI	mps	multiplier	ΔY
1.	5	.13	—	—
2.	15	$\frac{1}{4}$	—	—
3.	-10	$\frac{1}{3}$	—	—
4.	-6	$\frac{1}{4}$	—	—

Suppose that we know the following leakages. What is the size of *mps* and the multiplier?

Taxes	20%
Imports	5
Retained Profits	10
Savings	5

Solution: total leakages = 40%; m.p.s. = .40;

multiplier $\frac{1}{.40}$ or 2.5

5. Now figure these:

Taxes	15%
Imports	10
Retained Profits	5
Savings	3

Total leakages = ——

mps   = ——

multiplier   = ——

6.

Taxes	15%
Imports	-1
Retained Profits	24
Savings	20

Total leakages = ——

m.p.s.   = ——

multiplier   = ——

7. Here is a different problem. Investment shows the following changes:

Residental construction	+10 billion dollars
Nonresidential construction	+5
Equipment	+3
Net inventories	-5

Total changes in investment = ——

8. Leakages are as follows:

Taxes	30%
Savings	5
Imports	5
Retained Profits	10

Total leakages = ——

9. GNP is $900 billion before the changes in investment shown in 7 and the leakages given in 8. What will be the new GNP?

Solution: Step 1. What is the total amount of ΔI?

Step 2. What is the total amount of leakages?

Step 3. Substitute these figures in the standard multiplier formula.

10. Further problem—we have changes as follows:

Residential construction	−5 billion dollars
Nonresidential construction	+15
Inventories	−10
Equipment	+20

Leakages are:

Savings	10%
Taxes	25
Imports	5
Retained Profits	10

Before changes in I, GNP = $900 billion. What will be the effect of ΔI? _____

Answers

	multiplier	ΔY
1.	7.7	38.5
2.	4	60
3.	3	−30
4.	4	−24

5. Total leakages = 33%, m.p.s. = .33, multiplier = 3
6. Total leakages = 60%, m.p.s. = .6, multiplier = 1.67
7. Total changes in investment = 13 billion
8. Total leakages = 50%
9. The new GNP will be 900 + (2 X 13) = 926
10. The effect of ΔI will be to raise GNP from $900 to $940 billion.

A REVIEW QUIZ

Put a check under T (True) or F (False). T F

1. The purchase of a used tractor is an example of real investment.   _ _
2. The purchase of GM common stock is not an example of financial investment unless the money is used by GM for real investment.   _ _
3. The multiplier describes the effect

T F

that added spending has on income via consumption spending.   _ _
4. The rise in income resulting from an addition to spending gradually levels out.   _ _
5. The higher the leakages, the higher the multiplier.   _ _
6. If new spending is $1,000 and the *mps* is 25 percent, the multiplier will be 75 percent.   _ _
7. We can have a multiplier effect from any increased expenditure, not just increased investment.   _ _
8. The reciprocal of .20 is 5.   _ _
9. An increase in tax rates would increase the multiplier.   _ _
10. The multiplier is important in explaining the effect of abrupt changes such as we find in inventories.   _ _

Answers:

1. F (a used tractor is not part of current GNP)		
2. F	5. F	8. T
3. T	6. F	9. F
4. T	7. T	10. T

Here are a few multiple choice problems. Work them out carefully.

The U.S. builds a research station in a small isolated country. It spends $1 million in one outlay. The m.p.s. of the country is .25. Each "round" of spending takes about three months. The total income of the country before the U.S. began its operations was $100 million.

_ 1. What is the size of the country's GNP immediately after the first disbursements have been made?
  a. $100,000,000
  b. 101,000,000
  c. 104,000,000
_ 2. What is the size of the country's income one year after the U.S. expenditures take place?
  a. $100,000,000
  b. 104,000,000
  c. indeterminate

_ 3. Assuming that no further U.S. expenditures occur, what will be the income of the country (ceteris paribus) two years later?

a. $100,000,000

b. 101,000,000

c. 104,000,000

_ 4. What will be the size of the additional saving generated by the U.S. expenditures after one year?

a. $4,000,000

b. zero

c. $1,000,000

The U.S. now decides to spend $1 million annually on the maintenance of the research station.

_ 5. What will be the new level of permanent income in the country?

a. $100,000,000

b. 101,000,000

c. 104,000,000

_ 6. What will be the new level of savings annually generated in the country?

a. $1,000,000

b. zero

c. $4,000,000

_ 7. In actual fact, most multiplier expenditure takes place with the first round, and a great many leakages occur with the second round. Assume that the leakages with the first round are .10 and with the second round .50. GNP is $1 trillion. A government spending project pours $100 billion into the country on January 1. What will be the (annual) rate of GNP on February 1, after one round of expenditures?

a. $1,100,000,000

b. 1,900,000,000

c. 1,190,000,000

_ 8. What will be the annual rate of GNP after two rounds, say in March?

a. $1,190,000,000

b. 1,900,000,000

c. 1,235,000,000

_ 9. Assume that your *mps* is .25 and that your income is $10,000. You suffer a cut in pay of $1,000. The amount you will spend for consumption will fall by

a. $1,000

b. 2,500

c.   750

_10. If a community of a million people had an *mpc* of 1.00 and expenditure in this community increased by $1, the eventual increase in income would be:

a. $1,000,000

b. 1.00

c. infinity

_11. Suppose the community had an *mps* of 1.00. What would the eventual increase in income be?

a. $1,000,000

b. 1.00

c. zero

Answers:

1. $101,000,000. No multiplier effect; just the GNP plus the injection.

2. $104,000,000. GNP plus the multiplier $(1/.25) \times$ injection.

3. $100,000,000. The effects of the injection have disappeared; we are back to the GNP from which we started. All the expenditures ended up as someone's savings.

4. $1,000,000.

5. $104,000,000. Instead of disappearing, the effects of the $1 million injection are steadily reintroduced. It is Case 2 above, on a permanent basis, instead of 3.

6. $1,000,000. The difference is that in Case 4, the savings were made for one year only. Now they are made year after year.

7. $1,190,000,000. The base GNP is $1,000,000,000. To this we add the initial expenditure of $100,000,000 plus one round of respending at an *mps* of .10, or $90,000,000. Total: $1,190,000,000.

8. $1,235,000.

Now we have GNP $1,000,000,000 + expenditures $100,000,000 + first round at *mps* of .10, or $90,000,000 + second round of $90,000,000 × *mps* of .5 or $45,000,000. Total: $1,235,000,000.

9. $750.

You cut your consumption by the change in income × *mps* or by −$1,000 × .75 = 750.

10. infinity

11. $1.00.

If nobody ever saved anything, after an (infinite) length of time, the dollar would have travelled around enough to create infinite incomes. If the *mps* is 1.00, the community saves all its income. The first person who gets the dollar keeps it, and that's an end to the matter.

26

The Motivation of Investment

LEARNING OBJECTIVES

Here is what you should look for in this chapter:
1. An understanding of the difference between autonomous and induced investment.
2. An understanding of the acceleration principle.
3. An understanding of how the rate of interest helps to determine the size of investment.

There are two major problems to be reviewed in this chapter. One of them is the problem of the *acceleration principle* (also called the *accelerator*). The other is the many-sided problem of *the relation between investment and the rate of interest*.

The reason we study the problems separately is that sometimes investment behaves as a dependent variable, responding to events elsewhere in the economy: the accelerator is a particularly interesting instance of such investment. At other times, investment behaves as an independent variable, responding to motivations that lie outside the normal scope of our economic analysis, for instance, the invention of a new product or production process. In these cases (and in the case of induced investment as well), the rate of interest plays an important role in determining *how much* investment will occur.

THE ACCELERATOR

Induced investment has a special interest for us because it gives us an explanation of the uneven behavior so characteristic of much investment spending. Investment induced by changes in consumption typically reveals a "wave-like" pattern that we call *the accelerator* or *the acceleration principle.*

Let us see this wave-like motion by tracing through the effects of rising consumption on investment. (We can imagine the investment taking place in inventories to service a rising demand, or in machines to support a rising level of output.) In the following model, we make three critical assumptions:

1. We assume that it requires ten units of capital to supply 100 units of consumption. (We could use any ratio, as long as we leave it unchanged during the period in which we are interested: what is important is a *fixed capital-output ratio.)*

2. We assume that our *capital wears out regularly,* so that part of it must be replaced each year to maintain the existing stock: machines depreciate; depleted inventories must be replaced; and so on. Our model uses a 10 percent depreciation rate, but any other would do.

3. We assume there is *no slack in the system* –

no extra supplies of inventories or under-utilized machines we could draw on to satisfy a rise in demand.

Now to the model in Table 26-1.

Let's go through a few periods before you complete the chart. Our model begins in year one with everything in balance: consumption is 100, which requires 10 units of capital. In this year one-tenth of our capital wears out and is replaced, but there is no need for net investment. Total demand for capital goods is therefore one unit (one machine; one batch of inventories), all of which is for replacement purposes.

Now fill in the chart, as we go along. Year two repeats the same story; nothing changes. Action begins with year three. Now consumption rises to 110. The additional 10 units of consumption require a new unit of capital – an additional machine or larger inventories. We see this in column three, where "total capital required" has risen to 11, and in column five, where we now have net investment of 1 – the investment in the new unit. On the other hand, *replacement* investment is unchanged. Only one unit of the

TABLE 26-1

1	2	3 Total Capital Required	4 Replacement Investment	5 Net Investment	6 Total Investment
Year	Consumption				
1	100	10	1	0	1
2	100				
3	110	11	1	1	
4	120	12			
5	150		1	3	
6	160				
7	170				
8	170				
9	160				
10	150				

old capital has worn out and must be replaced as before. Thus total investment has risen to ____ .

Year four is just like year three. But with year five consumption rises by 30 units. The need for capital equipment therefore jumps from 12 units to____, and new investment accordingly rises from 1 unit to 3. As before, however, there is no change in replacement, and therefore total investment – now_____ units – is altered only by changes in new investment.

Now comes the critical year six. Consumption has risen by____ units. This will require____ units of additional capital. Net investment will therefore be ____ units. Replacement is still ____units. Therefore, total investment is ____units. *Notice that total investment has now* fallen, *even though consumption is still rising!*

Year seven should give you no problem: it is a repeat of year six. But now comes year eight. Consumption ceases to grow. Capital requirements will therefore also not grow. We will still replace one old unit of capital, but there will be zero net investment, and total investment will have fallen to____.

Year nine is worse still. Consumption now falls. Our capital requirement also falls: we now possess 17 units of capital inherited from year eight. This is one more unit than we need.

Therefore, not only will there be no net investment, but there will be no need to replace the unit of capital that wears out in year nine. Replacement investment is zero, and so is total investment. Year ten is another year with the same problem.

First check your filled-in problem against the answers in Table 26-2.

Do you see a wave-like movement in total investment? You will if you plot the movement of consumption and total investment on the chart in Figure 26-1. (note: plot *C* against the left-hand scale; *I* against the right-hand). Notice that investment turns down *before* consumption.

We get an added touch of dynamics by adding a multiplier to our accelerator. In the following table (Table 26-3) we show the levels for total investment in the model we have been using:

This time, fill in the columns showing the change in investment (ΔI), multiply this by the multiplier given by an m.p.c. of .5, and show the change in income. Obviously nothing happens until year three. Then investment increases by 1 unit; this is multiplied by____, to give an increase of ____ units of *Y*. Pay special attention to year six. Here the change in *I* is negative, and the multiplier will *decrease income* by the leverage of a .5 m.p.c. We won't work out the middle

TABLE 26-2

1 Year	2 Consumption	3 Total Capital Required	4 Replacement Investment	5 Net Investment	6 Total Investment
1	100	10	1	0	1
2	100	10	1	0	1
3	110	11	1	1	2
4	120	12	1	1	2
5	150	15	1	3	4
6	160	16	1	1	2
7	170	17	1	1	2
8	170	17	1	0	1
9	160	16	0	0	0
10	150	15	0	0	0

FIGURE 26-1

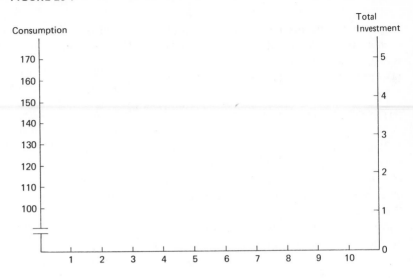

columns for you, but the answers for the last column should read: 0, 0, 2, 0, 4, -4, 0, -2, -2, 0.

Can you see how an even more complicated business cycle model could be constructed, using these changes in income as the sources for further changes in induced investment?

AUTONOMOUS INVESTMENT

Induced investment leads us into the mechanism of the business cycle; autonomous investment leads us to consider the interest rate. The reason is that autonomous investment behaves as an independent variable, not related to previous changes in the economic system. *Autonomous investment anticipates demand; induced investment follows it.* Yet the *amount* of investment that a new invention or some other autonomous stimulus will produce is related to the interest rate. (Note: we *know* from econometric studies that interest rates are an important factor in certain investment decisions, such as housing or

TABLE 26-3

Year	Total Investment	Change in I (Indicate + or −)	(Given m.p.c. = .5) Change in Y
1	1		
2	1		
3	2		
4	2		
5	4		
6	2		
7	2		
8	1		
9	0		
10	0		

long-term investments in utilities. We do not have econometric evidence with respect to manufacturing investment, but we think that interest rates may also play a significant role here.)

INTEREST AND INVESTMENT

What is the relation between the rate of interest and the amount of investment? The overall answer is very simple: *the lower the rate of interest, the more investment we can expect.* One obvious reason is that it is cheaper to borrow money for investment purposes as interest rates fall. Thus, the general demand function for investment looks like Figure 26-2 below:

FIGURE 26-2

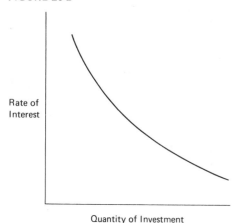

Rate of Interest

Quantity of Investment

When we look behind this overall relationship, however, we learn a number of important things about the investment process.

TIME DISCOUNTING

The first thing we discover is the phenomenon called *discounting future returns.* The idea is very simple. It is that a given sum of money that will come to you "tomorrow" is not worth as much today. Would you pay $100 *today* for an assured

return of $100 a year hence? Ten years hence? Of course not. There are two reasons for this:

1. *There is a risk* that the money tomorrow will not come to you. Perhaps the promise to pay will be broken. Perhaps you will be dead.

2. *There is an opportunity cost to waiting,* even if there were no risk. If you had $100 today, you could invest it. If the rate of interest were 10 percent, you would have $110 a year hence, and well over $250 in ten years. Therefore it would only be worth while to offer just over $90 today for $100 a year hence, since at 10 percent the $90 will amount to $99 after one year. If you *do* pay $100 for a bond whose future redemption price is $100, it is only because it pays enough interest to cover your opportunity cost.

Because of these reasons all of us discount future income. In Figure 26-3, the graph shows the difference between the flow of expected income from an investment, and the discounted value of that flow — the amount of money we would lay out today to have a claim on that future income.

FIGURE 26-3

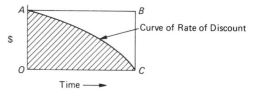

The rectangle *OABC* represents the discounted value of expected future income: say interest on bonds, or earnings from an investment. The shaded area shows the value *today* of that future income.

THE MARGINAL EFFICIENCY OF INVESTMENT

These considerations enter into investment decisions. A businessman discounts the expected returns from an investment before he decides whether to make the investment or not. He must decide whether the discounted returns from an investment will justify his initial outlay. Typically he will have a number of alternative investment projects among which to choose. Some appear so profitable or so certain, or so quick to "pay off," that even a very high rate of discount will justify their cost. Others will appear less profitable. As Figure 26-4 shows, there will be some investments (projects *A* and *B*) that will cover their costs even if the rate of discount is very high: others, such as Projects *C* and *D* will cover their costs only if the rate of discount is much lower. The graph on the right shows a generalization of this into a curve of *marginal efficiency of investment.*

THE RATE OF INTEREST

Now the question is: how many of these projects will be put into effect? Here is where the rate of interest enters. For our businessman has an alternative to putting his money into capital goods. He can buy bonds of varying degrees of safety that will pay him a stated return. Hence he compares the marginal efficiency of a given investment with the interest income he could earn on a bond of roughly the same degree of risk. If his discounted investment returns bring in more than the bond, he will put his money into investment; if not, he will buy the bond (or perhaps simply hang onto the cash).

In Figure 26-4, suppose the appropriate rate of interest is *OX*. Draw a line from *X* through both diagrams. Will Projects *A* and *B* be undertaken? Will *C* and *D?* Show on the generalized diagram how much investment will correspond to interest rate *OX*. Now suppose the rate falls to *OY*. Explain to yourself why *C* and *D* are now worth undertaking, and show the increase in total investment on the generalized curve.

Finally, suppose that the profit outlook improves. Perhaps this will be for political reasons – the government may decide to tax earnings less. Perhaps it is for technological reasons – it becomes cheaper to build capital projects. This means that Project *A* would repay its cost even if it were discounted at a higher rate than before, and of course the same applies to Projects *B, C,* and *D.* You can show this by adding a dotted extension to each project. What does that do to your generalized m.e.i. curve? At the same rate of interest (*OX*) will you invest more or less than before?

TWO LAST REMARKS

1. Don't forget that we cannot clearly establish this interest-rate investment relationship, except in certain cases, such as residential housing, where it is very clear. We have reason to think that the quantity of manufacturing investment also responds positively to a lower interest rate, but there is an econometric puzzle in trying to demonstrate it.

FIGURE 26-4

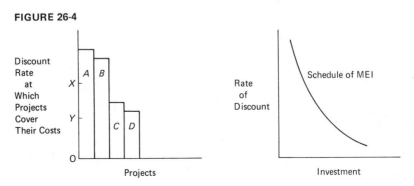

2. We have not mentioned the subject of *exports*. This is because we will study them when we get to foreign trade. We introduce them in this chapter because exports behave like autonomous investment, insofar as they constitute a volatile source of demand for GNP, from which multiplier effects result, just as with any added spending. In studying the demand for GNP, exports are a new *category* of expenditure, but a category that presents no new problems for our present analysis.

QUIZ

Put a check under T (True) or F (False).

T F

1. Autonomous investment means investment taken in response to changes in expenditure.
2. The accelerator relates changes in income to changes in investment.
3. It is possible for total investment expenditures to decline even though consumption expenditures are increasing.
4. It is impossible for *net* induced investment to be zero as long as consumption is rising.
5. Replacement investment cannot fall to zero as long as depreciation continues.
6. The rate of interest influences investment because higher rates of interest tempt investors to undertake capital projects.
7. Interest cost is a major consideration for residential construction.
8. Time discounting means that we will never pay $100 today for a bond that will pay $100 in ten years, even if it pays us interest in the meantime.
9. Time discounting involves the opportunity cost of waiting.
10. The marginal efficiency of investment refers to the return that a capital investment must yield, so that its discounted earnings just cover its present cost.

T F

11. The marginal efficiency of investment can change if expectations change or if technical factors change.
12. The rate of interest provides a guide against which to measure the marginal efficiency of various investment projects.
13. If the rate of interest rises, the marginal efficiency schedule shifts to the left.
14. The marginal efficiency of investment describes *expectations* about profits.
15. If the marginal efficiency schedule shifts, we will undertake a different quantity of investment even though the rate of interest remains unchanged.
16. If all investment projects had exactly the same expected future incomes, the m.e.i. schedule would be a horizontal line.
17. If there were no risk whatsoever associated with investments, we would not need to discount future earnings.
18. Exports affect GNP because they are a source of demand for output.
19. A change in exports will lead to a larger change in GNP because of the accelerator effect.
20. The accelerator and the multiplier together offset one another, to "dampen" what would otherwise be severe swings in spending.

Answers:

1. F	8. F	15. T
2. F	9. T	16. T
3. T	10. T	17. F
4. F	11. T	18. T
5. F	12. T	19. F
6. F	13. F	20. F
7. T	14. T	

Government Demand

27

LEARNING OBJECTIVES

Four main questions should lie at the center of your study:

1. Do you clearly understand the difference between government expenditure, including services, and government purchases? Do you also understand that "government" includes state and local, as well as federal spending?

2. Do you see how government spending can close a demand gap?

3. Do you grasp the idea of demand management? This involves the dynamics of the automatic stabilizers as well as the problems of time lags, the efficacy of public spending vs. tax cuts, and the categories of public spending.

4. Do you *really* see why an internally held government debt is different from a private debt or an externally held debt? Be sure and look at the last reading (on Deficit Spending) to test your knowledge.

Three problems emerge from this chapter and its short sequel on the arms subeconomy: a problem of *vocabulary;* an *analytical* problem of the mechanism of intersectoral cooperation; and a *policy* problem on the uses of the public sector. Let us consider them in turn.

VOCABULARY

We have not much used these review exercises previously to stress vocabulary. But vocabulary becomes of such importance in speaking of government demand that it seems useful to highlight some of its verbal pitfalls. Basically, the trouble arises because the term "government spending" has three meanings, each of which carries very important consequences for tracing the effects of public action.

1. Federal vs. state and local spending

When we speak of "government spending," it is vitally important_to know whether we refer to *federal, state, and local* activity or just to *federal* activity. In particular, bear in mind that "government" in the national income accounts covers *all three categories* of expenditure, so that "*G*" in the GNP identity equation does *not* just refer to federal spending.

2. Expenditures vs. purchases

The second source of difficulty arises from the fact that *transfer payments* are a major addition to government spending (meaning the spending of all three government subsectors). Roughly speaking, one-third of all government spending is for transfers; two-thirds are for purchases of goods and services. *Remember:* only government purchases contribute to production; transfers merely shift purchasing power from the government sector to the household or business sector. The *G* in the GNP refers to *purchases* by federal, state, and local authorities. Transfers do not show up in the GNP equation. Therefore expenditures can rise, if transfers increase, without any rise in *G*.

3. Categories of expenditure

The third source of confusion with regard to government spending is that it covers such diverse activities. Government purchases are the mainstay of our arms economy; they are also the mainstay of our educational system. Government transfers are the backbone of our welfare system (including Social Security); they are also the source of many special privileges, such as subsidies for certain private enterprises, crop supports, and so on.

Only an expert on public affairs can be expected to master the complexities of the public portion of the national income accounts. But every student should be permanently warned that the words "government spending" must always be carefully examined to see what they mean, before leaping to conclusions on the basis of unanalyzed statistics.

THE ANALYTICAL PROBLEM

We are now so well along in macroeconomic analysis that the analytical issue posed by government spending poses little difficulty. We understand that government purchases of goods and services constitute one of the four categories of final demand for GNP. Increases or decreases in that demand give rise to multiplier effects, exactly as do increases or decreases in investment or exports. By borrowing from the public and spending the proceeds, government purchasing can serve as an offset to a demand gap, exactly as with the business sector.

What is perhaps most important, in this regard, is that government spending, financed by borrowing, can offset a demand gap whose origin is insufficient *business* spending, as Figure 27-1 shows. (For simplicity's sake we assume no household saving, and have rearranged the sectors to make the diagram simpler to draw.)

AUTOMATIC STABILIZERS

A second analytical element in our study of government demand is the role of the *automatic stabilizers*. The automatic stabilizers refer to a "built-in" tendency for the government sector to act *against* the movement of GNP. When GNP rises, income taxes tend to rise faster than GNP because families move up into brackets where the marginal tax rates are higher. Therefore consumer spending is dampened because householders find their tax liabilities growing. At the same time, as GNP rises, certain kinds of transfer

FIGURE 27-1

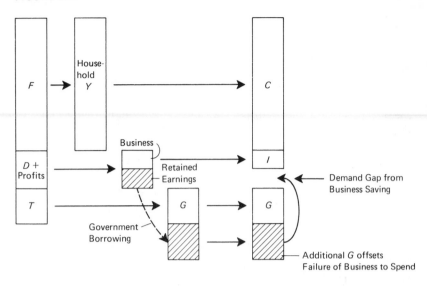

payments, especially unemployment compensation, or welfare payments, or agricultural support payments, are likely to diminish, thereby decreasing the contribution of government expenditures to the incomes of the household and business sectors.

Thus, as GNP rises, the structure of government tax and expenditure programs tend to act as a brake. Just the opposite effect occurs when GNP falls. Now tax liabilities fall even more rapidly, freeing some household funds for consumption spending, while at the same time transfer payments for unemployment, welfare, and the like tend to increase, bolstering the spending power of the private sector.

DEMAND MANAGEMENT

The last important issue is that of demand management – using the public sector as an instrument to achieve or maintain a desired level of GNP. Here we leave the clearcut world of diagrams and formulas, to enter the ambiguous world of reality. The problem is not that the diagrams or formulas are inaccurate, but that we must now find the empirical data to fill in the boxes and flesh out the variables, and this poses

enormously difficult problems for economic policy.

Let us review very briefly what some of those problems are:

1. Time lags

When does a recession "begin"? Even long after a recession, economists will argue about the correct date for its onset. All the more difficult, then, to recognize its "beginning" when government officials must operate from current data, much of which is inaccurate, incomplete, or already outdated.

Worse, it takes time to set into motion the machinery of demand management. Expenditure programs cannot be launched on twenty-four-hours notice. Congress may not quickly agree to cut or raise taxes. Thus we must recognize two lags: a "recognition lag" – the time it takes before an administration is convinced that corrective public action is needed; and an "implementation" lag – the time it takes to turn the faucets of government spending or taxing on or off. These lags may last many months and greatly complicate the problem of applying demand management at the right time and in the right amount.

221

2. Tax cuts v. expenditure increases

Second, what kind of demand management should be used? Raising (or lowering) taxes has more or less the same general effect on GNP as lowering (or raising) expenditures, but the differences between the two policies are also pronounced. Tax *cuts* are probably quicker to apply (if Congress is willing) than expenditure increases. On the other hand tax *raises* may be more difficult to bring about quickly than expenditure cuts!

Moreover, tax cuts typically benefit groups and income strata different from those expenditure increases benefit — but again this may vary according to the kind of program that is advocated. A cut in sales taxes would help the poor; a cut in income taxes helps the rich, speaking proportionately. An increase in road-building is likely to pump money into the lower-income brackets; an increase in federal research and development funnels money into the upper-income brackets.

What you should try to learn at this juncture is not the complex pros and cons of all these measures, but the fact that there *are* pros and cons, and that the choice of the best fiscal policies is a difficult and uncertain one.

3. Controlling the public budget

We focus on the problem of demand management because the public sector is the only component of final demand for GNP that is directly under the control of our political system. We cannot (or at least in democratic economies, we do not) *directly* regulate consumer or business spending, even though we seek to influence both kinds of spending by taxes and other measures. But we do directly control public spending and taxing. Thus government expenditures and taxes become key tools for the regulation of total demand.

But we must not be misled into thinking that we have complete control over the public budget. As the text explains, the public sector has its own inertias and propensities and "unmanageable" areas. We have the problems of RUOs (relatively uncontrollable outlays), such as the flow of Social Security payments that are now directly geared to the cost of living. We have problems such as fiscal drag. There is the very difficult matter of deciding how much money to transfer to the states (grants-in-aid), and how to — or whether to — influence the manner in which they use that money.

Thus, whereas demand management is the most important means by which modern market economies can regulate their overall economic activity, the degree of control over the economy is often disconcertingly small. We shall study this problem further when we reach the problem of inflation.

QUIZ

First, the good news. There seems no point in giving you a quiz on the subject matter of this chapter. The analytical material is easy (although some of the policy issues are very difficult). Instead, we suggest you look at a few readings that follow: one on the war economy; one on problems of fiscal policy; one on deficit spending (which goes with Chapter 28).

Next, the bad news. It seems time for a full-scale quiz on the matters from Chapter 22 on. This quiz (which follows the readings) will cover some matters in the chapter we have just finished, as well as some in Chapter 28, so we're afraid you won't quite get away scot-free.

ARMS FOR A TIME OF PEACE

Murray L. Weidenbaum

Murray Weidenbaum has been an Assistant Secretary of the Treasury Department, and has written widely about the problems of controlling defense expenditures. Here is an appraisal of the military sub-economy by a thoughtful critic.

A fundamental change in public attitudes toward the military is occurring in the United States. That stirring phrase "Arsenal of Democracy" has been consigned to the archives. Defense is on the defensive.

The military establishment is experiencing a crisis in legitimacy. Many factors have contributed to this situation — the protracted Vietnam War, racial tensions, PX corruption, drug abuse, and a general reduction of operational effectiveness. In an effort to offset these negative influences as we move toward an all-volunteer armed force, the government has raised military pay sharply and attempted to improve the living conditions of military personnel. The initial impact has been to overwhelm the military budget, squeezing badly the funds available for modernization of equipment. Yet unless the more fundamental and noneconomic issues of morale and motivation are dealt with, it will take baseball-star salaries to attract young men of the caliber needed.

Concern about the rise of a military-industrial complex is a related factor undermining public support of the military establishment. The magnitude of the sheer waste in military activities Between 1957 and 1970, 81 major weapons projects were canceled after $12 billion had been incurs the wrath of every citizen and taxpayer.

From *Challenge* (September/October, 1973), pp. 22-27.

spent on them. Waste of economic resources on such a scale is very serious.

Still, that is not the most adverse effect. How were other countries, such as the Soviet Union, to know — while we were working on these new weapons — that the projects would eventually be canceled? The record shows that they did indeed try to keep up with the Americans: the Russians have, for example, been producing ICBMs and nuclear submarines at a record rate. It is hard to think of anything that reduces our true national security more than building a new weapon that does not work or ultimately is abandoned but that meanwhile has evoked a strong response by a rival power.

CHANGING POWER RELATIONS

Paradoxically, during the same period of growing American disenchantment with military matters Russian military efforts have accelerated. As a result, a basic shift has taken place in the relative balance between the two superpowers. The USSR is now in a relatively stronger position vis-á-vis the United States than it was ten or even five years ago. We can debate whether the Russians are ahead of us or not, but it does seem clear that the USSR is making a determined effort to catch up, if not to overtake, the United States.

The Russians now have about 1,618 ICBMs compared with our 1,054. Under the SALT agreement, we can have no more than 44 modern submarines with 710 missile-launchers against their 62 modern submarines with 950 missile-launchers. The sheer poundage of the Soviet stockpile of nuclear warheads is greater – by about two to one. But we clearly have retained our lead in the number of warheads – 5,700 compared with 2,500 – and we believe that ours are more accurate. Also, our fleet of long-range bombers is much larger, 531 compared with 140.

The United States is no longer the unique possessor of overwhelming strategic/nuclear power. The USA and the USSR now both have the ability to exterminate the human race. This has created an almost involuntary interdependence. Although we continue to compete vigorously, the nature of the conflict does not permit resolution by victory, in the classic sense. But there is still very grim competition for position and world influence.

This is a difficult environment for us to learn to live in. Future conflicts are likely often to be resolved through third nations or by nonmilitary means – economic and technological competition, propaganda, and maneuvering in international political forums. Our military and political allies often become our economic and technological rivals: witness our changing relations with the Common Market and Japan. The assured availability of energy sources may become more important than the precise number of ICBMs in place.

NATURE OF THE
AMERICAN RESPONSE

The budgetary prospect for federal programs, military and civilian, is not one of liberality. We have literally mortgaged for many years the future fiscal dividends that are yielded by economic growth. As a rising share of our resources is devoted to welfare, environment, and other domestic considerations, the military budget for the remainder of this decade is likely to be a declining portion both of total government spending and of the national economy. Any aboslute dollar increases will be eaten up by pay raises and other inflationary factors. Thus, our ability to maintain a competitive military position in relation to the USSR may well become attenuated, unless the Russians decide to slow down their buildup of strategic weapons.

There are numerous domestic side effects of this shift in national budget priorities from warfare to welfare. One of the important though unintended impacts is a reduction in government support of science and technology. If further expansions in the budgets of civilian agencies continue to be dominated by welfare transfer payments and other low-R&D activities – as is the present case – the role of the government as patron of science and technology will diminish. A million dollars of Social Security payments just does not generate the kind of demand for R&D that a million dollars of military or space spending does. No civilian patron appears to be waiting in the wings to support this force so vital to our national growth and progress.

Despite sloganeering to the contrary, the United States is hardly becoming a garrison state. The Department of Defense is still the largest employer in the economy – although substantially less so than it was a few years ago. Yet its total manpower requirements, including workers in defense industries, come to 7.5 percent of the U.S. labor force. Thus, over 92 percent of the nation's working population produce goods and services to meet civilian needs.

The military is still the largest customer of American business – again, not as large as it was several years ago. Yet its total purchases come to 6.5 percent of the GNP. Over 93 percent of the nation's output is thus oriented to civilian demand. Very few of the top military contractors now depend on defense work for as much as one-half of their sales. This is a major change from a decade ago, when many of them received two-thirds or more of their business from the Pentagon. Key defense contractors that receive most of their business from customers other than the Pentagon include Boeing, McDonnell Douglas, North American Rockwell, Martin-Marietta, Northrop, and United Aircraft.

Contrary to popular mythology, the giants of American industry do not monopolize defense contracts. The three largest industrial corporations – General Motors, Standard Oil of New Jersey, and Ford – each obtained defense contracts equal to 2 percent of its 1970 sales. Sixteen of the 50 largest industrial firms had military sales so small, if any at all, that they did not appear on the Pentagon's list of 100 top contractors for 1970 (it took yearly military sales of at least $32 million to make the list).

In one recent year, among the top 100 defense contractors, the 27 giant corporations with assets of $1 billion or more received only 25 percent of the dollar volume of awards. The 30 medium-size companies with assets ranging from $250 million to $1 billion received the largest share – 58 percent of the awards.

DOMESTIC IMPACT OF OUR CHANGING SECURITY ENVIRONMENT

The nature of the challenges facing our society is changing. The external military threat has not receded; but new challenges have arisen which relate to the basic stability of our internal society. The social, ecological, and political strains have become increasingly severe. Our resources are not unlimited, but we can meet this combination of external and domestic challenges by making some hard choices.

It will take four key actions on the part of the United States to meet these domestic challenges and, at the same time, provide adequately for national security:

1. *Dedicating a major portion of our resources to dealing with the urban-racial-poverty cluster of problems.* This is necessary in order to restore our national sense of well-being and domestic tranquility. The national "blood pressure" has been reduced during the past four years, but the fundamental problems that erupted in the late 1960s remain with us. The answer is not more handouts – what economists call direct income redistribution: what we really need is more investments in human productivity and effectiveness, ranging from formal education to on-the-job training in the private sector.

2. *Developing public support for applying a sufficient portion of our resources to maintaining our military strength so that we adequately protect our national security.* There is nothing more wasteful than a fitful stop-and-go approach to military spending. We must avoid both crash efforts and excessive cutbacks such as those that followed World War II, which lead only to subsequent crash efforts to catch up. We must examine our military needs and resources in a far more objective manner. We should avoid equating support for higher military spending with greater patriotism – or, conversely, a simple-minded association of advocacy of less military spending with goodness of soul and worthiness of character.

3. *Overhauling the present wasteful methods of maintaining the military establishment.* The public just does not want to support the inefficient status quo, and there is no reason why it should. Let us try the private-enterprise approach. Existing procedures require defense companies to behave like government arsenals, with a proliferation of expensive reporting and paper work. The nation does not get the benefit of the innovation and efficiency that we expect from the private sector, but rather the cost overruns and late deliveries that we associate with government arsenals. The proposed "disengagement" of detailed government control would

also mean less government subsidy and support to these companies.

Even if more effective procurement approaches are developed, the military will still have to learn to pick and choose among alternative weapons possibilities, rather than take the more costly route of merely wanting more. The Appropriations Committee of the House of Representatives — no nest of radicals or doves — recently provided some pertinent observations: "The tendency in the Department of Defense too frequently is to add new programs as required but to resist the termination of the old programs which were valuable at one time but are now marginal at best."

We must face up to the unpleasant fact that the McNamara "revolution" in the Pentagon has not lived up to expectations. The resultant avalanche of paper instructions and staff organizations has delayed rather than improved military decision-making. Streamlining the "overhead" will help slow down the growth of the military budget.

Another area of potential economy is in the underutilized forces — the National Guard and the Reserves. Only about one of twenty National Guardsmen actually served in Vietnam. That war seems to have passed the Reserves by almost entirely, except for a small call-up in 1968. It is hard to justify taking unwilling and untrained draftees into the armed forces at a time when supposedly willing and trained volunteer members of the Guard and Reserves are not being used. If the Department of Defense did not need these forces to any substantial degree for the protracted Vietnam conflict, what are we saving them for?

A proper concern for economy and efficiency should not overlook the basic structure of the armed forces. There are more three- and four-star generals and admirals in uniform today than at the height of World War II, when the military establishment was four times as large. This proliferation of grade has been continuing at a rapid rate.

Utilizing disproportionately large amounts of the military budget for personnel costs (which are rapidly approaching a three-fifths share) may result in a well-paid, nattily dressed, and attractively housed service that lacks the modern equipment necessary to provide a realistic deterrent to potential aggressors.

Since 1964, military pay and personnel costs have exactly doubled, rising from $21 billion to $42 billion. Meanwhile, total outlays for modernization (research and development, procurement, and construction) have gone up less than the amount needed merely to offset the inroads of inflation. A restoration of balance between operating costs of the military establishment (mainly pay) and modernization outlays is badly needed.

4. *Finding the money to finance new high-priority civilian programs.* We can have both guns and butter provided we eliminate much of the flab and fat that have developed in our government structure. We can make a good start by reducing or eliminating the $70 billion in subsidies the federal government bestows each year on a host and variety of beneficiaries which can afford to do without the special federal handout. There are too many of these fiscal sacred cows, now sheltered from annual review, and they should be deprived of their privileged status.

A firm effort is needed to eliminate government spending that results from "the dead hand of the past." Many of the subsidies are vestiges of the 1930s and 1940s. Rereading the original justifications is like hearing an echo from a different age:

- To deal with the problem of low wages in the construction industry (the Davis-Bacon Act). Low wages in the building trades in the 1970s?
- To deal with the lack of an inventory of metals for extended war production (the stockpile of "strategic" materials). Protracted trench warfare in the 1970s?
- To deal with the lack of electricity on American farms (low-interest loans by the Rural Electrification Administration). No electric lighting in the 1970s?

These and many government programs like them have outlived their usefulness. They do not correspond to the realities and priorities of this decade. They should be given an honorable discharge or, better yet, a suitable burial. The federal government can and should respond to new and changing priorities, military and civilian. We can do so without a substantial tax increase, but only by taking the difficult action of cutting back older, lower-priority programs.

SECURITY WITH FLEXIBILITY

Military spending has continued at a high level for two decades. There is no likelihood of significant reduction in the near future. The role of the military establishment has become a substantial and more or less normal factor in the American economy. Simple-minded opposition to any "war machine" and uncritical attachment to the status quo are equally misguided. We must continually reappraise the role of the military establishment in our changing society of shifting priorities.

Particularly as a result of the Vietnam War, a new and more cautious approach toward the military objectives this nation can expect to achieve is developing. This points to a lower U.S. military profile in the 1970s. No country is likely to be Number One across the entire spectrum of international rivalry and competition. In the future, the American tent will not be quite so gloriously sited on the highest hill.

In light of our existing arsenal of ICBMs, B-52 bombers, and impregnable ballistic-missile sub-marines, it is hard to agree with those who worry about the United States' quickly becoming a second-rate military power. Neither does overkill accurately describe our current position, although that may have been the situation a few years ago. Our present military posture seems to be adequate to the uncertainties of the world we live in, with reasonable margins for error and safety.

It is vital that the United States maintain a strong research and development effort to prevent "technological surprises" on the part of any potential aggressor. A variety of programs is needed to develop new systems to deal with the potential threats to our key strategic retaliatory capacity — threats which can only arise in the future. But this is not an argument for moving new systems into production and operation before the threat materializes. For if we do, then it would be the United States, not the Soviet Union, that accelerates the arms race.

We are in a new arms age. As Vietnam vividly demonstrated, a large and well-equipped military establishment is important, but it does not suffice. National security comprises something that is both more and less than formal military strength — the will and morale of the people. A society that shows itself capable of promptly meeting challenges, domestic and foreign, demonstrates its basic strength.

A society that meets standards of fairness toward and concern for its many citizens simultaneously bolsters its overall security. It is a society well worth the necessary investments in arms to defend it.

Deficit Spending

28

LEARNING OBJECTIVES

You should be able to:
1. See the difference between *deficits* and *losses;*
2. Understand the distinction between *external* business debts and *internal* government debts; and
3. Formulate a conclusion regarding the advantages and disadvantages of governmental deficit spending.

PRIMER ON GOVERNMENT SPENDING

Peter L. Bernstein / Robert L. Heilbroner

In 1963 President Kennedy startled the nation with the suggestion of a tax cut planned to create a deliberate government deficit as a stimulus to a sagging economy. Two economists, one a coauthor of this book, the other Peter L. Bernstein, a noted financial analyst, wrote a brief "Primer on Government Spending" to explain this heretical proposal. At the end of the book they posed this quiz, which every reader of The Economic Problem *should pass with flying colors.*

As all good primers should, this one now presents a small test in which the reader can measure his mastery of the subject. The quotation that follows is a paraphrase of an address by a well-known and respected man who disagrees with the position taken in this book. Each of his arguments has been marked with a number. The reader should first attempt to answer these arguments himself. He can then consult our own numbered replies. Nothing would make the writing of this book more worthwhile for its authors than to find that our readers have put the matter better than we have.

As a practical businessman I have sense enough to know that when you spend more than you take in, something is radically wrong. (1) It's even more wrong that we are spending our children's and our grandchildren's money. (2) The history of deficit spending is a history of failure — we have had twenty-eight deficits in the past thirty-four years, to no effect. (3) Most of us do not worry about the debt only because it is so big we can't comprehend it; if it were smaller we would be more concerned because then we would understand its dangers better. (4) A few economists, I know, would have us believe that the debt is unimportant because we "owe it to

From Robert L. Heilbroner and Peter L. Bernstein, *A Primer on Government Spending* (New York: Random House, 1963).

ourselves," whatever that means. (5) Well, I have an old-fashioned conviction that debts have to be paid back some day. (6) If the holders of these federal promises to pay should lose their confidence in the government, we would have the most terrible conomic collapse ever seen. (7) I conclude then that the greatest moral danger facing our country at the moment is the danger of deficit spending. (8)

1. Not wrong: impossible for any length of time. One has to *borrow* the difference. The question really is, can one borrow safely? Is it "radically wrong" for the American Telephone and Telegraph Company to have spent many tens of billions more than it has taken in since the end of the war?

2. Neither the government nor the Telephone Company is spending our grandchildren's money. Whether the money they spend is raised through borrowing, taxing, or higher rates for phone calls and postage stamps, the money comes out of our pockets today. If our grandchildren have to pay off these debts, they will of course pay them off to one another.

3. Some of these deficits have been too small to have much impact on the economy. Even the $10 billion deficit proposed by President Kennedy for the fiscal year 1964 is a smaller proportion of the Gross National Product than

some of the deficits we incurred during the 1930s. In addition, recent experience indicates that the economy grows faster when the government runs a deficit and slower when revenues exceed outlays.

4. Ridiculous. To the extent that we worry about it, we worry because it is too big. But what does "too big" mean? Relative to other debts in the economy and to the production of goods and services, our national debt today is considerably more modest than it was fifteen years ago. Remember that 95 percent of both interest payments and repayments of principal go to American citizens; if the debt is "too big," then we must be "too rich" because we own "too many" government bonds.

5. To whom do we owe it, if not to ourselves? Only 5 percent of the debt is held outside the United States, and this is admittedly a problem, even if a small one.

6. Of course, each of us as individuals has to meet our obligations as they come due. So do corporations and states and cities and the federal government. But as long as we continue to meet those obligations regularly and as long as we have the resources to draw upon to make certain that we can meet them, what is to prevent us from paying off an old obligation by incurring a new one? Many users of consumer installment credit, most public utility companies, most states and municipalities, and the federal government all employ this technique.

7. This is true of the holders of any security — that is why the stock market "crashes" and this is why runs on banks develop. Panic is usually self-generating, so responsible citizens should hesitate about suggestions of this sort unless they are on certain ground. Many governments have had national debts much heavier than ours in relation to the size of their economies — Great Britain in the nineteenth century is a good example of this — without doubts as to the soundness of government obligations ever coming up. Panics of the type suggested here occur only when the government is overthrown or when the economy itself is disintegrating due to war, revolution, or some other form of complete disorganization.

8. There is one greater danger — ignorance masquerading as morality.

TEST ON CHAPTERS 22 TO 28

Ten easy questions

__ 1. The main reason why a public debt differs from a private debt is that

    a. it can be repaid.

    b. it is internally held

    c. it covers deficits.

__ 2. When we use the GNP formula, $C + I + G + X$, the term G stands for

    a. federal plus state and local purchases.

    b. all government expenditures.

    c. federal expenditures only.

__ 3. A multiplier effect relates

    a. any change in expenditure to a change in income.

    b. any change in income to a change in investment.

    c. a change in spending to a change in saving.

__ 4. The automatic stabilizers dampen economic swings because

    a. taxes change faster than GNP and expenditures move against GNP.

    b. taxes change slower than GNP and expenditures move with GNP.

    c. government policy allows us to control GNP.

__ 5. The marginal efficiency of investment describes

    a. physical productivity of capital.

    b. the rate of interest.

    c. expected profits on investment.

__ 6. The accelerator won't work if

    a. consumption rises unevenly.

    b. there is underutilized capital.

    c. autonomous investment is not forthcoming.

__ 7. The marginal propensity to save is

    a. the reciprocal of the m.p.c.

    b. the complement of the m.p.c.

    c. the complement of the average propensity to save.

_ 8. The size of the multiplier depends entirely on the

    a. average propensity to consume.

    b. marginal propensity to consume.

    c. average propensity to save.

_ 9. A demand gap arises because

    a. incomes do not equal costs.

    b. receipts do not equal expenditures.

    c. expenditures do not equal incomes.

_10. If GNP = 100, m.p.s. = .5, and exports +10, investment − 5, gov't − 5:

    a. there will be no change in GNP.

    b. GNP will rise.

    c. GNP will fall.

Ten Hard Questions

Put a check under T (True) or F (False).   T F

11. If the m.p.s. is a constant, the average propensity to save must also be constant.

                      — —

12. Even if the average propensity to consume is very high, the multiplier will be small if the marginal propensity to save is also high.

                      — —

13. Induced investment, because it results from a *previous* change in consumption, exerts no multiplier effect.

14. GNP = $Y + T + D$

                      — —

15. $\Delta Y = \dfrac{1}{1 - \text{m.p.c.}} \Delta I$

                      — —

16. If Social Security payments rise, there is no change in the G term in the GNP formula.

                      — —

17. Over time, the marginal propensity to save must decline, because the average propensity to consume remains roughly constant.

                      — —

18. Although we describe them as independent variables, both I and G have some characteristics of dependent variables.

                      — —

19. If General Motors absorbed all the enterprises in the nation, it could engage in deficit financing much like a government.

                      — —

20. The marginal efficiency of investment is really a kind of demand curve for capital goods.

                      — —

The Determination of GNP

29

LEARNING OBJECTIVES

Here we learn about the interplay of the supply of and demand for GNP. This teaches us:
1. The supply curve of income is a 45° line.
2. The demand curve for output is the sum of $C + G + I$.
3. Their intersection establishes the equilibrium level of GNP.
4. At the equilibrium level, leakages equal injections.
5. A change in the demand curve changes the level of GNP, in accordance with the multiplier.
6. The slope of the leakage (savings) curve depicts the multiplier.

Here is the chapter we have been waiting for, where the supply and demand for GNP finally meet. It is a lengthy chapter, but its length results mainly from the fact that the same ideas are presented several times and in several ways. Here we can go directly to the core of things, to be sure that you understand clearly how the forces of supply and demand create an equilibrium level of GNP.

PHYSICAL VS. MONETARY GNP

Our chapter begins by presenting an explanation of how supply and demand interact to bring about an actual physical volume of output – a GNP in tonnages, if you will – given various physical amounts of inputs (man-hours of labor and machine hours of capital). This brings us back to the idea of the aggregate production function that we last studied in Chapter Twenty-one. We recall that the aggregate production function that we last studied in Chapter 21. We recall that the aggregate production function was a *short-run supply curve* for total output, showing us how much GNP could be produced as we increased inputs of land, labor, and capital. In our last half dozen chapters we have been talking about the demand curve for output, and it now remains only to combine them.

What does the demand curve for output look like? It is not a downward-sloping curve because we are not relating the quantity of GNP to the "price" of GNP, but to the inputs of factors to make GNP. The more factors we employ, the larger will their demand for GNP be. From the shape of the propensity to consume schedule, we know the demand for consumption goods will not rise as fast as income and will not fall below a "bottom." This enables us to draw a generalized demand curve (which we will investigate again, Figure 29-1), giving us a picture of an equilibrium GNP.

As we know from the text, we will soon be working with a different set of supply and demand curves for GNP, both expressed in *dollar*

FIGURE 29-1

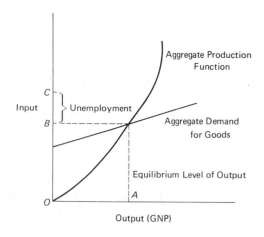

Output (GNP)

values. Why, then, do we begin with the aggregate production function?

The answer is that Figure 29-1 makes clear that an equilibrium volume of GNP – a GNP where the demand for output is just equal to the supply of output – need not be a volume that is large enough to bring full employment. In the figure, we might have *OC* amount of factors seeking production, but as we can see, only *OB* will be employed. Later we will talk of equilibrium levels of GNP in terms of expenditure levels, but here we get a chance to look directly at the physical outputs and the physical quantities of goods demanded, and to see that there is no necessary connection between equilibrium outputs and desired states of employment.

THE 45° DIAGRAM

Now we move to the conventional manner of showing GNP equilibrium. Because it is very important for you to understand this, we present it in a semiquiz form, so that you can test your comprehension as we go.

First, we want to convert our aggregate production function, which is a schedule of inputs of labor and machine hours, into a schedule of incomes. Therefore we will relabel the axes in Figure 29-2, with GNP, as before on the horizontal axis, and GNI on the vertical axis.

Exercise 1. What is the relation between GNP and GNI? It is an _____ . Suppose that the money value of $C + I + G + X$ is \$1,500,000,000. What must be the value of GNI?_____ . Suppose that GNP falls to \$1,000,000,000. What is the value of GNI?_____ Do you understand that GNI is by definition always equal to GNP? Complete the two definitional equations that establish this identity: $C +$_____ $\equiv F +$

Exercise 2. Draw a supply curve of *incomes* on the graph above. On the horizontal axis, mark off a level of GNP = *OA*. On the vertical axis,

FIGURE 29-2

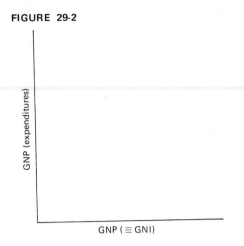

GNP (expenditures)

GNP (≡ GNI)

expenditures on _____ , _____ , and _____ (we can forget exports for simplicity's sake). In the short run we assume that the demand for *I* and for *G* are fixed, but we know that the demand for *C* is a function of income. We call this function the _____ .

Exercise 4. Draw a total demand function for GNP, in the graph above, showing that it is made up of a fixed demand for *I* and *G* and a growing demand for *C*. Now check yourself so far against Figure 29-3.

Exercise 5. In the space below draw in just the total supply curve for incomes and the total demand for output.

mark the corresponding level of GNI = *OB*. What must be the relation of *OA* and *OB*?

Do the same for another level of GNP = *OX,* and GNI = *OY.* Indicate the points on the graph, where *OX* = *OY* and *OA* = *OB.* Draw a line through these points down to the origin. What must be the angle of this line? _____ Do you clearly understand the meaning of this line? *It says that for any GNP there will be a supply of incomes that is equal to the GNP.*

Exercise 3. Now for the demand function. Total demand for GNP will be the sum of

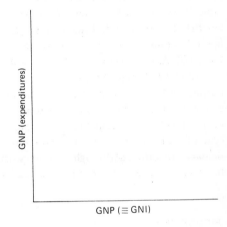

GNP (expenditures)

GNP (≡ GNI)

FIGURE 29-3

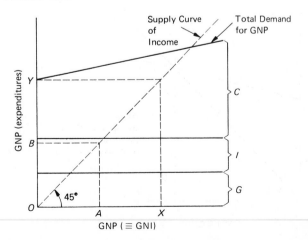

GNP (expenditures)

Supply Curve of Income   Total Demand for GNP

Y

B

45°

O   A   X

GNP (≡ GNI)

C

I

G

Draw a dotted line from their intersection to the output axis, labeling the intersection point *B* and the equilibrium amount of output *A*.

Now we will do something not in the text. The length of the line *OA* represents a certain amount of *C + G + I* (we will ignore exports). Arbitrarily mark off *OA* into three sections, representing these three flows of output. The height of the vertical line *AB* represents a certain amount of cost (or income, the same thing), *F, T,* and *D*. Arbitrarily mark off *AB* into these three costs. Now, can you prove that *C + G + I* must equal *F + T + D*?

The proof is simple. Connect point *B* with the income axis, marking the place *C*. Because we are starting from our 45° line, we know that *OA* must equal *OC*. We also know that *OC* is the same length as *AB* (we drew *OC* to be the same length). Therefore it follows that the *C + G + I* line (*OA*) must be exactly equal to the *F + T + D* line (*AB*). Any problem? See Figure 29-4.

Exercise 6. Would this be true if we chose an output level to the right of the equilibrium? Let us try it in Figure 29–5. Here the money value of output is *OA*. This means that the incomes or the cost of that output is *OC*. But now look at the demand function. Although output worth *OA* has been produced, only output _____ has been

FIGURE 29-5

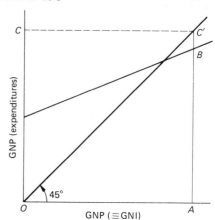

demanded. Some of the *C + G + I* represented by the line *OA* has not been bought. In fact, we can see that the size of the unbought output must be *CB. This is our demand gap.*

Exercise 7. Try it with an output level to the left of equilibrium. See Figure 29-6.

What is the value of output? _____ What is the value of income produced? _____ What is the value of demand for output? _____ Is demand smaller than, equal to, or larger than output? What is the value of the excess of demand over the costs of output? _____

FIGURE 29-4

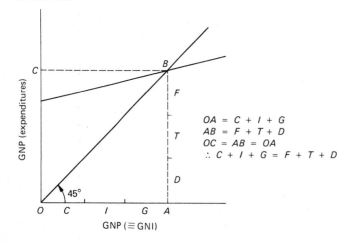

$$OA = C + I + G$$
$$AB = F + T + D$$
$$OC = AB = OA$$
$$\therefore C + I + G = F + T + D$$

FIGURE 29-6

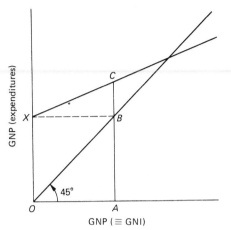

Exercise 8. How about leakages and injections? Can we explain equilibrium in these terms? Once again let us use our familiar diagram in Figure 29-7 and let us assume that the value of output is *OA*. What is the value of *incomes* (costs) at *OA?*_____ What is the value of expenditure (demand)? _____ Are all incomes being spent?_____ The difference must be a leakage, _____ . Further, can you see that at all levels of GNP above equilibrium, incomes will be larger than expenditures? *If income is not being spent, it is being saved.* Lightly color in the triangle that represents

FIGURE 29-7

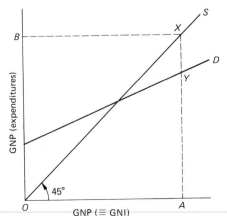

leakages. Can you see why these leakages will force GNP back to equilibrium?

Now suppose that we wanted to raise GNP to *OA*. We could do so by offsetting the leakages with injections. In the language of our earlier chapters, we could close a demand gap with added investment or with additional government spending. Assume that we do increase expenditures. Draw a new demand curve *D'D'* for GNP that will make *OA* an equilibrium level for GNP. At what point will the new demand curve *D'D'* cut the supply curve? _____ Can you see that there are no longer any leakages at point *X?* The leakage triangle has been pushed to the right as the demand curve has risen. *OA* is now a stable equilibrium because total demand _____ equals total supply_____ . See the completed diagram in Figure 29-8.

Exercise 9. There is a simpler diagram to show the crosscurrents of leakages and injections (or savings and investment). This is a diagram that concentrates only on the dynamic elements in GNP and ignores the passive element of consumption. It is really a diagram that shows the interplay between our leakage triangle and our injection band, as Figure 29-9 shows. Here it is obvious where the equilibrium GNP will lie. We can see that any higher GNP would be impossible because net leakages would cause GNP to contract; and any level below would be equally impossible because net injections would cause GNP to rise. For practice, draw vertical lines from points *X* and *Y,* and compare the leakages and injections for each.

Exercise 10. We want to add a last touch to our graphic analysis – the multiplier. Let us do it on both diagrams in Figure 29-10. Here we show the same economy in equilibrium at *OA,* in two diagrams. In both diagrams demand jumps by the amount ΔD, and a new equilibrium is established at *OB.* Now, with the *same* increase in demand, ΔD, could the level of GNP rise to *OC?*

If we forget about the diagrams for a moment, of course it is possible. A given injection can give us a small or a large change in GNP depending on

FIGURE 29-8

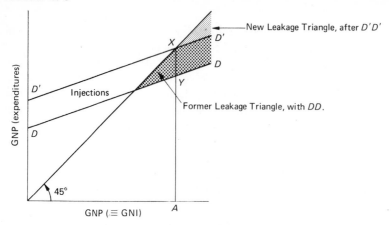

New Leakage Triangle, after $D'D'$

D'

D

X

Injections

Y

Former Leakage Triangle, with DD.

D'

D

GNP (expenditures)

45°

GNP ($\equiv$ GNI)

A

whether the multiplier is large or small. In turn the multiplier depends on the leakage fraction, the m.p.s. And in turn the leakage fraction is shown on a diagram by the *slope of the demand line,* or *the slope of the savings line.* In the diagram at the right draw in two leakage curves that would correspond to a high multiplier and a low multiplier, passing both curves through on the GNP line.

Obviously the high multiplier line will slope far to the right of the low multiplier line. Drop a line from the point where each cuts D' to the GNP axis, and compare how the *same* increase in investment (from D to D') has brought different

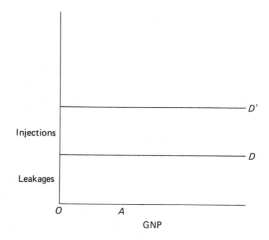

Injections

D'

D

Leakages

O A

GNP

FIGURE 29-9

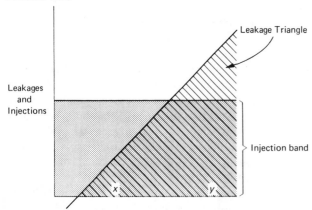

Leakage Triangle

Leakages and Injections

Injection band

x y

238

equilibrium positions for GNP. Do you remember the multiplier formula? _____
Can you see that the distance from D to D' corresponds to ΔI? That the change from OA to the new equilibrium position for GNP corresponds to ΔY? That the slope of the line you have drawn is the graphic equivalent of *mps*?

FIGURE 29-10

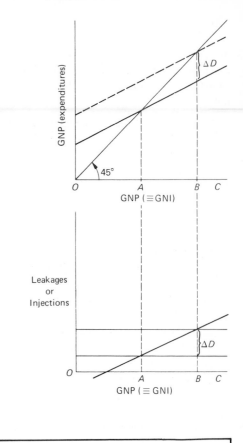

A NOTE ON INTENDED AND UNINTENDED *S* AND *I*

In our review exercises we do not usually go over material in the boxes. But just a word on ex ante and ex post savings and investment.

1. *In the national income accounts S and I are defined to be equal at any level of income.* (Savings is income minus consumption; investment is income minus consumption: *S* and *I* are thus identities.)

2. In real life, people try to save and to invest various amounts. *These intended (ex ante = "looking forward") flows of S and I are almost surely not equal.*

3. *At any moment in time, intended savings and investment are accompanied by unintended savings and investment.* Examples: a family may intend to save $1000, but because its income rises or falls, it finds that at a given moment its actual savings are only $500 or $1500. (It may later remedy this, but for the moment, total savings are larger or smaller than intended savings.) Or a merchant may desire to invest in $1000 worth of inventory, but because business is better or worse than he expected, his actual inventories may be lower or higher than he planned. It is his actual change in inventory that counts as "investment" in balancing the national accounts, although this change may not be what he intended, or what he will try to achieve in the future.

4. *Equilibrium diagrams show how changes in the level of income will bring about*

equality in the flows of intended saving and inestment. Changes in income bring about equality by giving rise to unintended saving and investment, which change people's minds about their subsequent actions.

5. *When we talk about the dynamic forces that change income we always speak of ex ante, intended* S *and* I, *and we analyze the effects of savings flows that are not identical with investment flows.* When we analyze a given income (at any level), we discuss it in terms of the national income accounts in which savings and investment are always identical. Sometimes we can identify the "unintended" portion of investment (usually in inventory swings); more often we cannot.

QUIZ

Are you ready for a quiz, after this long exercise? It's probably a good time to consolidate your knowledge, so do this test carefully and thoughtfully.

__ 1. In Figure 29–11 the demand for output is
   a. *AB.*
   b. *OA.*
   c. *BC.*

__ 2. The cost of output is
   a. *AB.*
   b. *OX.*
   c. *AC.*

__ 3. The multiplier is
   a. indicated by the slope of *XB.*
   b. indicated by the slope of *OC.*
   c. indeterminate from the diagram.

__ 4. The line *OC* is
   a. the aggregate production function.
   b. the supply curve of income
   c. the demand curve for output.

__ 5. the line *XB* represents
   a. $C + G + I + X.$
   b. $F + T + D.$
   c. both of the above.

FIGURE 29-11

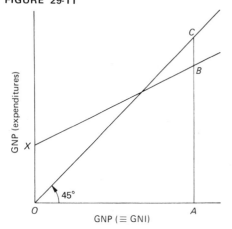

__ 6. At output *OA,* the diagram shows
   a. a demand gap.
   b. a demand surplus.
   c. an equilibrium.

__ 7. The line *OX* represents
   a. the "bottom."
   b. dissaving to sustain demand when income is zero.
   c. both of the above.

__ 8. A fall in injections would lengthen
   a. *OA.*
   b. *BC.*
   c. *AB.*

__ 9. The 45° line shows that $F + T + D = C + G + I + X$
   a. at equilibrium only.
   b. at all values for GNP.
   c. when there is no leakage triangle.

__10. The diagram indicates
   a. where full-employment GNP should be.
   b. how much unemployment there will be
   c. where GNP will settle.

TEN MORE QUESTIONS, ALL DIFFICULT ONES
                                  T F

11. An equilibrium GNP is determined solely by changes in the demand curve. __ __

12. The supply curve of income never changes its slope. __ __

13. Equilibrium income results from the interplay of injections and leakages. __ __

14. Given injections, the multiplier is determined solely by leakages; given leakages, solely by the size of injections. __ __

15. The GNP diagrams show adjustment over time. __ __

16. At equilibrium levels for GNP, leakages are less than injections. __ __

17. The aggregate production function is always a 45° line. __ __

18. A 45° slope on a leakage curve means a multiplier of 1. __ __

T F

19. Intended investment in the long run determines the size of savings because it establishes the level of income.

20. There is no difference except exposition between the formula for the multiplier and the slope of the leakage curve.

— —

— —

1. Intended savings always are larger than actual savings.

2. Savings and investment are always equal, ex post, regardless of the size of income.

3. Intended savings and investment are brought into equality at any moment in time by unintended saving and investment.

4. Intended saving and investment tend toward equality over time because of changes in income.

5. Ex ante, if savings equal investment, income will not change.

— —

— —

— —

— —

— —

Answers:

1. a	8. b	15. F
2. c	9. b	16. F
3. a	10. c	17. F
4. b	11. T	18. T
5. a	12. T	19. T
6. a	13. T	20. T
7. c	14. T	

Answers:

1. F	3. T	5. T
2. T	4. T	

Money

30

LEARNING OBJECTIVES

Here is what you should concentrate on:
1. What is the supply of money?
2. What is a bank's "excess reserve"?
3. How do bank loans expand through the system?

4. How does the Federal Reserve change the money supply? Be sure you understand the technique of open market operations.

This chapter introduces us to the mysteries of money — and, in particular, to how the supply of money is expanded and contracted in our fractional reserve banking system, and to how the Federal Reserve System maintains control over the supply of money.

WHAT IS MONEY?

It is whatever we use to make payments with. In particular, we call money currency outside the banking system (any money inside the banking system counts as part of its reserves, which are

not money) plus the total of checking deposits. Thus, if you deposit some currency in a bank and, accept a checking account for it, the total money supply has not changed as of that instant. Savings deposits or government savings bonds that can be cashed at a moment's notice are important liquid assets of the public called "near money," but they do not technically qualify as part of the money supply, because we do not carry out business or personal payments with them. So if you deposit your currency in a savings account at a commercial bank we would have to say the total money supply had decreased.

HOW DOES THE MONEY SYSTEM WORK?

The following exercise leads you step-by-step through the T account analysis. A clear grasp of how the banks work as a single system to supply us with money requires some review and practice. With pencil in hand follow through the T account analysis.

First we open up a brand new bank (called Bank A) by depositing $100,000 of currency and checks in it. Suppose our bank sends the whole amount of its initial deposits to the Federal Reserve Bank. (Actually, of course, it will keep some in its own vaults as till money.) What will our bank's balance sheet look like? Very simple:

Bank A

Assets	Liabilities
Cash and at Fed + $100,000	Deposits + $100,000

Now our bank is perfectly liquid – but it would not be making any money.

How can a bank make money? It can lend or invest part of its deposits. How much? That depends on the reserve ratio established by the Federal Reserve Board. Let us say that the reserve is set at 20 percent.

Our bank has $100,000 in deposits. With a 20 percent reserve ratio it must keep how much as reserves?_____. How much will it therefore be able to lend or invest?

Suppose now that our bank decides to lend out an amount equal to its full excess reserves of $80,000 by opening a new checking account in Mr. Smith's name.

Here is what its T account looks like when it has done so:

Bank A

Assets	Liabilities
Cash and at Fed $100,000	$100,000 (original depositors)
Loan 80,000	80,000 deposit of Mr. Smith

Note that Mr. Smith's signed loan agreement is an asset of the bank. It is exactly mirrored by a new liability – the new deposit of Mr. Smith. Note also that total deposits have now gone up to $180,000. Is there enough reserve to cover this at 20 percent? Decide for yourself:

Total deposits _____

20 percent of deposits _____

Reserve: Cash and at Fed _____

There is more than enough. Now what happens? Mr. Smith draws out his deposit to pay a large contract fee to Mr. Jones who banks at Bank B. What does Bank A's T account now look like?

Bank A

Assets	Liabilities
Cash and at Fed $20,000	Deposits $100,000
Loan 80,000	

What has happened? Mr. Smith has drawn $80,000 out of his account, and this sum has also disappeared from our "cash and at Fed" asset. Bank B has sent the check to the Fed to be "cleared" where they debited Bank A and credited B for $80,000.

Is our Bank A still within the law? Figure for yourself:

Total deposits _____

20 percent of deposits (required reserve) _____

Cash and at Fed _____

All is well. But what of the $80,000 check that Mr. Smith sent to Jones? Jones deposits it at Bank B. Now let us trace the changes in Bank B's T account (we will forget its previously existing assets and liabilities):

Bank B

Assets	Liabilities
Cash $80,000	Deposits $80,000 (Jones)

Bank B now has excess reserves. You figure them out:

Its required reserves (at 20 per cent) are _____

Its excess reserves are _____

Suppose Mr. Doe now comes into Bank B seeking a loan. Bank B will open a $64,000 account in his name, so that its T account will look like this:

Bank B

Assets	Liabilities
Cash and at Fed $80,000	Deposits: Mr. Jones $80,000
Loan to Doe _____	Mr. Doe _____

Bank B still has more than enough reserves, as you can quickly figure:

Its deposits are now _____

Its required reserves are _____

Its excess reserves are _____

Now it is Doe's turn to draw down his deposit created by the loan. Suppose he pays $64,000 to Mr. Roe who banks at Bank C. What does Bank B's T account now look like?

Bank B

Assets	Liabilities
Cash _____	Deposits: Mr. Jones _____
Loan _____	
	Mr. Doe _____

You had better check yourself on this. Cash is now $16,000 (the original $80,000 minus the $64,000 withdrawal). Deposits are $80,000; Jones' deposit is unchanged and Doe's is down to zero. Bank B's required reserves are therefore 20 percent of _____ , or _____ . Its remaining cash is _____ , which is exactly 20 percent of its deposits.

By now you have the idea and it should be little trouble to fill out Table 30–1 below showing what happened after Bank A made its first loan. First fill in the table, then check with the answer below.

TABLE 30–1

	Additions to Assets	Additions to Liabilities
Bank	New Loans	New Deposits
A	$80,000	——
B	——	——
C	——	——
D	——	——
E	——	——
F	——	——
G	——	——
H	——	——
Total ——		Total ——

Answers:

TABLE 30–1

	Additions to Assets	Additions to Liabilities
Bank	New Loans	New Deposits
A	$ 80,000.00	$100,000.00
B	64,000.00	80,000.00
C	51,200.00	64,000.00
D	40,960.00	51,200.00
E	32,768.00	40,960.00
F	26,214.00	32,768.00
G	20,971.00	26,214.00
H	16,777.22	20,971.52
		16,777.22
Total	$332,891.14	$432,891.14

THE MONEY MULTIPLIER

If we had carried the above table to Bank Z its addition to the money supply would have been tiny. How much will the total addition to deposits be when the new loans approach zero? The formula is exactly like the multiplier:

$$\text{New deposits} = \frac{1}{\text{reserve ratio}} \times \text{original increase in money.}$$

In this case the original increase was $100,000 and the reserve ratio was 20 percent or 1/5. Therefore the total amount of new money that can be created is

$$\frac{1}{1/5} \times \$100,000 = \$500,000$$

As the text demonstrates, this money-creating system works the same way in reverse.

What is the difference between the national income multiplier and the banking multiplier? The national income multiplier is concerned with the successive respendings of money in the production of goods and services. The banking multiplier simply creates new money.

CONTROLS OF THE FEDERAL RESERVE SYSTEM

We know that the Federal Reserve exists mainly to control the supply of money. How does it do so? The Fed has three important tools in its kit and the first two are simple to understand:

1. The Fed can instantly create excess reserves or can wipe them out by *lowering or raising the required reserve ratio.*

Suppose Bank A's T account looks like this:

Assets		Liabilities
Cash	$20,000	Deposits $100,000
Loan and Investments	80,000	

If the Fed lowered reserve ratios to 15 percent, what is A's required reserve? _____ Its actual reserve? _____ How much can it now lend or invest? _____

2. Changing the discount rate can influence banks to be easy or tight with their lending policies because it will be cheaper or more expensive for member banks to borrow extra reserves from their Federal Reserve Banks.

3. The last tool is the most important control to grasp. The Fed can buy or sell government bonds on the open market. Let us begin by going back to the original deposit of $100,000 in Bank A. Actually, opening that brand new bank did not increase the supply of money at all! Why? Because all the deposits that started our bank in business must have come from existing currency in the possession of the public or, more likely, from checks the founders drew on other banks. When Bank A started up in business, somewhere else in the economy other banks were poorer by the amount that A was richer

Obviously new money could have been created only if the original deposit for Bank A had *not* come from another commercial bank. Where could it have come from? *From the Federal Reserve Bank itself.* When the Fed buys bonds, it does not pay for them with a check on a commercial bank. It pays for them with a check drawn on itself! When these checks are deposited in commercial banks, they constitute additional deposits that are not offset by decreases in deposits in other banks.

T ACCOUNTS OF THE FED*

To create money through bank credit is remarkable, but to create also the reserves behind that money is uncanny. To understand how it works let us follow through the changes in the T accounts of a Federal Reserve District Bank (say, the district bank in New York). A simplified T account on a given day might look like this.

The FED's T Account

Cash deposits of members $100,000,000	Deposits owed member banks $100,000,000

Now assume the Board of Governors of the Federal Reserve System wants to expand the reserves of the banking system. To do so, the Board's Open Market Committee purchases $1,000,000 in government bonds.

Working through bond dealers around the country, the Fed buys bonds from a large number of sellers. Suppose we take notice of one seller, Mr. Brown, who does business at our original Bank A. We left Bank A after it had loaned $80,000 to Smith (who paid Jones who banks at Bank B), and you will recall that after Bank B cleared its check against A, Bank A was left with a T account as follows:

Bank A

Assets	Liabilities
Cash and at Fed $20,000 Loan $80,000	Deposits $100,000

*The following analysis is not in the text, but it is simple to follow, and will help your understanding of the Fed's operations.

Now let us return to Mr. Brown, who has just sold a $10,000 bond to the Fed. Brown deposits the $10,000 check in Bank A. The Bank sends the new deposit along to the Fed for addition to its reserves. Bank A now has a T account of:

Bank A

Assets	Liabilities
Cash and at Fed $30,000 Loans 80,000	Original deposits $100,000 Deposit of Mr. Brown 10,000

You should notice one thing particularly: As the result of the Fed's purchase of bonds, Bank A has increased its deposits from $100,000 to $110,000 and its deposits at the Fed from $20,000 to $30,000. To cover deposits of $110,000 only $22,000 in reserves is required. As a result Bank A now has excess reserves of $8,000, which it can lend and send through the multiplying process.

Next observe what has happened to the T accounts of the Federal Reserve Bank.

The FED's T Account*

Assets	Liabilities
Cash deposits of members $100,000,000 Securities bought from Mr. Brown 10,000	Deposits owed members $100,000,000 Deposits from Brown's bank (Bank A) 10,000

*For simplification we ignore the fact that there are twelve different Federal Reserve District Banks, and that it is unlikely that the checks from bond purchases would all land in one of them. The effect on the money supply of the country is the same whether it is concentrated in one Federal Reserve District Bank or spread about through several.

In similar fashion all the rest of the $1,000,000 comes back to the Fed just like the $10,000 from Mr. Brown. When all of the sellers of bonds have deposited their checks and their banks have deposited them at the Fed the T account of the Fed is:

The FED

Assets	Liabilities
Deposits from member banks $100,000,000	Deposits owed member banks $100,000,000
Government bonds just bought 1,000,000	Deposits from the banks of bond sellers 1,000,000

At this point banks all over the country have taken $1,000,000 in Federal Reserve checks, their customers have $1,000,000 more in deposits, and the banks have added $1,000,000 to their reserves at the Fed.

But this is just the "first round" of the money-creating process. Bank A, as we noticed above, had $8,000 excess reserves from the $10,000 worth of bonds its customer, Mr. Brown, had sold to the Fed. Obviously, in the economy as a whole there are banks with $800,000 of excess reserves ready to lend for the "second round" of the multiplying process. When the second round has been completed the T account of the Fed would look — *just like the last one!*

Why would there not be a new additional $800,000 in the assets and liabilities on the Fed's T accounts? Because the $1,000,000 in deposits *simply gets shifted about into the reserves of different banks when loans are made, but the total deposits with the Fed do not change.* The banks lending $800,000, of course, lose that amount of reserves to other banks. But it is simply a bookkeeping operation of the Fed to debit the reserves (deposits) of some banks and

credit others. The total on deposit with the Fed remains the same. Only its ownership shifts about as the total of new loans rises.

QUIZ

Our chapter covers a number of matters besides the mechanism of monetary expansion and Federal Reserve control. Most of these are not difficult. We will simply assume that you have grasped them, and will test you on these matters, as well as the problems we have just covered.

___ 1. The money supply consists of
   a. checking accounts and cash in banks.
   b. currency in the hands of the public plus checking accounts.
   c. currency in the hands of the public plus checking accounts plus cash at Fed.

___ 2. In anticipation of Christmas, the public usually withdraws large amounts of cash from its checking accounts. The result is to
   a. increase the supply of money.
   b. decrease the supply of money.
   c. leave the supply unchanged.

___ 3. The main purpose of changing reserve ratios is to:
   a. protect the public.
   b. control the amount of money.
   c. protect the banking system.

___ 4. A bank can lend or invest an amount equal to
   a. its deposits.
   b. its reserves.
   c. its excess reserves.

___ 5. The limit to the expansion of the money supply is determined by
   a. reserve ratios.
   b. discount rates.
   c. bond yields.

___ 6. All banks working together can expand the money supply because
   a. they do not lose their deposits from the total system.

b. they cannot face a run on the whole system.

c. they make loans to each other.

_ 7. If a bond is issued with a value of $1,000 and a "coupon" (a stated interest payment) of $50, and the bond sells, after issuance, at a price of $1,025, the yield has

a. gone up.

b. gone down.

c. stayed the same.

_ 8. When the Fed sells bonds,

a. it decreases the money supply.

b. it increases it.

c. it does not affect it.

_ 9. By raising reserve ratios, the Fed

a. creates excess reserves.

b. diminishes excess reserves.

c. leaves them unchanged.

_10. Open market operations affect the banking system because

a. banks receive deposits from or give up deposits to an institution that is not another commercial bank.

b. banks gain or lose deposits from one another.

c. this changes reserve requirements.

_11. The Fed is most effective when it tries to

a. increase bank loans.

b. decrease bank loans.

c. no difference.

_12. An elastic money supply would not be needed if

a. all prices were free to move instantly.

b. all prices were sticky.

c. all prices moved in the same direction.

Answers:

1. b	5. a	9. b
2. c	6. a	10. a
3. b	7. b	11. b
4. c	8. a	12. a

A TRUE-FALSE QUIZ   T F

1. If you draw money out of a savings account, you increase the supply of money.   _ _

2. The amount of actual currency in a commercial bank is less than its required reserves.   T F _ _

3. The reserves of banks at the Fed can be converted into currency by the owners of these deposits.   _ _

4. The process of buying bonds sends yields down.   _ _

5. Required reserves are the difference between the assets of a bank and its liabilities.   _ _

6. When a bank makes a loan, it simultaneously acquires both an asset and a liability.   _ _

7. A bank that loaned more than it was permitted to by law would probably find that its reserves were no longer at the required level.   _ _

8. A bank with excess reserves will only lend or invest if it is profitable to do so.   _ _

9. The multiplier formula for an increase in money is: $\Delta M = r \times \Delta D$, where M is money supply, r the reserve ratio, and D net deposits.   _ _

10. Fluctuations in bond yields result from changes in bond prices.   _ _

11. The discount rate serves as a means by which the Fed can bring quick changes in bank reserves.   _ _

12. When the Fed buys government bonds, it does not pay for them with a check on a commercial bank.   _ _

13. The gold cover today applies only to Federal Reserve Notes (that is, printed currency).   _ _

14. Printing money does not increase the money supply.   _ _

15. Any contractual price is "sticky."   _ _

Answers:

1. T	6. T	11. F
2. T	7. T	12. T
3. T	8. T	13. F
4. T	9. F	14. T
5. F	10. T	15. T

A DAY OF OPEN MARKET OPERATIONS

Paul Meek

*One of the ways in which monetary policy is put into effect
by the Federal Reserve is through "open market operations."
These operations are the fine-tuning instruments of the
monetary system. Here Paul Meek describes a day of open market
operations and discusses the considerations that guide
the policymakers.*

The Manager of the Federal Reserve System Open Market Account has made his decision. He will buy about $250 million in United States Treasury bills, which mature within the next twelve months. The time is just before noon on the Tuesday before Thanksgiving Day. In a room on the eighth floor of the Federal Reserve Bank of New York, six securities traders gather around an officer of the Securities Department to receive instructions.

Each of the six returns to his seat around a U-shaped trading desk. Each presses a button on a telephone console with wires linked to the nation's 20 or so primary dealers in United States Government securities. The trader's ring sounds a buzzer in the trading room of one of the three or four Government securities dealers he has been assigned to call.

"Jack," says the Reserve Bank's trader, "What can you offer in bills for cash delivery?"

Taking a quick look at the list of Treasury bills which the dealer firm owns, Jack replies, "Bill, I can offer you for cash $5 million of January 9 bills to yield 4.45 percent – $10 million of January 23 bills at 4.50 – $10 million of March 20 bills at 4.90 – and $8 million of May 15 bills at 5.12."

From Paul Meek, *Open Market Operations* (New York: Federal Reserve Bank of New York).

Bill says, "Can I have those offerings firm for a few minutes?"

"Sure."

Within a few minutes the "go-around of the Government securities market is completed. Each of the six Reserve Bank traders records the results of his three or four calls on special forms that the officer-in-charge attaches to a board until the full array of individual dealer offerings is before him. Addition quickly shows that dealers have offered $482 million in Treasury bills for sale for cash – that is, with delivery and payment that very day.

A glance at a list of the Federal Reserve System's current holdings enables the experienced Reserve Bank officer to choose the issues likely to be most useful for future System operations. Seeking the best – that is, the highest – yield on each issue, the officer checks a large quotation board across the open end of the U-shaped trading desk. This shows yields to maturity as they were in the market just before the "go-around" began. After selecting the specific offers he will accept, the officer informs the traders and they return to their telephone consoles to tell the dealers.

"Jack, we'll take the $5 million of January 9 bills at 4:45 and the $10 million of January 23 bills at 4:50, both for cash; no, thanks, on the others."

Within thirty minutes from the time the initial decision was made, all the calls have been completed. The manager has selected and purchased $242 million in Treasury bills for cash. The leg work and the paper work remain. On the same day, messengers from the commercial banks that handle the dealers' paper work will deliver to the Federal Reserve Bank of New York the specific Treasury bills purchased and the Federal Reserve, in turn, will credit on its books the reserve accounts of the banks concerned. The banks will credit the dealers' accounts with them with the proceeds of the sale.

The day's open market purchases will not retain their separate identities in the Federal Reserve System's weekly report on the monetary system. They will be merged with all other operations conducted during the week which ends on Wednesday, the next day. The figures, normally released to the press at 4 P.M. on Thursday in New York and Washington, will be released this week on Friday afternoon because of the holiday.

The next morning many officers of banks, financial corporations, and business concerns will turn automatically to the weekly Federal Reserve statement appearing in leading newspapers to see if there have been any significant shifts in the reserve positions of the nation's banks. All who are charged with raising money or investing funds for their firms know that changes in the availability of bank reserves normally have a major impact on the cost and availability of borrowed money in the national market for credit. They will spot the Federal Reserve's large open market purchases in the pre-Thanksgiving week and ask themselves: "Is the Federal Reserve only moving to make it possible for the banks to meet the public's seasonal demands for cash and credit? Or is it moving to increase – or reduce after allowance for seasonal factors – the ability of banks to extend credit?" Such questions can rarely be answered on the basis of a single week's figures. Only over a period of several weeks will

financial men be able to sort out any gradual shift in Federal Reserve policy from transitory fluctuations in bank reserves.

The Federal Reserve System uses open market purchases and sales of United States government securities as its most flexible means of influencing bank reserve positions and the availability of bank credit. These operations are continuously directed at two objectives. The first is the workaday one of heading off the stresses imposed on the monetary mechanism by seasonal, regional or accidental shifts in money flows. The second is the basic long-run goal of promoting a healthy domestic economy – one marked by a high, but sustainable, rate of economic growth, high employment, and reasonable price stability. In other words, the Federal Reserve System employs open market operations both to assure that the nation's monetary machinery runs smoothly and to encourage realization of the nation's economic potential.

ALL PART OF A DAY'S WORK

Each day presents a new challenge to the Manager of the Open Market Account. Yet each day has much in common with every other day. Let us go back to that Tuesday before Thanksgiving Day and follow the developments which led to the purchase of $242 million in Government securities. On such a day, as on all days, the Manager must bear in mind the current directive and the consensus of the last FOMC [Federal Open Market Committee] meeting. Let us suppose that the directive states that "open market operations should continue to foster money and credit conditions conducive to sustainable economic expansion," and that these broad objectives are to be pursued by maintaining about the prevailing conditions in the money market.

The main outlines of the task which lies ahead are at least roughly visible to the Manager early on Tuesday morning. He has before him the preceding day's projections of the behavior expected of the factors affecting reserves over the coming three weeks. . . . . Tuesday's projections will be available a bit later at about 10:45 A.M. The projections are based upon the behavior of reserve factors over the same calendar period during the past five years and take into account any special factors such as a foreign purchase of gold.

Yesterday's projections indicate that the decline in float at the month-end is expected to combine with the seasonal rise in currency in circulation during the next week to draw reserves in large volume from the banking system. A seasonal rise in required reserves associated with higher loan demands may add slightly to the drain on reserves. It thus appears that the Manager will have to supply reserves in substantial amounts just to maintain the existing degree of firmness in the money market. Indeed, the day before, Monday, the Manager provided $280 million in reserves by making $65 million in repurchase agreements with dealers early in the afternoon, after buying $215 million in Treasury bills outright for cash in the morning.

Dealer Conference

At 9:15 A.M., two officers of the Securities Department hurry to a tenth-floor conference room to meet with one or two representatives of a Government securities dealer firm. Dealers confer every business day on a rotating schedule with the Reserve Bank officers directly responsible for the conduct of open market operations. At these conferences, the dealers comment on market developments and on any matter of interest to the firm. The Reserve Bank officers listen and ask questions.

This morning, representatives of three dealers are scheduled to appear, one after the other. At the first conference, a senior partner of a dealer firm observes that the market has been rather quiet during the last few days, and that he has been rather disappointed by the lack of corporate demand for Treasury bills. He finds that insurance companies and pension funds are holding off on bond purchases until the $100 million bond issue of the XYZ Corporation due to be offered on Wednesday hits the market. The dealer gives his views on whether the Treasury should issue short-term or long-term securities, or both, in meeting its cash needs, and indicates the kind of reception he thinks the market would give the new issues. After answering questions asked by one of the Reserve Bank officers, the dealer departs at 9:30 A.M.

Two representatives of a second dealer firm enter the conference room. Among other things, these representatives indicate that while the market as a whole has been quiet, their firm has handled some sizable transactions in the last few days. They feel that many investors have large cash positions and are merely waiting for more attractive yields. One also feels that conditions in the money market were a little tight yesterday afternoon even after the System's intervention; his firm had to pay a relatively high interest rate to obtain financing for its position through loans and repurchase agreements negotiated with banks and others. The second firm's representatives leave at 9:45 A.M., and the vice president in charge of the dealer operations of a New York City bank enters. The third conference covers much the same ground. The last dealer departs at 10 o'clock, and the Reserve Bank officers return to their offices to prepare for the daily call from the U.S. Treasury.

The Treasury Call

Each morning shortly after ten, the Fiscal Assistant Secretary of the Treasury uses the direct telephone line linking the Treasury and the New York Reserve Bank to compare notes with the Manager or his deputy on the outlook for the Treasury's cash balance at the Reserve Banks.

Their objective is to try to smooth out fluctuations in the Treasury's balance at the Reserve Banks and to minimize disruptive effects of changes in the balance on member bank reserve positions. They estimate the amount of funds that need to be transferred from the Treasury's Tax and Loan accounts at commercial banks to the Reserve Banks in order to maintain a fairly stable working balance in the face of checks they expect to be presented for payment at the Reserve Banks. (The Treasury channels a large part of its receipts from taxes and from sales of its securities through Tax and Loan accounts to reduce the sudden impact of these large flows on bank reserves.)

Today, the Assistant Secretary tells the Reserve Bank officer that his projections of daily Government receipts and expenditures indicate that the Treasury will need to transfer $100 million from Treasury Tax and Loan accounts at about 80 large commercial banks across the country (the Class C banks) to its account at the Federal Reserve Bank. This will be in addition to calls previously scheduled on Tax and Loan accounts at other commercial banks. The Reserve Bank official notes that projections of the New York Bank's staff point to a need to call about $140 million to maintain the Treasury balance at about the desired level. However, since bank reserve positions are expected to be under pressure from seasonal factors, the Reserve Bank officer and Assistant Secretary agree that the call be limited to 15 percent of the previous night's Treasury balances at the "C" banks – about $96 million.

The conversation over, the Reserve officer dials another officer in the Bank to inform him that the Treasury has decided to make a special call today on the "C" banks. By 11 A.M., the large banks will have been informed that they must transfer 15 percent of the Treasury's deposits with them at Monday's close to their district Reserve Banks. . .

Getting the "Feel" of the Market

In the meantime, the Government securities market has become active. At the Trading Desk, opening quotations are beginning to come in. Several of the traders around the Desk are talking to dealers to learn if any trend is developing. Other traders have a pretty good fix on orders to be executed for foreign accounts or for Treasury trust accounts. Reports have arrived from the research and statistics departments on dealer positions and on the previous day's reserve positions and Federal funds transactions of eight major banks in New York City and 38 banks in other cities. On hand also is a complete nationwide picture of the reserve positions of member banks as of Monday's close, including information on the distribution of reserves among money market banks and other reserve city and country banks.

Shortly after 10 A.M., two young ladies bring the quotation board up to date with "runs" of price and yield quotations obtained from telephone calls to securities dealers. The Federal Reserve's traders already know from their conversations with dealers what the board shows – that the market is steady with few changes either up or down. They also know that there has been little trading except for the professional activity of the dealers who are testing each other's markets by occasionally "hitting a bid" – selling securities at the price bid by another dealer. About 10:45 A.M., the Desk receives the first tentative quotation on Federal funds. The quote is 5¾ percent, a shade higher than yesterday's rate of 5½ percent, which exceeded the 5¼ percent discount rate at which member banks can borrow from their Reserve Banks.

One member of the staff calls each of the nonbank dealers to find out the volume of funds needed to replace loans maturing today or to finance securities for which payment must be made today. A few minutes before 11 A.M., his tabulation shows that the dealers need loans of about $750 million to finance their present securities holdings. Money was available at yesterday's close at 6 percent, but the dealers are not too sure about today. Several think money may be harder to get and more expensive.

. . .

[After collecting various additional statistics] the officers hurry to an adjoining office to participate in a very important telephone conversation – the Federal Reserve conference call, which takes place at about 11:10 A.M.

The Conference Call

"Washington and Minneapolis are standing by," announces the telephone operator, completeing the three-way telephone hookup that each morning enables the Account Manager to review developments with a member of the Board of Governors in Washington (or his representatives) and one of the Reserve Bank presidents currently serving on the FOMC. Sitting in on the conversation in New York today are the president of the Bank, the Manager of the System Account, and the officers of the Securities Department. One of the officers seated directly behind a telephone microphone speaks:

"Conditions have changed somewhat since we spoke yesterday. The Government securities market opened steady this morning with very few changes in prices and rates, and with little activity, but Treasury bills now seem to be in increasing supply so that yields are rising. There are some indications that long-term investors are holding off to see how the market will take the $100 million bond issue of the XYZ Corporation tomorrow. Our first tentative information on Federal funds showed a bid of 5¾ percent, ¼ percent above yesterday's closing rate, and word just received from the Trading Room indicates that funds have now begun to trade at 5-7/8

percent. Dealer financing needs this morning are about $750 million. The banks have raised their call loan rates on dealer loans from 6 percent to 6¼ percent.

"Yesterday, bank reserves dipped slightly despite our action to supply reserves. The outlook is for a sharp decline in reserves today and tomorrow as currency in circulation increases and float declines. New York City and Chicago banks are under pressure and have been heavy buyers of Federal funds on each of the last three business days. Banks in several other major cities show reserve deficiencies. Today's call on the "C" banks will withdraw $96 million and will probably add to pressure on the money-market banks."

The officer then reads the Manager's proposed plan for the day:

"In view of the expected stringency in reserves, the Account plans to purchase securities for cash. If the market continues to tighten, we may buy as much as $200 million of Treasury bills. Repurchase agreements with the dealers can be used to supply additional reserves if needed."

The conversation is, of course, more detailed than the above colloquy, and conclusions are supported by a marshalling of facts. Prospective developments in the next couple of days and weeks are discussed. Participants in Washington and Minneapolis may report additional information and express their views as to the appropriateness of the proposed action.

By 11:30 A.M., the call is usually completed. . .

The Decision

Shortly before noon conditions in the market begin to jell rapidly, indicating a sharp increase in reserve pressures. The Federal funds rate jumps to the 5-7/8 percent and dealers, New York City banks and other participants in the funds market report that funds are hard to find. Dealers report a pickup in commercial bank selling of short-term securities. Dealer portfolios have increased substantially even though the dealers have been lowering the prices they are willing to pay for bills (with a consequent increase in yields). At the same time, they have not been able to make any progress in meeting their financing needs by borrowing from their out-of-town contacts even though they have been offering to pay 6 percent for money. In fact, given the additional bills they have had to buy, they now need $850 million to pay off maturing loans and to pay for the securities they have bought.

The Manager reviews the evidence: "The market has really started tightening up. We had better move in right away in size to prevent this from getting out of hand. Let's go in and buy about $250 million in Treasury bills for cash today."

The Manager of the System Open Market Account has made his decision. Six securities traders gather around an officer of the Securities Department to receive instructions. As we have seen, within thirty minutes the Reserve Bank's traders purchase $242 million in Treasury bills for cash in a "go-round" of the market. A summary report from the New York Reserve Bank of the day's developments and System action will be on the desks of the Board members and all Reserve Bank presidents on the following morning.

The officers continue to watch the situation after the "go-around" is completed at around 12:20 P.M. The Federal funds rate eases back to 5¾ percent bid for a time, but then the brokers report that the bid appears to be building while the supply available remains limited. Given the persistence of tightness, the Manager approves the recommendation of the Desk officers that the System purchase about $300 million of Treasury and Federal agency securities under overnight repurchase agreements. By 1 P.M. the additional injection of reserves has been made — bringing the day's total to $542 million. A better balance returns to the Federal funds market, but the officer will not know until the next day whether the shortage of reserves reflected a sharper-than-expected drop in float or something else.

The market may debate whether the day's action was designed simply to head off the developing strain in the market or whether it had broader policy significance. The market may not be able to be sure on that score until it can look back on several weeks of action and see if a cumulative easing of bank reserves overlays the weekly fluctuations not ironed out by System operations. But for today it is sufficient that the reserve strains which threatened to become acute have disappeared. The crisis is over before it really got started.

Tomorrow is another day. . . .

Money and the Macro System

31

Now that we know what money is and how its supply is controlled, we want to find out how money "works." That will take us into a three-stage journey. The first stage is to master the old-fashioned quantity theory of money. That's very easy. The next stage is to learn about the relationship between the supply of money and the demand for money — a relationship that is expressed through the rate of interest. That is more complicated. The last is to acquaint ourselves with some of the problems of money management. That's not difficult in a technical sense, but in actual fact it is the hardest problem of all.

THE OLD QUANTITY THEORY

Let us quickly review the quantity theory. In its classic formulation, it is an identity:

$$MV \equiv PT$$

Why is it an identity? Well, M times V means the supply of money multiplied by the number of times the supply is spent. If the supply is $1 million and it is spent twice, MV = $2 million. What does PT mean? P stands for the average price of, and T for the number of units of transactions. PT must therefore stand for the total sales value of goods: if P is $10, and T is 200,000, PT would be $2 million. Why, then, is MV identical with PT? Because the sales value of all goods must be identical with the value of all money spent. You can't spend money without buying something. You can't sell something without receiving money.

FROM IDENTITY TO THEORY

The quantity equation was used, however, not to establish an identity, but to express a theory. The theory was that prices were a direct function of the quantity of money: $P = f(M)$. The theory assumed therefore that V and T were constants, or near-constants. V was assumed to be a constant because the original quantity theorists assumed that people spent money with regular frequency; T was thought to be a constant because they believed that the economy was always at full employment, and therefore T was "fixed" (at least in the short run) by the capacity of the economy. It followed therefore that by increasing or decreasing M, you would directly affect the level of prices P.

Both these assumptions have been discarded by economists today. We know that V is capable of considerable variation, especially in the short run: people can hoard money, which reduces V, or they can go on "spending sprees" that will raise it. That is, as we shall see below, they can use money for liquidity or transactions purposes. More important, we now know that the economy will not always gravitate toward capacity output, so that T is capable of wide short-run variations.

It is this second fact that is decisive in causing us to reject the old quantity theory. The concept of GNP in equilibrium at levels less than full employment leads us to divide the effect of a change of M into two sharply contrasting cases (with a third intermediate band), as we show below:

High Unemployment		Low Unemployment
$\Delta M \to \Delta T$	$\Delta M \to \Delta P + \Delta T$	$\Delta M \to \Delta P$

As the figure shows, when unemployment is very high (as in a severe depression) changes in money tend to be reflected mainly in changes in *output* rather than in prices. When unemployment is moderate, a change in M leads to changes both in output and prices. And when unemployment is low, ΔM leads mainly to changes in prices. In our next chapter we will look into this relationship further as one explanation for inflation.

THE SUPPLY AND DEMAND FOR MONEY

The breakdown of the old-fashioned quantity theory leads us to the next problem of this chapter: how does an increase in M affect *expenditure;* To put the question differently, what is the functional link between M and MV? From our chapter we know that r, the rate of interest, is the missing link. What is the nature of this linkage?

The answer introduces us to two different kinds of demands for money: demand for money to make *transactions* and demand for money for *financial* purposes. What is the relation of r to each?

The relation is very clearcut for transactions. The less expensive money is, the more people demand it for direct expenditure. When we say that money is less expensive, we mean that the rate of interest is lower – you can borrow more cheaply. Thus, the demand for money for spending presents us with a demand curve exactly like that for any commodity. See Figure 31-1.

FINANCIAL DEMAND

The demand for money for financial purposes also looks like a regular demand curve, but the role of the rate of interest is different. We hold money for financial purposes in order to be "liquid" – to have cash reserves either for precautionary reasons or for speculative reasons. We call this desire to be liquid *liquidity preference.*

Why do we wish to be more liquid — to hold our financial assets in cash rather than securities — when the interest rate is low? *Opportunity cost* gives us the answer. When interest rates are high, we sacrifice considerable interest income by keeping our financial assets in cash: at an interest rate of 10 percent, we give up an income of $100 a year by keeping $1000 in the bank. When interest rates fall, the sacrifice is less:

FIGURE 31-1

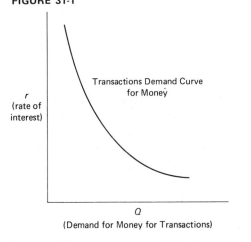

Transactions Demand Curve for Money

r
(rate of interest)

Q
(Demand for Money for Transactions)

at 2 percent, we give up only $20 a year. Therefore, the lower the interest rate, the less the inducement to invest in securities; or (what is the same thing) the more the inducement to be liquid.

FIGURE 31-2

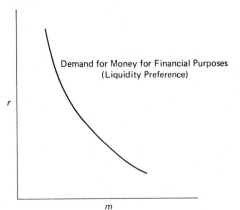

Demand for Money for Financial Purposes
(Liquidity Preference)

r

m

Putting the two demand curves together, we can see that the demand for money for both transactions and liquidity purposes gives us a downward-sloping curve.

FIGURE 31-3

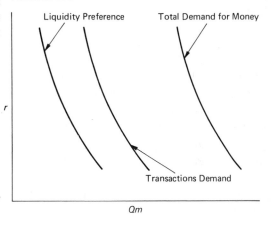

Liquidity Preference   Total Demand for Money

r

Transactions Demand

Qm

THE RATE OF INTEREST

Our analysis is useful in two ways. First, it explains how the rate of interest is determined by the interplay of the supply and demand for money. Second, it shows us how an increase in M leads to an increased MV.

Let us take the first question. In Figure 31-3 we show our demand curve for money (we show the total curve, disregarding the transaction and financial divisions), and the supply of money. Note that the supply of money is an inelastic curve. It is the quantity of checking deposits and currency in the hands of the public — a quantity that is "exogenously" determined, that is, directly established by the monetary authorities.

We begin with a supply and demand situation in which a given rate of interest, OA, exists. As we can see, this is a rate that just equates the amount of money people wish to hold with the amount that exists, OX. Now suppose the authorities increase the supply of money by buying government bonds with Federal Reserve checks. The supply curve of money shifts to the right, as our graph shows.

TRANSACTIONS EFFECT

Now what happens? First, let us consider the transactions effect. As banks find their deposits increased, they will have larger excess reserves. They will compete with one another to lend those reserves, thereby reducing the cost of borrowing. Individuals and firms will increase their borrowings to spend more for automobiles, housing, plant and equipment, inventories, and the like. *Note that competition among banks will tend to push down the rate of interest.*

LIQUIDITY EFFECT

Second, liquidity. As a result of the government's operations, the public will have larger deposits than previously. But looking at our demand schedule for money, we find that at interest rate *OA,* the public only wants *OX* amount of money (for both transactions and liquidity purposes). The public now holds more cash balances (*OY*) than it wishes to hold. It will try to get rid of its unwanted cash by buying bonds.

The effect of buying bonds is to drive up bond prices, and to lower yields. A $1,000 government bond paying $50 yields 5 percent. If the demand for bonds increases, its price will rise, say to $1,100. But the $50 interest payment does not change. Rather, $50 now represents a yield of 4.5 percent ($50 ÷ $1,100). The fall in yield is therefore the same thing as a fall in interest rates: formerly you could get 5 percent for government bonds; now you can get only 4.5 percent. At a lower interest rate (*OA*) the opportunity cost of being liquid is less. Some individuals will decide to remain liquid — that is, they will be content to hold more cash than they would have held at a higher rate.

Thus we can see how the increase in *M* leads

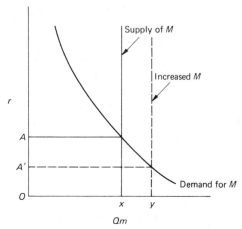

FIGURE 31-4

to an increase in both transactions and in cash holdings (liquidity). To be sure you understand, let us trace the process once more, this time with you answering questions as we go. (In case of doubt, there are answers given below.)

1. People want money for two different purposes. One purpose is to make _____ , the other to be more or less _____.
2. Let us consider transactions. As the price of money, or the _____ rate, falls, it becomes _____ to borrow.
3. As the interest rate falls and it becomes cheaper to borrow, the transactions demand for money_____. Conversely, if interest rates rose, we would expect the demand for transactions balances to _____ .
4. The second source of demand for money is for _____ purposes. We hold more or less cash for precautionary or speculative reasons, according to our schedule of_____ _____ preferences.
5. When the rate of interest is high, there is a high _____ cost for being liquid. This cost is the _____ income that we will forego.
6. As the rate of interest falls, we therefore expect the demand for financial balances to _____ .
7. Adding together transactions and financial demands, we can construct a demand curve for money that shows the relation between the rate of interest and our wish to hold

cash. This curve shows that as interest rates rise, the demand for money _____ .

8. The supply of money is established by the _____ .

9. If the supply of money is decreased, banks will be less willing or able to make _____ . Competition among individuals or firms will send the rate of interest on loans _____ .

10. If the supply of money is decreased, individuals or firms will find that their cash balances are _____ than they used to be.

11. When cash balances are less than they used to be, individuals or firms will try to _____ their cash holdings by _____ securities.

12. Selling securities (or buying them) does not increase the amount of _____ . But it does affect the _____ on bonds. This is because selling securities will send their prices _____ .

13. As security prices fall, yields on securities _____ . For example, a $1,000 bond paying $100 a year yields _____ percent. If the security now falls in price to $900, the $100 a year represents a yield of _____ .

14. As yields increase, the opportunity cost of being liquid _____ .

15. At a higher opportunity cost for liquidity, individuals will be content to hold _____ _____ money.

16. The rate of interest is therefore changed because the amount of money in existence is not the same as the amount people are willing to hold at a going _____ .

17. The effort to become more liquid or less liquid results in changes in bond yields, which are the same thing as the _____ .

18. When the authorities increase the supply of money, money becomes cheaper for two reasons: (1) banks have _____ reserves and compete to make more _____ ; and (2) the public holds more _____ than it wants, and tries to get out of cash into _____ , sending yields _____ .

19. An increase in the supply of money therefore gets used in two ways. Part of it is directly used for more _____ ; and part of it ends up in larger _____ balances.

20. A decrease in the supply of money results in less money being used for _____ ; and in _____ balances held for _____ . The smaller balances for liquidity are agreeable to the public because the decrease in money has caused the _____ _____ to rise.

Answers:
1. transactions; liquid
2. interest, cheaper
3. rises, fall
4. financial (or liquidity), liquidity
5. opportunity, interest
6. rise
7. falls
8. monetary authorities
9. loans, higher
10. smaller
11. increase, selling
12. money, yield, down
13. rise, 10, 11+
14. rises
15. less
16. rate of interest
17. interest rate
18. excess, loans, cash, securities, down
19. transactions, liquidity
20. transactions; smaller, liquidity, interest rate.

MODERN MONETARY DILEMMAS

There has been a great deal of interest in monetary theory in recent years. This is partly the result of a new and more sophisticated version of the quantity theory, which suggests that an increase in M results *directly* in an increase in MV (without the complicated mechanism of a change in the interest rate and its effects). The so-called "monetarists" hold that increasing the quantity of money will induce a larger volume of expenditures, because the public tends to spend more when its cash holdings rise. There is still a great deal of controversy as to the importance and nature of this "liquidity" effect.

MONEY MANAGEMENT

By far the most difficult part of this chapter concerns the problems of adjusting the money supply to bring about whatever changes in expenditure the monetary authorities seek.

This is a problem that needs more than technical analysis. To give you a feel of what monetary management is all about, we suggest you go through the reading after the short quiz that follows.

QUIZ

Ten Easy Questions: T F

1. $M \equiv PT/V$ __ __
2. The quantity *theory* implies constants for V and T.   __ __
3. Unemployment is incompatible with the original quantity theory that ΔM leads to ΔP.   __ __
4. All additional expenditure can be inflationary at full employment except consumption.   __ __
5. Increases in M affect MV via the rate of interest.   __ __
6. The demand for transactions balances varies inversely with the rate of interest.   __ __
7. The rate of interest measures the opportunity cost of liquidity.   __ __
8. Selling securities to increase cash balances increases the supply of money.   __ __
9. When bond prices rise, so do bond yields.   __ __
10. A shift in liquidity preferences can occur even though the rate of interest is unchanged.   __ __

Answers:

1. T	5. T	8. F
2. T	6. T	9. F
3. T	7. T	10. T
4. F		

Ten Hard Questions: T F

1. A rise in liquidity preferences, ceteris paribus, will lead to a higher rate of interest.   __ __
2. An increase in the supply of money will cause investors to absorb larger cash balances for liquidity.   __ __
3. The modern quantity theory asserts that transactions are a direct function of cash balances.   __ __
4. At all times the demand for financial balances plus the demand for transactions balances must be equal to the supply of money.   __ __
5. The function of a change in the interest rate is to induce the public to hold the amount of money that it must hold, whether it wishes to or not.   __ __
6. ΔV has no effect on M.   __ __
7. ΔM has no effect on V.   __ __
8. Historically, M has increased faster than P.   __ __
9. Individuals can directly affect the rate of interest if their transactions spending increases.   __ __
10. An increased volume of output requires an increased velocity of money.   __ __

Answers:

1. T	5. T	8. F
2. T	6. T	9. T
3. T	7. F	10. F
4. T		

DOES MONETARY POLICY MATTER?

Peter L. Bernstein

*Here is what monetary policy and its problems look like
from the viewpoint of someone who is a trained economist
and a professional consultant on business and investment
matters.*

Everyone has become a Fed watcher. This was once a relatively exotic pastime, engaged in by only a few people in the investment world . . . but it has now blossomed into a full-time activity for the masses . . . The ability to express the minute-by-minute jiggles in all the variables in terms of annual-average-percentage-rates-of-change is the true hallmark of the new monetary expert.

Now, in our opinion, this proliferation of monetary expertise has created two problems. In the first place, we all know that what we all know gets discounted so rapidly in the marketplace that it loses most of its forecasting value. That is bad enough. Perhaps even more serious, the experts have become so infatuated with monetary data and so obsessed with Federal Reserve policy, that they tend to forget there is a great big economy out there. The future trend of business activity depends on a lot more than the latest average-annual-percentage-rate-of-change in one or another of the monetary variables.

We have no intention of renewing the stale debate on whether money matters. Of course it does: no one has yet devised a successful substitute to use in paying our bills. The more we have of it, the easier it is to finance expenditures and, consequently, the greater the likelihood of an expansion in output or prices or both — and vice versa.

Nevertheless, after years of controversy and miles of computer printouts, no one — not even

Arthur Burns or Milton Friedman — has any precise idea of what the proper relationship should be between money and business activity, the speed with which changes in money influence business activity (or whether instead business activity influences the changes in money), or the nature of the transmission process between monetary variables and business activity. This means that exclusive concentration on monetary data can lead the forecaster to confuse cause and effect, to make poor timing judgments, and to overlook autonomous forces in the real economy that can overwhelm the monetary forces, at least in the short run.

Even today, most people must admit that John Maynard Keynes occasionally knew what he was talking about, and Keynes put major stress on the inevitable slippages between changes in money supply and changes in business activity. The slips "twixt cup and lip" to which he referred in a famous passage occur primarily because of what he described as liquidity preference, or the changing desires of millions of individuals and business firms to hold money rather than to spend it. Shifts in liquidity preference functions, in turn, depend upon both

---

[1] If transactions balances rise, the additional money used for expenditure must come from smaller liquidity balances. Unless liquidity preferences shift, this will mean that individuals will be selling securities to try to get more spending money. Selling securities will lead to a rise in yields (interest rates).

longer-term and relatively predictable institutional changes in the use of money (such as the willingness to substitute other types of liquid assets like time deposits, short-term Treasury issues, and commercial paper, or the use of credit cards and automatic overdraft facilities) and upon shorter-term and less predictable changes in *expectations.*

If we are willing to recognize how difficult it is to understand the impact of monetary policy in the past, then we must face up to the even greater difficulty of predicting its impact on the future. The difficulty in analyzing the past arises on two scores that appear to be different but are in reality only variations on a common theme: (a) on what period of time do you base your analysis, and (b) when is the relationship between money and business activity "too high," "too low," or "just right"? Unfortunately, this relationship is like cream cheese and jelly on a cracker – if you have too much of one, you always seem to end up adding too much of the other in an effort to come out even.

Let us look at some recent data to illustrate this point. In view of the rapid increase in business activity relative to the pure money supply over the past twenty-five years, we prefer to look at these trends in terms of what is known as M_2, that is, the total of demand deposits, currency outside banks, and time deposits other than large CDs at commercial banks. Increasingly in recent years, the public has tended to transfer excess checking account balances into these time accounts in order to take advantage of the interest paid on such accounts. "Aha!" cries the convert to monetarism, "See how neat the relationship is! Years of rapid monetary increase are followed by years of rapid GNP growth, as night follows day, and vice versa. Furthermore, you can see that when the growth in money significantly outruns the growth in GNP, as in 1967 and 1971-72, it leads to those unsustainable and inflationary surges that ultimately bring us into the times of trouble."

	Annual % Change*		
Year	M_2	GNP	GNP per $ of M_2 **
1965	8.7	8.0	2.40
1966	5.3	10.9	2.45
1967	10.2	5.8	2.41
1968	9.2	8.8	2.45
1969	2.3	7.6	2.43
1970	8.0	4.9	2.48
1971	11.2	7.6	2.38
1972	10.8	9.7	2.35
1973	9.7	11.5	2.40

*Annual % change based on year-end figures.
**GNP per $ of M_2 based on average value of M_2 for the year.

The table also shows the Federal Reserve in a desperate attempt to deal with the cream-cheese-and-jelly dilemma. They jammed on the monetary brakes in 1966 to offset inflationary GNP growth in 1965 and nearly ran us into a recession in 1967; consequently, they had to flip-flop back to generous monetary expansion in 1967-68, but the inflationary results of that pushed them back to restraint in 1969; this was followed by the recession of 1970, which necessitated another flip-flop in 1971-72; not surprisingly, they subsequently felt the urge to go back to a policy of restraint in 1973, whose imminent reversal is now anxiously awaited by one and all. Fine-tuning the economy with monetary policy does seem to be a most difficult task.

Many people have argued, in fact, that we had the defeat of inflation within our grasp in both 1966 and 1970. The Fed, however, chronically afraid of overkill, appears to have chickened out and made matters even worse than they had been before the period of restraint.

But the table also raises as many questions as it appears to answer. For example, what is the appropriate span within which to measure the impact of monetary policy? A quick look at the table shows that monetary expansion after 1969 averaged significantly higher than before 1969 (6.5 percent a year from 1965 to 1969 and 10.0

percent from 1969 to 1973, to be precise), which would seem to lay a lot of blame for the current inflation at the door of the Federal Reserve. Suppose, however, that we took the periods 1964-68 and 1968-73. Monetary growth averaged just 8.5 percent a year in *both* periods, although the rate of inflation was surely much greater in the latter period; thus, a lot depends on which dates you use as starters and finishers before you draw any conclusions.

Furthermore, what is the "right" relationship between GNP and money? When do we have enough money to finance economic growth and still too little to finance inflation? The table suggests that we tend to run into slow growth when we are doing more than $2.45 of business for every $1 of money supply and that we get an inflationary push when we are doing $2.40 or less of business activity for every $1 of money supply. Yet even this rough guide is by no means a complete answer, for it means (a) that the Fed must have perfect forecasting ability as to what both variables will be if monetary policy is to be right on the mark, and (b) that there exists in fact some preordained supply of money relative to some given level of GNP that will satisfy the public's desire for liquidity over and above the immediate needs of financing current expenditures.

Unfortunately, we simply don't know what level of liquidity makes individuals and business firms comfortable. All we do know is that the economy is a lot less liquid relative to the volume of business than it was twenty years ago. And we also know that liquidity preferences change over time, that experiences like 1966 and 1969 in such quick succession make businessmen and financial institutions even more eager to hold liquid assets, and that, finally, inflation itself reduces the purchasing power of money and thus makes any given supply of money appear smaller than it did in the past. In view of all these considerations, can we say that the Fed was wrong in easing so much in 1971-72, particularly in view of the sluggish pace of the recovery during most of 1971?

As we mentioned above, there is also a great big economy out there. For example, the surges in consumer spending for durables after 1960, in 1968, and from mid-1971 to mid-1972 were motivated by a variety of factors, of which liquidity was only a minor part; yet, they may have had as much or more to do with the acceleration in business activity than anything the Fed was doing. Similar comments would apply to the economic slowdowns of 1966 and 1970, which were preceded by tight money episodes but were also accompanied by declines in consumer spending for durables that, again, were motivated by much more than liquidity considerations; history is now repeating itself here.

We want to stress that we have no intention of minimizing the importance of money or of monetary policy, particularly when policy runs to extremes of ease or restraint. The point that we believe must be made, however, is that (a) the liquidity needs of the economy are unstable and therefore difficult to forecast; (b) this means that the Fed operates in an environment characterized by constant uncertainty, and, consequently, (c) forecasting both Fed policy and its impact on that great big economy may be a practical impossibility.

In short, forecasting the supply of crude oil, soybeans, hogs, rainfall, babies, paper, customers for automobiles, gold hungry gnomes, or phthalic anhydride is far from easy, but forecasting any one of them may be far more rewarding than forecasting the supply of money.

32

33

The Problems
of Inflation
and Unemployment

These chapters deal with the most difficult problems of modern economic society. Yet there is very little in these chapters that presents a new *analytical* challenge to us. We learn about Phillips curves, about zero-sum games, and about the problems of technological unemployment, but all of this calls on our previously earned knowledge rather than teaching us new concepts.

There is a reason for this. Until these chapters we have been advancing across fairly well-explored terrain. But inflation and unemployment, although old problems, are not "well-explored" concepts. There is a great deal that we do not understand clearly about both problems. To put it differently, when we apply our macroeconomic tools to them, we get results that do not lend themselves to successful economic policy.

Therefore we are not going to review the subject matter of these chapters here. Instead, we would like you to learn something about these problems as they appear to contemporary econo-

mists. The best way to "master" the problems of inflation and unemployment is to read the diverse views of economists, as if you were sitting on a Congressional Committee, listening to a body of expert testimony, much of which contradicted itself. The readings are interesting and worth your time. We hope you will profit from them.

FOLD NO MORE, SWEET DOLLAR

Russell Baker

Russell Baker's column in the New York Times *has kept economists (and many others) laughing and thinking for many years.*

With the dollar undergoing the monetary equivalent of surgical sex change, this is a good time for the Government to do something about coin reform.

It is clear by this time that the greenback is an antique, and ought to be done away with. When derelicts brace you on the sidewalk, murmuring, "Buddy, can you spare a dollar for a cup of coffee?" it should be clear even to a Republican Secretary of the Treasury that it is time to adapt to reality.

The obvious solution is to turn the dollar bill into a coin. The grocer treats it as loose change; why shouldn't the government? Men who keep their folding money in billfolds have probably noticed lately that wallet pockets in their clothes now wear out faster and faster. This is because of

From *The New York Times* (March 5, 1974). ©1974 by The New York Times Company. Reprinted by permission.

the accelerating frequency with which the wallet has to be slid out and in over increasingly expensive fabric as demand for dollar bills becomes increasingly insistent.

The current melodrama of the dollar's eerie shrinkage provides the publicity music necessary for coin reform, but we should not be contented with transmutation of paper into brass. The old coins — quarters, nickels, pennies — have been out of date a long time. Total reform is overdue.

Consider the quarter. An antique. Originally created for heavy tipping. Headwaiters, Pullman porters who had seen you through an overnight trip. After the inflation which followed World War II, its status declined from elegance to bourgeois businesslike serviceability. It flourished to tip cab drivers, doormen, waitresses in lunch joints, to buy a shoeshine, a magazine. Now it is wrong for everything.

People who once tugged forelocks at a quarter tip may now aim it at your head — there is an incivility inflation, too — if it isn't accompanied by at least a dime, and maybe a nickel more. The quarter no longer fits. Its replacement should be a coin worth about 37½ cents. It could be called a "Tipper."

Magazines that only yesterday used to be yours for a quarter now require 53 cents before they will yield up their secrets. (How to have hip fat surgically removed; latest trends in adultery; bad news about the dollar; the time Liz and Dick almost bumped into Jackie off Gibraltar.) The price rise is due to inflation and the 6 percent sales tax, which is spreading across America like the elm blight.

The logical move at the mint is to stop making pennies. Pennies don't buy anything anymore anyhow. Even penny candy nowadays costs two cents for considerably less than a penny's worth. Also stop making nickels.

In its day the nickel was a truly great coin. That buffalo! That fantastic Indian in profile! That good silver feel! And the beautiful precision of the thing! It was created for only two specific purposes — but what a magnificent two they were!

It bought a bus, subway or streetcar ride. And it bought the "Saturday Evening Post" with its weekly testament to the soundness of the dollar.

Well, the streetcar is gone, and most of the buses, and those that remain cost 40 or 50 cents per ride. And the "Post" is gone, too, with the soundness of the dollar, and gone with all these wonderful things is the whole point of the nickel.

What replacement? Instead of the penny, a 3-cent piece. The ideal coin to pay the universal 6 percent sales tax, especially since nothing nowadays costs less than 50 cents, even penny candy if you want to get a really honest penny's worth.

The nickel, by mint decree, would become the new 50-cent piece. This way it would again serve the functions it was made for — buying magazines and local transportation. The present 50-cent piece would be eliminated for the dollar coin. A coin any bigger would weigh too much and wear out coin pockets too fast. Moreover, everything that used to cost 50 cents now costs a dollar anyhow, so there is no point in retaining the 50-cent piece.

Money men can probably find flaws here. A case can be made that instead of a dollar coin, there ought to be a 99-cent coin, in view of the American merchant's passion for pricing sale items at $1.99, $2.99, $3.99 and so on up to $10 billion and 99 cents. Alternatively, the coin might be made worth $1.06, to build the sales tax payment right into the currency.

That is for experts to settle. The basic need, however, cannot be winked away by Treasury bureaucrats. We abolished the rumble seat, didn't we? Why be sentimental about the greenback? Let's make it a coin which men can drop on a plastic table and, hearing its "clack!", be moved to smile and say, "Sound as a yen!"

THE ECONOMICS OF THE
NEW UNEMPLOYMENT

Martin Feldstein

*Professor Feldstein recently testified before the Joint
Economic Committee of the Congress on ways and means of
reducing unemployment. Here are some of the (surprising)
data and the (unorthodox) conclusions of that testimony with
respect to the problem of youthful unemployment.*

Most macroeconomic analyses of unemployment are based on ideas about the causes and structure of unemployment that are inappropriate and out of date. The basic framework of Keynesian economics, conditioned by the experience of the 1930's, has always emphasized the inadequacy of aggregate demand as the source of unemployment. The conventional view of post-War unemployment might be described as follows: "The growth of demand for goods and services does not always keep pace with the expansion of the labor force and the rise in output per man. Firms therefore lay off employees and fail to hire new members of the labor force at a sufficient rate. The result is a pool of potential workers who are unable to find jobs. Only policies to increase the growth of demand can create the jobs needed to absorb the unemployed."

This picture of a hard core of unemployed workers who are not able to find jobs is an inaccurate description of our economy and a misleading basis for policy. A more accurate description is an active labor market in which almost everyone who is out of work can find his usual type of job in a relatively short time. *The problem is not that these jobs are unavailable but*

that they are often unattractive. Much of the unemployment and even more of the lost manpower occurs among individuals who find that the available jobs are neither appealing in themselves nor rewarding as pathways to better jobs in the future. For such individuals, job attachment is weak, quitting is common, and periods without work or active job seeking are frequent. *The major problem to be dealt with is not a chronic aggregate shortage of jobs but the instability of individual employment.* Decreasing the overall rate of unemployment requires not merely more jobs, but new incentives to encourage those who are out of work to seek employment more actively and those who are employed to remain at work. As I shall explain below, an important part of these incentives is a change in the kinds of jobs that are available.

It is difficult to replace our old notions about demand-determined unemployment by this new view. Let me therefore describe in more detail some of the characteristics of American unemployment during the past decade. I will begin with the experience of the total labor force and then consider differences among demographic groups.

First, the duration of unemployment is quite short. Even in a year like 1971 with a very high unemployment rate, 45 percent of those unemployed had been out of work for less than five

From *The Public Interest,* No. 3 (Fall, 1973), pp. 3–42. ©1973 by National Affairs, Inc.

weeks. In 1969, this proportion was almost 58 percent. Similarly, very few are without jobs for as long as 27 weeks; in 1969 this was 4.7 percent, and in 1971 it was 10.4 percent of all the unemployed.

Second, loss of jobs accounts for less than half of total unemployment. In 1971, only 46 percent of the unemployed had lost their previous jobs. In the more favorable market conditions of 1969, this proportion was only 36 percent. The remainder are those who voluntarily left their last jobs, are reentering the labor force, or never worked before. In 1969, with an overall unemployment rate of 3.5 percent, losing one's job contributed only 1.2 percent to this figure.

Third, the turnover of jobs is extremely high. Data collected from manufacturing establishments show that total hirings and separations have each exceeded four percent of the labor force per month since 1960. Moreover, the number of quits has consistently exceeded layoffs during the past five years. Even with the high unemployment of 1971, more workers quit manufacturing jobs than were laid off.

DEMOGRAPHIC DIFFERENCES

Perhaps the most important characteristic of our current unemployment problem is the differences in unemployment experience among demographic groups. The unemployment rates in certain groups are not only very high but are also quite unresponsive to changes in the aggregate demand for labor. This implies that fiscal and monetary policies that drastically cut the unemployment rate of mature men would still leave a high overall unemployment rate.

To study these differences I have estimated the relation between the unemployment rate in each demographic group and the concurrent unemployment rate for men over 24 years of age. This rate for mature men provides one of the best measures of cyclical variation in labor market pressure. Table 1 presents the results of this analysis. Column I gives the 1971 unemployment rates in eight different demographic groups, ranging from four percent for white men to 32 percent for non-white teenagers. Column II shows the sensitivity of each unemployment rate

TABLE 1.   Differences in Unemployment Experience Among Demographic Groups

Demographic Group	I Unemployment Rate, 1971	II Sensitivity to Rate of Mature Men*	III Unemployment Rate When Mature Men* Unemployment is 1.5 Percent
Males, 16-19	16.7	1.45	11.4
Females, 16-19	17.4	0.26	13.7
Whites, 16-19	15.2	1.03	10.8
Nonwhites, 16-19	31.8	0.26	24.5
Males, white, 20+	4.0	0.92	1.7
Males, nonwhite, 20+	7.3	2.33	3.3
Females, white, 20+	5.3	0.59	3.2
Females, nonwhite, 20+	8.7	0.99	6.1

*The mature men unemployment rate refers to all men over age 24.

to labor market pressure (i.e., the change in that specific unemployment rate that would occur when the rate for men over 24 years of age changes by one percent). For example, a one percent fall in the unemployment rate for mature men would lower the teenage male unemployment rate by about 1.5 percent. A change in aggregate demand, therefore, has a greater absolute effect on the teenage unemployment rate than on the rate for mature men. Nevertheless, variations in aggregate demand account for a relatively small fraction of the high level of teenage male unemployment. Even if the rate for mature men were depressed to 1.5 percent — below the level reached at any time in the post-War period — the analysis implies that the male teenage rate would be at about 11.4 percent. This is shown in Column III. Although the absolute sensitivity of male teenage unemployment to changes in aggregate demand is a serious problem, it is the very high level of the cyclical troughs that prevents macroeconomic policy from reducing that unemployment to a level below five percent. . . .

The evidence presented in this section can be summarized briefly: *The current structure of unemployment in the American economy is not compatible with the traditional view of a hard core of unemployed who are unable to find jobs.* Even with the high unemployment rate of 1971, the durations of unemployment were short, job losers accounted for less than half of unemployment, and quit rates generally exceeded layoffs. An examination of the past experience of individual demographic groups indicates very substantial variation in the response of unemployment rates to aggregate demand and implies that even an extremely tight labor market would leave some groups with high unemployment rates. The next three sections examine why these unemployment rates are not more sensitive to aggregate demand and suggest possible policies to deal with these problems.

UNEMPLOYMENT AMONG YOUNG WORKERS

Unemployment rates for young persons seem outrageously high. In 1971, male teenagers had an unemployment rate of 16.6 percent. Even among those aged 20 through 24, the unemployment rate was 10.3 percent. If unemployment in these groups could be reduced to the same rate as for mature men, the overall rate would fall by more than one third. . . .

Youth unemployment is not primarily due to inadequate demand. Statistical analysis indicates that the unemployment rate of young persons would remain high even in a very tight labor market. There are two main sources of the chronic high unemployment in this age range: (1) unnecessarily slow absorption of new entrants and (2) low job attachment among those at work. Because of the slow absorption, a very significant part of the unemployment of young workers is among new entrants to the labor force and others who are seeking their first full-time job. New entrants to the labor force spent an average of 9.1 weeks until their first employment. Among teenagers, new entrants contributed 6.7 percent to the unemployment rate; new entrants therefore accounted for 40 percent of total teenage unemployment.

The single most effective way of reducing unemployment among new entrants as well as improving the quality of first jobs would probably be the establishment of a special Youth Employment Service. The British experience with such a program suggests its potential impact in America. In a recent year in which approximately 280,000 boys between 15 and 17 entered the labor force, the Youth Employment Service arranged 200,000 employment placements for boys in that age group. While some of these placements are not for new entrants, the magnitude of the British achievement is enormous. Part of their success is due to their direct contact with students: Nearly 80 percent of school leavers who are not going to universities are interviewed in school by the Youth Employment Service.

I would favor a federal program that reimbursed states for the cost of operating a Youth Employment Service that met certain federal standards. The Service should be separate from the regular Employment Service and should deal only with persons below 21 years of age. Although available to those who have already left school, it should focus mainly on an active program of advising and placing those who are about to leave. A participant state should require each student to be interviewed by the Youth Employment Service before he graduates from high school or is allowed to leave school legally. Making a Youth Employment Service an integral part of the educational system should facilitate the transition from school to job. The knowledge that everyone entering the labor force is seen by the Youth Employment Service would encourage employers to list jobs that are not now given to the regular Employment Service. If those leaving school are more aware of the options open to them, they are more likely to find a job with which they will be satisfied. They will not only find a better job in this way, but will also be less likely to leave that job in an illusory hope of improving their position.

THE INSTABILITY OF TEENAGE EMPLOYMENT

The second source of unemployment — the high rate at which young men and women lose jobs, quit jobs, and drop out of the labor force — is both a more serious problem and a more difficult one to solve. Much of the unemployment among experienced young workers occurs not because jobs are unavailable but because they are unattractive. For many young workers, the available entry-level jobs are also dead-end jobs. They offer neither valuable training nor opportunities for significant advancement within the firm. Since employers have made no investment in these workers, they do not hesitate to lay them off whenever demand falls. Since comparable jobs are easy to find, these young workers do not hesitate to quit. The growth of our economy during the past few decades now permits relatively high wages even for those with entry-level jobs. Among the young and single, these high wages encourage an increased demand for leisure. If the content of the job and the structure of the firm's employment policy do not outweigh this, job attachment will be weak and quit rates high.

All of the evidence points to this highly unstable character of employment, rather than to any long-term difficulty in finding jobs, as the primary source of unemployment among experienced young workers. First, the mean duration of unemployment is much lower for this group than for the rest of the labor force. Even in 1971, when the mean duration for all unemployed was 11.4 weeks, among 16-21 year olds the mean was only 8.5 weeks; while 24 percent of all workers were unemployed for more than 15 weeks, only 15 percent of 16 to 21 year olds were. Second, unemployment among job leavers and those reentering the labor force is much more important for younger workers than unemployment among job losers. In 1971, job leavers and reentrants contributed 7.1 percent, or more than two thirds, of the unemployment among teenage experienced workers.... A survey that followed the same group of young men from October 1966 through October 1968 found that approximately one fourth of black 16-20 year olds had three or more spells of unemployment and about half had two or more inter-firm shifts during the 24 months. Among whites the proportion experiencing at least one spell of unemployment was similar (after educational differences are taken into account), but multiple spells of unemployment were less common. Still, one fifth of whites and two fifths of blacks between 16 and 24 who were completely out of school experienced some unemployment during those two years despite the very low overall national unemployment rate.

STUDENTS AND NONSTUDENTS

Why is employment so unstable and labor force attachment so weak in this age range? . . . I believe that a fundamental reason is the types of jobs that are available and the lack of adequate reward for stable employment. I will return below to discuss this in more detail and to suggest possible remedies. First, however, I want to emphasize two ways in which the figures overstate the magnitude of the social and economic problem of unemployment among young people.

Part of the high quit rates and rates of leaving the labor force merely reflects the impact of our educational system and the seasonal character of the labor force activity of students. Those who have not stopped their formal education seek full-time employment when schools are closed and may also seek different part-time jobs during the school year. Since attending school is the major activity of more than 23 percent of the labor force between 16 and 21 years of age, the peculiar labor market behavior of that group has a substantial impact on the statistical picture of youth unemployment. If those who are looking only for part-time work are not counted in the unemployed, the unemployment rate for 16-21 year olds in 1971 drops from 15.0 percent to 10.2 percent. Moreover, many of those who leave school and take jobs later return to being full-time students. High unemployment among young Americans is therefore in part a reflection of our commitment to providing many more years of schooling than is common in other countries, and is a price we pay for a very fluid educational system which encourages people to move back and forth between full-time work and full-time education.

In considering the gap between the unemployment rates of young persons and of more mature workers, it is important not to lose sight of their differences in motivation and attitudes. Most young workers have no family responsibilities and may continue to live with their parents. It is significant that the 1971 unemployment rate for 16-24 year old males who were classified as "household heads" was only 6.4 percent while all others in this age-sex group had an unemployment rate over 16 percent. Although today's high wage rates provide a substantial reward for working, they also permit a comfortable standard of living with significantly less work or less responsible work than was required 20 years ago. Many young persons want more leisure than is consistent with full-time employment and a permanent attachment to a particular firm. They prefer to alternate between working and other activities rather than to seek and hold permanent employment. These remarks are not intended as criticism. The behavior of these young persons is seen in better perspective by comparison with our student population. The major activity of over 40 percent of 16-21 year-olds is attending school. The academic schedule provides frequent long vacations. For those in higher education, the daily routine is varied and the individual is generally free to choose his own activities and pace of work. Perhaps much of the high turnover and voluntary labor force withdrawal among young nonstudents reflects an attempt to enjoy the same freedom and occupational irresponsibility that we take for granted in our student population of the same age.

The extremely high unemployment rates are therefore not quite what they seem. They reflect the peculiar labor force behavior of students and the temporary and voluntary unemployment that young people can afford in an affluent society. Despite this, I believe that there does exist a real and serious problem. The high turnover rates and voluntary unemployment are also a response to the unsatisfactory type of job that is available to many young workers. These are often dead-end jobs with neither opportunity for advancement within the firm nor training and experience that would be useful elsewhere. The young worker's incentive to stay at work is often further reduced by a seniority system that implies that the newest employees are most likely to be laid off during the next small business downturn. Moreover, the lack of sufficient opportunities to begin careers leading to high-paying jobs or to obtain valuable on-the-job training in industry and business is no doubt responsible for an excessive reliance on formal education. I shall not venture to guess how many of our college students might be served better by working than by going to school if more adequate jobs were available.

THE MINIMUM WAGE AND OPPORTUNITIES FOR TRAINING

At the root of this problem is the hard economic reality that firms cannot afford to offer useful on-the-job training to a broad class of young employees. A firm can generally provide the opportunity to acquire new marketable skills — by on-the-job training, detailed supervision, or even just learning by experience — only to a worker whose net product *during the period of training* is at least equal to his wage. Unfortunately, the current minimum wage law prevents many young people from accepting jobs with low pay but valuable experience. Those who come to the labor market with substantial skills and education need not be affected by the minimum wage. They are productive enough to permit employers to pay at least the minimum wage while also providing further training and opportunities for advancement. But for the disadvantaged young worker, with few skills and below-average education, producing enough to earn the minimum wage is incompatible with the oppor-

tunity for adequate on-the-job learning. For this group, the minimum wage implies high short-run unemployment and the chronic poverty of a life of low-wage jobs.

In this way the minimum wage law has an unambiguously harmful effect on some young workers. Even if an individual were willing to "buy" on-the-job training by taking a very low wage for six months or a year, the minimum wage law would not permit him to do so. It is unfortunate and ironic that we encourage and subsidize expenditure on formal education while blocking the opportunity for individuals to "buy" on-the-job training. . . .

The burden of this effect of the minimum wage law falls most heavily on the disadvantaged. Because they bring little to the labor market, they are able to obtain little in exchange. It is clear from the few successful programs in training the disadvantaged that for some time these workers produce little if any net revenue over the costs of training. A job at the minimum wage will not permit any significant amount of training. The disadvantaged youth for whom more formal education is unsuitable is therefore forced into dead-end jobs without training or opportunities for advancement. In the short run, this means high absenteeism, high quit rates, and high turnover. The long-run effects are even more serious. The lack of additional training for those who start with low skills makes them part of the permanent poor. For the disadvantaged, the minimum wage law may have the ironic effect of lowering lifetime incomes by a very large amount.

Note that this view of the harmful effects of applying the minimum wage law to young workers is quite different from the usual proposition that the minimum wage law creates unemployment because at the established level the supply of workers exceeds the demand. The evidence on that is ambiguous. It is clear that there is no lack of jobs in the sense that nearly any young person can get a job, but it is not certain that they *all* could. The important point is that, because of the minimum wage law, many of the jobs that are available do not provide young workers and their employers with an incentive for stable employment.

The problem then is to remove the barrier to better on-the-job experience and training that is currently posed for some young workers by the minimum wage law. There are a variety of ways to do this. The method that one prefers depends in part on whom one wants to bear the cost of these better job opportunities. One obvious solution would be to modify the minimum wage law so that its full force does not apply to young workers. This would put the full cost of the better training on the young workers themselves. Although there is strong opposition to changing our current minimum wage system, the case for a minimum wage is clearly the weakest when applied to young workers. At best, the minimum wage is an administratively simple way of providing a minimum annual income for every family with a full-time working member. It suffers even in this context from its failure to relate that income to family size. This is particularly relevant to young workers who are single and who often live with their parents.

YOUTH EMPLOYMENT SCHOLARSHIPS

There are, however, two practical objections to relying solely on a reduction in the minimum wage for young workers as the means of facilitating better job experience. First, some young workers could simply not afford to take a job that would provide adequate training and experience. The low incomes associated with such jobs would effectively exclude those with family responsibilities. Single individuals who had to support themselves would also be eliminated from the best programs; the cost of some successful training programs has been so high that without a direct subsidy employers could

offer little more than a "tuition-free education." Second, many of those who could both afford and benefit from a low-wage job with training would not take the opportunity. Uncertainty about the future value of the training and impatience for immediate income would lead many to jobs with higher pay but less useful experience. Some form of subsidy is therefore necessary if sufficient on-the-job training is to be achieved. Given the substantial direct and indirect subsidies that are now given to students, a program of subsidies for young workers is only equitable. Such subsidies would also help to reduce the current distorting incentives to choose formal education rather than learning on the job.

The advantage of removing the minimum wage barrier to training could be achieved without any change in the minimum wage if a subsidy were paid to employers for all young workers. This would, however, be a very inefficient way to deal with the problem because it would provide the same subsidy regardless of the young person's family income. Such a program would either yield relatively little useful training or be very expensive. A more reasonable solution would be to combine a decrease in the minimum wage with a stipend that is related to the financial situation of the young worker and his family.

A wide variety of alternative programs, differing in the degree of control that the government exercises over the individual's training, could be designed. *Central to all such programs would be a Youth Employment Scholarship paid to young workers as a supplement to their wage income.* At one extreme, each individual would receive his scholarship and make whatever job arrangements he wished. The program would rely on the individual worker to select the job that offered him the most valuable combination of training and current wage. The danger, however, is that because of uncertainty, ignorance, or impatience, many would fail to take advantage of the opportunity to acquire training and would seek the highest current wage. At the other extreme are arrangements like the current JOBS program in which the government contracts directly with firms to provide specific training to individuals selected in a particular way. Neither the rate of acceptance of this program in the business community nor the end results for the trainees have been encouraging. The contract route places undue emphasis on the formal characteristics of the program and puts the government in the inappropriate role of buying specific educational services rather than of subsidizing suitable job settings for young workers. Along the spectrum of possibilities between these two extremes are different combinations of prior approval, supervision, and incentive payments.

PROSPECTS FOR INFLATION IN THE UNITED STATES

Albert T. Sommers

Albert T. Sommers, economist for the prestigious Conference Board, writes his own introduction to this interesting analysis:
"The literature on inflation is getting richer every day, and while it still presents, at least to me, a very imperfect diagnosis, it has already moved into remedial therapy. But I am not at all satisfied that the diagnostic work is complete, and since both therapy and prognosis depend upon the diagnosis, my comments therefore take the form of a kind of Q and A on the origins of the inflation now raging (not too strong a word) throughout the developed world."

In an old story form that seems to be revived and adapted for each oncoming generation, a group of assorted individuals is asked to write an essay on the elephant; their essays reveal their obsessive preoccupations. In modern dress, for example, an oil executive would write on the "elephant and the depletion allowance," a reporter from the *Washington Post* on "the elephant and Watergate." And the modern economist, of virtually any nationality, could now be depended upon to write his essay on "the elephant and inflation."

From The Conference Board *Record* (July 1974).

It was, of course, not always thus. In the 1930s, his essay most certainly would have been on "the elephant and unemployment"; even as recently as eight years ago he would have addressed himself to "the elephant and the payments deficit."

Certainly the greatly increased attention to inflation can be explained in part by the acceleration of inflation itself.

But while simply the *rate* of inflation may account for most of the popularity of the subject, the past several years have provided some disconcerting evidence that inflation is a process, rather than a rate; that it appears to be indigenous to the developed economy of the late 20th century, and, even more ominously, that it may be inherently cumulative. The problems of unemployment having been overpowered by expansionary public policies throughout the free world, inflation has emerged as the putative residual disaster – the Achilles heel – of the modern economy.

The debate over inflation, its causes and cures, goes on at two very different levels. Among professionals, and in the inner councils of policymakers, the question appears as a tough, durable, perhaps fundamental issue confronting the nation. In the press, which draws on the public releases of policymakers, inflation appears as a monthly struggle to interpret each oncoming price index as a passing reflection of temporary and nonrecurring developments. But if the record of the past half-dozen years tells us anything, it is that inflation is now a deeply rooted, inherent phenomenon of the mixed economy, and we delude ourselves, as well as the public at large, if we allow each new price statistic to distract our attention from the great underlying phenomenon.

THE NATURE OF THE PRESENT INFLATION

First of all, is this special, non-recurring inflation? Certainly part of the 11% rate of general inflation being experienced in the United States can be traced to special circumstances.

A rise in agricultural prices has certainly accentuated the behavior of price indexes in early 1974. The agricultural price increase has, in an ingratiatingly conventional way, induced a considerable rise in the prospective supply. (These days, I get a warm, nostalgic feeling whenever any market behaves the way the textbooks say it should.) It is not unreasonable to hope that agricultural prices will be stable in the last half of 1974.

Similarly, although not quite so comfortably, the energy scarcities which have accounted for another large increment in general prices may be near their peaks; certainly we can hope that petroleum product prices will not be behaving in late 1974 as they have behaved over the past several months. There is also much truth in the proposition that all of the great consuming nations of the western world have been operating at very high levels of activity over the past year, and that this coincidence of cycles has temporarily augmented world demand, particularly for raw commodities, with price consequences that no national set of policies can fully accommodate. The relative devaluation of the dollar over the past three years has, of course, directed a more than proportionate component of worldwide inflation into the U.S. system, thus elevating our rate of inflation toward the higher rates that have prevailed in Western Europe.

But it is hard to take much comfort from the argument that our present inflation is solely attributable to such special conditions. Excluding both farm prices and energy costs, the U.S. price level has risen sharply whenever the administration of the direct controls has made it possible – in early 1973 under Phase 3, and in late 1973 and early 1974 under Phase 4. In early 1974, for example, virtually every component of the industrial wholesale price level in the United States has been accelerating. In March [1974] the acceleration is formidably visible in what is perhaps the single most important component of the price structure, at least insofar as the durability of inflation is concerned – that is, in the capital goods that dictate the overhead costs of the future.

While it may be politically comfortable to point to international inflation as an unreachable component of domestic inflation, this poses only another question: Why has inflation accelerated throughout the developed world?

Here the monetarists offer a simple answer to what they take to be a simple question.

Cross-sectionally – that is, country by country – the rate of inflation appears to be moderately well correlated with the rate of growth of money supply; ergo, the growth of the money supply causes inflation, and the way to end it is to reduce the growth rate of the money supply. Bernard Shaw once said that to every question there is a simple answer; the trouble is, it is always wrong.

The monetarist explanation for worldwide inflation seems to me to be dangerously simplistic. It is not at all clear that the causality runs in the direction assumed by the explanation. On all of the evidence it is, I think, a more tenable hypothesis that it is the inflation that is causing the rise in the money supply, rather than the other way round. The occasional efforts in the United States and elsewhere to stop inflation by control of the money supply seem to stop everything *but* inflation, and out of the debris of such experiments emerge more inflation, more money and more inflationary legislation.

Next question: Isn't inflation simply an excess of demand over supply, and isn't that temporary, as it appears always to have been in the past?

Answer: "Scarcity" is certainly a useful word in any appraisal of inflation, but it is a description, not an analysis. The analytic issue is *why* scarcity has appeared across the whole developed world. Moreover, it is not at all clear in the historical record of recent years that scarcity and inflation are uniquely associated; both Europe and the United States have experienced a considerable degree of inflation in time periods when resources in general were not in scarce supply.

If, then, the acceleration of inflation in the United States and the rest of the world cannot largely be explained by non-recurring events, or diabolical or misguided monetary policy, and if scarcity describes but does not explain it, where do the real sources of inflation lie? The answer, unfortunately, is very large and complicated. Unlike past cyclical inflations, modern inflation is only partly economic in nature. Its real essence

is a historical, sociological, institutional phenomenon, rooted in the nature of a mixed economy, and the laws (not just the legislation) that dictate the behavior of a mixed economy.

ECONOMICS: MIXED AND MIXED-UP

A mixed economy is a very complex social organism; it stands in somewhat the same position, in respect of the free-market economy of the early 20th century, that man occupies in respect of the animal kingdom. The emergence of the mixed economy out of the automatic, self-adjusting, naturally cyclical free markets developed in the course of the industrial revolution has interesting parallels with the emergence of man out of the unconscious, self-adjusting world of nature.

In Byron's words, man is "half dust, half deity"; the mixed economy is half the competitive world of nature, and half the socialized world of conscious planning. Both combinations have their problems, and inflation is one of the problems of a mixed economy.

The ways in which inflation is generated in a mixed economy are so interconnected that it is hard to describe them in sequence, without simplification and repetition. I offer here not a definitive description, but a series of views of this complex process.

THE GESTATION OF INFLATION

The mixed economy is an uneasy and unstable blend of opposites: of the free market, and planning; of competition, and cooperation; of private, and public; of freedom, and security; of incentive, and equality. It should be obvious, of course, that the elements of these pairs are in a trade-off relationship. The more we want of one member of the pair, the less we can have of the other. Unfortunately, the mixed economy cannot bear to treat these pairings as trade-offs. It seeks to maximize both elements in the pair, rather than to optimize their relationship. In the process, it is forever over-budgeting its available resources; it lives in a continuous condition of superheated over-commitment.

The mixed economy wants, for example, all public goods and all private goods at the same time. While it cheerfully legislates a rapid rise in the social goods to be provided by government (total social costs in the United States have risen from 2% of GNP in 1929 to about 18% today), it continues to measure its performance in terms of conventional private per capita consumption, and any flagging of the rate of consumption stimulates another stream of pro-consumption legislation and credit policy. In the end, of course, the price level is left to rationalize this contradiction, and it does so by rising.

The mixed economy – this is almost embarrassingly obvious, but it requires restatement in any discussion of modern inflation – is politically oriented toward consumption, even at the expense of investment. When policy sees a need for stimulation, it ordinarily stimulates consumption; when it sees a need for restraint, it tends to restrain investment. The consumption flows carry heavy political armor; the investment flows are exposed to the slings and arrows of a kind of short-circuited morality which treats present consumption as a human need, overriding future consumption. Consumption is, of course, the one insatiable demand in the system; there is no insatiable demand for capital goods, or inventories, or for most forms of government spending (social spending by government is, of course, a cousin of consumption).

The consumption bias of the mixed economy is in violent contradiction with its social goals; this is one of the main roots of monetary inflation (since monetary authorites are in the end compelled to provide enough funds for both) and of price inflation itself. In this sense, as in many others, a rise in the money supply and in inflation are not in a causal relationship with

each other; they are joint consequences of the underlying characteristics of the mixed economy.

SOCIALLY MANDATED INFLATION

A second major aspect of the mixed economy that generates inflation is its dedication to full employment. A credible commitment to full employment has powerful real as well as psychological impacts, all of them inflationary. The security implied by the commitment tends to erode saving propensities, and augment borrowing propensities. At the same time, the commitment dismantles some of the aspects of the labor market that used to warrant the term "labor market," in that it rejects unemployment, and the risk of unemployment, as an element in the determination of wages, without putting anything else in its place. Under our present institutional arrangements, the effort to obliterate the business cycle and cling closely to full employment is in an inexorable trade-off with the rate of inflation: the more eagerly we pursue full employment, the higher the rate of inflation.

Finally, it must be noted that all of the new goals of the mixed economy, not just the full-employment objective, hold a potential for inflation: educational goals, medical service goals, security goals, pension goals, urban rehabilitation goals, housing goals, environmental goals – all of the objectives imposed on the system from outside the free market require diversion of resources from the free market. They accordingly require an arraying of priorities utterly foreign to the free market, and an ethic by which to array the priorities.

It is a pallid understatement of the fact to say that the U.S. political system does not readily lend itself to the rational arraying of economic priorities. Instead, it rushes off in all directions at once. Even where we seemingly legislate the resources to meet the goals, as well as the goals, we subsequently bargain our way out of the costs through political and market power, each group voting for the new priority, and then bargaining itself out of the costs, in what has been aptly called "a shell game." In the end, of course, after monetary policy has indulgently provided everybody with the monopoly money to bid for the resources, inflation makes the final allocations.

Two other points should be noted. The inflationary bias of the modern mixed economy might be at least moderately reduced if new tools of policy were to be developed to meet this kind of institutional inflation. In other words, if it were possible to legislate away some of the contradictions between our conventional celebration of personal freedom, on the one hand, and the increasingly centrally planned goals of the system, the rate of inflation could be importantly reduced. In fact, a certain amount of such anti-inflationary institutional change is now required in order to offset the continuing *pro-inflationary* changes induced in our institutions by inflation itself — such as escalation of wages, Social Security payments, welfare payments, unemployment compensation, minimum wages and, most recently, private pensions. One need not be an entirely cock-eyed optimist to see some hope here.

The Congress is making some progress on rationalizing its budgeting procedures; it is conceivable that a Congress in the near future will recognize the enormous burden of under-depreciation now facing the corporate sector, by revising the acceptable methods of depreciation accounting; and there is a growing body of sophisticated and even conservative opinion that the full-employment commitment would be a lot less inflationary if it were accompanied by a suitable public employment program, to help relieve the Federal Reserve of its present impossible two-front war against both inflation and unemployment.

Modernizing our institutions to meet the needs of the mixed economy might also involve shifting the tax burden toward consumption and away from income, providing the Executive Branch with discretionary tax powers, and examining whether the Federal Reserve should not be equipped with additional powers affecting the direction of credit, and not simply the aggregate volume of credit supply.

But in appraising the future of inflation over the next several years, we should not be superficially optimistic. Several years ago it became apparent that the inflation of the early 1970s was not simply a consequence of misguided fiscal policy during the Vietnam War. It is clear now that our current inflation is not just farm products, or crude oil, or devaluation of the dollar, or a coincidence of international cycles. Inflation is as fundamental a part of the mixed economy as the full-employment commitment and the new social mandates that have invaded economies throughout the western world.

ESCALATING INTO DANGER AND DISORDER

These observations do not readily translate into estimates of the inflation rate in the middle 1970s. But as a rough rule of thumb, I would suggest that the general rate of inflation in the United States, apart from temporary, accidental dislocations of supply, will run between 6% and 9% in the middle 1970s — nearer the lower end of this range when activity falls somewhat short of full employment, or is rising at less than its long-term potential, and near the upper end of this range when it is at or close to full employment, or rising at faster than its long-term potential. Moreover, I would argue that this band of three percentage points is still drifting upward, because the system that generates the inflation is still being subjected to more pro-inflationary institutional change than anti-inflationary change.

Only very powerful national leadership, that can deflect our national attention from immediate consumption demands toward the more remote, less easily appreciated interests of the future, can hope to shift this net rate of institutional change, and it is not easy to see such a political outcome over the next several years.

There are, to be sure, wide differences of opinion among economists about the seriousness of any given rate of inflation, about whether it is possible to accommodate comfortably to any rate of inflation as long as it is fully anticipated; and about whether any given rate of inflation, whether anticipated or not, is or is not likely to accelerate. Without at all suggesting that these are sterile debates, I offer a firmly held judgment of my own: namely, that a high and rising rate of inflation augments consumption at the expense of investment, and therefore conduces to scarcity, and is therefore self-reinforcing. At the same time, a high rate of inflation, by inhibiting investment, inhibits real growth; in so doing, it makes more difficult the process of gradual equalization of incomes to which all developed nations are rather firmly dedicated for both ethical and political reasons; and we therefore should not be surprised to find a high rate of inflation increasingly associated with social disorder.

In the middle 1970s, inflation has emerged as the principal social and economic challenge to the western world. I do not think we should allow ourselves to relinquish this serious view of inflation even if, as seems quite possible, the statistical rate of inflation falls sharply later in 1974, as the temporary effects of increases in farm product prices and perhaps petroleum prices as well disappear from the published indexes.

Problems of Economic Growth

34

LEARNING OBJECTIVES

The only technical point to master is the idea of *balanced growth.* More important is the realization that growth is a two-edged sword, bringing *benefits* and *dangers.* You should bear this major problem in mind as you study the readings that follow.

Our last chapter in macroeconomics takes us to profound issues, especially with regard to the relation between economic growth and welfare, and economic growth and environmental safety. We shall not discuss these matters in this review section, for we have little to add to what is in the text. We recommend that you peruse the readings that follow this short exercise.

But there is also an analytical problem of importance that we would like to go over. This is the problem of balanced growth — of determining what rate of growth will match rising output with just the right amount of rising income.

MARGINAL CAPITAL-OUTPUT RATIO

The basic idea, once grasped, is simple enough. Each act of investment has a double-edged result. On the one hand, it increases *incomes* via the familiar multiplier mechanism. On the other hand, it also increases *capacity,* or potential output. *The question that balanced growth asks us to solve is the rate of growth of investment that will keep the rise in expenditures equal to the rise in output.*

This introduces us to a term we first met early in out study of macroeconomics, the marginal capital-output ratio. Unlike the multiplier, which tells us the results of *behavior* — namely, the effect of our savings propensities — the marginal capital-output ratio is a technical fact of life. It tells us how much capital it will take to produce another unit of output.

For example, suppose that it requires an investment of $4 million in a building to get $1 million of new rentable space (output). In that case, the marginal capital-output ratio is $4 million ÷ $1 million or 4. If it takes on $2 million of investment to bring into cultivation an area that will yield $1 million in crops the marginal capital-output ratio would be 2. In a manufacturing establishment it is often as low as 1: only $1 million in new capital is needed to bring about $1 million in output.

We can write this relationship as follows: $\sigma = I/\Delta O$, where σ, or sigma, stands for the marginal C/O ratio. From this definition, we can also derive a very useful relationship needed to solve the question of balanced growth. *We can inquire how large an increase in output we can expect from a given investment.* By turning around our equation, we get: $\Delta O = I/\sigma$. For example, suppose we know that $I = 100$ and $\sigma = 4$. What would ΔO be under those circumstances? _____ Or suppose that I was 100 and σ was 1. In that case, how large would ΔO be? _____ You can see that the same size investment can give us large or small increases in output, depending on σ: 25 in the first case, 100 in the second.

Now, how do we relate this information about output to income? The steps are not hard.

1. We begin with our familiar multiplier formula. This will tell us by how much income will increase, given an increase in investment. The multiplier formula is: $\Delta Y =$ _____ (you can abbreviate 1/m.p.s. to $1/s$, if you like).

2. Now we write down the equation we have just learned that tells us how much *output* will increase, given I and σ: $\Delta O =$ _____ . Note that our multiplier formula is interested in *increases* in investment, whereas our output formula is interested just in investment. This is because only *increases* in investment give rise to increases in income, whereas even an unchanged rate of investment will increase our output capacity.

3. Now we want to find the conditions under which $\Delta Y = \Delta O$. In other words, we want to know what relationship our key terms, s and σ, must have to one another. All that is required is some elementary algebra:

if $\Delta Y = \Delta O$
and if $\Delta Y = 1/s\Delta I$
and $\Delta O = I/\sigma$
then it follows that
_____ = _____ when income and output increase equally.

4. Now take the result, $1/s\Delta I = I/\sigma$, multiply both sides by s (to get s and σ on the same side) divide by I, and we end up with: _____ .[1]

Now let's understand clearly what this means: First, we have now found *the conditions for balanced growth,* in which we will be creating just enough incomes to enable us to buy back the increased goods.

Second, we can see that the solution requires a *certain rate of increase of investment, $\Delta I/I$.*

Finally, we can see that the required rate of increase of investment depends on two things: how large the s fraction is, and the size of σ.

Let's now apply this in a few examples:

Suppose that $\sigma = 2$ and $s = .5$. How fast would investment have to increase to keep income growing as fast as output? Our formula tells us that the answer is s/σ, or $.5/2 = .25$. Investment would have to grow at a rate of 25 percent a year to give us balanced growth.

[1] $\Delta I/I = s/\sigma$

Suppose that $\sigma = 4$ and $s = .5$. Then how fast would investment have to grow? The answer is s/σ or ___ / ___ = ___ %.

Suppose that $\sigma = 4$ and $s = .25$. Then rate of change in investment ($\Delta I/I$) must be ___ / ___ = ___%.

Can you now answer the following questions?

1. The larger the multiplier, the _____ (larger/smaller) must σ be to keep $\Delta O = \Delta Y$.
2. The smaller the multiplier, the _____ (larger/smaller) must σ be to keep $\Delta O = \Delta Y$.
3. The larger the marginal capital-output ratio, σ the _____ (smaller/larger) must s be to keep $\Delta Y = \Delta O$.

Answers to these are below. But the principle is clear. If we have a small s, we have large multiplier. Therefore, the increase in income will be relatively large. We therefore need a lot of output per unit of additional investment to keep balance in the economy. Conversely, if s is large, we will have a _____ (large/small) multiplier. Income will grow relatively _____ (fast/slowly). For balanced growth we must therefore have a _____ (large/small) increase in output per unit of investment. This will take _____ (large/small) σ. (*Answers*: small, slowly, small, large.)

Our formula for balanced growth is not easy to apply to the data of the economy. But it highlights for us an important principle: *The rate of growth of investment is a key element in balancing increases in demand with increases in supply.* Perhaps we can now see why. The rate of growth of investment is $\Delta I/I$. The numerator of this fraction, ΔI, works its way into the demand side of our economy through the multiplier, I/s. The denominator, I, affects the supply side of the economy through the marginal capital-output ratio, σ. By varying the proportion of ΔI to I, we can keep in balance our spending propensities and our supply capabilities.

Answers: 1. smaller, 2. larger 3. larger [a large s means a low multiplier]

Thus, just as a certain amount of investment was the critical element in closing a demand gap, *growth* in investment is the critical element in closing the "growth gap" – the gap between rising incomes and rising outputs.

QUIZ

___ 1. The marginal capital-output ratio relates
   a. investment with increases in output.
   b. increases in output with increased investment.
   c. increases in output with income.

___ 2. The smaller is σ,
   a. the more investment it takes to get a unit of output.
   b. the less investment it takes to get a unit of output.
   c. the more income it takes to buy a unit of output.

___ 3. If s is the leakages fraction, the larger s is,
   a. the more will income change with a change in investment.
   b. the less will income change with a change in investment.
   c. the more will output change with an increase in spending.

___ 4. As a condition of balanced growth,
   a. increased investment = increased output.
   b. increased income = increased output.
   c. increased investment = increased income.

___ 5. An economy with a slow rate of growth of investment will not have enough demand to buy its increased output unless
   a. s is small and σ large.
   b. s is small and σ small.
   c. s is large and σ small.

TRUE AND FALSE   T F

6. The capital-output ratio has no effect on changes in income.   __ __
7. The lower the marginal capital-output ratio, the faster will output grow per unit of I.   __ __

	T	F
8. Changes in technology that lower σ mean that incomes must increase more rapidly to keep balanced growth.	—	—
9. σ is a technical, s, a behavioral variable.	—	—
10. Balanced growth means no unemployment.	—	—

Answers:

1. a	5. a	8. T
2. b	6. T	9. T
3. b	7. T	10. F
4. b		

THE WAGES OF GROWTH

E. J. Mishan

Professor Mishan of the London School of Economics is one of the first economists to warn against the dangerous side effects of growth. Here he takes a somber look at the question of whether continued economic growth is apt to bring more harm than good.

Though I pose the question, whether continued economic growth is physically possible, it could be rephrased more sensibly as follows: under what conditions, and for what length of time, is an x percent rate of growth possible for a particular area? Put more generally yet, what time-paths of economic growth, as conventionally measured, are physically possible for an economy having particular economic endowments and institutions?

Alas, we have no methods as yet by which we can produce convincing answers to such questions. Indeed, it is entirely possible that we shall be unable, even in the future, to ascertain the physical limits to economic growth until we experience some manifest deterioration of living standards or incur some ecological catastrophe.

From "Ills, Bads, and Disamenities," *Daedalus,* (Fall 1973), pp. 64-69, 72-73, & 79-82. Reprinted by permission of *Daedalus,* Journal of the American Academy of Arts and Sciences, Boston, Massachusetts, Fall 1973, the *No-Growth Society.*

The best we can do today is to infer tentatively, from highly simplified global models using controversial assumptions about future technological progress and about world reserves of materials, that growth at present rates, either of population or of industrial output, cannot continue for much more than a century.

Whether or not they believe these conclusions realistic, all the people debating this issue recognize that we inhabit all too tiny a planet. Most of them are alarmed at current population trends; the prospect of some fifteen billion human beings swarming over the planet in fifty or sixty years' time is not an inviting one. With the existing population of about four billion souls, we are already getting in each other's way and stepping on each other's toes. Assuming the mobility indices continue to rise — car ownership in Western Europe increasing at about 8 percent per annum, air travel at about 10 percent — the mounting frustrations of travelers and the resentments of indigenous populations may break out in civil disturbances.

Apart from population growth, though aggravated by it, there are the familiar problems of pollution, food supplies, and the depletion of natural resources. Although there have been some local improvements over the last quarter of a century – there is, for example, less sulphur dioxide (though much more carbon dioxide) in the air of London than there was twenty years ago, and some (possibly mutant) species of fish have recently been discovered in the murky waters of the Thames – nobody seriously challenges the fact that air and water pollution exist on a larger scale today than ever before in man's history. The global scale of pollution not only destroys flora and fauna but spoils the food we eat. Chemical pesticides enter our bloodstream either directly through our consumption of chemically sprayed plants or indirectly through our consumption of cattle that ingest them. The poisoning of rivers destroys fish in estuaries and renders the flesh of the survivors increasingly toxic to humans.

Turning to material resources, in particular fossil fuels and metals, a common estimate is that, if present consumption trends persist, we shall run out of oil by about the end of the century even allowing for the discovery of new reserves, and of all but a few of today's "essential" metals within about fifty years. Indeed, at current rates of usage, all known reserves of silver, gold, copper, lead, platinum, tin, and zinc will have been used up within· a couple of decades.

The conventional economic response to the threat of depleting resources is twofold: to quote history in illustration of the principle of resource substitution and to affirm faith in the future of technology and "the wit of man." Concerning the first, economists will point out that the shortage of a resource leads to a rise in its price which induces manufacturers to replace it by other materials that, though less suitable, are now less expensive. The less successful the search for suitable substitutes, however, the higher the resulting costs of the finished goods in question, and the smaller the amounts bought by consumers.

But all this takes place in the world of theoretical constructs. The real world may turn out to be less accommodating. Historical examples, such as those given by Barnett and Morse, cover about a hundred years of recent history and contain few examples apart from the apparent success story of fuels: wood to coal, coal to oil, and oil (hopefully) to nuclear power. I say the *apparent* success story since it may not prove feasible to maintain, much less increase, per capita consumption of energy much further unless we discover economical means of disposing safely of the vast amounts of heat and radioactive wastes generated by nuclear power stations. Neither can one be very optimistic about the impending exhaustion, simultaneously, of a large number of widely used metals. Only in theoretical models are substitutes always available. It is entirely possible that some of these metals will rise steeply in price, thus drastically reducing their use and the output of products that depend upon them, without any tolerable substitute being discovered. There will be no comfort to be had from traditional doctrines when we are brought up sharply against the unalterable facts of the physical universe.

TWO REASONS FOR SKEPTICISM ABOUT TECHNOLOGY

Over the future of technology a great question mark hangs, and for much the same reason. Two hundred years of scientific discovery and innovation have imbued us with a faith that man will eventually conquer. Thus, whenever some of the less happy consequences of modern technology and its products are brought to our attention – 140,000 automobile deaths a year, the ecological disasters of DDT, the genetic effects of Thalidomide – or whenever account is taken of the increasing risks to which humanity is now exposed, the habitual response of technocrats is to transmute the risk into a "challenge" or to quote some historical piece of "doomsdayism." Yet if, as philosophers are agreed, there are no laws of historical development, the proposition must be extended also to the development of science and technology. We cannot be sure of technological progress either. Man may, then, become engaged endlessly in some kinds of research that, in the nature of things, cannot come to fruition.

Apart from these real possibilities, there are at least two reasons for feeling less than sanguine about the future of technology. First, the unprecedented scale of the current exploitation of the earth's finite resources makes virtually a qualitative difference between the situation today and that of yesterday. For this reason alone, deriding yesterday's Jeremiahs affords little consolation. Time works vast changes, and the alarums of today should not go unheeded simply because those of yesterday were premature. The apprehensions of an octogenarian about his impending demise are not to be soothed by reminding him that he thought he was going to die when he was twenty.

To pursue the same analogy, the discovery that some poet was lamenting the disappearance of the English countryside at about the time of Chaucer is, in itself, no answer to those who lament today for the same reason. The English countryside can indeed disappear. It is, in fact, being irreparably destroyed. Again, from the observation that the fears of Malthus and others were premature at the turn of the nineteenth century, it does not follow that the earth can comfortably support any size of population. And however abundant the earth's reserves of fossil fuels and minerals, their continued mining must eventually exhaust them, and faster than we are prone to imagine. Sustained rates of growth build up to incredible magnitudes. If, for example, actual reserves turn out to be four times as great as we estimate today, the current growth of

consumption could be maintained for only fifteen years longer than it could according to current estimates. To take another example, if the growth of air travel in Western Europe maintains its pace, there will be about fifteen times as much air travel at the end of the century as there is today, and more than sixty times as much in another fifteen years. I need hardly remark that the trend is unlikely to continue at such rates for many years – though not because governments are far-sighted enough to take measures to discourage the trend. Owing to limitations of air and ground space, commercial attempts to maintain the expansion of air travel will run into difficulties long before air travel has multiplied fifteenfold.

In sum, we of this generation are already being pressed against the inescapable limitations of a finite planet. Whether or not we succeed in stabilizing population in time, we cannot continue much longer to use up space, to ransack the earth's resources and to fill its air and waters with effluent with the reckless abandon that has characterized our activity since the industrial revolution. The implications of this new situation can be crucial for technology, for its development over the last 200 years has been based on physical conditions that no longer obtain: virtually unlimited resources and a virtually unlimited assimilative capacity of the biosphere. It remains to be seen how technology will cope when abundance in these repects gives way to constriction.

The second reason for feeling less than sanguine about the contribution of technology in maintaining the existing growth rates is that we are moving into an area of increasing uncertainty. In order of diminishing tractability we can list four types of global risk, none of which existed before the industrial revolution.

(1) Insofar as the chief effluents poured into the air, lakes, rivers, and coastal waters are known and their toxic effects understood, they

can be effectively curbed in a number of ways, of which enforcing minimal standards of purity may well be the most economic. The success of this method depends upon the efficacy and frequency of monitoring, and on the severity of the penalties exacted for failing to comply. What economists do not sufficiently allow for, however, are the limits to our present knowledge. There cannot be many effluents whose full range of toxic effects are known to us. Moreover, in consequence of rapid chemical innovation, new gases and fluids are being produced whose effects on the ambient environment and on our health may not be discernible for many years, and possibly only after substantial and irreversible damage has been done.

(2) To these risks that we run from pushing on in a state of semi-ignorance, we may add (a) those arising from the indiscriminate use of chemical pesticides such as DDT, from the gradual dissipation of the protective ozone mantle by the gases emitted in supersonic flight, and from the accumulating deposits of synthetic material that resist absorption into the ecological cycle, and (b) those arising out of the growing assortment of chemical compounds appearing each year on the market, about whose ultimate biological and genetical effects, taken singly or in combination, we know next to nothing. Nor can we reasonably expect to detect the dangers in time. Luckily, the mutilative potential of the medically recommended sedative, Thalidomide, was discovered before it became a genetic calamity – and then, not by doctors or scientists, but by a private citizen working on a hunch. We may not be so lucky with a number of other common drugs on the market. If, after a number of years, the death or sickness of a small proportion of the human population can be traced to some new substance or to some new combination of substances, it will be likely that the disease is latent in a much larger proportion of the population. What is more, it may not be

possible to find an adequate antidote in time, and even if one is found in time, its side effects may eventually prove to be more dangerous than the disease it is intended to cure.

(3) The third category of risk arises from our diminishing immunity to contagious diseases – a consequence, ironically, of the apparent success of modern medicine. Just as many insect pests have, over the last three decades, successfully adapted themselves to withstand, or even to thrive on, once powerful pesticides, as too, are micro-organisms, with their faster rate of reproduction, and therefore of mutation, becoming resistant to the action of penicillin, antibiotics, etc. The ultimate effect of "miracle drugs," it appears, is, through the irrepressible mechanism of natural selection, to breed "miracle microbes." But this powerful adaptive mechanism of the micro-organisms that are man's most ruthless foe does not take us "back to square one." The situation is in reality worse. For under favorable conditions, the human body, aided perhaps by older methods of treatment, could often enough cope with the old strain of germs. Once new strains have appeared in response to the initial efficacy of new drugs, the human body may no longer be able to cope alone even under favorable conditions. Perforce it may have to depend entirely on new and "more powerful" drugs, but drugs yet to be discovered. And there is no assurance that they will be discovered in time, and no assurance that, if discovered, they will not again be rendered useless within a short period by new strains of microbes. It may transpire, then that the much lauded achievements of medical science will have succeeded only in starting a race for survival between man and microbe in which the advantages seem to lie with the microbe.

(4) The fourth and the greatest immediate risk in the foreseeable future is that humanity will perish as a result of the great scientific

discoveries of the last thirty years inasmuch as they have presented man with the means of illimitable thermonuclear destruction and bio-chemical warfare. Within the next decade the power of instant annihilation of all life over vast areas will be within the destructive capacity of the governments of some thirty nations, including many of the smaller nations that are led by unstable regimes which may continue to include adventurers and fanatics. Introduce into this already inflammable situation the possibility of accident, military bungling, or bluff carried too far, and the chances of humanity surviving the end of the century do not look particularly strong . . .

Finally, we might more reasonably be asking if life is becoming more enjoyable or if we are becoming better or more contented people in consequence of economic growth. Bearing in mind the facts of human nature, we could reflect on current economic and social developments in particular areas and endeavor to obtain clues about the extent to which the modes of living they give rise to accord with, or conflict with, man's biological and psychic needs. And by speculating about technological and economic developments over the foreseeable future, we can debate whether, on balance, we are likely to be better people, or more contented people, over the next few decades. This seems to me the more promising area of inquiry, and the one to which I suggest we direct our attention.

Obviously we cannot *prove* propositions about the decline in social welfare as one can prove, for example, that a significant rise in the price of beef, *ceteris paribus,* will cause a drop in the maximum amount of beef that people are willing to buy. In debating social welfare, sub-jective judgments are required – judgments of fact, and possibly also judgments of value.

Let us move now toward the hub of the problem by asking an apparently naive question: Why cannot a rise in GNP, or rather in real per capita income, be accepted as an index of an increase in society's welfare? The theoretical economist's short answer is that the sufficient conditions that would allow a translation from GNP to social welfare are not met.

First, the identical population would have to remain in being during a period over which GNP rises. If the period extends to two generations, and each person in the second generation has more goods than some corresponding person in the first, the economist can only report that fact. Since he eschews interpersonal comparisons, he is unable to declare that persons in the second generation experience more welfare than those in the first. Secondly, and for the same reason, the economist cannot state that a person whose real income has grown over time is better off unless it is also known that his tastes and his capacity for enjoyment have remained unchanged.

These conditions do look rather austere, and in his practical recommendations the economist has a tendency to overlook them. Provided that people are not working harder and that the distribution of the aggregate product among the population is no less satisfactory, a rise in real per capita income is commonly regarded as conferring benefits on society, even though its size and age composition are changing. I would be persuaded to go along with this, were it not for the fact that quite a useful proportion of our national resources is devoted expressly to per-suading people to change their tastes – not always for the better – and were it not for another proviso . . .

SOME OBJECTIONS OF GROWTHMEN

Let me pause in passing to consider some misunderstandings of the environmental issue. Of late, it has been asserted that the new surge of concern about the environment is no more than a cover under which the middle classes are trying to hang onto their privileges, that it has nothing to offer to the working classes or the poor.

Strangely enough, the same person may also be found arguing that in order to make *desirable* environmental improvements it is necessary to maintain and, if possible, to increase the rate of economic growth.

One can indeed think up environmental improvements that would benefit largely higher income groups, but for the most part these are undertaken by such groups at their own expense and initiative. Insofar as the improvements entail cleaner air, quiet, and purer water, there is no reason to suppose that the schemes proposed do not extend such benefits also to the poorer members of society. In fact it is plausible to believe that the poorer citizens benefit more than the richer ones who can always move with far less inconvenience than the poor from any district that is sinking in the scale of amenity. If, on the other hand, the revenues raised for environmental benefits happen to involve a greater proportional reduction of the income or purchasing power of the poor than of the rich there need be no difficulty in altering the tax structure in order to restore equity. This should present no financial difficulty inasmuch as the strict economic case for reducing pollution requires that aggregate benefits exceed costs – a condition that has to be met, incidentally, quite irrespective of the distribution of incomes.

As for the alleged need for more of this GNP stuff, as a condition for performing good works – removing the accumulated filth in the environment, reducing poverty in the cities, healing the sick, comforting the aged, educating the young – we find that the same arguments were used in the fifties; indeed, similar arguments have been used in justification of growing richer, individually or socially, as far back as Adam Smith. Since we can count on the poor always being among us – the relatively poor, that is – we shall never lack for an excuse to push onward with GNP.

The obvious weakness of this line of defense is simply that we would not need to grow in order

to do good works if we were just a little less reluctant than we happen to be to share what we have more equally with the less fortunate in the community. Had we stronger moral principles, or more patriotic virtue, neither of which, however, find much encouragement in the ethos of an affluent society, the bulk of the population would recognize at once that already it had enough to spare for good works. People would recognize that forever putting off the day of reckoning by claiming the need to grow richer is as transparent an instance of self-deception as that of the miser who claims the need to hoard more so as eventually to give more to charity. One need bear in mind the vast current expenditures on "demerit goods" – the "expendables," "regrettables," the "inimicals" and "near-garbage" that absorb so large a proportion of our resources – to recognize the moral implications of society's political choices.

And yet the case for spending more on environmental improvement would hold even if no such "demerit" goods were produced by the modern economy, and if our moral behavior as a community were already impeccable. As I have indicated above, the economic case for such improvements presumes, indeed requires, an excess of social benefit over resource cost. The case for their introduction then depends no more on the rate of economic growth than it does upon the level of aggregate income or its distribution. Whatever the rate of economic growth – positive, zero, or negative – and whatever the aggregate level of income and its distribution, if there is an economic case for reducing pollution levels or enhancing the environment, the case is for doing so now.

Finally, insofar as ecologists and environmentalists reject sustained economic growth as a desirable social goal for the West, they are reminded by economists of the difficulties that arise when the economy does not grow. In each of the short-lived periods of stagnation of the American economy, for instance, there has been an appreciable rise in the number of unemployed, a decline in the share of labor income (except perhaps during the prolonged depression of the thirties), particular hardship among the poorest section of the populace, a frustration of people's expectations, and increased conflict among the working classes. But these recessional features are not pertinent to the issue. For they are peculiar to a growth-bound economy, one in which a period of no growth or decline in growth arises from market failure and inadequate monetary and fiscal policies, and necessarily entails unemployment, stagnation and, consequently, increased frustration. Those concerned primarily with the quality of life have never proposed to create unemployment in the growth economy as a means of slowing economic growth. Rather they seek to persuade the public to abandon the pursuit of economic growth in favor of a stable or steady-state economy within which there is explicit consideration of the factors that enhance the quality of life. The

actual means whereby a steady-state economy is to be brought into being – the rationing of raw materials, the controls on technology etc., – and the level of affluence to be sought are important subjects of discussion. But in the existing state of social awareness, they are perhaps premature. Immediate concern must be with the revolution in thought and feeling that is necessary if men's aspirations toward the good life are ever to be realized. Thus the aim of the ecologist and environmentalist is not a no-growth economy per se. It is to win *acceptance* by the public at large of a no-growth economy. Once the ethics of a no-growth economy are accepted and the competitive striving for more, ever more, is a thing of the past, it will be that much easier to remove the wretched poverty that still lingers in Western countries, to redirect expenditure away from current extravagance and waste, and to bring about a more equal distribution of income . . .

FOULING THE NEST

Peter Passell/Leonard Ross

How dangerous is the process of growth? Potentially it is very dangerous, argue the authors of this reading – but many of these dangers can be avoided by intelligent public policy. In their book The Retreat from Riches *Professors Passell and Ross argue that growth is the most practical political means of eliminating poverty, and that controlled growth should therefore remain a high objective on the national agenda.*

If the ecology movement has often been comically trendy, it is also deadly serious and, perhaps, the most important and hopeful variety of reformist politics left in this country. Decades of progressive degradation of the environment had been ignored – or, more commonly, exacerbated – by the agencies of government. Palliatives had often made the problem worse. Interstate-highway construction temporarily speeded traffic but made Americans ever more dependent on the automobile. Federal subsidies paid for hundreds of local treatment plants to cut the flow of raw sewage into our waterways; but the rivers did not become much cleaner, and the treated waste itself created a new pollution hazard by fertilizing microscopic water-plant life. Pittsburgh reduced its industrial air-pollution problem with tough regulations on smokestack emissions, but permitted new pollution hazards to arise by virtually abandoning mass transit. Eventually, this record of social neglect and mishap drove conservationists, the young, and even the doyens of the Establishment to despair. As Aurelio Peccei, a Fiat executive, put it, "We have entirely lost the capacity for guiding the

From **Peter Passell and Leonard Ross**, *The Retreat from Riches* (New York: The Viking Press, 1971), pp. 20-35.

complexities of society: one can see signs everywhere."

To many liberals, this history was sobering but was no basis for being fatalistic. The chances for real environmental protection have always been compromised by confused planning and halfhearted financial commitments. Now that the electorate was aroused, work could begin in earnest. Surely, went the weary but plausible argument, the nation that sent a submarine under the polar icecap and a man to the moon can save Lake Erie.

A growing and well-publicized group of environmentalists challenge this common-sense assertion. They predict that a modest shuffling of priorities, a few billion dollars reassigned to antipollution or mass-transit programs, will have little effect. This pessimistic vision is a sober prophecy by respectable scientists who are convinced that we can no longer count on being bailed out by progress. The harsh realities of scarcity, they argue, make it imperative that we stop environmental problems at their source, that we slow the gluttonous engine of economic growth. Technology may work fine in outer space, but it offers scant hope of redeeming the sins we have committed against our earth-bound biosphere.

Indeed, technology has inadvertently magnified pollution while increasing economic output: deadly mercury-waste production has jumped dramatically since World War II, mostly as a consequence of the demand for chlorine. Synthetic pesticides, so effective in raising crop yields, threaten to reach man in toxic doses. The substitution of tough plastic packaging, impervious to chemical breakdown, for frailer cardboard means that litter remains intact unless somebody picks it up.

Could we, perhaps, grow without reliance on this defiling technology? Again, the new view is pessimistic. Growth, the environmentalists say, is drastically limited by the availability of resources. Man's appetite for depletable minerals is increasing so rapidly that most reserves could be exhausted within a few centuries. Fossil fuels — the coal, oil, and natural gas that provide virtually all of our energy — are being used up a thousand times faster than nature creates them. World supplies of crucial metals such as tungsten, zinc, nickel, aluminum, and lead are far from infinite; projected industrial demand can be accommodated from known reserves for less than one hundred years.

Even before we run out of raw materials or poison ourselves with alien technology, casual abuse of the environment may well trigger rapid natural changes with disastrous consequences. The world, some scientists conjecture, is speeding toward an ecological judgement day on which seemingly trivial violations of nature will threaten the existence of man. By this reasoning, to assume offhandedly that economic growth can go on forever is suicidal.

Predictions of imminent doom may be speculative, but they are even more frightening than prophecies of a more gradual end through resource exhaustion. And behind the strong language are some reasoned, scientific arguments. Ecologists tell us that the biological accident that created and continues to sustain man is only thinly defended against disaster. Carbon, oxygen,

and nitrogen, critical to life, are shuttled between earth, air, and living organisms through delicate ecological chains. Almost any economic activity disrupts these chains — the bigger the scale and the more modern the organization, the more disruptive it is. Coal is burned, increasing the carbon dioxide and smoke in the air. Insects are exterminated with pesticides, cutting off a food source for numerous higher life forms. Natural vegetation is cleared for farming, reducing the amount of oxygen released into the air, increasing the rate of moisture loss from the soil, and modifying the capacity of the land to resist erosion. Underground rivers are tapped for irrigation, lowering the water table. The consequences of these disruptions are rarely understood before major environmental changes are under way. The ecological chains are so complex and interwoven that we have only primitive knowledge of the effect of severing a link or two. A few examples culled from the list of hazards are illustrative.

Phosphorus and nitrogen compounds from modern laundry detergents, processed sewage, and fertilizers are pumped into lakes and rivers. Innocuous in themselves, these chemicals disrupt the balance of animal and vegetable life in large lakes. Colonies of microscopic algae feast on the nutrients and then die, leaving great masses of organic wastes on the lake bottoms. At unpredictable intervals, these wastes can siphon off much of the natural oxygen supply in the water. The result: rapid changes in the lake's capacity to sustain aquatic life. Lake Erie has been particularly vulnerable to this process. Some types of fish have disappeared altogether, while all fish catches are down sharply. Thanks to a doubling of plant-nutrient discharges over the past decades, other important lakes and coastal fishing waters are not far behind.

Consider another ecological snare. Every use of coal or oil to generate heat discharges the by-products of combustion into the atmosphere. Of course, the local effects are obvious to any city dweller who endures his daily measure of filth. But scientists suspect that far more subtle changes to the environment are taking place. Natural combustion creates heat, carbon dioxide, and smoke as it consumes oxygen. Atmospheric carbon dioxide, in any conceivable concentration, is harmless to any form of life, but it affects the capacity of the earth to radiate heat absorbed from the sun. The gas creates a sort of greenhouse effect in which solar energy can enter the atmosphere but is prevented from leaking back into space. By the year 2000, thanks to man's use of fossil fuels, atmospheric carbon dioxide will increase by one fifth, tending to raise the surface temperature of the earth by perhaps one degree. At the same time, however, the average level of smoke particles in the atmosphere will increase, acting as a shield against solar radiation. Thus the smoke tends to cool us, but no one knows on balance whether the earth's temperature will go up or down.

Atmospheric temperature has little direct effect on our lives — a few degrees one way or another would hardly be noticed. Yet those small changes might affect weather patterns and, in turn, change the size of the polar icecaps. A major temperature increase could melt enough ice to flood the low countries of Europe and all of the world's major harbors. A decrease could trigger a new ice age.

Similarly, the introduction of supersonic commercial aircraft will have unknown effects on the upper atmosphere. Once in operation, these SSTs will emit exhaust particles and water vapor into the stratosphere, thereby changing its natural capacity to reflect solar radiation and perhaps seriously affecting the climate. Moreover, some scientists forecast a dramatic change in the energy-filtering capacity of the stratosphere, which would permit more ultraviolet rays to reach us and thereby multiply the incidence of skin cancer.

The list of imponderable hazards can be extended further. Modern agricultural methods permit enormous improvements in crop yields through the use of fertilizers, pesticides, and irrigation. They constitute the main weapons of the so-called "Green Revolution." Yet all of these measures threaten to defile the environment. Fertilizer washed off the soil is an important cause of stream and lake pollution; it is also a suspected threat to infants when it infiltrates drinking water. Pesticides, such as DDT, work their way through the food chain and collect in birds and animals; current, low-concentration levels have already reduced fish supplies in some areas. Major irrigation projects rarely have a benign effect on local ecologies, and occasionally have produced disaster. The Aswan dam on the Nile has induced a snail-population explosion spreading a debilitating disease to the peasants who work near the river. And all of these environmental difficulties may be just a preview of coming detractions; even if all industry were to shut down tomorrow, the impact of existing pollution would not be known for decades.

This vision of future economic growth is thus quite grim. We seem trapped in a pattern of rapidly increasing pollution and rapidly decreasing resource reserves, complicated by the omnipresent danger of ecological disaster. If history is adequate evidence to judge the future, the technology that has permitted us our economic miracles will sabotage all efforts to break out of the circle.

Given this scenario, the alternatives for avoiding collapse are very limited. Further expansion of economic output would appear intolerable; in fact substantial contraction might be inevitable. Anthony Lewis probably speaks for most environmentalists when he writes, "The conclusion of the scientists [is that] . . . there is only one way to avoid the pattern of boom crashing into earthly limits. That is to moderate all the interconnected factors: population, pollution, industrial production. The essential is to stop economic growth."

It is difficult to quarrel with much of the environmentalists' message. Economic growth has been pursued in ignorance of the environmental costs. As a British scientists' broadside in *Ecologist Magazine* sees it: "Industrial man in the world today is like a bull in a china shop . . . [who has] set himself the goal of reducing it to rubble in the shortest possible time." By pretending that the problems don't exist, we have tempted the gods to anger. At best, we could end up waist high in pollutants without the resources to provide even the necessities. At worst, we could trigger disastrous changes in climate or earth chemistry that could make the planet unfit for human life.

But in prescribing an end to growth as the remedy, the doomsday environmentalists have made an error not so different from those who would ignore the implications of ecology altogether: the past is an uncertain measure of the future. Though growth has been associated with the rape of the biosphere for the last few centuries, this does not mean that we are powerless to sever the association. The real problem is maintaining some perspective on an issue that seems to beg for ideological commitment. To a large extent, the arguments about ecology and growth have been made at the expense of reason. Either one must agree with the environmentalists who assert that stopping growth is the key to survival, or one feels compelled to defend the idea "that conditions are getting better not worse . . . that the danger today resides in the Disaster Lobby . . . who are undermining the American system and threatening the lives and fortunes of the American people."

The temptation to choose sides is undeniably strong: that we are close to doomsday makes little intuitive sense to the majority in a nation conditioned to a toaster-oven in every kitchen and a car in every garage; that the world can go on as it is appears equally absurd for converts to the cause. Yet should neither view turn out to be correct, the penalties of choosing either extreme will be considerable. If the alarmists are right, a policy of business as usual will mean disaster. But if they are wrong, a policy of deliberately halting

economic growth would unnecessarily condemn much of the world to permanent poverty. Any remotely probable redistribution of current output would leave most of the world with an annual income of less than $500.

Perhaps the best way of presenting the case for a middle position is to examine the assumptions behind the most ambitious scenario of doom offered to date, *The Limits to Growth,* by a team of computer specialists led by Dennis Meadows. Produced under the auspices of the Club of Rome, a self-styled "invisible college" of elite international corporation executives and technocrats, this volume has caught the attention of the press with its dramatic prediction of world economic collapse within decades unless the engine of economic growth is slowed to idle.

The Limits to Growth approaches the problem of forecasting the future straightforwardly enough, employing the time-honored technique of computer-aided mathematical simulation. Simulation has proved invaluable as a device for testing engineering designs at little cost and no risk to lives. Instead of simply building a prototype aircraft and seeing if it flies, the airplane's characteristics are condensed down to a series of computer equations that simulate flight. The Apollo moon rocket made thousands of trips on an IBM machine before it was even built. Economists also use simulation, though their successes have been modest. Thanks in part to our rather crude understanding of how the economy works, simulation models have a spotty record in using current data to predict national income, unemployment, and inflation even a year or two in advance.

But *The Limits to Growth* is cast from a more heroic mold than any engineering or economic study. The Meadows team focuses its attention on the whole world, and extends its time horizon to centuries. Factors that the researchers believe influence population and income are boiled down to a few dozen equations. The crucial variables – population, industrial output, raw-materials reserves, food production, and pollution – all interact in ways that are at least superficially reasonable: population growth is limited by food output, health services, and pollution; industrial and agricultural growth are limited by resource availability and pollution. *Limits* is thus able to create a hypothetical future based on knowledge of the past.

As a first approximation of that future, the *Limits* study assumes that the world is incapable of adjusting to problems of scarcity. Technology stagnates and pollution is ignored, even as it chokes millions to death. In their grim scenario, resource scarcity, rather than environmental decay, delivers the *coup de grace*; world reserves of vital elements (silver, tungsten, mercury, etc.) are exhausted within forty years. Around 2020, the pinch becomes tight enough to cause a fall in per-capita income. A few decades later, malnutrition and lagging health services abruptly reverse the climbing population trend. By the year 2100, the resource base has shrunk so badly that the world economy is unable to sustain even nineteenth-century living standards.

Rather than demonstrating the need to halt economic growth, the scenario only plausibly illustrates the obvious need for continued scientific progress to sustain current levels of prosperity. The quality of life in the future surely depends on the progress of technology and, to some degree, on our willingness to slow population growth. But that should come as no surprise to developed nations of the world where people are already enormously dependent on modern techniques. If the telephone company were restricted to turn-of-the-century technology, 20 million operators would be needed to handle today's volume of calls. Or, as the editor of *The Economist* put it, an extrapolation of the trends of the 1880s would show today's cities buried under horse manure.

By the same measure, the simulation provides some insight into the probable hazards of continued population growth. Large families are a luxury in the developed nations; population growth reduces the possibility of privacy for

many and causes genuine hardship for those at the bottom of the economic ladder. Thanks to the new technology of birth control, the problem may be eliminated altogether without government interference. But, for the less developed countries, the population explosion may wipe out all the gains from output growth, and thereby condemn them to unending poverty.

The authors of *Limits* and many environmentalists have much more in mind than these simple lessons, however. They are out to show that pollution, malnutrition, and population growth cannot be attacked directly, but only by stopping economic growth. They argue that any reasonable modification of their assumptions to account for new technology, nonpolluting industrial processes, and population control might postpone collapse but would not avoid it. Under the most sanguine conditions imaginable, the Meadows team contends, "The limits of growth will be reached sometime within the next hundred years. The most probable result will be a rather sudden and uncontrollable decline in both population and industrial capacity." Even if technology doubled known resources and crop yields, pollution were cut by three-fourths, and birth control eliminated all accidental pregnancies, growth would turn out to be self-limiting. In no more than a century, the collective weight of food shortages, raw-material depletion, and pollution would reverse expansion. The only way to avoid collapse and its attendant miseries is to halt growth now.

It is no coincidence that all the *Limits* simulations end in collapse. A close examination of their technique reveals the weakness of the doomsday arguments. As in any simulation, the results depend on the information initially fed to the computer. And the *Limits* team fixes the wheel; no matter how many times you play, there is only one plausible outcome. Critical to the model is the notion that growth creates stress (on the environment, on mineral and agricultural resources) which multiply geometrically. Like compound interest on a savings account, these stresses accumulate at a constantly accelerating pace: every child born is not only another mouth to feed but another potential parent, every new factory not only drains away resources but increases our capacity to build more factories. Geometric (or, as mathematicians prefer to call it, exponential) growth must eventually produce spectacular results. If the Indians who sold Manhattan three hundred years ago for $24 could have left their money untouched in a bank paying 7 percent (a number chosen no more arbitrarily than many in *Limits*), they would have more than $25 billion today.

While the world model hypothesizes exponential growth for our future industrial and agricultural activities, it places arbitrary, nonexponential limits on the technical progress that might accommodate them. New methods of locating and mining ores, or recycling used materials, are assigned the ability to do no more than double reserve capacity; agricultural research can do no more than double land yields; pollution can cut emissions from each source by no more than three-fourths. Hence the end is inevitable. Economic demands must outstrip economic capacities simply because of the assumption of exponential growth in the former.

The basic idea is hardly new. The Reverend Thomas Malthus made a similar point two centuries ago without benefit of computer printouts or blinking lights. Malthus argued that people tend to multiply exponentially while, at best, the food supply increases at a constant rate. He expected that starvation and war would periodically redress the balance. The cause has never been long without spokesmen. In the 1920s, John Ise recast the Malthusian dilemma in terms of natural resources; twenty years ago, the issue was resuscitated by the Truman Administration's Paley Commission report on resource scarcity.

It is true that exponential economic growth cannot go on forever if technology does not keep up or if resources are exhausted. If technology is going to fail us, we must save ourselves much

misery by stopping before we reach the limits, but there is no particular criterion beyond myopia on which to base that speculation. Malthus was wrong; food capacity has kept up with population. The Paley Commission was wrong; there are no signs of a general shortage of raw materials. While no one knows for certain, technical progress does not seem to be slowing down. The best econometric estimates suggest that is indeed growing exponentially.

Not only are natural-resource reserves and technology calculated on the most conservative assumptions in *The Limits to Growth,* but the world economy is assumed to be incapable of adjusting to shortages once they appear. This is largely due to the absence of prices as a variable in the projection of how resources will be used. In the real world, rising prices act as an economic spur to conserve scarce resources, providing profit incentives to use cheaper materials in their place, stimulating private efforts to discover new ways to save on resource inputs, and making renewed exploration attempts more lucrative. In fact, natural-resource prices have remained low, giving little evidence of coming shortages; mineral prices have roughly kept pace with industrial prices for the past one hundred years. The reasons are not hard to find. Technical change has dramatically reduced exploration and extraction costs in spite of the scarcity of high-grade ores – the mining operation that took one hundred man-hours in 1929 used only forty-five in 1957. And technology continues to widen the opportunities to substitute plentiful materials for scarce ones: plastics for metal; synthetic fibers for natural; irrigated, chemically treated land for naturally fertile; etc.

Of course, nature does pose some constraint on economic output. The earth is finite; hence, in some sense, there are limits. But those limits may be so distant that they need not concern us any more than the fact that the sun will burn out someday casts a shadow on our lives. Most scientists agree that the ultimate limit must be calculated in terms of the availability of energy.

In effect, energy can make up for raw-material scarcity. Given enough energy, minerals can be reclaimed from under the sea, or from sea water itself; trace minerals could be recycled from scrap or garbage. With enough energy, we could even extract minerals from other planets.

Conventional sources of energy are confined to fossil fuels (coal, oil, natural gas) and fission fuels (uranium). While supplies of these are much larger than is generally known — Canada's tar sands and Colorado's shale-rock-oil deposits dwarf the great oil reserves of the Persian Gulf — expected use rates could still exhaust them within one thousand years. However, the infant technology of nuclear fusion already shows signs of freeing us from the constraints of conventional energy sources. It is possible that nuclear-fusion reactors, in essence controlled hydrogen bombs, can provide safe, cheap, virtually limitless power within decades. The fuel for nuclear fusion is hydrogen, an element as available as sea water. No one has yet been able to generate a fusion reaction in the laboratory, let alone in a commercial power plant — the technical problems of heating hydrogen to millions of degrees within a tiny fraction of a second are staggering. But the goal now appears within reach — close enough so that at least one American corporation is developing a fusion reactor without government subsidies.

If the natural-resources-limits argument is a red herring, what of the danger of ecological disaster? Here *The Limits to Growth* simulation can offer little hard evidence. The Meadows team simply assumes that abatement practices will at best reduce pollution by three-quarters. Yet that goal could be accomplished using techniques that exist today, and it ignores the promise of innovations that are being developed. Relatively pollution-free autos can be built if we have the political will to insist; electric power can be generated with minimal pollution if we are willing to pay a reasonable price.

This does not mean, of course, that ecological damage should be dismissed outright as the ultimate limit to growth. But in their fervor to publicize the dangers of ignoring the environment altogether, many ecologists have overstated the case. Survival may demand some modification in our behavior. However, that need not mean an end to economic growth.

Much of the recognized global ecological threat comes from known contaminants — smoke, high-altitude fuel combustion, pesticides, fertilizers — which can be attacked directly without opting for an end to economic expansion. A large portion of industrial air pollutants can be eliminated without crippling production; high-cost natural pesticides (quickly broken down by the elements) and the new technology of genetic weapons against insects can replace DDT and its deadly cousins; water eutrophication can be controlled by limiting fertilizer runoffs, phosphate-detergent use, and sewage-treatment-plant dumping. Some kinds of economic activity might be banned altogether — supersonic jet aircraft probably fit the category. But such limits hardly imply the end to growth.

Subtler forms of environmental damage caused by economic activity — weather change due to power generation is a prime candidate — are possibilities, but the best scientific evidence suggests that the probability of their reaching critical or irreversible levels in the next century has been exaggerated. One 1970 study, sponsored by MIT, weighs the merits of the doomsday scenarios and finds them wanting. Its report, based on the work of experts from a dozen disciplines ranging from meteorology to law, catalogues the possible global threats and finds none that constitutes a clear danger. But should we eventually identify specific threats to the global ecology, it is likely that solutions short of stopping the machinery of economic growth will be found. The most important lesson of ecology is caution; each step toward more sophisticated technology risks transgression against nature. But that same expansion of technology gives us the ability, if not the will, to recognize and avoid the hazards.

BUDDHIST ECONOMICS

E. F. Schumacher

*This intriguing article bears directly on the question of
growth and happiness. Its author was for twenty years the
top economist and head of planning of the British Coal Board,
as well as an articulate advocate of workers' control
of industry.*

Economists themselves, like most specialists, normally suffer from a kind of metaphysical blindness, assuming that theirs is a science of absolute and invariable truths, without any presuppositions. Some go as far as to claim that economic laws are as free from "metaphysics" or "values" as the law of gravitation. We need not, however, get involved in arguments of methodology. Instead, let us take some fundamentals and see what they look like when viewed by a modern economist and a Buddhist economist.

There is a universal agreement that a fundamental source of wealth is human labor. Now, the modern economist has been brought up to consider "labor" or work as little more than a necessary evil. From the point of view of the employer, it is in any case simply an item of cost, to be reduced to a minimum if it cannot be eliminated altogether, say, by automation. From the point of view of the workman, it is a "disutility"; to work is to make a sacrifice of one's leisure and comfort, and wages are a kind of compensation for the sacrifice. Hence the ideal from the point of view of the employer is to have output without employees, and the ideal from the point of view of the employee is to have income without employment.

The consequences of these attitudes both in theory and in practice are, of course, extremely

From E. F. Schumacher, *Small Is Beautiful* (New York: Harper Torchbook, 1973), pp. 50-58.

far-reaching. If the ideal with regard to work is to get rid of it, every method that "reduces the work load" is a good thing. The most potent method, short of automation, is the so-called "division of labor" and the classical example is the pin factory eulogized in Adam Smith's *Wealth of Nations*. Here it is not a matter of ordinary specialization, which mankind has practised from time immemorial, but of dividing up every complete process of production into minute parts, so that the final product can be produced at great speed without anyone having had to contribute more than a totally insignificant and, in most cases, unskilled movement of his limbs.

The Buddhist point of view takes the function of work to be at least threefold: to give a man a chance to utilize and develop his faculties; to enable him to overcome his ego-centeredness by joining with other people in a common task; and to bring forth the goods and services needed for a becoming existence. Again, the consequences that flow from this view are endless. To organize work in such a manner that it becomes meaningless, boring, stultifying, or nerve-racking for the worker would be little short of criminal; it would indicate a greater concern with goods than with people, an evil lack of compassion and a soul-destroying degree of attachment to the most primitive side of this worldly existence. Equally, to strive for leisure as an alternative to work would be considered a complete misunderstanding of one of the basic truths of human existence, namely that work and leisure are complementary parts of the same living process and cannot be separated without destroying the joy of work and the bliss of leisure.

From the Buddhist point of view, there are therefore two types of mechanization which must be clearly distinguished: one that enhances a man's skill and power and one that turns the work of man over to a mechanical slave, leaving man in a position of having to serve the slave. How to tell the one from the other? "The craftsman himself," says Ananda Coomaraswamy, a man equally competent to talk about the modern west as the ancient east, "can always, if allowed to, draw the delicate distinction between the machine and the tool. The carpet loom is a tool, a contrivance for holding warp threads at a stretch for the pile to be woven round them by the craftsmen's fingers; but the power loom is a machine, and its significance as a destroyer of culture lies in the fact that it does the essentially human part of the work." It is clear, therefore, that Buddhist economics must be very different from the economics of modern materialism, since the Buddhist sees the essence of civilization not in a multiplication of wants but in the purification of human character. Character, at the same time, is formed primarily by a man's work. And work, properly conducted in conditions of human dignity and freedom, blesses those who do it and equally their products. The Indian philosopher and economist J. C. Kumarappa sums the matter up as follows:

If the nature of the work is properly appreciated and applied, it will stand in the same relation to the higher faculties as food is to the physical body. It nourishes and enlivens the higher man and urges him to produce the best he is capable of. It directs his free will along the proper course and disciplines the animal in him into progressive channels. It furnishes an excellent background for man to display his scale of values and develop his personality.

If a man has no chance of obtaining work he is in a desperate position, not simply because he lacks an income but because he lacks this nourishing and enlivening factor of disciplined work which nothing can replace. A modern economist may engage in highly sophisticated calculations on whether full employment "pays" or whether it might be more "economic" to run an economy at less than full employment so as to ensure a greater mobility of labor, a better stability of wages, and so forth. His fundamental criterion of success is simply the total quantity of goods produced during a given period of time. "If the marginal urgency of goods is low," says Professor Galbraith in *The Affluent Society,* "then so is the urgency of employing the last man or the last million men in the labor force." And again: "If . . . we can afford some unemployment in the interest of stability – a proposition, incidentally, of impeccably conservative antecedents – then we can afford to give those who are unemployed the goods that enable them to sustain their accustomed standard of living."

From a Buddhist point of view, this is standing the truth on its head by considering goods as more important than people and consumption as more important than creative activity. It means shifting the emphasis from the worker to the product of work, that is, from the human to the subhuman, a surrender to the forces of evil. The very start of Buddhist economic planning would be a planning for full employment, and the primary purpose of this would in fact be employment for everyone who needs an "outside" job: it would not be the maximization of employment nor the maximization of production. Women, on the whole, do not need an "outside" job, and the large-scale employment of women in offices or factories would be considered a sign of serious economic failure. In particular, to let mothers of young children work in factories while the children run wild would be as uneconomic in the eyes of a Buddhist economist as the employment of a skilled worker as a soldier in the eyes of a modern economist.

While the materialist is mainly interested in goods, the Buddhist is mainly interested in liberation. But Buddhism is "The Middle Way" and therefore in no way antagonistic to physical well-being. It is not wealth that stands in the way of liberation but the attachment to wealth; not the enjoyment of pleasurable things but the craving for them. The keynote of Buddhist economics, therefore, is simplicity and non-violence. From an economist's point of view, the marvel of the Buddhist way of life is the utter rationality of its pattern — amazingly small means leading to extraordinarily satisfactory results.

For the modern economist this is very difficult to understand. He is used to measuring the "standard of living" by the amount of annual consumption, assuming all the time that a man who consumes more is "better off" than a man who consumes less. A Buddhist economist would consider this approach excessively irrational: since consumption is merely a means to human well-being, the aim should be to obtain the maximum of well-being with the minimum of consumption. Thus, if the purpose of clothing is a certain amount of temperature comfort and an attractive appearance, the task is to attain this purpose with the smallest possible effort, that is, with the smallest annual destruction of cloth and with the help of designs that involve the smallest possible input of toil. The less toil there is, the more time and strength is left for artistic creativity. It would be highly un-economic, for instance, to go in for complicated tailoring, like the modern west, when a much more beautiful effect can be achieved by the skilful draping of uncut material. It would be the height of folly to make material so that it should wear out quickly and the height of barbarity to make anything ugly, shabby or mean. What has just been said about clothing applies equally to all other human requirements.

The ownership and the consumption of goods is a means to an end, and Buddhist economics is the systematic study of how to attain given ends with the minimum means.

Modern economics, on the other hand, considers consumption to be the sole end and purpose of all economic activity, taking the factors of production — land, labor, and capital — as the means. The former, in short, tries to maximize human satisfactions by the optimal pattern of consumption, while the latter tries to maximize consumption by the optimal pattern of productive effort. It is easy to see that the effort needed to sustain a way of life which seeks to attain the optimal pattern of consumption is likely to be much smaller than the effort needed to sustain a drive for maximum consumption. We need not be surprised, therefore, that the pressure and strain of living is very much less in, say, Burma than it is in the United States, in spite of the fact that the amount of labor-saving machinery used in the former country is only a minute fraction of the amount used in the latter.

Simplicity and non-violence are obviously closely related. The optimal pattern of consumption, producing a high degree of human satisfaction by means of a relatively low rate of consumption, allows people to live without great pressure and strain and to fulfill the primary injunction of Buddhist teaching: "Cease to do evil; try to do good." As physical resources are everywhere limited, people satisfying their needs by means of a modest use of resources are obviously less likely to be at each other's throats than people depending upon a high rate of use. Equally, people who live in highly self-sufficient local communities are less likely to get involved in large-scale violence than people whose existence depends on world-wide systems of trade.

From the point of view of Buddhist economics, therefore, production from local resources for local needs is the most rational way of economic life, while dependence on imports from afar and the consequent need to produce for export to unknown and distant peoples is highly uneconomic and justifiable only in exceptional cases and on a small scale. Just as the modern economist would admit that a high rate of consumption of transport services between a man's home and his place of work signifies a misfortune and not a high standard of life, so the Buddhist economist would hold that to satisfy human wants from faraway sources rather than from sources nearby signifies failure rather than success. The former tends to take statistics showing an increase in the number of ton/miles per head of the population carried by a country's transport system as proof of economic progress, while to the latter – the Buddhist economist – the same statistics would indicate a highly undesirable deterioration in the *pattern* of consumption.

Another striking difference between modern economics and Buddhist economics arises over the use of natural resources. Bertrand de Jouvenel, the eminent French political philosopher, has characterised "western man" in words which may be taken as a fair description of the modern economist:

He tends to count nothing as an expenditure, other than human effort; he does not seem to mind how much mineral matter he wastes and, far worse, how much living matter he destroys. He does not seem to realize at all that human life is a dependent part of an ecosystem of many different forms of life. As the world is ruled from towns where men are cut off from any form of life other than human, the feeling of belonging to an ecosystem is not revived. This results in a harsh and improvident treatment of things upon which we ultimately depend, such as water and trees.

The teaching of the Buddha, on the other hand, enjoins a reverent and non-violent attitude not only to all sentient beings but also, with great emphasis, to trees. Every follower of the Buddha ought to plant a tree every few years and look after it until it is safely established, and the Buddhist economist can demonstrate without difficulty that the universal observation of this rule would result in a high rate of genuine economic development independent of any foreign aid. Much of the economic decay of south-east Asia (as of many other parts of the world) is undoubtedly due to a heedless and shameful neglect of trees.

Modern economics does not distinguish between renewable and non-renewable materials, as its very method is to equalize and quantify everything by means of a money price. Thus, taking various alternative fuels, like coal, oil, or wood, or water-power: the only difference between them recognized by modern economics is relative cost per equivalent unit. The cheapest is automatically the one to be preferred, as to do otherwise would be irrational and "uneconomic." From a Buddhist point of view, of course, this will not do; the essential difference between non-renewable fuels like coal and oil on the one hand and renewable fuels like wood and water-power on the other cannot be simply overlooked. Non-renewable goods must be used only if they are indispensable, and then only with the greatest care and the most meticulous concern for conservation. To use them heedlessly or extravagantly is an act of violence, and while complete non-violence may not be attainable on this earth, there is nonetheless an ineluctable duty on man to aim at the ideal of non-violence in all he does.

Just as a modern European economist would not consider it a great economic achievement if all European art treasures were sold to America at attractive prices, so the Buddhist economist would insist that a population basing its economic life on non-renewable fuels is living parasitically, on capital instead of income. Such a way of life could have no permanence and could therefore be justified only as a purely temporary expedient. As the world's resources of non-renewable fuels – coal, oil and natural gas – are exceedingly unevenly distributed over the globe and undoubtedly limited in quantity, it is clear that their exploitation at an ever-increasing rate is an act of violence against nature which must almost inevitably lead to violence between men.

This fact alone might give food for thought even to those people in Buddhist countries who care nothing for the religious and spiritual values of their heritage and ardently desire to embrace the materialism of modern economics at the fastest possible speed. Before they dismiss Buddhist economics as nothing better than a nostalgic dream, they might wish to consider whether the path of economic development outlined by modern economics is likely to lead them to places where they really want to be.

TEST ON CHAPTERS 29–34

__ 1. Equilibrium for GNP is determined by
   a. the interplay of leakages and injections.
   b. marginal capital output ratio and investment.
   c. the supply of money and liquidity preferences.

__ 2. Which of the following is *not* an identity
   a. $GNP = MV$.
   b. $GNI = C + G + I + X$.
   c. ex ante S = ex ante I.

__ 3. The multiplier plays a crucial role in determining
   a. the capital-output ratio.
   b. the rate of balanced growth.
   c. the effect of M on P.

__ 4. The 45° line relates
   a. costs to expenditures.
   b. GNI and GNP.
   c. demand for GNP to supply of GNP.

__ 5. The effect of openmarket purchases by the Fed is to
   a. create excess reserves.
   b. decrease reserves.
   c. lower bond yields.

__ 6. If a bank has deposits of $100,000, and the reserve ratio is 20%, it can
   a. lend $40,000 and invest $60,000.
   b. invest $80,000.
   c. create new deposits of $100,000.

__ 7. When bond prices fall
   a. yields fall.
   b. yields rise.
   c. yields remain unchanged because the bond pays the same amount.

_ 8. At higher interest rates
   a. opportunity cost of liquidity rises.
   b. transactions demands rise.
   c. bond prices rise.
_ 9. An increase in the quantity of money causes holders of liquidity balances
   a. to buy bonds.
   b. to sell bonds.
   c. to hold portfolios unchanged.
_10. A nation with a low growth rate in investment and a low multiplier will be better off with
   a. a high capital output ratio.
   b. a low capital output ratio.
   c. makes no difference.

TRUE-FALSE

T F

11. The aggregate production function relates GNP and GNI. _ _
12. At all levels of output GNI equals GNP. _ _
13. The equation for the increase in money resembles that for the multiplier. _ _
14. The Federal Reserve is most effective when it seeks to expand bank loans. _ _
15. The demand for money is determined partly by the need to finance output, partly by the desire to keep speculative and precautionary cash. _ _
16. It is possible for the Fed to create money, but for MV to remain unchanged. _ _
17. The rate of interest is the price that will induce the public to hold a certain amount of money. _ _
18. An inflationary buying spree does not change the amount of money. _ _
19. The Phillips curve relates the volume of output to the rate of unemployment. _ _
20. Inflation and unemployment are trade-offs because both are zero-sum games. _ _

THE BEFORE-AND-AFTER TEST IN MACROECONOMICS AGAIN

Here is your second chance at the before-and-after test. Naturally, we hope you did poorly "before" and will do well "after." We have asked ourselves what a student should do who actually did worse "after" than "before." We have two answers: (1) sell your textbook to a used bookstore; (2) leave economics. (Or should *we* leave economics?)

Place a check under T (True), F (False), or ? (Don't Know).

T F ?

1. The amount of money in the economy increases when people draw money out of their checking accounts.

2. Inflation is "zero-sum" game – a process in which there must be as much gain as there is loss.

3. One of the most effective remedies for recession is to encourage people to consume more.

4. A main cause for recession is that not enough incomes are paid out to buy back the output of the economy.

5. One of the principal sources of economic growth is the increase in skills and knowledge.

6. It is unsafe for the government to run up a huge deficit for the same reason that it is unsafe for a family to incur a huge debt.

7. The more rapidly we spend money, the more money there is.

8. The main purpose of the Federal Reserve System is to safeguard the nation's currency.

9. Inflation in the United States has been less severe than in Europe.

10. A national debt, owed by a country's citizens, can safely be of any size, since we owe it to ourselves.

11. Banks can actually create new money by loans.

12. It is possible for employment and unemployment both to increase at the same time.

13. An economy that is no longer growing will also be an economy that is no longer polluting the environment.

14. The main purpose of gold is to provide a national backing for currency.

15. Gross national product is a measure of national well being.

16. As a result of consumer credit, the households of the nation spend more than their total incomes.

17. When we buy stock on a stock exchange, our purchase usually helps a company finance its expansion.

18. The chief argument against an unbalanced government budget is that the government can't spend money it doesn't have.

19. More spending is the way out of a recession.

20. An economy at full employment will have less inflation than an economy in which there is unemployment.

Answers:

1. F	8. F	15. F
2. T	9. T	16. F
3. F	10. T	17. F
4. F	11. T	18. F
5. T	12. T	19. T
6. F	13. F	20. F
7. F	14. F	

As before, score –5 for each wrong answer; –3 for each "don't know."

Score ——
Score before ——

INTERNATIONAL ECONOMICS

BEFORE-AND-AFTER-TEST ON INTERNATIONAL ECONOMICS

Here is another of these tests whose purpose is really to test ourselves as teachers as well as yourselves as students. International economics is a complex field and therefore we will not expect you to know (or not to know) as much about it as in micro- or macroeconomics. The quiz is short, but we hope fun. Try it, this time, because there are only ten questions, scoring yourself with – 10 for errors and – 6 for "don't knows," and enter the results on the bottom of page 350.

T F ?

1. One of the striking changes in recent international economics has been the huge surge of exports from the so-called multinational corporations.
        — — —
2. The chief danger of international trade is that one nation, by virtue of its cheap labor *and* capital, will be able to undersell the rest of the world without buying anything in exchange.
        — — —
3. A tariff is a tax levied on imports and therefore borne wholly by foreign nations.
        — — —
4. Despite the deficits incurred by the United States during the early 1970s in its international transactions, the overall balance of payments always balanced.
        — — —
5. A nation usually exports goods from industries in which its domestic wage levels are lowest.
        — — —
6. A country pays for its imports by sending its money abroad, and gets paid for its exports by receiving foreign money that is sent from abroad.
        — — —
7. The world operates its international exchange on a gold standard.
        — — —
8. If one country, say Japan, can undersell another, say the United States, in every line of production, the U.S. could not hope to have a profitable international exchange with Japan.
        — — —
9. A country cannot import more goods than it exports for a prolonged period.
        — — —
10. The rational objective for any nation is to maximize its exports.
        — — —

Score _____

Answers:

1. F	5. F	9. F
2. F	6. F	10. F
3. F	7. F	
4. T	8. F	

The Gains From Trade

35

LEARNING OBJECTIVES

The subject of the gains from trade is an important one. Zero in on:
1. The idea of comparative advantage.

2. The trading range within which mutually profitable exchange can take place.
3. The arguments pro and con tariffs.

Two problems lie at the heart of this chapter: comparative advantage and the tariff question, but the latter is really only a specific obstruction of the former. Hence let us be sure that we understand the essence of the comparative advantage argument.

Suppose we have two countries with equal populations, which we shall call Superia and Inferia; and let us suppose that Superia, as the name suggests, is more efficient than Inferia in the production of everything — "everything" being the two commodities both countries offer in international trade: wheat and corn.* Here is a table showing what the countries can produce

when their labor forces are equally divided between the two occupations.

Obviously Superia can outproduce Inferia in every commodity. Her labor in wheat is twice as productive as Inferia's; in corn one and one-half times as productive. How, then can trade possibly be worthwhile?

*It is worth stressing again a point mentioned in the text that not every commodity produced in a country can enter international trade because of the *transportation costs* involved. Bricks may be made more cheaply in Superia than in Inferia, but it may cost too much to bring them across the border, so that Inferia continues to make its own.

We answer the problem by looking at the *opportunity costs* of the two nations, and here

	Superia	(tons)	Inferia	Total (tons)
Wheat	100,000		50,000	150,000
Corn	300,000		200,000	500,000

we discover the vital clue. Opportunity costs are different in the two countries. Superia could double her wheat production, assuming constant returns, by moving her workers out of corn, but she would have to give up *3 tons of corn for the gain of a ton of wheat*. In Inferia a similar movement of workers out of corn into wheat would cost *4 tons of corn for 1 ton of wheat*. Corn is *relatively* abundant in Inferia, and, therefore, it is in corn that she has a *comparative* advantage. On the other hand, wheat is *relatively* abundant in Superia, and in that crop lies her comparative advantage.

You can work this out for yourself. Suppose that both countries shift their work forces entirely into wheat:

	Superia	Inferia
Wheat	200,000	100,000
Corn	—	—

Suppose that both countries shift their work forces entirely into corn:

	Superia	Inferia
Wheat	—	—
Corn	600,000	400,000

1. To gain its additional 100,000 tons of wheat, how much corn has Superia had to relinquish? _____
2. How much corn does Inferia relinquish for its additional 50,000 tons of wheat? _____
3. To gain *one ton* of wheat, how much corn must Superia give up? _____

4. Inferia? _____
5. To gain *one ton* of corn, how much wheat would Superia have to give up? _____
6. Inferia? _____
7. In which product does Superia have a *comparative* advantage? _____
8. In which does Inferia? _____

Let us review the answers to the above questions in terms of the relative *money* prices for wheat and corn that we would find prevailing in each of the two countries. If you bought one ton of corn in Superia, you could have bought one-third of a ton of wheat with the same money, but in Inferia you could have bought only one-fourth of a ton of wheat. So wheat is *relatively* high priced in Inferia, which must mean that its *comparative* advantage is in corn. In Superia, on the other hand, wheat is *relatively* cheap, so it is in wheat that its *comparative* advantage lies.

9. Now suppose that Inferia devotes all her resources to corn (400,000 tons produced) and that Superia shifts over enough of her workers to produce 50,000 more tons of wheat. What will the new production schedules look like?

	Superia	Inferia
Wheat	150,000	0
Corn		

10. Taking Superia and Inferia together, has their joint corn output increased? _____
11. Their wheat output? _____
12. Now, how will the trade between the countries be priced? To begin with, let us take Inferia, which has given up 50,000 tons of wheat. What is the *largest* amount of corn she will be willing to trade from her present increased production of corn to get back her 50,000 tons of wheat? In ton-for-ton terms, what is the highest price she will pay in corn for a ton of wheat? _____
13. Superia has given up 150,000 tons of corn to raise 50,000 tons of additional wheat. What

is the highest price in wheat that she will pay for 150,000 tons of corn? _____

14. Can you now establish a trading range between corn and wheat within which trade can take place? What is it? _____

15. Can you clearly explain why trade is not profitable on either side of that range? _____
_____
_____
_____

Does this make clear the concept of opportunity cost?

16. It is now easy to put prices on the products. We know that one ton of wheat will not sell for less than _____ of corn or for more than _____ of corn.

17. Suppose that wheat sells for $100 per ton. What must be the trading range for corn?
_____
_____

Answers:

1. 300,000 tons (of corn equals 100,000 tons of wheat in Superia)
2. 200,000 tons (of corn equals 50,000 of wheat in Inferia)
3. 3 tons (of corn equals one ton of wheat in Superia)
4. 4 tons (of corn equals one ton of wheat in Inferia)
5. one-third ton (of wheat equals one ton of corn in Superia)
6. one-fourth ton (of wheat equals one ton of corn in Inferia)
7. wheat
8. corn
9.

	Superia	Inferia
Wheat	150,000	0
Corn	150,000	400,000

10. Joint corn output has increased from 500,000 tons to 550,000 tons.

11. Joint wheat output is unchanged at 150,000 tons.

12. See answer 4 above.

13. See answer 3 above: for the 150,000 tons of corn Superia has given up, she will pay anything up to 50,000 tons of wheat.

14. The trading range must be somewhere between one ton of wheat for three of corn and one of wheat for four of corn.

15. On either side of this range one country or the other would fall back on the *opportunity* it has of producing all its own consumption in both wheat and corn.

16. three; four

17. Corn must be between $25.00 and $33.33 per ton or there will be no trade.

TARIFFS

The main argument made in favor of tariffs is that they protect domestic workers against low-paid foreign labor. Is this true?

The argument overlooks a critical question: why is foreign labor low paid? Or conversely, why is American labor highly paid?

Once we ask this question we see that wages reflect the *general level of productivity* of labor in the industries of a nation. An industry that is hurt by imports is essentially in the same position as an industry that *cannot compete with other domestic high-productivity industries.* It is the highly productive auto worker in Detroit who is causing the textile mill worker in South Carolina to suffer, because the level of automobile wages pulls up American wages in general, thereby exposing the relatively unproductive Carolina textile worker to the competition of textile labor abroad.

The answer to the low-wage-competition problem is, therefore, to help the textile worker find other, higher productivity, employment. This is true whether we are talking about foreign trade or not. In this way we will move our resources to the point of highest return, and thereby give our consumers the benefits of inexpensive goods. To "protect" the textile worker by a tariff means:

1. We are supporting behind a tariff wall resources that should and could make a larger contribution to output elsewhere;
2. We are taxing the American consumer to maintain an efficient industry; and,
3. We are depriving another nation of its ability to earn dollars that could be spent on the goods in which America is relatively productive and, therefore, exports.

Thus the argument for free trade is essentially an argument for *efficiency.* Note, however, that the argument assumes that we can maintain a level of *full employment,* and that we will retrain or relocate the textile worker in an occupation where he will make more than his present pay. The free trade doctrine also assumes that we are not an underdeveloped nation seeking to establish a necessary industrial nucleus, and willing to subsidize "infant" industry by tariffs until it gains economies of scale and can maintain itself in international competition.

The argument for free trade thus applies more comprehensively to mature, developed nations than to underdeveloped ones.

QUIZ

__ 1. Opportunity cost means
   a. the additional output that could be gained from resources otherwise employed.
   b. the value of the production given up by moving resources from their present use.
   c. the advantage that one nation has over another in production.

__ 2. If the opportunity costs of two nations, producing, say wheat and corn, are the same,
   a. trade between them is pointless.
   b. trade would still be useful because one nation might be a more efficient producer in both areas.

   c. trade between them would follow the normal principle of comparative advantage.

__ 3. Comparative advantage means that
   a. two nations usually have different opportunity costs.
   b. one nation is usually more efficient than another in all areas.
   c. one nation usually has natural advantages in production of some product.

__ 4. If two nations trade, each will
   a. export the good in which it has a comparative advantage.
   b. import the good in which it has a comparative advantage.
   c. export the good whose opportunity cost is greatest.

__ 5. The effect of trade will
   a. shift outward the combined production possibility curves of both countries.
   b. keep *p-p* curves unchanged, but locate both nations at different points on these curves.
   c. move both nations beyond their post-trade *p-p* frontiers.

__ 6. The price at which a good will be traded will be
   a. determined by the opportunity cost of the good offered.
   b. determined by the opportunity cost of the good sought.
   c. both of the above.

__ 7. Tariffs have the economic effect of
   a. altering opportunity costs within a nation.
   b. altering comparative advantages among nations.
   c. neither of the above.

__ 8. The arguments for free trade
   a. place producers' advantages above consumers'.
   b. place consumers' advantages above producers'.
   c. stress national advantages over international.

__ 9. An industry threatened by imports suffers because of

a. the wage levels of foreign producers.

b. the costs of production of foreign producers.

c. its relative inefficiency compared to other domestic producers.

_10. The effects of a tariff are felt by

a. foreign producers.

b. domestic consumers.

c. both of the above.

True-False Questions

T F

11. Imported goods probably come from industries whose wage level is high in the exporting country. _ _

12. A tariff is a subsidy to domestic producers. _ _

13. Tariffs impose transition costs on domestic industry. _ _

14. The argument for free trade is one of efficiency, not equity. _ _

15. From a welfare standpoint, imports are a gain, not a loss. _ _

T F

16. The main difficulty with free trade is internal mobility. _ _

17. The gains from free trade assume full employment. _ _

18. Trade is a zero-sum game, if imports balance exports. _ _

19. The argument for infant industries is based on long run declining average costs as a result of enlargement of scale. _ _

20. The gains from trade may be unequally distributed among the trading partners. _ _

Answers:

1. b	8. b	15. T
2. a	9. c	16. T
3. a	10. c	17. T
4. a	11. T	18. F
5. a	12. T	19. T
6. c	13. F	20. T
7. b	14. T	

36

The Problem of International Transactions

LEARNING OBJECTIVES

A few central ideas will help clarify this chapter.

1. How is an export (or an import) financed?
2. What is "foreign exchange"?
3. How does a change in exchange rates affect exports or imports?
4. What are the main categories of the balance of payments?
5. How are "deficits" in the balance of payments financed?

How do we know if the goods of a foreign country are cheap or dear compared with our own goods? The answer is, "By finding out the *rate of exchange* – the rate at which we can swap our money for theirs." Hence the key to understanding foreign trade, in addition to understanding the principle of comparative advantage, is knowing how the exchange rates are determined.

EXCHANGE RATES

Like all prices, exchange rates reflect supply and demand. What creates a "demand" for foreign exchange? Suppose that you wish to import British sweaters. Can you send a check in dollars to the English manufacturer? (Would you take a check in pounds if you sold something to an English purchaser?)

To get the pounds to send to your English supplier you go to your bank and buy pounds. Note these steps:

1. Dollars are transferred from your checking account to the account of a British bank which is kept in a United States bank.
2. The British bank in England, which has gained dollars in its U.S. deposits, now pays out pounds to the British seller.

Note that the British bank has gained dollars in an American account. These dollars arising from foreign trade are called *foreign exchange.*

How would we gain our foreign exchange to buy in Britain? Suppose that you sold a piece of machinery to a British buyer. He would go to his bank in England and draw a check in pounds on his account. This check would go into the British account maintained by an American bank, and the American bank would then send you a check in dollars. Where is the foreign exchange? It is the pounds that now reside in the British account of the American bank. *Foreign exchange means the supplies of any nation's currency that are held by other nations* – as checking accounts.

If exchange rates are free to move, the rate of exchange can rise or fall like any price. Suppose that two countries – Superia and Inferia again – wish to trade and that the home prices of their products are as shown in the table:

	Superia (kronen)	Inferia (dinars*)
Wheat (bu.)	10	6
Corn (bu.)	8	4

*1 kr = 1 d

Can trade take place? Everything depends on the rate of exchange.

Suppose that 1 krone equalled 1 dinar.

1. What would be the price (ignoring transport costs) of Inferian wheat in Superia? _____
2. What would be the price of Superian wheat in Inferia? _____

3. What would be the case with Inferian corn in Superia, as compared with their domestic corn? _____
4. Which country would be selling, which buying? _____
5. As a result, would balances of Inferian owned kronen be piling up in the banks of Superia, or balances of Superian owned dinars in the banks of Inferia? _____

_____

6. Think carefully: (1) Which country will be exporting? (2) What will be the financial result of these exports (that is, in which country will checks be written that go into the other country's local bank account)?

_____

_____

_____

7. Will Superia be able to go on buying Inferia's cheap products long? Why not? _____

_____

8. What will happen when Superia's importers seek to get Inferian dinars after a while? As dinars get scarce, will their price go up? ____

_____

9. Instead of getting 1 dinar for 1 krone, will you get more or less dinars for a krone? ____

_____

10. Suppose that after a while you have to pay 2 kronen for a dinar. Is Inferian wheat still cheaper than Superian? _____

11. Is Inferian corn profitable to import into Superia? _____

_____

12. What must be the dinar-krone trading range in order for trade to take place? (You know that if it takes 2 kronen to get a dinar, Superia can no longer afford to buy anything.) Now what is the extreme in the other direction? That is, what is the lowest amount of kronen that an Inferian must get for a dinar to allow him to buy anything in Superia? _____

13. Suppose an Inferian gets 1 krone for a dinar. Can he buy anything more cheaply in Superia? Suppose he could get one and one-half kronen? Six dinars would then buy how many kronen? _____ Would wheat still be too dear? _____

14. Suppose the exchange rate went to 1.7 to 1, so that 6 dinars got you 10.2 kronen. Could you now buy wheat advantageously in Superia? _____

15. The limits of the exchange rate for two-way trade to take place are thus:

   1 dinar must exchange for less than ____ kronen and for more than _____ kronen.

Answers:

1. 6 kronen

2. 10 dinars

3. Inferian corn would be 4 kronen in Superia, domestic corn would be 8 kronen

4. Inferia would be selling, Superia buying

5. Inferian owned kronen would be piling up in the banks of Superia

6. checks will be written by Superian buyers to pay their banks, who then will pay the Inferian sellers with checks from the deposits of dinars that the Superian banks have in the banks of Inferia

7. the deposits of Inferian dinars owned by Superian banks will be used up

8. yes

9. less

10 no

11. no, domestic and imported corn would cost the same

12. One and two-thirds kronen for 1 dinar. Then Inferia could buy Superian wheat

13. 9

14. yes

15. 2; 1 2/3

DETERMINATION OF EXCHANGE RATES

We have seen how exchange rates determine whether a foreign product is cheaper or more expensive than a domestic one. But how are exchange rates themselves determined?

The answer, as so often before in our analytic work, is provided by supply and demand. Here the trick is to think of the foreign currency as if it were only so many units of a commodity called "dinars" or "marks" or "pounds." Then it is easy to understand the demand curve for this foreign "currency-commodity." The cheaper it is, the more units of the commodity will be demanded, for example by importers or investors.

The supply side is trickier to grasp. Now you have to put yourself in the shoes of a foreigner for whom "dollars" are a commodity. From his point of view, the price of dollar-commodities goes in the opposite direction from the price of his own currency-commodity from *our* point of view. When Japanese yen are cheap – that is, when *we* get more units of yen for a dollar – the dollar becomes dear in Japan because a Japanese gets fewer units of dollars for each yen. Conversely, when yen are expensive in dollars, dollars are cheap in yen. It follows that when American importers are demanding fewer yen because of its high price, Japanese importers are demanding more dollars because of its low price! We can see this in Figure 36-1.

FIGURE 36-1

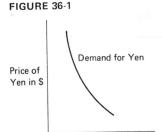

Price of Yen in $

Demand for Yen

q of Yen

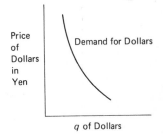

Price of Dollars in Yen

Demand for Dollars

q of Dollars

From here there is only one step left. Every time an American buys (demands) yen, he is offering (supplying) dollars. Every time a Japanese buys (demands) dollars, he is supplying yen. *Thus the American demand curve for yen becomes a supply of dollars in Japan, and the Japanese demand curve for dollars becomes a supply curve for yen in the United States.* As we can see in Figure 36-2, this gives us a supply and demand curve for both markets, where the exchange value of the currencies is simultaneously determined.

CHANGING EXCHANGE RATES

Understanding the mechanics of exchange rates requires a good deal of familiarity with the world of foreign exchange, and we won't go into it further here. What is important to note, however, is that an increase in the demand for Japanese goods will shift the demand curve for yen to the right (don't forget these curves are really opposite sides of a coin). This will result in a higher price for yen and a cheaper price for dollars, as you can see by pencilling in such a shift in Figure 36-2. The yen will *appreciate,* and the dollar will *depreciate.* Japanese goods will therefore become more expensive in the United States, and American goods cheaper in Japan.

Imports from Japan will tend to diminish; American exports to increase.

An important result follows. Let us suppose that the United States and Japan each exported only one good to the other and had no other financial dealings. We can see that under these conditions, the total value of Japanese sales to the United States would have to be equal to the total value of U.S. sales to Japan. If that were not the case, one country or the other would be acquiring more of the currency of its trading partner than it wanted. Competition among banks would soon raise the price of one currency and lower the price of the other, until quantities supplied and demanded were equal. No balance of payments problem of any kind would arise. The only important question would be the quantity of (say) cameras and wheat that importers in each country would get. In real terms, there might be very substantial problems connected with international trade, but financial problems of the kinds we experienced in the early 1970s could not exist.

BALANCE OF PAYMENTS

These so-called balance of payments problems can only occur when the prices of currencies are fixed, or sticky, so that they cannot

FIGURE 36-2

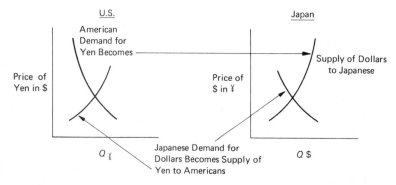

move up or down to clear the market. Our text explains how these imbalances arise, but let us tackle the same problem here from a slightly different point of view.

We begin by stressing that every item in the official balance of payments is entered twice. The first entry shows the actual value of the transaction, and places the transaction in its appropriate category – a merchandise transaction or a government transaction, a long- or short-term capital transaction, or whatever. The second entry shows how the item was financed. This almost always takes place by changes in short-term capital. As we know, every U.S. export involves the transfer of foreign currency into a U.S. bank account abroad. It is therefore financed by a gain in short-term credit for the United States. So, too, every import into our country is financed by moving American dollars into the hands of a foreign-owned bank account in the United States. This entry of dollars into a foreign-owned account is a short-term credit for foreigners.

Now let us see how balance of payments problems can arise by tracing four items, as each gets entered twice in the balance of payments accounts. The four transactions are:

1. The U.S.A. buys $1,000 worth of German goods.
2. Germany sends us $500 worth of dividends.
3. We pay $600 to Germany for food consumed by our army stationed there.
4. We acquire $400 worth of German shares.

Now trace each transaction by its identifying number in the balance of payments in Table 36-1. You will see two things: (1) although the overall balance of payments always balances, (2) *the amounts of short-term credit* (foreign exchange) *that are gained or lost by the two trading partners need not be equal.*

Notice that the United States has gained $900 in short-term capital – that is, in new deposits in U.S.-owned accounts in Germany. But Germany has gained $1,600 in deposits in German-owned accounts in the United States. On balance, the United States has lost $700 more in short-term credits than it has gained. It has a balance of payments "deficit" of this amount.

How is this deficit financed? Basically there are two ways:

1. We can sell the Germans $700 worth of gold or Special Drawing Rights. This would show up as follows:

TABLE 36-1. Balance of Payments

Receipts from Foreigners (Credits)	Payments to Foreigners (Debits)
2. $500 in dividends from Germany	1. $1,000 in imported goods
4. $400 in shares of a German company	3. $600 in military supplies
1. $1,000 of short-term capital (deposits of that amount added to German-owned bank account in U.S.A.)	2. $500 in short-term capital (deposits of that amount move into a U.S.-owned bank account in Germany)
3. $600 in short-term capital ($600 added to a German-owned bank account in a U.S. bank)	4. $400 in short-term capital (as in 2 above)
Total $2,500	Total $2,500

Receipts from Foreigners (Credits)	Payments to Foreigners (Debits)
$700 in gold exports	$700 in short-term capital (deposits of that amount in a U.S.-owned bank account in Germany)

As a result we can see that: (1) the overall balance still balances (it *always* does); and (2) *there is now a balance in short-term credits.* We have gained as much in U.S.-owned accounts as we have paid into German-owned deposits. The "deficit" is gone.

2. There is also another way. We can persuade the German Central bank to hang onto its extra $700 in American deposits. As long as the central bank of any country is willing to allow its holdings of a foreign currency to pile up without demanding "payment" in gold, no deficit problem arises.

Until the monetary crisis of the early 1970s, balance of payments deficits were settled either by gold flows or by increases in holdings of currencies, mainly U.S. dollars. We will follow what happend to that arrangement in our next chapter. However, let us be sure that we understand the mechanics of the international payments before we plunge into the problems of international economics. Working through this exercise should help.

1. Suppose you are an American importer of Swiss watches. Watches in Switzerland cost Sw. Fr. 100. The exchange rate is $1 = 4 Sw. Fr. What is the cost of the watch in dollars (transportation, tariff and other costs ignored)? _____

2. If the Swiss franc appreciates, will you get more or fewer francs per dollar? (Think carefully.) _____

3. Suppose that the franc rises (appreciates) until you only get 3 fr. per $1. How much do watches now cost (in dollars)? _____

4. Will your demand for francs rise or fall if the franc appreciates? _____

5. From the Swiss watchmakers' point of view, do dollars get more or less expensive, when the exchange rate goes from $1 = 4 Sw. Fr. to $1 = 3 Sw. Fr.? _____ .

6. If $1 = 4 Sw. Fr., what is 1 Sw. Fr. worth in dollars and cents? _____

7. When the franc appreciates to 3 Sw. Fr. per dollar what is 1 franc worth in dollars? _____

8. Suppose that the Swiss watchmakers import American boxes in which to package their watches. When the Swiss franc appreciates, do American boxes become cheaper or dearer? _____

Answers:

1. $25	4. fall	7. 33¢
2. fewer	5. cheaper	8. cheaper
3. $33.33	6. 25¢	

Now let us go through a brief drill on the balance of payments. Below is a series of transactions. Enter them in the balance of payments form (on the next page), making sure that you enter each item twice, first as a transaction (in the proper category) and again in the short-term credit category. (All figures below are in millions).

1. The United States exports $100 worth of goods

2. The United States imports $50 worth of transportation

3. U.S. travellers spend $25 abroad

4. U.S. corporations send $95 home in dividends

5. Payments for American armed forces abroad come to $40

6. American companies invest $80 abroad. (Remember: a capital export is a *gain* in our claims and therefore a *credit* when it is first entered as a transaction.)

Then answer these questions, and check with the completed table on page 321.

1. What is the balance on merchandise account? _____

2. What is the balance on goods and services account? _____

3. What is the balance on current account?

_____

Balance of Payments

	Credits +	Debits −
Merchandise	—	—
Services	—	—
Unilateral transfers	—	—
Long-term capital	—	—
Short-term capital	—	—
	—	—
	—	—
Total, all items	—	—

4. What is the balance on long-term capital account? _____
5. What is the balance on current a/c plus long-term capital? _____
6. What is the balance on short-term capital? _____
7. What is the total balance? _____

Answers: Each figure is different, so you should have no trouble tracing the numbers back to the original questions.

Try this True-False Quiz to see how much of this chapter you have now fully mastered: T F

1. Comparative advantage in a commodity will not lead to trade if exchange rates are fixed. — —
2. Changes in the rate of exchange can offset comparative advantage. — —
3. If the U.S. dollar appreciates, imports into the United States get cheaper. — —
4. When the pound depreciates in terms of the franc, an Englishman gets more francs for a pound. — —
5. It is to the advantage of a nation's importers to have its currency depreciate. — —
6. The demand for German marks in Swedish kronen is the same as the

Balance of Payments

	Credits +	Debits −
Merchandise	100	
Services	95	50
		25
Unilateral transfers		40
Long-term capital	80	
Short-term capital	50	100
	25	95
	40	80
Total	370	370

Balances	Balance	Items in Balance +	−
1. Merchandise a/c	+100	100	0
2. Goods and services	+120	100 95	50 25
3. Current a/c	+ 80	100 95	50 25 40
4. Long-term capital	+ 80	80	−
5. Current a/c plus long term capital	+160	80 80	
6. Short-term capital	−160	50 25 40	100 95 80
7. Total balance	0	all items	all items

   T F

supply of Swedish kronen in German marks. — —
7. At an equilibrium exchange rate, the volume of exports equals the volume of imports. — —
8. At an equilibrium exchange rate, the value of all demands for a currency will equal the value of all supplies of that same currency. — —
9. There can only be an imbalance in the total balance of payments under fixed change rates. — —
10. Central banks are the agencies through whose actions surpluses or deficits of currencies are financed. — —

T F

11. Under a floating or free exchange rate, the supply of and demand for exchange will be equilibrated for current accounts, regardless of capital transactions. — —

12. Deficits or surpluses in current accounts must be matched by surpluses or deficits in short- and long-term capital accounts. — —

13. Gold "balances" the balance of payments because it counts like an export and for no other reason. — —

14. Deficits or surpluses in the balance of payments, under fixed exchange rates, result in central banks gaining or losing exchange. — —

15. When the United States pays for the upkeep of a foreign military base, it acquires net supplies of the foreign currency in its bank accounts in that country. — —

16. There is no analytical significance in the total balance of payments. — —

17. It would be possible for a country to have a large surplus of exports over imports, and therefore to have

T F

a balance of payments problem, even under free exchange rates. — —

18. A fixed exchange rate can give rise to a shortage of exchange, exactly as a price ceiling can give rise to a shortage of a commodity. — —

19. The balance of payments allows us to see the supplies and demands for foreign exchange that originate from different groups within a nation. — —

20. A shortage of liquidity means that a nation cannot persuade other nations to accept its currency as a reserve currency. — —

Answers:

1. F	8. T	15. F
2. T	9. F	16. T
3. T	10. T	17. F
4. F	11. F	18. T
5. F	12. T	19. T
6. T	13. T	20. T
7. F	14. T	

37

The International Monetary Problem

We are not going to review with you the various ways of coping with a surplus or deficit in the balance of payments. Instead, here are three readings that will show you the problem as it actually appeared in the mid-1970s.

THE DOLLAR AND BRETTON WOODS:
A POST MORTEM

Robert Warren Stevens

*Professor Robert W. Stevens, an expert on international trade
and finance, provides insight into the decline of the
dollar and the demise of the Bretton Woods agreement of
1944 in which the post World War II exchange system was established.*

One of the most dramatic events of our time has been the meteoric decline of the dollar. As much as the administration and some financial writers may try to smooth over the fact of its decline by pointing out aspects of its new position that may be regarded favorably from the U.S. point of view — such as its being free now to be devalued "just like any other currency" — the fact remains that the devaluation of the dollar and the monetary system's lapse into floating exchange rates were events that the U.S. government has been determined to prevent from happening over the past quarter-century.

So whatever "bright side" we may be asked to look upon today, the new regime is exactly the opposite of what mainstream bankers and economists have been telling us for decades to regard as a well-functioning international monetary system. Not so long ago the dollar was, by universal agreement, anything but "just another currency"; our government bargained hard in international monetary forums to maintain some very special privileges for it when it was, in the words of the U.S. Treasury, "the linch pin" of the international monetary system.

My intention here is neither to deliver a eulogy on the past glories of the dollar nor to

From *The Banker's Magazine,* 89 Beach Street, Boston, Mass. 02111 (Summer, 1973).

debate the merits of, for example, floating exchange rates versus a fixed exchange rate system. Instead, I propose to look back briefly at the dollar and the Bretton Woods international monetary system to see whether we can throw any new light on what happened to them.

HOW DID THE DOLLAR OVERHANG ARISE?

The overhang of dollars held outside the United States has arisen from a long series of deficits in the U.S. balance of payments, going back to the early 1950s. As we are often reminded, a balance of payments deficit occurs when more dollars go out of the country than foreign residents send back into the country. If this happens year after year, foreigners' holdings of dollars keep accumulating until they have more than they want, and there is a dollar glut.

A balance of payments statement is drawn up in order to show for what purposes U.S. residents and foreign residents are sending dollars out of the country and sending them back to the country, respectively. So and so many dollars go out to pay for imports of Toyotas, purchases of foreign companies, and American tourists' expenditures versus so and so many dollars coming in to pay for Boeing stratocruisers, soybeans, and to bring home the profits on American investment abroad.

If we are to understand what happened to the dollar, we must unravel a balance of payments statement, at least part way, in order to find out. But, we are warned, although the U.S. balance of payments statement is a very important financial document (one of the most important of our time, in my opinion) it is also a very complicated statement, to be understood only by an inner circle of the cognoscenti. In its current form of presentation, it comes out in the form of *six* balances, and the supporting tables may run to more than twenty-five pages of figures in the Commerce Department's *Survey of Current Business.* But like some other complicated documents, it has a central core of meaning that is not hard to grasp. In this discussion, we will be interested only in that central core of meaning.

One of the leading characteristics of the U.S. balance of payments for the twenty-one years from 1950 to 1970 (before it got churned up by the events leading to the two devaluations of the dollar) was that, year in and year out, the United States earned comfortable surpluses from exports of goods and services to the rest of the world. Nevertheless, the country ended up with balance of payments deficits in almost every year. We shall find the key to the dollar's difficulties only if we can separate out the large dollar outflows that more than gobbled up the country's net earnings on goods and service exports for twenty years.

When the problem is viewed in this way, the conclusion is often reached that the country had balance of payments deficits for twenty years because outflows of dollars for foreign aid, for the government's foreign military spending, and for private foreign investment were larger than its earnings from exports of goods and services. These three large outflows of funds, then — foreign aid, the government's foreign military spending, and private foreign investment — are

pictured as the villains of the balance of payments drama. Each outflow has been very large in its own right. Taken together, they have simply overwhelmed U.S. net earnings from exports of goods and services.

Examining the Balance of Payments

This is a good place to begin thinking about the balance of payments, because it groups all transactions into four major accounts that, between them, determine the final result: net U.S earnings on goods and service exports being overwhelmed by outflows under the other three headings. The record for the twenty-one years 1950-1970 showed a remarkably stable pattern of relationships among these four accounts — goods and service exports showing net earnings which were more than offset by outflows of funds under the other three headings.

This is only a place to start thinking about the problem, however; as usually presented, these outflows are shown on a gross basis and are compared with net goods and service exports. This is not only a questionable accounting practice, but it also may lead to a misunderstanding of what is going on in the balance of payments. Since a balance of payments focuses on the net balance between money flows in and money flows out, we will learn more about what causes the balance to be adverse if we look at net flows rather than gross flows.

The simplest way to convert the three balance of payments villain accounts from gross flows to net flows is to link each major outflow to the corresponding inflows, or paybacks, that it generates. Private foreign investment generates payback flows of fees, royalties, and investment income; foreign aid generates payback flows of interest and principal repayments of foreign aid loans; and the Pentagon launched a major foreign arms sales program in the 1960s to generate income from arms sales as an offset to its foreign military spending. For the present purpose, we can treat these foreign military sales as a payback flow associated with foreign military spending.

In Table I, the associated paybacks for each one of our three major dollar outflows are shown as percentages of the gross outflows that gave rise to them. That is, fees, royalties, and investment income are shown as a percentage of gross U.S. private investment outflows in the two periods 1960-1964 and 1965-1970, and similarly with repayments of foreign aid and with foreign military sales as a percent of foreign military spending. The three villain accounts are shown to differ drastically in the extent of their villainy when they are viewed in terms of their net impact, as in Table I. It is apparent that both private foreign investment and foreign aid generate paybacks much larger than their initial outflows of funds, and that these paybacks exceeded outflows very substantially in the latter part of the decade. The heavy net balance of payments cost of foreign military spending stands out in this table because of its small percentage payback compared to the other two major outflows. This difference should come as no great surprise, because unlike private foreign investment and foreign aid, foreign military spending does not involve any repayment obligations, not does it add to income-earning productive capacity abroad as the other two do.

It does come as a surprise to many people to realize that foreign aid did not impose a net burden on the U.S. balance of payments in the 1960s. On the contrary, in the course of the decade, foreign aid came around to making a net contribution to the balance of payments, which had become substantial by the end of the decade.

The transformation of foreign aid from a net cost to a net benefit in the balance of payments occurred as the result of three long-run trends. In the first place during most of the decade nearly all foreign aid was through purchases that the recipient countries were required to make in the U.S. In 1970, for example, the Agency for International Development (AID) purchased in the U.S. 98 percent of the commodities it supplied as foreign aid. Thus, nearly all foreign aid dollars are paid to U.S. residents, not to foreigners. Second, more foreign aid is being supplied in the form of loans and less as grants than in earlier years, and these loans must be repaid with interest. Third, since the flow of new foreign aid is declining while interest and principal payments from earlier aid extensions are rising, U.S. receipts of interest and principal repayments now exceed the outflow of new foreign aid dollars by a wide margin. This margin amounted to $1.4 billion in 1970.

Table I places the cause of the net balance of payments deficits of the 1960s in a different perspective from the one shown in most balance of payments analyses. It shows that, if we focus on the net effects of the three large gross outflows that are usually regarded jointly as the main causes of the deficits, we find that only one cause is left – the government's foreign military spending.

TABLE I. Payback Percentages in the Balance of Payments of U.S. Private Foreign Investment, U.S. Government Nonmilitary Grants and Credits, and U.S. Foreign Military Expenditures

	1960–64 Average	1965–70 Average
U.S. private foreign investment	102	157
U.S. government nonmilitary grants & credits	150	281
U.S. foreign military expenditures	19	28

This same conclusion emerges if we take a different, somewhat more complex, approach toward isolating the net balance of payments. In Table II, the underlying details of the official statistics are consolidated according to a different organizing principle from the one customarily used by the Commerce Department officials who prepare the government's estimates of the balance of payments. In Table II, the deficit is broken down in order to show what parts of it are accounted for by the U.S. private sector and the government sector, respectively. These are the same categories used by government statisticians in estimating the gross national product. However, in the usual presentation of balance of payments statistics, the roles of government and private sectors are not shown separately.

It can be seen that in 1960-1970 the private sector earned abroad an average of $1.3 billion a year (Line 3), while the U.S. government sector ran up annual deficits averaging more than 2.5 times as much — $3.4 billion a year (Line 7). Within the private sector alone during this period, earnings of foreign exchange on current account (mainly from its net exports of goods and services) were $1.3 billion larger on the average than its net exports of long-term capital.

This means that if the U.S. government had merely broken even in its international transactions, the U.S. balance of payments would have been in surplus instead of in deficit in the decade of the 1960s.

Within the U.S. government sector, Table II brings out the heavy preponderance of military spending abroad by the government, just as Table I does. In the eleven-year period shown, military spending accounted for 88 percent of all net foreign spending by the government ($3.0 billion ÷ $3.4 billion). Contrary to a widespread impression, though, the heavy role of military spending was not due solely to the Vietnam war. On the contrary, military spending was also the dominant factor in the years before the Vietnam escalation began in 1965-1966.

WHY WAS THE COLLAPSE OF THE BRETTON WOODS SYSTEM INEVITABLE?

The Bretton Woods monetary system was definitely based on the dollar as the key currency because only the dollar was freely convertible into gold. Other currencies maintained

TABLE II. Summary of U.S. Basic Balance of Payments, 1960–70 Annual Average (Alternative Format)

	$ Billion 1960–70
(A) Private Commercial Transactions	
(1) U.S. net earnings on current account, commercial transactions only	$+3.6
(2) Private long-term capital transactions	−2.3
(3) Basic Balance, U.S. private sector (lines 1 + 2)	+1.3
(B) U.S. Government Transactions	
(4) Military transactions, net	−3.0
(5) Nonmilitary grants & credits, net	+0.1
(6) All other government, net	−0.5
(7) Basic balance, U.S. government (lines 4 + 5 + 6)	−3.4
(8) U.S. Basic Balance of Payments deficit (lines 3 + 7)	−2.1

a second-degree gold convertibility, as it were, through their convertibility into dollars. Moreover, because monetary gold stocks were inadequate during most of the post–World War II period, many other countries held dollars in their official international monetary reserves as a substitute for gold. This practice, although very widespread, was a violation of Gresham's Law — two separate forms of money cannot for long circulate side by side because sooner or later one of them will become more valuable than the other and disappear into hoards. "Bad money drives out good," as the textbooks say.

The possibility that Gresham's Law would go into operation someday against the dollar was the sword of Damocles that hung over both the dollar and the Bretton Woods system. First in March, 1968, then in August, 1971, and most recently [early in 1973], to many holders of dollars, gold and/or continental European currencies came to seem more valuable than dollars and they rushed out to dispose of their excess dollar holdings. On each of those occasions came a moment of truth for the dollar. On each occasion, the dollar was in deeper trouble than before.

WHAT IT MEANS

What conclusions can we draw on the basis of this brief look into history?

Concerning the dollar, we can say that its meteoric decline was due not primarily to any weakness of the U.S. economy but on the contrary, to the foreign policy of the U.S. government. In the foreign policy sphere the problem was military spending, not foreign aid. In a period dominated by the cold war, the U.S. government spent abroad for military purposes

more foreign exchange than the rest of the U.S. economy was able to earn.

The government's attitude toward spending on the cold war during most of the 1950s and 1960s was the same as if it were spending on a hot war: it believed survival was at stake (whether it was or not), and it was unwilling to have its spending restrained by "mere" economic and financial considerations. It was in this frame of mind that Washington allowed the dollar to go into its meteoric decline. Washington gave top priority to fighting the cold war. Civilian considerations, including the role of the dollar in the world economy, were of secondary interest.

Most U.S. balance of payments analysts were not fully aware of the role of foreign military spending in bringing down the dollar because the official balance of payments statistics do not distinguish between foreign spending by the private and public sectors, respectively.

Concerning the Bretton Woods system, we can now see that the International Monetary Fund was not much more than a forum for international consultation superimposed upon a key currency international monetary system, with the dollar cast in the role that, for many years, had been played by the pound sterling. When the key currency fell, the Bretton Woods system, of course, came tumbling down with it.

The situation is rich in irony. Consider, for example, that the founding fathers of the Bretton Woods system thought they were creating machinery to handle international commercial transactions. When we recall that the last thing they thought they were setting up was an internation monetary mechanism to handle military transfers out of the United States, we are impressed that their creation was able to last as long as it did.

GOLD

Peter L. Bernstein

*Peter L. Bernstein, who in the readings for Chapter
Thirty-one asked "Does Monetary Policy Matter?," now
turns his attention to some causes behind the current
meteoric rise in the price of gold.*

I must in all fairness begin this essay with a warning: Although on occasion some people have been good enough to consider me an authority on the subject of gold, and although I have in fact written extensively about it, my formerly unblemished forecasting record has become badly blemished over the past three years. Like most economists, I have believed that men were capable of managing their affairs in a rational manner, despite temporary aberrations; given this premise, gold seems like a foolish medium to use as a technique of control. As history teaches us, gold becomes meaningful only when men in general and their governments in particular seem incapable of ordering their affairs. Unfortunately, in the unprecedented chaos that rules the world today, the explosion in gold prices should perhaps have been less of a surprise to us than it has been.

Be that as it may, here is a further warning: I have consulted no other "experts" in preparing this analysis. I have no faith in what they can tell me. I am reminded, in fact, of the old story about the man who asked Baron Rothschild to explain gold to him. "Only two people understand it," replied the Baron, "a director of the Bank of England and an obscure clerk in the Bank of France. Unfortunately, they disagree!"

The price of gold has more than quadrupled in the free market over the past four years and has just about doubled in the past twelve months. The basic reasons for this are clear enough, but the consequences are more obscure. It is this aspect of the matter that we shall attempt to illuminate here.

First, however, a few introductory observations may be helpful. The most important of these is the peculiar physical and chemical properties of gold itself, which make gold such a singularly appropriate thing to hoard. Gold is chemically inert, which means that – unlike other metals – it barely reacts at all to oxygen and therefore never tarnishes. This not only provides its magical and beautiful luster, but it also means that gold can be kept for centuries under any and all conditions without any visible deterioration whatsoever.

Furthermore, gold has extraordinarily high density. A small amount weighs a lot and therefore packs a lot of value. The world's entire monetary gold stock weighs only about 50,000 tons, which contrasts, for example, with the 400,000 tons *a day* produced by the U. S. steel industry. The classic gold brick, which takes up less space than half a dozen legal-sized yellow pads, was worth $14,000 at the old price of $35 and would fetch about $60,000 in the free market today. Contrast this by visualizing a bushel of wheat that now brings about $6 or an equivalent weight of copper currently worth about $20.

At first glance, gold at $35 has no more significance or importance than gold at $150. It has some peripheral impact, such as raising the value of South African annual production by some $4 billion or increasing the asset value of those people who bought it at lower prices. It is likely to reduce the demand for gold watches and jewelry and to make engaged couples think twice before they invest in wedding bands. Like any product, those who hold gold and produce it benefit from a higher price, while those who use it have to pay more or economize on its use. In general, however, the world can go on about its business regardless of the price of gold, for its use in all but a tiny part of the world's production of goods and services is negligible. This of course is entirely different from the impact of an increase in the price of oil or wheat or copper.

And yet, something profound has happened. Except for gold producers, who want to sell it and convert it into money just as the producer of any article must do, gold has lost a vital function in its role as money: it has ceased to be a medium of exchange – a means for making payments and settling up debts. Today it is only a store of value, moving only into hoards instead of greasing the wheels of commerce.

Although most individuals who hold gold have always hoarded it and considered it their ultimate asset in case of total disaster, gold has nevertheless functioned primarily as an international medium of exchange, through which nations settled up their payment imbalances with one another. It is this function that has atrophied as a result of the high free-market price for gold.

No central banker or treasury minister would be so foolish as to sell another nation an asset for forty-two dollars an ounce that the buyer could then readily sell for a price way above that in the free market. The seller would do just as well to sell the gold himself for foreign exchange in the free market and settle up his debts that way. Consequently, central bankers and treasuries are attempting to settle their international payments

deficits in any way possible other than by dipping into their gold reserves.

As a result, one important method of balancing international accounts is inoperative. This means that pressures on exchange rates are more intense than they would be if this facility were available – and that governmental financiers must find new ways of tiding themselves over when their nation is spending abroad more than they are receiving from foreigners. This is why we see such uneasiness in the international financial markets and why the achievement of a new international payments system is so difficult.

Of course, one might ask why the central bankers fail to take advantage of the high price of gold in the free market: why don't they sell it in exchange for foreign currencies that they may need in the future to cover deficits in their balance of payments? Since, among monies, gold is the top tier par excellence, and since we have just had proof that the top tier of other financial assets can deteriorate in value with dramatic suddenness, I should think that at some point the temptation to take advantage of the emotionally charged atmosphere of the free market will be too great for the central bankers to resist. There must be some price that will ultimately appear to be "too high."

Unfortunately, however, the hoarding fever attacks everyone who touches gold, even taciturn and pipe-smoking central bankers. In a kind of Gresham's Law analysis, central bankers are reluctant to exchange gold for the currency of any country when inflation continues to drain away the purchasing power of currency and bank deposits. Yet, although this may seem like "sound" financial policy, it is pure speculation nonetheless, for they are simply betting that the price of gold will continue to rise faster than the prices of goods and services. Meanwhile, they are not only failing to earn any interest on their gold hoards – a not insignificant consideration – but they are also engaged in a tulip-bubble type game in which the price of the commodity in which they are speculating bears no relationship whatsoever to any productive purpose.

Indeed, any commodity specialist will tell you to go short when inventories are equal to more than twenty-five years' production, which is in fact the relationship between the high hoards of the central banks and current levels of new gold production. In other words, the prevailing free-market price is based upon false scarcity resulting from the central bankers' hesitancy to part with their hoards, which in turn is a consequence of expectations of still higher prices. Any reversal in expectations will bring about an abrupt and cataclysmic decline in the price of gold.

Thus, the opportunity costs and risks of holding gold obviously increase with each upward step in its price. Any security portfolio manager will testify from hard experience that this calls for prudence and moderation rather than blind assurance and greed. The Greater Fool Theory, as we have all learned too well, is a dangerous game to play for too long.

To the extent that gold is used by governments or by hoarders to finance the purchase of goods and services, an increase in its price adds to inflationary pressures. Gold is money, after all, and the higher it goes in price, the more purchasing power it commands. The effect is the same as though everyone holding a five-dollar bill could tomorrow buy twenty dollars of merchandise with it – he has more purchasing power while everyone else has no less. With more dollars chasing the same amount of goods, prices would inevitably tend to rise.

When we follow the process through, however, its ultimate impact is less clear. If gold circulated freely as a medium of exchange, then surely those people and governments who hold it could buy more with it when it commands $150 of purchasing power than when it commands $35. They could either coin it and pay it out in the marketplace for whatever they wanted to buy, or they would deposit it in their bank

accounts, just as they deposit coin and currency, and write checks against it. This is in essence what the Treasury does when the value of its gold stock is written up from, say, $35 an ounce to $42.

But gold does *not* circulate as a medium of exchange. The only fixed and stated value that it has (as a five-dollar bill has a fixed value of five dollars) is the official price, which is less than one-third of the current free-market price. If holders of gold use gold as a medium of exchange with a fluctuating value, much more gold would be coming to market. Consequently, its price would begin to decline as the dishoarding process took place, its purchasing power would shrink correspondingly, and its inflationary impact would be lessened by the same token.

The hoarder of gold who decides to spend his profits could of course always sell his gold to a central bank – but he would receive in return only forty-two dollars of spendable currency. This means that he would continue to offer his gold in the free market as long as the free market price were above forty-two dollars, but, as we have already seen, the process of offering gold in order to use it as a medium of exchange would mean an increase in supply relative to demand and a decline in its price/purchasing power.

Many people have wondered what would happen if the Arabs insisted on payment in gold before they would sell any of their oil.

No one knows how much gold coin and bullion exists outside the vaults of central banks, but a rough guess would suggest $30 billion at current free-market prices. This is clearly insufficient to cover the cost of oil imports to the industrialized world for very long (the United States alone was importing at an annual rate of more than $8 billion before the [1973] (embargo), even if it were all available for the purpose.

In other words, the Arab demands could be met only if the central bankers were willing to use their gold holdings to cover the balance of payments deficits that we are incurring vis-à-vis the Arab states. Since they would obviously be unwilling to give the Arabs the additional windfall of exchanging gold for oil at forty-two dollars an ounce, the official price of gold at that point would probably jump to somewhere near the then free-market price or even higher. This would give the industrialized countries at least $200 billion in gold to exchange for oil.

How much better off would the Arabs be as a consequence? Like King Midas, they would have exchanged one of the world's most truly valuable assets — oil — for a sterile, speculative, and unproductive asset — gold. The more they insist on this fruitless goal, the more the price of gold will increase and the fewer ounces of gold they will receive for each new barrel of oil.

Ultimately, the problem shakes down to precisely the form it takes when the Arabs take payment in currencies rather than gold: in both cases they give up a real asset for a financial asset. Financial assets cannot feed you, clothe you, house you, or transport you. Unless they produce a stream of income, they have no ascertainable value — like stocks that never pay a dividend, they will in fact be highly volatile in value. Unless, therefore, they have a claim on real assets that are productive, they are essentially speculative tulip bulbs. This means, then, that no matter what form of payment the Arabs take for their oil, they will ultimately have to exchange the oil for something productive and useful or they will be caught in the Midas syndrome.

Our own feeling, now tentatively supported by others, is that hoarding of everything is reaching the panic stage. This means in turn that it will be far overdone, resulting ultimately in a dangerous and unpleasant process of dishoarding. In that process, however, those who will be hurt the most will be those who hold assets whose intrinsic value is the least.

In short, the high price of gold is a symptom of chaos rather than a cause of it: its consequences are peripheral rather than determining. Nevertheless, no one should ignore or minimize the manifestations it provides of greed, anxiety, and lack of faith in one's fellow man. We are tragically reminded of the greatest temper tantrum in history, when Moses came down from Mount Sinai with the most rational code of conduct for men to live with one another in harmony:

The tables were the work of God and the writing of God. And it came to pass as soon as Moses came nigh unto the camp, that he saw the golden calf and the dancing, and Moses' anger waxed hot and he cast the tablets out of his hands and brake them beneath the Mount. And Aaron said, "Let not the anger of my lord wax hot: thou knowest the people, that they are set on mischief." And Moses returned unto the Lord and said, "Oh, this people have sinned a great sin and have made them gods of gold." And the Lord said unto Moses, "When I visit, I will visit their sin upon them," and the Lord plagued the people because they made the calf.

Excerpted from Exodus,
Chapter 32.

THE INTELLIGENT READER'S GUIDE TO THE INTERNATIONAL MONETARY MUDDLE: HOW THE INTERNATIONAL MONETARY SYSTEM DEVELOPED, AND WHY IT DOESN'T WORK TOO WELL

Anwar Shaikh

This reading needs no explanation. It is written by an economist who specializes in international economics.

The paradox of money, this most practical of things, is that its usefulness depends exactly on the faith we place in it. Money is, after all, a social convention, accepted by all of us in exchange for goods or services precisely because we take for granted that it can be reexchanged at some later date for other goods or services. Undermine this implicit "faith" and you undermine the whole structure of economic activity it supports.

We have nowadays, by and large, become accustomed to the idea that within any country, *domestic money* need not be backed up by some precious metal in order for us to have the necessary "faith" in it. But even the most casual observer of the international scene can see that it would be difficult to carry over this faith to international monies. It is easy to understand, therefore, why even today the international acceptability of any national currency depends largely on the "backing" this currency has. Which brings us to gold.

GOLD

Historically, gold and silver have been the traditional supplies of money in the West. But

From *Challenge* (March/April, 1974), pp. 52-56.

the new production of these precious metals very seldom kept pace with the rapidly increasing demand for money engendered by the economic growth of Western countries. As a consequence, there was a gradual shift away from gold and silver *domestic money* toward currency *backed* by gold and silver reserves, which in turn led to today's notion of domestic currency backed largely by "faith."

Internationally, the same pressure led to drastic devaluations of many currencies with respect to gold; over a long period of time, from roughly the thirteenth century to the nineteenth century, the price of gold in terms of most national currencies rose steeply, so that any given quantity of gold was equivalent to a rising quantity of international money.

In spite of all this, the supply of gold proved inadequate, and after World War I it became increasingly common to back up international monies with *reserves which included quantities of some "key currencies," primarily the pound sterling.* Thus the ratio of "key currency" reserves to annual imports, for all countries as a whole, rose from 2 percent in 1913 to 11 percent in 1928, ushering into the international monetary system the gold-(foreign)-exchange standard — *as well as setting the stage for its collapse!*

The basic problem with the gold-exchange standard, *then and now,* is that it works only if the "key currency" countries are willing to let their own reserve positions decline. For instance, in the 1920s, as foreigners accumulated pounds, they acquired claims on London's gold reserves, since pounds were backed by British gold. Because these gold reserves did not grow as fast as the foreign claims on them, Britains's reserve position deteriorated; confidence in the pound, which is what made it a key currency in the first place, also deteriorated, *and with it confidence in the system itself, since the pound sterling was a major component of international reserves.* By 1928 Britain's reserve rates (of gold reserves to foreign claims on them) had fallen to less than 25 percent.

Robert Triffin, the well-known specialist on international monetary affairs, put it this way: "The increasing use of foreign exchange balances as a remedy to world illiquidity under the new gold exchange standard had thus fatally weakened the reserve position of the country on which the system was primarily dependent for its continued operation. The collapse of the major key currency of the system in 1931 inevitably sucked other countries into the whirlpool, and entailed the temporary breakdown, not only of sterling, but of the international monetary system itself" (*Gold and the Dollar Crisis: The Future of Convertibility, p 67*).

DOLLARS

Since World War II, the dollar has supplanted the pound as the single most important "key currency," accounting for some 55 percent of the growth in world monetary reserves. And with this rise in importance has come the concomitant pressure on the liquidity of the dollar. Since the end of World War II the United States has been running a chronic deficit in its balance of payments, i.e., spending more abroad than it made abroad.

In the beginning this deficit was considered acceptable on both sides of the Atlantic as necessary expenditures for postwar reconstruction, for aid to the less developed countries, and for the conduct of the Cold War, so that foreign central banks were willing to finance these deficits *primarily* by holding on to dollars they received, rather than "cashing" them in for U.S. gold – in effect, accepting short-term IOUs from the United States. Thus, from 1949 to 1965 the gold stock of the United States dropped by only 33 percent, while its liquid liabilities rose over 300 percent! After 1965, however, a substantial portion of U.S. deficits were due to the escalation of the Vietnam war and American penetration or takeover of European business firms, activities which European nations generally considered far less acceptable reasons for financing a deficit. As foreign willingness to hold dollars declined, the pressure on the dollar, and therefore on the whole international gold-dollar system, increased significantly.

THE IMF AND PAPER GOLD

In 1967, the British pound, faced with similar problems, devalued, and set off a world monetary crisis. A stampede for gold occurred as hoarders sought to convert dollars and pounds into gold at a rate that would have stripped Fort Knox within weeks. As a direct consequence, in March 1968 all gold payments from official central banks to the free market were suspended. Since then there have been two kinds of gold (the "two-tier gold system"): that held by a central bank of a government, transferable only to *another* central bank at $35 an ounce; and that held by private individuals or firms, which may be bought or sold on the free market, generally at a price higher than $35.

The two-tier gold system described above is at best a stopgap measure, designed to protect official gold reserves from the onslaughts of the market. In effect it confines these reserves within the member nations of the International Monetary Fund (IMF), since none of the ten major members (The Club of Ten) may buy gold from any nation that deals with the free market in gold. (The exception to the "boycotted" gold suppliers is South Africa, which can sell to the IMF at the fixed parity of $35 an ounce what it doesn't sell on the free market.) Obviously, with each $35 requiring an ounce of IMF gold as backing, and the official gold supply stagnant or increasing slowly, the expansion of world trade would soon be brought to a halt. Thus in 1970, having temporarily stemmed *this* tide, the IMF adopted a new plan to expand world reserves by creating "paper gold."

The basic idea was to create reserve assets, which would then be allocated to IMF members in proportion to their initial contribution to the Fund. These allocations, known as special drawing rights (SDRs), were to be used by members to settle their international balances with one another, thereby supplementing gold and they key currencies as "backing" for international money. Thus, for instance, by 1971 U.S. reserves had expanded by about $1.6 billion in SDRs. Not enough by a long shot, as it turned out!

THE BEAT GOES ON

Meanwhile, the central problem remained unchanged. At best, the two-tier gold system had succeeded in protecting American gold reserves only from the free market, not from claims by other member nations of the IMF. It therefore relieved the pressure on the dollar only briefly. Similarly, the creation of "paper gold" (SDRs) increased U.S. reserves somewhat, which again took some pressure off. But the growing U.S. deficit continued to pile up more and more dollars in foreign central banks, so that foreign claims on U.S. gold continued to grow. In a short while the United States had more or less used up its "paper gold" in paying off a small fraction of these claims, and even its gold bullion reserves

began to fall. In 1970 a new annual high in U.S. deficits ($10 billion) was reached, and by the first six months of 1971 the deficit was up to $12 billion, an annual rate of $24 billion. The run on the dollar was on!

Once again stopgap measures were quickly put into effect. In August 1971, the U.S. Treasury stopped redeeming in gold even those dollars held by foreign central banks and in December 1971, the U.S. dollar was devalued by 8.57 percent relative to gold (about 11 percent relative to currencies like the Japanese yen and West German mark, which were simultaneously revalued upward). This stopped the drain of gold from the United States and temporarily eased the strain on the dollar. In addition, measures were taken to cut back U.S. imports (by raising tariffs, and thus making foreign goods more expensive within the United States), and expand U.S. exports (through the wage-price freeze, in the hope that U.S. prices would rise more slowly than foreign prices, making U.S. goods relatively more attractive to foreigners), so that the basic cause of the problem, the U.S. balance of payments deficits, might be ameliorated somewhat. But even the successful elimination of U.S. deficits would hardly solve the problem. After all, if none of the key currency countries ran deficits, world reserves could only grow as fast as *gold* reserves, and it was the inadequacy of gold reserves that led nations to use key currencies as reserves in the first place!

THE CURRENT MUDDLE

It is obvious that if some countries are running deficits in their balance of payments, others will be running surpluses. The U.S. deficit, for instance, has its counterpart in Japanese and German surpluses, among others. Therefore, one way to reduce U.S. deficits would be for Japan and Germany to *appreciate* their currencies relative to the dollar. If, for instance, the Deutschemark were to cost more dollars than before, German goods would cost more to Americans, and American goods would cost less to Germans. Thus the U.S. deficit would be lessened as its imports decreased and exports increased. Of course, Germany would then be selling less goods to the United States *and* the rest of the world (presuming all other currencies stay tied to the dollar) – which would lead to unemployment in German industries, and political problems for the government.

Many countries in fact suspect the United States of being primarily concerned with forcing appreciation on persistent surplus countries, thereby avoiding its responsibility to cut back its own huge deficits. As it currently stands, the U.S. dollar is no longer convertible into gold (since Nixon suspended convertibility in August 1971, during the run of the dollar). so that the U.S. deficits for Vietnam and multinational corporate expansion abroad are not countered by any direct economic pressure to end these deficits. Meanwhile, the surplus countries find that U.S. dollars spent there add fuel to inflationary pressures, so that they must either accept these or let their currency appreciate – which would lessen their trade not only with the United States but with the rest of the world as well!

In spite of these serious differences, all sides agree that there is a basic need for international monetary reform. It is increasingly clear to everyone concerned that the alternative to reform is a collapse of the system itself. But, as history teaches us, it is by no means certain that reform will in fact take place before a collapse.

DIRECTIONS OF REFORM

At the moment, the United States is very reluctant to restore the convertibility of the dollar into gold, for fear of another run on its reserves. It therefore takes the position that some rules for changing the present situation must *first* be agreed upon before any steps are taken to restore dollar convertibility. This would mean agreement on two major principles: first, on rules which will prevent IMF member nations from running persistent surpluses or deficits, these rules to be backed up by sanctions, if necessary; and second, on a method for *creating* and expanding international reserves at a rate suitable to the growth in world trade. On this second principle the consensus among member nations seems to favor some method similar to the current IMF practice of creating "paper gold" (SDRs), though not all nations agree on "paper gold" as the *only* international reserve, since this would place them at the mercy of the SDR allocation rules of the IMF.

There is little reason to expect that any general agreement will be reached in the next two years. Crises in the system will undoubtedly continue to occur, which may generate pressures sufficient to create a consensus before collapse.

POSTSCRIPT: THE LATEST CRISIS

On February 12, [1973] as this article was on its way to the printer, the U.S. announced another devaluation of the dollar. Thus in the last fourteen months the value of the dollar has fallen from 1/35th of an ounce of gold to 1/38th in December 1971, and then to less than 1/42nd of an ounce currently. It is a sign of the times that just prior to the devaluation, in an unprecedented move, casino operators in the Portuguese Province of Macao refused to accept American dollars!

The previous devaluation agreement of 1971, hailed by President Nixon as "the most significant monetary achievement in the history of the world," proved to be little more than a palliative. 1972's balance of payments deficit turned out to be in the order of $10 billion and the balance of *trade* deficit was $6.4 billion, the highest ever. As is to be expected, these facts did little to strengthen the credibility of the dollar, and in the first two weeks of February, some 7 billion dollars were unloaded in exchange for German marks and Japanese yen, precipitating the latest devaluation. What happened in the current crisis is basically what happened in the last one, and what most probably will happen in the next. At any rate, these crises certainly do help build up pressure for reform!

The

Multinational

Corporation

38

LEARNING OBJECTIVES

There is much more we don't know about multinationals than we do know. Hence your best learning objective is to become aware of the *complexity of the issues* posed by multinational corporate production.

The multinational corporation is an enormously important new element in international economics. We still do not understand fully its long-term implications, but here is a considered view of the impact of the multinational.

MULTINATIONAL CORPORATIONS: PROFILES AND PROSPECTS

Burton Teague

As the following article suggests, economists and policymakers around the world are increasingly turning their attention to the multinational corporation. Burton Teague, of the research staff of the National Industrial Conference Board, presents some of the conceptual and political issues involved.

Despite their significant and essential contribution to gross world product, multinational corporations are not thoroughly and objectively understood. Because of the wide variety of the breed, they have, as yet, no generally accepted definition. To quote Antonio Knoppers, senior vice president of Merck & Co., "It [the multinational corporation] has something in common with happiness or misery. No one can define it, but you always know when it is there." Mr. Knoppers adds that it is an "enterprise that sees the world, or a goodly portion of it, as its market, and acts to make the most of its opportunities on an supranational basis." He groups these enterprises into: *International Corporations* (with substantial foreign investment but a predominant home base), *Multinational Corporations* (whose sales abroad are about equal to domestic sales), and *Transnational Corporations* (which have lost their national identity through wide international ownership). . . .

[C]urrent definitions of multinational corporations essentially depend on the criteria by which they are being judged. It is also evident that "the present legal framework has no comfortable, tidy receptacle for such an institution," each component of a locally registered corporation in the chain of the multinational company has a separate nationality.*

Despite its defiance of ready description, however, most multinational corporations are easily identifiable. The *Directory of American Firms Operating in Foreign Countries* in 1969 listed approximately 3000 American companies with interests in 114 foreign countries. Over half of the 1000 companies on *Fortune's* first and second "500 largest" lists operate abroad. But, according to a U.S. Department of Commerce study, 60% of U.S. direct foreign investment was accounted for by the 50 largest, 70% by the 100 largest, and 90% by the 300 largest corporations.**

GLOBAL RESULTS

If multinational corporations cannot be defined theoretically, they can be identified by what they achieve. The consolidated gross sales of the 528 international, multinational, or transnational companies that were identified on the *Fortune* lists range from $52 million to over $24

*Professor Detlev Vagts, *Harvard Law Review,* Feb. 1970.
**Survey of Current Business, October 1968.

billion, with global net income after taxes ranging from a deficit of $38 million to a profit of almost $2 billion. Their individual worldwide operations employ from 400 to almost 800,000 people, their assets run from about $6 thousand to over $250 thousand per employee, and they have direct operations in from only one to 75 or more foreign countries.

In a separate, related Conference Board survey of 267 of these 528 companies, roughly 24% can be classified as engaged in the automotive, machinery, tools and related industries abroad; about 24% are engaged in chemical, oil, drug and similar undertakings; 20% in enterprises related to aerospace, electrical and electronic, and other high-technology activities; about 12% are in mining, metals, building materials and construction industries; and the remaining 20% in the production of various consumer products including food, apparel, tobacco, paper, glass, books and so on.

Of the 267 companies who responded to the Board's questionnaire, about 65% expect their foreign operations to expand more rapidly than their domestic. The remaining 35% say they expect their foreign business to grow hand-in-hand with, or slower than, their domestic operations. Of those expecting faster growth abroad, 50% report their business overseas now contributes from 25% to over 50% of their consolidated gross sales. Of those less sanguine about foreign prospects, 50% report their current overseas operations now contribute less than 15% to total operating results. Over twice as many companies in the automotive, machinery, and tools industry group; the chemical, oil group; and the high-technology group expect faster growth abroad than those who did not. The forecasts are approximately even among companies in mining, metals, and consumer products.

Because of the vast range of difference in the operating results the 528 international companies achieve, their activities are difficult to bring into focus. A statistical distribution of these companies in terms of gross sales shows the top

of the range to be 480 times the bottom. Almost one-half of the companies range between $100 million and $800 million in sales. The 10% at the top vary by a factor of almost 15 times, while, conversely, the 10% at the bottom vary by a factor of only a fraction over one (Table 1).

In measurement by Net After Taxes, there is also almost 1800% spread between the minimum and the maximum of just the top 10% of the range of the distribution. However, median company earnings of the group are between $10 million and $25 million (Table 2).

When the 528 companies are ranked by Return on Investment, the variation among the top 10% of the companies is about 875%, but the typical (median) ROI is just under $11 million (Table 3).

The data suggest that there may be some correlation between sales, net, and return, and other possible categories of measurement. The same companies were therefore ranked by: (1) Gross Sales, (2) Total Assets, (3) Net Income After Taxes, (4) Number of Employees, (5) Geographic Dispersion (number of countries of foreign operation), (6) Assets per Employee, (7) Return on Investment, (8) Ten Year Growth Rate, and (9) Total Equity Invested.

A high ranking in one of these categories is by no means assurance of high ranking in all the others, to be sure, but there is in fact a high degree of correlation between all the categories of measurement which are obviously related to physical and financial size: Sales, Assets, Equity, Number of Employees, etc. There is also some

TABLE 1.   International Companies: Distribution by Gross Sales ($ millions)

Range	Number of Companies	Percentage
From $1,700 to $25,000	53	10
From 600 to 1,700	106	20
From 135 to 600	210	40
From 70 to 135	106	20
From 52 to 70	53	10
	528	100

TABLE 2. International Companies: Distribution by Net After Taxes ($ millions)

Range	Number of Companies	Percentage
From $90 to $1,711	53	10
From 29 to 90	106	20
From 5 to 29	210	40
From 2 to 5	106	20
From deficit to 2	53	10

correlation between these and Net Income, Geographic Dispersion, and Assets per Employee. However, these size measures are not closely related to Return on Investment and Growth Rate. Of those companies which are among the top 10% ranked by Gross Sales, over 90% are also among the top 10% in the ranking by total Assets and Equity Invested; over 80% are also top ranked by Net Income After Taxes; and over 70% by Number of Employees. But only about 40% were similarly ranked by Geographic Dispersion; about 20% by Assets per Employee; and less than 10% for both Return on Investment and Ten Year Growth Rate.

A similar ranking comparison by Number of Employees confirms and emphasizes these results.

A ranking by Geographic Dispersion reveals a high degree of correlation between this measurement and Net Income, Assets, Equity, and Sales; and a somewhat higher degree of correlation with Return on Investment than was the case with the other two comparisons.

It may be noted that there is a relatively high degree of correlation between top ranking in Gross Sales, Number of Employees, and Geo-

TABLE 3. International Companies: Distribution by Return on Investment (percentage)

Range	Number of Companies	Percentage
From 17.9% to 174.6%	53	10
From 13.1 to 17.9	106	20
From 8.7 to 13.1	210	40
From 4.6 to 8.7	106	20
From — to 4.6	53	10

graphic Dispersion. There is little correlation between any of these categories of measurement and Assets per Employee. This suggests that the multinational corporation may be either labor-intensive or capital-intensive with no strong trend in either direction characterizing their operations.

GEOGRAPHIC CHARACTERISTICS

Examining the whole list of *Fortune's* 1000 leading American industrial corporations makes it clear that Gross Sales of the international companies are related to the extent of Geographic Dispersion (Table 4).

Whether or not a company engages in international operations also correlates with its size. From an analysis of the same list of American corporations, it is apparent that if a company's gross sales are in excess of about $1 billion, the chances are 9 to 1 that the company will be engaged in foreign operations. Conversely, if its sales are under $60 million, the chances are better than 2 to 1 that it will be engaged solely in domestic operations (Table 5).

In terms of geographic areas, Canada is by far the most popular country for direct investment by U.S.-based international companies. Great Britain and Western Europe are not far behind.

TABLE 4. Rank of 528 International Companies Among the 1000 Largest Industrials

(Fortune's 1st and 2nd "500 largest")

All-Company Rank by Gross Sales	International Company in Rank (No.)	Average Number of Countries of Operation
1 — 100	90	18
101 — 200	80	12
201 — 300	69	8
301 — 400	57	6
401 — 500	46	6
501 — 600	41	5
601 — 700	42	4
701 — 800	36	4
801 — 900	38	3
901 — 1000	29	3

TABLE 5. Companies Operating Abroad by Volume of Sales

(Fortune's 1st and 2nd "500 largest")

Range Sales ($000,000)	Number of Companies	Percentage of International Companies	Percentage of Solely Domestic Companies
$1.154-$24.295	100	90%	10%
547- 1.153	100	80	20
312- 546	100	69	31
221- 311	100	57	43
162- 220	100	46	54
120- 161	100	41	59
94- 119	100	42	58
76- 93	100	36	64
63- 75	100	38	62
51- 62	100	29	71
Total	1.000	52.8%	47.2%

Australia and New Zealand appear to be gaining favor, with the countries of Latin America, Africa, and the East bringing up the rear.

THE U.S. INTERNATIONAL COMPANY IN PROFILE

The foregoing analysis makes it possible to bring the typical U.S.-based corporation into focus. First of all, it is most likely to be one of the giants of American industrial enterprise. While size alone does not dictate a move into foreign markets by direct investment, the mathematical probability of a company "going foreign" increases as size does. Typically, this international company (based on medians) has gross sales of about $275 million, a net after taxes of about $13 million, and almost 12,000 employees. It invests roughly $20,000 per employee and enjoys a return on its total investment of about 11%. It operates in Canada, Great Britain, Mexico, Australia, and either France, Germany, Italy, Switzerland, Belgium, Holland, or Japan, in that order of preference.

MULTINATIONAL CORPORATE IMAGES

The recorded operating results of multinational companies reflected in official statistics and estimates from informed sources, underscore and support the words of N. R. Danielian, president, International Economic Policy Association.* "There is no other instrumentality with the same flexibility, inventiveness, initiative, and effectiveness as the multinational corporation in undertaking the extraction, refinement, fabrication, transportation, and marketing [of the world's] resources. No armies, no governments, no foreign aid, no international institutions can match this achievement."

But not everyone shares this favorable and sanguine view of industrial multinationalism. Representative Hale Boggs, in his opening remarks to the Hearings beginning July 27, 1970, said:

*Professor John H. Dunning, University of Reading, England, Hearings before the Joint Economic Committee, Subcommittee on Foreign Economic Policy, 91st Congress, Second Session, July 1970 (Washington, D.C.: U.S. Government Printing Office, 1970) p. 794.

While business leaders have viewed [direct investment abroad] as a means of distributing the fruits of technology and managerial expertise more rapidly throughout the globe, spokesmen for organized labor have viewed multinational corporations as institutions exporting thousands of jobs. The U.S. government has also become concerned that American firms might be able to avoid administrative regulations by permitting their branches abroad to engage in activities that would not be permitted here. On the other hand some other governments have considered the attempt to impose U.S. antitrust statutes, balance of payments guidelines, and trade regulations on the foreign subsidiaries of American firms as an unjustified extension of U.S. sovereignty.*

The countervailing and conflicting pressures on international companies were dramatically described by Mr. Danielian:

They [multinational companies] are confronted with a diversity of political motivation – some of emotional origin, such as nationalism; others ideological, such as consumerism; and some even humanitarian, as in the case of welfarism – which subject them to a multiplicity of restrictions and taxation of varying levels in different countries. They have to do business in a variety of environments: the nation, state, common markets, free trade areas, preference systems, state trading blocs, and democracies of varying degree of popular representation.... They have to cope with controls over imports and exports, tariffs, nontariff barriers, diversity of tax systems and tax rates, different welfare schemes, a variety of employment policies, exchange controls, antitrust rules, and threats of nationalization and expropriation.

He then concludes, "Multinational corporations, the most important instrument of economic development, are left starkly alone, buffeted by the violent currents of world politics, with no support in public opinion, no

*Dunning, Hearings before the Joint Economic Committee, p. 745.

court of appeal, and often abandoned by their own governments."

Not unexpectedly, organized labor in the United States is disturbed by the rapid development of international companies. It is attempting to develop a countervailing force internationally by association with local labor organizations, bringing together U.S. and foreign unions into large federations as in the American past.

The first "danger" to which unions point is the cost in terms of American jobs. According to Nathaniel Goldfinger, director of research, AFL-CIO, citing Labor Secretary Schultz, 1.9 million jobs would have been required to produce the value of 74% of the imports into the United States in 1966. By 1968 the estimate would be 2.4 million jobs, and this does not include an untold number of jobs lost to American labor by the production of foreign subsidiaries of U.S. companies operating overseas, and foreign companies operating under license from U.S. companies.

A second aspect of international activity to which organized labor in particular takes exception is the growth of the "foreign satellite plant" concept. By this method companies can establish manufacturing facilities, usually in Canada or Mexico, where labor rates are lower. The more labor-intensive portions of the process can be accomplished there, and the semifinished product can be imported to the United States at low tariff rates for final processing.

HOST COUNTRY HOSPITALITY

The host country view of the multinational corporations, especially those based in the United States, is candidly expressed by Jean Jacques Servan-Schreiber, member of the French

Chamber of Deputies, publisher of *L'Express* (Paris) and author of *The American Challenge*. His point of view appears to be that of the whole European Economic Community and, to a degree, of the rest of the free world. He regards American penetration of European markets as an invasion, a form of colonialism reminiscent of that of the European colonial powers in the nineteenth century. Its growth, he contends, should be alarming to Europeans.

From 1965 to 1966, U.S. investment in the United States rose 17%; in the world at large, 21%; and in the EEC countries, 40%. The magnitude alone is reason enough for apprehension, many believe, but qualitatively it is additionally alarming. The U.S. subsidiaries control 15% of the consumer goods production in the EEC, 50% of the semi-conductors manufactured, 80% of the computer output, and 95% of the integrated circuit facilities. Moreover, the funds to do this, for the most part, are obtained from local capital sources. Of $4 billion invested by U.S. companies in Europe in 1965, 55% came from loans within the EEC, 35% from EEC government subsidies, and only 10% directly from U.S. sources.

It's the concentration of economic power in a few companies that should be most disconcerting to Europeans, according to Servan-Schreiber. Over half of the American-owned European subsidiaries are controlled by 340 of the top 500 companies on the *Fortune* list. They have the economic muscle to drain the capital market and the labor market, to ignore national boundaries, and to upset economic tranquility by ignoring cartels and knocking down prices, he claims.

Host countries have by no means adopted a uniform stance in this matter. The situation is viewed differently by bankers (who appreciate riskless investment), consumers (who appreciate lower prices), workers (who appreciate higher wages), and politicians (who appreciate the admittedly higher standards of living). Within government, the various ministries – labor, fi-

nance, industrial development, etc. – can be expected to support varying views. They will react differently to different kinds of transactions: investment inflows, repatriation of profits, technical and managerial inflow versus outflow, import versus export of capital goods, etc.

There is no overall uniform reaction one can point to – reactions trend from eager courtships through complacency to stirrings of envy and anger. However, a more complete picture can be obtained by noting the experience of several major countries where multinational corporations have made important inroads.

Canada

In Canada, U.S. investment has become a popular political issue. Of Canada's GNP, 23½% is export; of this, 70% goes to the U.S.A. About 25% of Canadian GNP is import, 73% from the U.S.A. Her manufacturing equity is 60% foreign owned, and of this, 46% is American. It is now common knowledge that many Canadians feel American dominance of their economy has deprived them of a degree of their sovereignty.

Japan

For years Japan has made it difficult for foreigners to set up controlled investments within her boundaries. She is now on the verge of becoming a capital exporter; as such she will be forced to relax barriers to foreign capital. But she is concerned about her trade and her competitive position. (Postwar wages have risen 10-15% per annum.) U.S. exports to Japan trebled in the last 10 years from $1.5 billion to $4.5 billion. Japan is the second largest trader with U.S.A. for both exports and imports.

Britain

The development in the United Kingdom is striking. In prewar Britain, U.S.-based companies controlled only 6% of the production, and drew 7% of the profits. In 1969 they controlled 14%

of the production, 20% of the capital formation, and 25% of the sales. Moreover, they now account for 80% of fresh investment capital, and 75% of that is directed to research-intensive industry. They are able to shift their work to low labor-cost countries, and the profit to low tax areas. (In the past 25 years U.S. firms have created 8000 subsidiaries throughout the world; their combined output is larger than that of any nation except the U.S., USSR, or Japan.) Britain has not reacted overtly to these developments, but this situation may change when British attention to the problems of EEC accommodation lessens.

Italy

In Italy income from foreign private investment, 80% of which is American, has grown from about $1.9 billion or 12% of annual merchandise exported in the period 1950-1954, to $8 billion of 22% of the merchandise exported today. Italians do not seem unduly exercised over this development, preferring to enjoy their own postwar economic recovery to a position of relative affluence.

Latin America

Direct investment remains a politically sensitive item, increasingly exposed to abrasive forms of nationalism; despite its obvious advantages as a vehicle for transferring capital to developing countries of Latin America. Roberto de Oliveira Campos, president, Banco de Investmento e Desenvolvimento Industrial, Sao Paulo, characterizes the behavior of developing countries toward foreign direct investment as schizophrenic: "We seem to like the fruits of the investments but not necessarily the presence of the investor." He classifies the several formulae being tried in Latin America to cope with multinational corporations as compulsory participation in the corporation by nationals ("Mexicanization"), mixtures of nationalization and expropriation (as in Peru and Bolivia), fiscal incentives to go public on the local financial markets (as in Brazil).

A REBUTTAL

Jacques G. Maisonrouge, president, IBM World Trade Corporation, offers a forceful rebuttal to foreign concern about the American Presence and to American labor leaders, however, saying:

Relatively few people appreciate the underlying reasons for the rise of the multinational company. They simply view the final result — large corporations that appear to spill over national boundaries from their own sheer momentum — and wonder if they are not some kind of threat. . . . It is a measure of human ingenuity that people on both sides of the Atlantic can view the same phenomena and reach diametrically opposite conclusions.

Some Europeans believe this pervasive presence can only be attributed to some formal U.S. plan to penetrate those sectors of national economies with advanced technologies and high rates of growth.

The truth is that a large proportion of U.S. investments has been made in technology-based industries not because of any single-minded U.S. strategy, but because these industries . . . went where the action was. They did this independently of each other.

Mr. Maisonrouge also points out that these decisions are not a choice between "manufacture abroad" and "export." The alternatives often are simply "manufacture abroad" or "give up a major portion of your foreign markets." And he emphasizes, "If U.S. companies did not manufacture abroad, those jobs simply would not exist." It is not a clear choice, by any means, between locating jobs abroad and keeping them at home.

FUTURE TRENDS

From this caldron of conflicting views, interests and strategies, does a central theme emerge? Apparently while everyone recognizes the benefits derived from the multinational corporations, some powerful forces are anxious, afraid, or angered by it. Such reactions generally lead, at the very least, to accelerated harassment. And it appears unlikely this can be prevented. Still, from the recommendations of authorities, the testimony of witnesses before Congress, and from an objective examination of the framework within which international corporations actually operate, some trends for the future can be discerned.

Before going further, however, one must not lose sight of the fact that the U.S. is not just a base for the international corporation. It is also a host. *Fortune* magazine lists 200 of the largest industrial companies *outside* the U.S. which in 1969 had sales ranging from over $355 million to almost $10 billion. Many of these are now familiar names here — Shell, Unilever, Philips, BP, Hitachi, Toyota, for example.

Some of the results obtained by such foreign companies as a group were more robust than those of the U.S. 500 list. To quote *Fortune,* "Sales of the 200 showed a sparkling 16.2% increase [over last year]. . . . This far outstepped the 500's gain of 9.7%." There is nothing to suggest a reversal of this growing penetration of U.S. markets in the future. Moreover, according to Harold Malmgren, former Assistant Special Representative for Trade Negotiations, Office of the President, the European Economic Community is now the largest trading unit in the world, and Japan is moving up fast. The big news, Pierre-Robert Goetschin of the Management Development Institute, Lausanne, Switzerland, points out, is that the European firms are growing rapidly and are no longer content to sit behind their national boundaries defensively. They are seizing merger opportunities in the U.S.A. Plainly, U.S.-based international companies must expect increasingly vigorous competition from other multinational companies, here at home as well as abroad.

Adding to the momentum, the EEC is pushing its boundaries further and further afield. Originally six countries (France, Germany, Holland, Belgium, Italy and Luxembourg), it now has association with Greece, Turkey, Morocco, Tunisia, Algeria, Spain and Israel. Deals are also being worked out with Lebanon, Egypt, and Argentina, and are being considered with Kenya, Uganda, Tanzania, Malta and Cyprus. Britain's membership is now assured, and Ireland, Norway, and Denmark are coming close, while Switzerland, Sweden and Austria are seeking associate status. Expectations are that the other EFTA countries — Finland, Portugal, Iceland and the British Commonwealth (Canada, Australia, New Zealand, India, Pakistan, Singapore, and Hong Kong) — will be accommodated now that their former partner, the U.K., has been admitted to the EEC.

CONTROLLING THE INTERNATIONAL

It is apparent host countries have already reacted to the American Presence by increased competition and by extension and expansion of the trading bloc concept.

But there is more, much more, they can do. For example, as a general rule multinational companies operate in specific foreign countries under cover of a closed local corporation. The laws relative to public disclosure of financial results are generally designed for large, publicly held corporations. The closed corporation was originally intended for small, family-type enterprises. As a result, the multinational company escapes the more stringent rules in this respect. Foreign parliaments could easily alter these regulations to include all large operations, regardless of the legal corporate structure.

Standard accounting procedures could be adopted to make it more difficult to move profits and costs around between corporations in the same multinational chain to suit the convenience of the parent company of the group. And other forms of regulation could be tightened. Such controls as anti-pollution rules, safety requirements, zoning restrictions and so forth offer fertile areas for harassment if local governments desire to use them.

Corporate requirements for a minimum number of local nationals on management boards are already in existence in some countries. This means of influencing the multinational company could be extended. Approval for new ventures could be withheld by local governments until the multinational company meets whatever conditions the local government may reasonably desire. We have seen recently how the oil-producing and exporting countries have succeeded in imposing much stiffer terms on the major oil companies. More countries may adopt such strategies and apply them to additional industries, or to such areas as capital flows, reinvestment requirements, earnings remittances, etc.

There is a growing concensus that accords with Professor Charles Kindelberger of M.I.T. who anticipates that the multinational company is going to face more rather than fewer problems in the future. However, U.S.-based international companies have evidenced remarkable hardihood in hostile environments in the past. They have flourished despite considerable regulation and harassment, and their own optimism seems undiminished. The U.S. Department of Commerce recently estimated that $15.3 billion will be invested abroad in 1971 by American firms. If this mark is reached, it will be an all-time high for a single year. This represents a 16% increase over the figure for 1970, which itself showed a 22% increase over 1969.

It should be noted that the region attracting the greatest capital flows is Europe, and it is expected to rise 27% in 1971 despite the U.S. government's attempt to reduce capital flow to that area. Conversely, in Latin America, where the U.S. government has exhibited a contrary policy, U.S. capital expenditure is expected to drop by 5% this year.

In view of the growth of multinational corporations, the interest of Congress is not surprising. The sheer magnitude of their combined impact on the international economy warrants it, aside from questions of balance of payments, monetary stability, and tariffs. There is even growing apprehension that the economic thinking in which the Bretton Woods Agreements, GATT, and the Kennedy Round were nurtured is no longer applicable.

Number of American Companies Operating in Various Countries of the World (Not Charted)

Country	Number of Companies
Rhodesia	42
Luxembourg	18
Ghana	13
Zambia	12
Iraq	11
Jordan	10
Syria	7
Barbados	6
Gabon	6
Mozambique	6
Angola	5
British Honduras	5
Central African Republic	5
Malagasy	5
Burundi	4
Cambodia	4
Cameroon	4
Chad	4
Congo Katanga	4
Guyana	4
Madeira	4
Malawi	4
Mali	4
Malta	4
Reunion	3
Senegal	3
Tanzania	3
Laos	2
Nepal	2
Surinam	2

Given an expanding world economy and the rise of the multinational corporation, national boundaries may follow the history of our state boundaries, which failed to confine the American corporation or prevent the growth of a national economy. Indeed, the present expansion of economic communities and trading blocs not only illustrates but accelerates the trend toward a worldwide economy, just as the development of the international corporation would appear to make the domestic corporation we have known just an overgrown specimen of local business.

TEST ON INTERNATIONAL ECONOMICS

Place a check under T (True) or F (False).   T F

1. Comparative advantage refers to opportunity costs and has no relation to exchange rates.   — —

2. The effect of trade is to shift production possibility curves outward.   — —

3. Trade enables one nation to take advantage of the lower opportunity costs of another.   — —

4. There are no sound economic arguments for tariffs.   — —

5. The balance of payments is a means for determining whether a nation's foreign exchange rate is too high or too low.   — —

6. An export of goods results in a gain in short-term credit by the exporting country.   — —

7. An export of capital from the United States results in a shift of dollars from foreign-owned accounts in the United States to American accounts in the United States.   — —

8. The only means of correcting a deficit in international transactions is a change in exchange rates.   — —

9. As long as a nation's currency is acceptable as a reserve currency, it can run a deficit in its balance of payments.   — —

10. Free or floating exchange rates make gold shipments unnecessary.   — —

11. The "classical medicine" cure for a balance of payments problem is devaluation.   — —

12. The devaluation of the dollar means that the dollar is declared to be worth fewer pounds or marks or yen.   — —

13. The multinational corporation differs from the international corporation because it emphasizes exports rather than overseas production.   — —

14. Under free exchange rates, we would expect a nation that persistently enjoyed a surplus on capital account to run a deficit on current account.   — —

15. A nation that exported large amounts of goods and that imported only small amounts could not also export capital in a free exchange system.   — —

16. Special Drawing Rights are a substitute for gold.   — —

17. The multinational corporation is almost exclusively an American phenomenon.   — —

18. The total value of imports (ignoring transportation and insurance costs) is an identity with the total value of exports.   — —

19. Foreign exchange consists of nondomestic currencies held by all countries.   — —

20. A devaluation of the dollar is exactly the same thing as an appreciation of the currencies of other nations.   — —

BEFORE AND AFTER TEST ON INTERNATIONAL ECONOMICS

Here is the last of the before-and-afters. It might be interesting for you to compare your comparative results in these tests in macro, micro, and foreign trade. In which field, judging by the results, have you learned the most? It would be our guess that the answer should be in the field of international economics, where misconceptions are greatest. Don't forget, score −10 for error, −6 for "don't know's".

Place a check under T (True), F (False), or ? (Don't Know).   T F ?

1. One of the striking changes in recent international economics has been the huge surge of exports from the so-called multinational corporations.   — — —

2. The chief danger of international trade is that one nation, by virtue of its cheap labor *and* capital, will be able to undersell the rest of the world without buying anything in exchange.   — — —

3. A tariff is a tax levied on imports and therefore borne wholly by foreign nations.   — — —

4. Despite the deficits incurred by the United States during the early 1970s in its international transactions, the overall balance of payments always balanced.   — — —

5. A nation usually exports goods from industries in which its domestic wage levels are lowest.   — — —

6. A country pays for its imports by sending its money abroad, and gets paid for its exports by receiving foreign money that is sent from abroad.   — — —

7. The world operates its international exchange on a gold standard.   — — —

8. If one country, say Japan, can undersell another, say the United States, in every line of production, the United States could not hope to have a profitable international exchange with Japan.   — — —

9. A country cannot import more goods than its exports for a prolonged period.   — — —

10. The rational objective for any nation is to maximize its exports.   — — —

Answers:

1. F	5. F	9. F
2. F	6. F	10. F
3. F	7. F	
4. T	8. F	

Score ———
Score before ———

SOCIOMETRIC
SYSTEMS

39

The Underdeveloped World

LEARNING OBJECTIVES

Learning about underdevelopment is a major task, and our chapter gives only a quick glimpse of a huge subject. Instead of trying to itemize the many issues in this chapter, think about these problems (to which there are no simple answers):

1. Why are so many countries desperately poor? Is it a question of resources? Climate? Economic systems? Social or political systems?
2. How can an *economist,* using his skills, help an underdeveloped country begin to develop?

There is little we can do to review this chapter for you. Instead, let us suggest a few readings, too long for this book, that you might profitably pursue if the subject interests you. None of them requires any more economic knowledge than you now have:

On population and food: Lester R. Brown, *In the Human Interest* (New York: W. W. Norton, 1974). A sober look into the problem of burgeoning populations and lagging food supplies, and a program for change.

On social stability: Albert Hirschman, "The Changing Tolerance for Income Inequality," *Quarterly Journal of Economics* (November 1973). A highly stimulating inquiry into the strains that development places on the different social classes in underdeveloped nations. (You can forget the mathematical appendix.)

On the relations of rich and poor countries: Paul Baran, *The Political Economy of Growth* (New York: Monthly Review Press, 1957), also paperback. One of the first and still one of the best radical analyses of imperialism.

A general review of the problem: Gustav Ranis (ed.), *The United States and the Developing Economies* (New York: W. W. Norton, 1973). A collection of readings that touches on many aspects of the problem.

Last, we give you here one reading that we think will interest you – a reading on the fascinating and still little-explored subject of Chinese development.

CHINA'S ECONOMY: A VIEW FROM THE GRASS ROOTS

Lloyd Reynolds

Lloyd Reynolds traveled through China in 1973. Sterling Professor of Economics at Yale, Dr. Reynolds has served as program director for the Ford Foundation and as an advisor to the Agency for International Development. His careful report therefore carries the weight of an experienced observer of economies in development.

The number of American economists who have been to China is about equal to the number of astronauts who have been to the moon, so each returning traveler can add something to our limited knowledge of that vast and complex country. These notes are intended to supplement the reports of previous visitors without repeating things which are generally known.

Our group of five Yale economists traveled from Hong Kong to Canton, Shanghai, Tientsin, and Peking. We talked at length with industrial managers, commune officials, and university economists. Like others before us, we were unable to gain access to provincial or national planning officials. We had to peer upward through the administrative structure from a grass-roots level. Hence our title.

FARM OUTPUT AND EMPLOYMENT

Chinese economic policy is quite pro-agriculture. Taxes on agriculture are moderate; prices paid by the state for farm products have been raised gradually, while prices paid by farmers have been stable or falling. The com-

From *Challenge* (March/April, 1974). Reprinted with permission from *Challenge*, the Magazine of Economic Affairs.

munes have considerable autonomy in running their own affairs. Supplies of fertilizer, farm machinery, and other modern inputs are rising rapidly in percentage terms, though from a low base.

The population of a commune equals that of a small American city. It is organized on three levels: the production team, the production brigade, and the commune as a whole. The production team, which includes 20 to 50 households, corresponds to a traditional village. It is the basic unit for production decisions and for distribution of farm income. After deductions have been made for the cost of purchased inputs, the government tax, and the contributions to a capital accumulation fund and a public consumption fund (covering education, health, and cultural activities), the remaining 60 percent or so of farm income is distributed — partly in cash and partly in grain — among the workers in the team. Allotments are made according to a system of "work points" that are based on quantity and quality of work performed. The production brigade is made up of 8 to 12 production teams and 400-500 households. The commune as a whole includes perhaps 10 production brigades and 4,000-5,000 households.

People at each of the organizational levels perform industrial and local government functions as well as agricultural work. This involves much overlapping of activities, and we tried to figure out what determines the division of labor among them. The most important clue is scale of operation. Thus the production team owns hand tools; the commune, large tractors and threshing machines (which are rented out to the teams on a fee basis). The commune runs a hospital; the production brigade, a medical clinic; and the production team, a pharmacy staffed by a "barefoot doctor." Primary schools are operated by the production team or brigade; high schools, by the commune. The production team may operate small workshops – 20 women in a room making place mats – while at the commune level one finds factories with several hundred workers.

OUTPUT AND PRICING

National planning is confined to crops of major importance: rice, wheat, vegetable oils, and industrial raw materials such as cotton. For these crops national targets are established in Peking, distributed among the provinces, and from there further distributed to the commune and production team levels. All marketed output is sold to state trading corporations ("state" meaning, in Chinese terminology, the national government) at a predetermined price. The sales quota of, say, rice for each team is set by making an estimate of output, apparently based on an average of recent years, and then deducting consumption requirements for household members on the basis of a standard ration. There is no problem about selling above-quota amounts in a good crop year. We did not press the question of who gets squeezed if the crop falls below the expected level. It appears, however, that considerable buffer stocks of grain are carried at all levels from the national government to the individual farm family. (Decentralized accumulation of such reserves is encouraged for defense reasons as well as for famine prevention.)

The system for less basic products is quite different. Communes located near urban markets (which were the only ones we visited) go heavily into vegetables, fruit, poultry, pigs, milk cows, and fish ponds. Their products are sold to municipal trading authorities at locally negotiated prices, and provide a substantial part of farm income.

The price paid to farmers for "national" crops is uniform throughout the country. The problem of "poor communes" is attacked by trying to raise their productivity rather than through the price system. The city price of foodgrains has remained unchanged for many years. Farm prices, on the other hand, have been raised moderately over the past decade to reduce the urban-rural income gap. At present, the city price and the farm price of rice are said to be equal, which would mean a state subsidy amounting to transportation and handling costs.

We asked whether relative prices for the major crops were ever varied to steer farmers' planting plans in a desired direction. This was strenuously denied. Planting plans, it was said, are guided strictly by physical output targets. Although these statements were doubtless sincere, there is evidence from other sources of limited use of price incentives. In 1971, for example, the purchase price was raised for bast fibers (those used for cordage, matting, and fabrics), oil seeds, and sugar. Farmers responded, and in the 1972 season there were substantial increases in output of these crops. For local products, too, the products in demand in the cities and the prices at which these can be sold must have an important influence on output. These prices also appear more flexible than those for national crops, retail prices being cut where necessary to move supplies of perishable products.

Farmers' private plots average about 7 percent of total farm acreage. These plots appear to be used mainly to grow vegetables and other products for the family's own consumption, but output can also be sold in free markets set up and regulated by the municipality.

EMPLOYMENT AND "LABOR SCARCITY"

In India and other densely populated Asian countries, underemployment in the rural sector is a chronic and growing problem. It was certainly a problem in the China of 1949. Yet despite a continued high rate of rural population growth, it is said that China has shifted from a situation of labor surplus to one of labor scarcity. This would have to mean that many more man-hours are being worked in the rural areas today than before 1949.

We inquired into possible sources of this increased employment. There seem to have been four main reasons. First is the marked expansion of small-scale industrial production (in workshops employing anywhere from 20 to 200 people) within the rural communes. In the Tientsin area, we were told that these activities employ about 20 percent of the available labor force. Again, in the commune we visited near Peking, which included 6,300 households and about 30,000 people, we were told that there were 2,700 people working in commune enterprises and 1,400 in workshops run by the production brigades. Part of these rural industries — tractor and implement repair workshops, fertilizer plants, brick kilns, cement plants, and power and waterpumping stations — produce for farm use, but part also turn out consumer goods for off-farm sale and even for export. At seasonal peaks of planting and harvest activity, most of these industrial workers go into the fields; but their main activity is factory work. They are paid, in cash or in work points, at about what they would receive for the same amount of time spent in farm labor.

Another reason for the labor scarcity in rural areas is the sizeable increase in labor time invested in infrastructure activities: roads, water control and irrigation systems, land terracing, reforestation, and the construction of schools, hospitals, and public buildings as well as housing.

These activities are organized mainly within the commune, but large-scale projects may be planned at higher levels and draw labor from several communes. The work is done mainly off season and, like the small-scale industrial production, helps take up the seasonal slack in labor demand.

Third, these infrastructure activities, especially improved water control, have made possible a considerable shift of acreage from single to double crops. They also make possible greater use of fertilizer and more sophisticated input "packages," which substantially increase crop yields. All this requires more labor.

Finally, there has been a marked diversification of farm activities into fruit and vegetable production and into animal husbandry, particularly in areas near city markets. These activities are more labor intensive than grain growing.

All in all, we concluded that the claims of full employment in the rural sector were valid. Some of this employment, to be sure, has a low yield per man-hour — for example, creating new land with great effort by carrying baskets of earth from some other area. There is doubtless a tendency to treat the available labor time as an overhead cost and to regard *any* addition to output as worthwhile.

ORGANIZATION AND MANAGEMENT OF INDUSTRY

Chinese industrial organization has a number of distinctive features. There is marked decentralization — most enterprises are "owned" at levels ranging from the provincial government down to the rural production team. There is a wide range of plant sizes for similar products. The differences correspond somewhat to the variation in ownership levels: large city factories operate under the provincial organization; small handicraft workshops, within a commune. A natural accompaniment is coexistence of different levels of technology, from quite advanced to completely traditional. While primitive techniques may eventually be abandoned as modern equipment increases, the elimination will clearly be gradual. Meanwhile, the Chinese do not seem to look down on traditional methods, or to be in a great hurry to get rid of them.

Geographic dispersion is another characteristic of Chinese industry. This is accompanied by an emphasis on local self-sufficiency. Provinces and counties incurring a deficit in a particular good which forces them to import from other areas are urged to raise production of that good and become more nearly self-contained. How far this autarkic tendency runs contrary to efficient division of labor and cost minimization and how far this is offset by gains in other directions are open questions.

Industrial enterprises, like all other Chinese organizations, are controlled by a "Revolutionary Committee" which includes representatives of all ranks in the plant. There is great emphasis on grass-roots discussion and mass participation. Research and development is carried out by "three-in-one teams" consisting of managers, technicians, and workers. The contribution of the workers was always heavily stressed in our discussions.

All this raises questions in the mind of a Western observer: To what extent is the emphasis on mass participation a verbal tribute to political ideals, and to what extent is it actually operative in plant practice? How substantial is the workers' contribution on technical matters? If an enterprise is to operate effectively, must not some members of the governing committee be "more equal than others"?

CONTROL, COORDINATION, AND PLANNING

The enterprises we visited were located in Tientsin and Shanghai, and they operated under the governments of those cities, which because of their size are the equivalent of a Chinese province. We can speak, then, only about industries controlled at the province level.

There are several layers in the management structure. For example, the watch factory we visited in Tientsin operates under the Tientsin Watch Corporation, which is under the Tientsin Light Industries Bureau, which in turn is subject to the government of Tientsin.

We had conflicting reports as to whether formulation of the annual output plan typically begins with targets passed down from above or with proposals passed up from below. In any event, at an early stage there are discussions in the factory and a proposal to the parent corporation. The corporation then presumably consults its governing bureau, and officials of the provincial planning commission and the provincial government also become involved (precisely how, we did not learn, since we were not able to interview members of these higher bodies). Eventually, a counterproposal is passed down from the corporation to the factory. There may be further back-and-forth discussion before a final consensus is reached. The whole process may take four to six months, and is usually not complete until the spring of the calendar year covered by the plan.

The annual plan includes a variety of targets: quantity, quality, and variety of output; gross value of output; employment and wage bill; total production cost; and planned profit. To the extent that management is obliged to choose among these, the quantity and quality of output seem to be regarded as most important. In deciding what varieties of, say, watches or carpets to produce, the factory relies on the judgment of the sales organization that distributes its product. "Market guidance" in this sense seems to be more prominent in Chinese planning than in traditional Soviet planning.

We had the impression — it can scarcely be more than that — that Chinese enterprise plans contain more leeway than Soviet plans. There seems to be less of a tendency to set unrealistic output targets or pressure the enterprise for performance in excess of plan while (sometimes) starving it on the input side. In line with the policy of deemphasizing material incentives, the workers and managers in a Chinese enterprise get no benefits for output in excess of plan, nor do they apparently suffer direct penalties for falling short of plan.

FINANCE

Production cost includes labor, materials, and depreciation (which we were told in one plant is calculated on a 25- to 33-year straight-line basis). Price-cost margins vary with the product in question. The Shanghai machine tool plant reported its profit rate as 10 percent (of production cost); the Tientsin carpet and woolen mills, 20 percent; and the watch factory, 50 percent. Profit goes completely to government and forms the major part of government revenue.

Since price and wage changes are infrequent, gains from productivity improvement tend in the short run to accumulate as profit. This may be one reason for high profit rates. There is a considerable lag between cost reductions and price cuts. Over the longer run, however, prices of some manufactured goods are reduced, though only every few years. Wages are also raised at intervals, as will be explained later.

Circulating capital to carry inventories is built into the firm's financial structure, and is apparently increased as output levels rise. One plant reported circulating capital as about 20 percent of annual output value. Emergency needs can be covered by borrowing from the State Bank, but the enterprises we saw had made little use of this source.

For allocations of investment funds, the province-controlled enterprises that we saw could apply to the provincial planning authorities for moderate amounts or to the national planning authorities for larger amounts. Requests are subject to review and are frequently cut. It was strenuously denied that the profitability of an enterprise is a criterion for investment allocations: "We do not work for profit." It is interesting, however, that the highly profitable Tientsin watch factory had received all the funds it requested for plant expansion in the current year. Actual construction of the new plant was being carried out not by the enterprise itself, but under a contract with the Tientsin Construction Bureau.

INDUSTRIAL WORKERS IN THE CITY

Jobs in a plant are classified into eight labor grades. The ratio of the highest to the lowest wage is about three to one, from about 40 yuan a month at the bottom to 110 yuan at the top. The average in the plants we visited was usually between 50 and 60 yuan, indicating that the labor force is heavily concentrated in the lower labor grades.

The manager usually earns little more than the most skilled worker, and may even earn less. Engineers, however, sometimes go as high as 150 yuan per month. The range for university teachers is about 70-350 yuan, but there are very few at the top rate. The highest salary in the country, that of top government officials, is reportedly 450 yuan; but the number enjoying these high salaries is small. In general, the earnings gap between manual and nonmanual workers seems to be less than in the USSR, and much less than in the United States.

Wage increases are relatively infrequent. There was apparently a round of increases in 1971 and again in 1973. These took the form of increases for the lowest two or three grades, with no increase for higher grades. The effect was rather like that of a minimum wage increase — a deliberate compression of the occupational wage structure in order to reduce income inequality.

The work week is usually six days, eight hours a day. Most plants operate two or three shifts, which is sensible in a capital-scarce country. Fringe benefits are quite generous: a number of paid holidays, and four-day breaks at the time of the two big national holidays on May 1 and October 1 (but no paid vacation); low-cost canteen meals in the factory; nurseries to care for small children while the mother is at work; employer contributions to the cost of medical care; two-month maternity leaves for women; long sickness leaves at full pay for everyone; early retirement – at age 55 for women, 60 for men – at 70 percent of salary. Retirement at these ages is optional, however, and a worker in good health can go on working longer.

We were struck by the fact that young people in the city want to become factory workers – this is the preferred job choice. There seem to be several main reasons. First, a period of time as a worker is the only way to "get on the ladder" for higher positions. You cannot go to college, become a foreman or manager, move up in the Party or the government or anything else without having first served your time on the factory floor (or on a farm). Second, a factory job is the best safeguard against having to go to the country, where work is harder and earnings are lower. Third, earnings are higher in a factory than in other city jobs or in farming. Finally, the exalted status of the worker in the official ideology may have a considerable effect on young, idealistic people.

FARMERS' INCOMES

We visited only two communes, and these were unusually prosperous communes near major cities. From our readings and discussion, however, the following propositions seem reasonable:

– Income distribution within a commune is quite egalitarian. Although people may receive more or fewer "work points" per day, depending on the job and their performance of it, the range

is not wide. Days worked in industrial enterprises on the commune pay a bit more than days spent in farm labor, but not much more.

– There is a wide range of incomes among communes, however, depending on soil fertility, water availability, climate, distance to market, and other factors. One sample survey in 1965 found that average income per worker in the richest commune studied was 3.4 times that in the poorest one. This wide variation in productivity is, of course, a general characteristic of less developed economies. Even in the United States income inequality in the rural sector is substantially greater than in the urban sector.

– The average level of rural incomes is substantially below that of urban incomes (again, a characteristic of virtually all economies, the gap being considerably wider in the less developed than in the more developed countries).

In short, China has not avoided some inherent sources of income inequality which can be remedied only gradually as a by-product of development. What the regime has accomplished is to cut off the extreme "tails" of the income distribution. There are no longer any rich people, nor is anyone allowed to fall below a minimum standard of living. It is government policy to continue reducing inequality over the years ahead. This is apparent in the gradual increase in farm procurement prices, in wage increases slanted toward the lower labor grades, and in increased supplies of heavily subsidized necessities – notably housing and medical care – which tend to equalize real incomes.

THE MINIMUM STANDARD OF LIVING

It is striking that a country as poor as China has managed to establish a guaranteed minimum level of living, something which the rich United States has still not accomplished. The main components of this minimum level are:

1. Free education, including a living allowance for college students (19 yuan per month, of which about 14 yuan go for food, the remainder for pocket money). Medical care is almost free. Employer and employee contribute to its cost, but these contributions total only 2 yuan per year. Thus education, health, and the private automobile (unobtainable in China), which all take a large bite out of the American consumer's budget, take virtually nothing from the Chinese.

2. A grain ration which varies somewhat with how much heavy labor one is doing, but seems to run in the range of 40 to 50 pounds per person per month. There is general agreement that this is as much as one can reasonably eat. Vegetable oils and the ever-necessary soy sauce are rationed at the rate of two-thirds of a pound per person per month. Vegetables appear plentiful. Consumption of fruits and animal products is still very low by our standards, but rising.

An interesting question is: If grain is in adequate supply, why is it still rationed? One answer we were given is that rationing provides a firm demand figure against which output targets can be measured. Further, since yields vary considerably from year to year, rationing may be considered a necessary standby device for poor years. Also, since grain reserves are apparently being accumulated gradually, the ration system is helpful on this front.

3. The ration of cotton cloth varies somewhat between warmer and colder regions, but seems to run from 15 to 20 feet of cloth per year. This is sufficient for a couple of suits of the standard tunic-and-trouser sort. In addition, more expensive and unrationed fabrics are gradually appearing, in a greater variety of styles and colors. We saw scarcely anyone who was not neatly and comfortably dressed, nor did we see anyone going barefoot.

There is some kind of housing for everyone, though most housing is still old and crowded. Large homes of the former bourgeoisie have been split into several apartments. Modern housing is being expanded in the cities, though there is obviously still a huge backlog of demand. "Modern" means an apartment of two rooms, plus a lavatory and a kitchen shared with another family, for a "three-generation" family of six or seven people.

The cost of these basic necessities is low enough for many families to have some income left over. This "discretionary income" can be used in a variety of ways. It can be used to brighten up one's home or one's clothing. It can be banked and accumulated for the purchase of expensive consumer durables such as a radio (50-75 yuan), a good wrist watch (150 yuan), a bicycle (120-150 yuan), a sewing machine (200 yuan), or even a television set (400 yuan). Another favorite use of extra money is for train travel to visit relatives, the ancestral village, or the big city. Chinese passenger trains are as popular and heavily utilized as American trains were in 1900.

LABOR MARKETS AND LABOR MOBILITY

There is no real labor market for urban factory workers. An enterprise can recruit labor and a worker can find work only through the municipal employment bureau. Hiring is mainly for replacement purposes, as workers leave through age or disability. Quit rates are phenomenally low. A worker can transfer only for "good reason." One acceptable reason is development of an entirely new plant or industrial region. In such cases an established enterprise sometimes "spins off" a new plant, sending part of its experienced work force as a nucleus for the new plant. The Chinese call this the "chicken and egg principle."

Except for such cases, a worker who shows a desire to leave is apparently subjected to social pressure by his peers, and in effect "talked out of it." This tends to produce a lifetime attachment to one enterprise not unlike the traditional Japanese system.

Social pressure to persuade the individual that what the state wants is really what he himself wants, or should want, is a pervasive feature of the society, extending to such matters as persuading families not to have more than two children, persuading people sent to the country that they really like farm work, persuading workers to stay on the job, persuading applicants for a vacant apartment that someone else has a better claim. How far this should be considered coercive or how far, on the other hand, it is a legitimate appeal to social conscience is perhaps best left to the philosopher. At any event, it seems to be quite effective.

The natural tendency of labor to flow from country to city is restrained in several ways. First is the industrial location policy. New industries are being located in suburban areas and in interior provinces of the country, to restrain big-city growth. Second, there are employment controls. One cannot get a job except through the central employment bureau, which will accept migrants from the country only if there is a genuine need for additional workers, and only if the existing urban labor supply has been fully mobilized. Also restraining urban migration are housing allocations. If a country worker applies for housing in the city, the first question is "Do you have a job?" If the answer is no, the applicant is back to square one. Finally, permission is also required, for rationing purposes, to change one's place of residence, and this is not easy to get. All in all, as one member of our group put it, "The worker's option space is very small." Unless one has relatives patient enough and affluent enough to house and feed him, it is simply not feasible to be unemployed in the city.

Because of this effective damming up of labor in the countryside, the ratio of China's rural population to total population has held steady at about 80 percent, instead of falling as it normally does in the course of economic development.

THE LEVEL OF INCOME

How well off are the Chinese, and how rapidly are living standards rising? The best estimates of China's national income, adjusted to Western definitions and converted at official exchange rates, place it at about $120 billion. Best guesses at population place it at some 800 million. Thus one arrives at a per capita income figure of $150.00

Taken literally, this would imply imminent starvation of the population. The error in the calculation arises from the fact that Chinese prices for basic consumer goods are much lower than U.S. prices; and the discrepancy has been increasing as prices in the United States and other countries continue to rise while the Chinese price level remains completely stable — indeed, is slightly falling. Thus the purchasing power of the yuan is much higher than the official exchange rate suggests.

Two members of our group could speak and read Chinese. With their aid we collected a good deal of price information in Shanghai, Tientsin, and Peking. A comparison of Chinese and American prices for standard food and clothing items suggests that the yuan, instead of being worth $0.50 (which is approximately the current exchange rate), is actually worth closer to $1.50.

We also secured a number of family budgets. A well-off worker's family in Shanghai, with husband and wife working, reported a monthly income of 150 yuan (certainly above average for industrial workers in general). We found out how much of this went for food, clothing, rent, and other items of consumption. On our return, we estimated how much it would cost for an urban American family to live in the same way. That would mean eating mainly cereals with very little animal products, using public transportation rather than a private car, living in a two-room apartment, and so on. The total came to about $400 per month, or $4,800 per year.

The main reasons for this wide gap, in addition to the lower Chinese price level for food and clothing, are that medical treatment in China is virtually free; house rents are heavily subsidized (apparently covering only maintenance costs with no capital charges); and bus transportation, utility services, and other incidental items are priced much below American levels.

THE GROWTH RATE OF INCOME

Official data have not been published since 1957, but Western estimates suggest that growth has continued at a respectable, if not sensational, rate. Professor Dwight Perkins, for example, estimates that from 1957 to 1972 agricultural output rose at an average annual rate of 3 percent, industrial output at 8 percent, and GNP at about 5 percent. In view of the fact that this span of years includes two periods (1958-61 and 1966-69) of marked political turbulence and economic reorganization, this is not a bad performance. It is, in fact, about the average rate of growth achieved since 1950 by the USSR and the East European socialist countries, and also (if we exclude the spectacular case of Japan) by the advanced capitalist countries.

The population growth rate is not known, but is usually estimated at something above 2 percent. Nor do we know the precise allocation of GNP increases among private consumption, public consumption, investment, and military purposes. Despite these uncertainties, it seems likely that personal consumption per capita has risen at something like 2 percent a year over this period. This improvement in living standards has meant a somewhat more varied diet, including a gradual increase in consumption of animal proteins; a slow rise in the percentage of the population living in newly constructed housing; and a growing surplus of family income over essential expenditures, a surplus which can be used for unrationed clothing items, furniture, travel, and consumer durables.

ECONOMISTS AND THE ECONOMY

One could say a good deal about the state of the universities and the teaching of economics. This is not a happy story. The universities are quite disorganized and are operating well below capacity. The curriculum in political economy is heavily ideological, aimed at transmitting doctrine rather than analyzing economic performance.

This kind of curriculum clearly does not produce industrial managers or economic planners. Yet large numbers of people – at national, provincial, and lower levels of government – are engaged in economic planning and administration. What kind of training do they have for these tasks? Are they simply "learning by doing"? It is, of course, a disquieting thought that an economy can get along without economists or, at least, without our kind of economist! But the suspicion cannot be entirely dismissed.

The economy itself is making modest progress; and on reflection, this is not really surprising. If labor resources can be fully mobilized, if people can be persuaded to work long and hard while accepting a low level of consumption, a country can produce an economic surplus for capital formation, public services, and military might. This is the story not only of China but of Meiji Japan from 1868 onward. The institutional setting, of course, was very different; but Emperor worship served somewhat the same function as Mao worship, and the economic results were quite similar.

The question for the future is whether sheer effort, accompanied by technological borrowing from other countries, will prove sufficient to sustain the momentum of economic growth. Will it not be necessary for China to strengthen the indigenous sources of technical progress? And will this not require a reversal of the present policy of downgrading the expert and the intellectual? The educated professional class is now deeply suspect as a source of potential opposition to the regime. But a complex industrial economy cannot get along without professionals, technicians, and managers. The resolution of this dilemma will strongly influence China's growth rate over the next generation.

From Market
to Planning

40

LEARNING OBJECTIVES

This chapter touches on the subject of central *planning*. You should review in your mind the mechanism of planning and contrast it with that of the market.

The question of the alternative ways of organizing economic systems is too vast to be adequately dealt with in an introduction to economics. As in our previous chapter, therefore, we suggest a few outside readings that may be of interest to you.

On Russian Planning: Marshall Goldman, *The Soviet Economy: Myth and Reality* (Englewood Cliffs, N.J.: Prentice Hall, Inc., 1968). A very readable and excellent overall survey of the Soviet Economic System.

On European planning: Andrew Shonfield, *Modern Capitalism: The Changing Balance of Public and Private Power* (Boston: Oxford University Press, 1969). An extremely interesting survey of the various planning devices used by capitalistic nations.

Last, we commend the next reading to you, as an effort to see the problem of economic organization from an overall perspective.

ECONOMIC LIBERTARIANISM

Kenneth Boulding

*Professor Boulding, one of the most original of modern
economists, suggests three ways in which an economy may be
organized. We suggest you peruse his suggestions with your
mind on the concept of "convergence" discussed in the text.*

I shall try to look at what I call the limits of libertarianism, particularly in regard to the role of exchange in the organization of society. I think freedom is a bit of a red herring here. The really crucial question is the role of exchange as an organizer. This is what the economic liberals, if we can call them that, care about. It is both the successes and the limits of this role of exchange which represent the real issue.

I recognize three major organizers in society. An organizer is something like a social gene. It is a relationship which organizes role structures in society and hence is capable of developing organization. I distinguish three of these organizers. I call them the threat system, the exchange system, and the integrative system.

THE THREE ORGANIZERS OF SOCIETY

The threat is an ancient organizer. This is the idea that you had better do something nice for me or I shall do something nasty to you. It frequently is effective. It can result in what I call the threat-submission system. This is found in the slave economy, for example. It is particularly powerful in the organization of civilization,

From Kenneth Boulding, ed., *Collected Papers* (Colorado Associated University Press, 1971).

which I regard as something resulting fundamentally from agriculture and exploitation. With agriculture, we get a food surplus from a food producer, and exploitation takes it away from him. Thus we get civilization, which I regard as a deplorable state of man, roughly from 3000 B.C. to 3000 A.D., which is now in the process of passing away. It is the condition where we have agriculture and a food surplus plus a coercive system which, through either the priest or the king, takes the food surplus away from the food producer. With this surplus we feed philosophers, armies, artisans and builders, and so make cities and civilizations.

Exchange is a much more powerful organizer with a much wider horizon. The threat system has a low horizon of development; it can produce classical civilization but it cannot do anything better. The exchange system is as old as the threat system. The first traders probably snuggled up to the temples, the forts, and the castles. They have always been despised. As Milton Friedman has said, the traders have always had a bad press. But they have gradually developed an enormous world-wide system of exchange and specialization which, as Adam Smith pointed out, makes everybody better off because exchange, if it is really free exchange, does not happen unless both parties are better off. This does not mean, of course, that there is no conflict in exchange, but that is another question.

The integrative system is harder to define, but I think it is at least as important as the other two systems. It involves such things as status, identity, love, hate, benevolence, malevolence, legitimacy — the whole raft of social institutions which define roles in such a way that you do things because of what you are and because of what I am, that is, because of some kind of status or respect.

The important thing about the integrative system is that it is a necessary matrix of the other two. The threat system is fairly ineffective unless it can be put into an integrative matrix, that is, unless the threats can be legitimized. Naked threats are extraordinarily ineffective as a social organizer. You have to coat them with a kind of plastic coating or something of legitimacy before they can be very effective. Incidentally, this is why we are so ineffective in Viet Nam, where we have an enormous amount of threat with practically no legitimacy. Exchange can take place only if there is an atmosphere of trust, confidence, respect and, indeed, equality. Exchange is an extraordinarily equalitarian institution in the sense that in exchange the two parties look eye to eye. In contrast, the threat system tends to produce inequality of status, with one party dominant and the other submissive.

Economic libertarianism quite rightly emphasizes the benevolent and developmental qualities of exchange. As Friedman suggests, it is perhaps the subtle nature of this system which causes it to have a bad press and to be unappreciated. But I argue also that the political weakness of libertarianism as a doctrine arises partly because of the failure of the libertarian to recognize explicitly that exchange is only one of the organizers of social life and that, if it is to operate successfully, it must operate in a setting in which both the threat system and the integrative system are realistically taken into account.

NO SOCIAL SYSTEM WITHOUT ALL THREE ORGANIZERS

No social system exists, I maintain, without all three organizers. Even if we take the most idealistic Utopian community, there is always an element of threat, for instance, of expulsion. Even in the family there is a certain element of threat. In any institution there are elements of exchange. There are always balance-of-payment problems. There is always a problem of terms of trade, of what you get for what you give. I argue also that in any social system there have to be some integrative elements or the system simply will not operate at all.

I suggest that the greatest threat to the exchange system is the claim that it can do everything. This leads to the equally absurd claim that it can do nothing. The real problem here is to appraise it in its setting and to get the right kind of setting for it.

I illustrate this with the problem of sexual relations. The market solution to this problem is prostitution. This usually is not regarded very favorably, even though it is an ancient industry and a very persistent one. But it is very difficult to build this into the integrative system, although there have been attempts to do so. For instance, in India there is (or was) temple prostitution, and in our society there is Hollywood. But there is always a little edge to this; we always feel that it is not quite respectable. And the reason is that the sexual relationship is a subtle and a complex one which involves large integrative elements. It is not just like buying a shirt; you do not "simply" buy this sort of thing, because it is too complicated, even though there are elements of exchange in it.

In marriage, for instance, the element of exchange is very fundamental; that is, if the balance of payments in a marriage gets out of whack, the marriage is in trouble. If one (or both) of the parties feels that he (or she) is giving everything and is getting nothing, a balance of payments problem exists. So there is a market element in a marriage, but it is wrapped up in an enormous integrative package of religion, ethics, love, security and all this great big ball of wax which I call the integrative system.

A slight element of prostitution carries over into many aspects of the exchange system. For instance, we do not really approve of mercenaries. We do not really approve of corruption, even though in political life in a highly politicized, centrally planned society the only thing that makes the thing work at all is corruption. If the threat system is overexpanded, the only way that the exchange system gets around it is by corruption. Even in this country I suspect that corruption has been an important, positive element in enabling people to do sensible things. If somebody sitting at a desk can prevent your doing something which is perfectly sensible to do and you consistently slip him something under the desk, this is the exchange system. Corruption is the market economy operating in political life. However, even though it is sensible, it has an element of prostitution about it. That is why we find it a little hard to approve.

MANAGEMENT OF THREAT SYSTEM A MAJOR WORLD PROBLEM

Perhaps one of the major problems that the world faces today is the management of the threat system, particularly in international relations. We are all aware that we are facing a major crisis in the international system. Traditional, unilateral national defense has really broken down as a system in the face of nuclear weapons. Nuclear weapons have done for national defense what gunpowder did for the baron. Europe is full of ruined castles. The reason they are ruined is gunpowder. You do not have to believe in the materialistic interpretation of history to believe that gunpowder made a great difference.

Certainly the weapons system has a profound impact on the social system. We cannot develop a

new weapons system without changing radically the whole social system, and we have developed a weapons system that is so new and so radical that no social institution will remain unchanged as a result. I am quite sure that what may be called the classical institutions of national defense have broken down. We realize this only dimly. We realize this through the development of interest in arms control and disarmament agencies, but we have not had the kind of disaster that will really bring this home.

Unquestionably we are heading for such a disaster. The probability that a large proportion of the people and property of the United States will be destroyed in the next 25 years is quite high. We all know this. We do not want to recognize it, but this is the plain fact of the matter. We have not adjusted our image of the world to the realities of the weapons system. There are still people who think they can live in castles; there are still people who think we can have civil defense. The plain fact is that this is nonsense. We are in a totally different world from the one into which you and I were born.

My great complaint against the economic libertarians is that they offer no solution to this problem, whereas traditionally they should. On the whole, the economic liberals of the 19th century, like Cobden and Bright, were anti-imperialistic and antimilitaristic, although in the absence of any really good theory of threat system they did not get far with it. Great Britain, which is supposed to be the home of economic liberalism, actually was the most militaristic country in the 19th century, judged by the number of wars it was engaged in. Even in the 19th century, economic liberalism was accompanied by an extreme willingness to use the threat system on people outside. The liberal is a man who does not believe in coercion at home, but who does believe in it abroad. This inconsistency seems to be at the heart of libertarianism, even in this country. It is an inconsistency that brings libertarianism into disrepute.

If the liberals are hawks rather than doves, then they are trapped in their own system, because hawkism leads to socialism. The only place where creeping socialism has been significant in the United States is the Department of Defense. This department actually is the second largest centrally planned economy in terms of GNP. If we list centrally planned economies we have, in order of size, the Soviet Union, the U.S. Department of Defense and then the People's Republic of China. The Department of Defense is full of bright young people, and their knowledge is terribly frightening. I sometimes wonder what would happen if Mr. McNamara were the Pope. The attempt to introduce rationality into what is fundamentally a heroic and nonrational organization can easily be quite disastrous.

The bright young people in the Department of Defense recognize that, in a sense, the jig is up and that they are not going to defend anybody. We must move toward arms control and disarmament if we are going to live; and if we do this, what becomes of the Department of Defense? What the bright young people in the Defense Department want to do is to keep this the 10% socialist sector of the economy that it now is, and divert it into the civilian economy. The Department of Defense, they argue, is the only place where we do not have to worry about labor unions; hence it can go in for all sorts of technology and is not trapped by all the restrictions of the civilian economy.

WELFARE STATE: EXPANSION OF THE INTEGRATIVE SYSTEM

The other weakness of economic libertarianism, I argue, is a failure to understand or to come to terms with the integrative system, especially as reflected in the welfare state. It seems to me there should be no hostility between the libertarians and the welfare state. They are strictly complementary goods, if they are prop-erly understood. This is because the welfare state represents an expansion of the integrative system in the sense that it involves the responsibility of each for all. This is an element in human life and in human motivation that cannot be denied and cannot be neglected.

There are, of course, things that are very worrisome about it. I agree absolutely with Friedman that most government activity in this direction subsidizes the rich against the poor. Most of our redistribution goes the wrong way. I can give you a shocking example – public education. I am an employee of a socialized industry, a state university. I always tell my colleagues in the business school that they had better be careful what they say, for they are employees of a socialized industry, too! Actually, I'm quite in favor of state universities. I am in favor of a mixed system here. We would not have had the quantity, or perhaps even the quality, of education that we have had if it had not been for this mixed system combining public and private institutions.

However, the whole public education system is a device for subsidizing the rich. I became particularly aware of this last year in Japan when I had to pay for the education of my own five children. This took 25% of my income, and was really quite rough. Now I am home and I find my taxes incredibly low. I am really being subsidized to the extent of $2,000 to $3,000 a year by the system of public education. And who is subsidizing me? It is the little widows and the orphans and all the poor little people who own little houses and who run rooming houses. Even though I am not rich, I am not as poor as they are. I am being subsidized by people who are considerably poorer than I am. Every time we try to redistribute income by subsidizing prices, this is what we run into.

We have the same thing in agriculture. Our whole agricultural policy is a device for sub-sidizing the rich at the expense of the poor. The poverty in agriculture arises from having little or nothing to sell. If you have nothing to sell, it does not matter what price you do not sell it at. So, if we "do something for agriculture" by raising prices, the more a farmer has to sell, the more he is subsidized by raising prices. So it is the rich farmer who gets most of the subsidy, and the poor farmer gets practically none.

There are many other examples of subsidy of the wealthy. I am not quite sure about the income tax. Some studies of the rich at our Survey Research Center, not yet published, are extraordinarily interesting. They reveal that the rich in this country are (a) almost inconceivably stingy and (b) quite surprisingly stupid. The extent to which they actually pay avoidable taxes is quite surprising.

NATIONAL STATE THE STRONGEST INTEGRATIVE SYSTEM

The national state is by far the strongest integrative system in the world today. One of the aspects of the integrative system is what may be called the "grants" economy. There are two parts to our economy: the exchange economy, in which you get a *quid* for a *quo;* and the grants economy, in which all you get is *quid* – you do not pay any *quo.* The grants economy is between 5% and 15% of the total American economy. It is difficult to tell precisely, because of the fact that many things that look like grants in the short run actually turn out to be exchanges in the long run. Most social security, as Friedman suggests, is a compulsory exchange rather than a part of a grants economy.

Even so, the grants economy is important and it is growing. Included in this economy are such things as foundation grants, government grants, pensions, relief payments, aid to dependent children and so on. The grants economy is extremely important in the family. The family is a grants economy of considerable magnitude. You do not expect your children to support you

in your old age anymore, that is, if you are wise. In the old days the family was a social security institution, but today it is not. You shovel money out to your children in great quantities, but you do not expect to get very much of it back. The family certainly is still far and away the most important element of the integrative system. After that is the national state.

Socialism is an incredibly weak integrative system, as the Chinese-Russian split indicates. The great "workers of the world" idea and the ideology about the common interests of the proletariat is just hogwash; there is nothing to it. The Russians have done practically nothing for the Chinese. They have lent them about one cent per Chinese per annum, and the Chinese have had to pay this back with interest at times when they were broke. No wonder the Chinese do not like the Russians! If I were a Chinese, I would not like the Russians either.

The socialist camp is a weaker integrative system than the French Union. The French shovel out 2% of their GNP to the old French colonies. Just look at a place like Cayenne. It lives almost wholly on French social security. That is its major industry. Its imports are about nine times its exports. The French are romantically generous; I cannot imagine why they do it. The British are almost as bad – or as good. And we do a fair amount of it ourselves – about ½ of 1% of GNP. But we do not shovel out nearly as much as the French; we are really very stingy.

The Christian church is an integrative system to some extent. And Judaism is a great integrative system. I sometimes think the Jews are the only generous people in the world. They are the only people who really work at it. For example, look at the way they have supported Israel. It is one of the most extraordinary examples of the grants economy in the integrative system.

In general, humanity represents an extremely weak integrative system. Note the United

Nations. The ordinary budget of the United Nations is about the same as that of the University of Michigan and only a quarter of that of the Department of Sanitation of the city of New York. In the exchange economy we get what we pay for, and we get the amount of world peace that we are willing to pay for. This is what we are prepared to pay for in the way of world integration, and this is why there is no real solution to any of our problems.

EXCHANGE ECONOMY NEEDS INTEGRATIVE MATRIX

I am suggesting that the exchange economy can operate successfully only if it is in a suitable integrative matrix. Schumpeter saw this very clearly. He argued that the reason capitalism will not survive is that nobody loves it. The institutions of the exchange economy do not produce in themselves the integrative system which will support it. The integrative system has to come out of religion, or nationalism, or education, or the family or something of that kind. Exchange in itself is such an abstract and stripped kind of relationship that it will not develop a very strong integrative system. Suppose you say, "Ask not what General Motors can do for you; ask what you can do for General Motors." This may be all right for General Motors, but it sounds a little silly. We do not expect exchange organizations to be very strongly integrative.

There is a bank in Michigan which had a motto, "The Bank That Puts People First." I have never believed this; if I believed it, I would take out my money and put it in another bank. I do not want a bank to put people first; I want it to put money first. I do not want a bank to be lovable; I want it to be efficient. I want it to be nice to me and not snarl at me; I do not mind bankers being polite, but I do not want them to slobber over me. There is a kind of abstract exchange relationship here which, within its

limits, is entirely legitimate. The world of bankers will not produce the kind of institutions which can support them; you have to rely on the other institutions to provide this.

Adam Smith saw this. I am very fond of Adam Smith. But it is rather depressing to go back to him, because it makes you realize how little we have learned. It has been nearly 200 years since he wrote, yet on the subject of economic development we have said little that Adam Smith did not say. He has a wonderful passage in which he denounces the division of labor. He has built up the advantages of the division of labor, exchange and how specialization produces wealth. Then he has second thoughts about it. Let me read this lovely passage:

The man whose whole life is spent in performing a few simple operations, of which the effects too are, perhaps, always the same, or very nearly the same, has no occasion to exert his understanding, or to exercise his invention in finding out expedients for removing difficulties which never occur. [There is the learning process. This is why we have to be free to sin. I agree with that.] He naturally loses, therefore, the habit of such exertion, and gradually becomes as stupid and ignorant as it is possible for a human creature to become. The torpor of his mind renders him, not only incapable of relishing or bearing a part in any rational conversation, but of conceiving any generous, noble or tender sentiment and consequently of forming any just judgment concerning many even of the ordinary duties of private life.

He goes on to say that a worker under these conditions is utterly incapable of being a citizen. Here is Adam Smith attacking the division of labor because it produces too much specialization. Actually, automation is going to get us out of this problem. It is the computers now that are torpid and stupid. A computer can be as stupid as it likes because we probably are not going to give it the vote for at least 50 years.

Then Adam Smith said: "No two characters seem more inconsistent than those of trader and sovereign." Here he is arguing for the idea that you cannot run a government as if it were a business; you have to keep business out of government. The people who make a Bible out of Adam Smith had better go back and read him again. They might find it disconcerting.

I agree with Friedman that the greatest enemies of the free market are businessmen and intellectuals. I hope that the cold war between them is reaching the stage of peaceful coexistence; I suppose this Conference is a sign of it. I hope even more that the cold war between business and government in this country will reach a stage of coexistence. A great problem of this country is that the business community is neurotic. It is neurotic because of the Great Depression. It had an enormously traumatic experience in the 1930s. As a result, the leaders of the business community today are depression-fixated in the same way that the leaders of government are Munich-fixated. These are our two greatest dangers today. Again, it is a matter of "learning things that ain't so." We do this all the time.

TWO CONCEPTS OF FREEDOM

Let me just add a note on the question of freedom. This is a crucial and important question. I suggest that there are three concepts of freedom. One is the concept of power. This is defined as "what limits behavior." It is very close to the concept of wealth itself. The wealthy are free and the poor are not. The Indian peasant has no freedom at all; he is in an absolute box. The most important road to freedom is development, it is just plain getting rich. This is a most important concept of freedom.

On the other hand, this is not the only concept of freedom. There are other things which limit us. There are legal limitations, moral limitations, and even psychological limitations that box us in.

There is another concept of freedom which is a matter of the legitimacy in our minds of the limitations that box us in. We are always going to have to operate within limitations; so long as there is scarcity, we cannot have absolute freedom. This is fundamental.

However, the question as to whether one accepts these limitations as legitimate is enormously important. For instance, I accept the limitation of the traffic light. We all stop for a red light. This is a limitation on our freedom, but we accept it because we recognize that it is a limitation which in effect produces more freedom. If we did not have any traffic lights we should probably be dead, and there is a nothing less free than being dead.

Let me give another example. I was in Japan and Korea last year, and I very much wanted to go to China. Because I am an American citizen, I could go to China.* If I were a Canadian or an Australian or a Britisher or a Frenchman, I could go to China. But because I am an American citizen my freedom is seriously impaired, and I am hopping mad about it. I feel that it is outrageous that the State Department can prevent me from going to China or to Cuba just because of a little thing like a passport. Every time I look at my passport I chafe mentally. I deny the legitimacy of this limitation upon my freedom.

Legitimacy is a much more important concept than power. It is a more important system than the threat system. It is the dynamics of legitimacy that really determine the future of the world. In our social system we have to understand how things gain legitimacy and how they lose legitimacy. I am quite in sympathy with the question which Milton Friedman raises: How is it that exchange, the free market, which is a very successful institution, finds it so hard to develop, keep, and retain legitimacy? I do not quite know.

*This was written before U.S.-Chinese relations were "normalized" by former President Nixon. [ed.]

The role of the market in finance and financial institutions is of particular interest. We have Yugoslav economists coming through Ann Arbor frequently. They all seem to say the same thing. They all say how wonderful Adam Smith is and they tell us that we do not appreciate the wonders of the free market and the price system. But if we ask them whether they are going to set up a stock exchange, they turn a bit shy. Nevertheless, in the socialist countries there is a very marked creeping capitalism developing because they are beginning to understand and appreciate the virtues and importance of the price system and of the market economy. But they are not showing any signs whatever of developing anything that looks even remotely like a free market in finance.

What we need is a cost-benefit analysis of the financial system. The financial system performs a real function which has to be performed in any society. If it is not done one way, it has to be done in another. But we do not really know the realtive costs and benefits of alternative methods of performing this function. When such a study is made, I shall not be at all surprised if the answer comes out on our side of the fence. Until we know the answer to this question, we are in a weak position in arguing with the Yugoslavs. There is a certain amount of evidence, I think, that bankers are richer than they need to be. Possibly we could get this kind of service more cheaply. There may be obstacles to freedom of entry. This may result in this particular service being performed more expensively than it really needs to be. But it might still be cheaper in the long run than a centrally planned economy.

SOCIAL SECURITY: LEGITIMATIZED COERCION

On the subject of social security, which I favor, I am prepared to quarrel with Friedman, who is a bit more radical than I am. He wants a negative income tax, or whatever he calls it. He wants to "shovel it out" regardless, and I am somewhat sympathetic to this. I wish somebody would try the pivoted income tax, one under which those above a certain income pay taxes and those below a certain income get subsidies. This would simplify the whole problem and we could get rid of all social security and all welfare payments and we would have an enormous amount of freedom. It would be fun to try such a system and see what would happen. It would satisfy the requirements of the integrative system that there are income limits below which people cannot be allowed to fall, and it would permit freedom which could be used wisely or unwisely.

The existing social security system is open to severe criticism on precisely the grounds that Friedman suggested; that it is, for instance, a bad bargain for the young. I am not altogether opposed, however, to the use of what might be called legitimized economic coercion. The tax system is a threat system. If there were no penalties for not paying taxes, and if we tried to run the government like the Red Feather, with voluntary contributions, it might involve difficulties. Even the United Fund has a bit of the threat system in it: You *want* to give to the United Fund, do you not, says the foreman. There is a bit of a tax element in it.

Friedman has neglected what might be called legitimatized coercion. We accept coercion because we are better off if everybody is coerced. Law is legitimatized coercion. There are certain aspects of life in which there are enormous advantages of monopoly. This may well be true in social insurance; if everybody is in it, it is much cheaper for everybody. Under such circumstances, where there are substantial economies of scale and substantial economies of monopoly, it may be perfectly rational to vote to be coerced.

But this is not inconsistent with the fundamental principles of economic liberalism, if economic liberalism involves a sensible appraisal of the value of exchange as a social organizer. If this is what being an economic liberal means, then I am an economic liberal. After all, my middle name is Ewart. I was born in Liverpool on the same street as William Ewart Gladstone. If that does not make me a liberal, what does?

Is Capitalism
the Problem?

41

LEARNING OBJECTIVES

As before, in these last chapters of our book, our objectives are to make you thoughtful, not to teach you a few more or less simple analytical concepts. Some people think that capitalism *is* the problem; others disagree. You should consider this chapter the first, not the last word on the subject. The following readings, covering a wide spectrum of political thought, may start you on your way.

CAPITALISM, FOR WORSE

Paul M. Sweezy

*One of America's leading Marxian economists argues that
American capitalism is an inextricable part of a world
system whose past performance has depended heavily on
war expenditure and whose future prospects are not bright.*

With few exceptions the economists of the capitalist countries, liberal and conservative alike, are agreed that in the nearly four decades since the publication of Keynes's *General Theory of Employment, Interest, and Money,* governments have been in possession of, and have successfully utilized, means to control the level of economic activity and prevent the occurrence of serious depressions. To quote Harvard's Nobel Prize winning economist Kenneth J. Arrow:

The new economic ideas of Keynes and his disciples have been translated into policy with almost unprecedented speed. The idea that the state, through its decisions to spend, tax, and regulate the supply of money, could reduce unemployment to levels far lower than those in the depths of previous depressions was accepted among both economists and political leaders, and has shown itself to work in practice with great success. In every advanced country, the post-World War II record is like that of a new economy. (*New York Times,* March 26, 1973)

Let us look for a moment at the U.S. record (I will return to the others later on). It is true that since World War II there have been no depressions comparable to that of the 1930s. But is this because economists and political leaders have put their heads together and decided upon appropriate spending, tax, and monetary policies to head one off every time it threatened? Or is it because there has been a tremendous increase in the general level of government spending, with

From *Monthly Review* (February, 1974), pp. 1-7.

armaments and war playing by far the largest part? (I presume that neither the economists nor the political leaders would wish to claim that the military spending is merely the form taken by Keynesian ideas when put into practice.)

To these questions our economist friends would probably reply that while for overriding political or foreign-policy reasons the requisite amount of government spending has in fact been for military purposes, if this had not been the case it would have been possible to spend a great deal more for welfare objectives, with much the same economic results. In their eyes, the theory of the controllability of the level of economic activity is therefore vindicated regardless of what the money is spent on.

If this were really so, however, would we not expect that the controllers, helped by the large military budget, would have had an easy time maintaining a reasonably satisfactory level of economic activity throughout the postwar period? Surely with 20 percent or more of the American people living below the officially defined poverty line and with such projects as decent low-cost housing, pollution control, and mass transportation crying out for vastly increased public outlays, there has never been any lack of worthy purposes for the controllers to turn their attention to. And yet it is a notorious fact that even in boom periods, as at the time of writing in June 1973, officially counted unemployment amounts to 5 percent or more of the labor force. Taking facts like this into account, one could be pardoned for suspecting that the whole "controllability" idea is a myth and that the military budget is after all the only rational explanation of the relatively (i.e., relatively to the 1930s) favorable economic record of the postwar period.

In order to test this hypothesis, my colleague Harry Magdoff and I conducted an "experiment."* Using common sense and generally conservative estimating methods, we calculated for the year 1970 the number of workers who were either unemployed or directly and indirectly dependent on military spending. We then added these figures and compared the results with the number of unemployed in 1938. (It should be noted that both 1970 and 1938 were years of recession following a long period of cyclical upswing and should therefore be fairly comparable.)

The problem was to get an estimate of real, as distinct from offically counted, unemployment, since everyone familiar with the subject knows that there is a large discrepancy.** Working from official data on labor force participation rates, which were steadily declining for male workers during most of the 1950s and 1960s, and making an adjustment for involuntary part-time workers, we concluded that a conservative estimate of real unemployment was 8.1 million (9.4 percent of what would have been the labor force if jobs had been available). To this we added those in the armed forces (2.9 million), civilian employees of the Defense Department (1.2 million), those employed in producing goods for the Defense Department (3 million), and those employed because of what economists call the multiplier effect, i.e., workers employed in satisfying the demand generated by the incomes of those directly employed by the military budget (7.1

*Reported in detail in "Economic Stagnation and the Stagnation of Economics." *Monthly Review* (April 1971).

**See, for example, the article on unemployment entitled "6 Pct. Is Only the Tip of the Iceberg" by A. H. Raskin in the *New York Times* "Review of the Week" section, June 25, 1972.

million). These items total 22.3 million. This is just over 25 percent of the 1970 labor force adjusted to include those not officially counted as unemployed.

This compares with an official unemployment figure of 19.0 percent in 1938. However, if we make adjustments for hidden unemployment at that time and add to the expanded total the relatively small number of defense-related employed, we would probably come up with a figure somewhere around 30 percent to compare with the 25 percent in 1970. All of which leads to the conclusion that, apart from military spending, things were a bit better in 1970 than in 1938. But not much, and certainly nowhere near enough to sustain the thesis that the economists and politicians are in effective control of the economy.

If my Keynesian friends wish to dispute these facts or estimates, I would be happy to hear from them. I confess, however, that I do not expect to. They like to talk about the record, but they are shy about subjecting it to a concrete historical analysis. In this connection it is worth noting, if only in passing, that they have not yet come up with a coherent theory of the Great Depression and why it was so much worse than any previous capitalist depression. Need I add that without such a theory it is quite impossible to provide any rational analysis of what might have happened in the postwar period in the absence of vastly expanded military spending?

At this point the Keynesians, with remarkable unanimity, shift their ground. What about the other advanced capitalist countries, they ask, and especially Germany and Japan, the two with the best growth and employment records and the lowest levels of military spending?

It is impossible to answer this question adequately in a brief essay, especially since, to the best of my knowledge, no one, and least of all the Keynesians, has made a serious effort to do so. I can therefore only indicate the general lines along which I believe an attempt at an answer should proceed.

Most fundamental here is the fact, too often forgotten by social scientists each working in his or her narrow specialty, that capitalism is a global system and not a collection of separate national economies. What happens in any part of the system affects to some extent what happens in all the others; and if the part in question happens to be by far the largest in the system, as is the case with the United States in world capitalism, the effect on some or all of the other parts is likely to be large and even decisive. The question, then, is to what extent the performance of the world capitalist economy, and especially the economies of Germany and Japan, has been determined by the relative prosperity of the United States during this period.

It is, I believe, beyond dispute that both the German and the Japanese economic "miracles" were launched in the boom which accompanied the Korean War, i.e., as a direct result of U.S. military spending and involvement. In the case of Germany, Heinz Abosch has written: "For the West German economy, the Korean War proved to be a remarkable stimulant: while the big industrial powers had to step up the production of armaments, Germany, still subject to the restrictions of the Potsdam Agreement, was able to increase her entire industrial output, thanks to the orders that poured in from all sides. As Professor [Henry] Wallich remarks: 'It was sparks from the Korean War that set German exports alight.' "* What was true for Germany was even more so for Japan which was the rear staging area for U.S. forces fighting in Korea and a direct recipient of large military orders. "In terms of the growth situation," writes Professor Tsuru, "the Korean conflict and the subsequent maintenance of 'special procurement' demand was a distinct boon."**

Of course it would not be possible to establish so close a continuing dependence of the German and Japanese economies on U.S. military spending. The booms touched off by Korea had much else to feed on: repair of war damage, renovation of capital equipment, and, perhaps most important, a veritable binge of "automobilization" similar to that which had sustained the U.S. economy in the 1920s. But continuing strong demand for German and Japanese exports remained a *sine qua non* of the prosperity of these countries, and it is difficult to believe that this export demand would have held up if the U.S. economy had once again sunk into a condition of low-level stagnation such as prevailed in the 1930s. It is well to remember that in that earlier period it was only military spending, first in Japan and Germany and only later in the United States, which pulled the capitalist world out of the Great Depression. In the post-war period I would argue that it has been military spending (plus other similarly motivated outlays such as economic subsidies to puppet and client states), so far largely but by no means exclusively centered in the United States, which has prevented the capitalist world from sinking into a new Great Depression. As an historical interpretation of these strife-ridden decades, I submit that this makes vastly more sense than the notion that the postwar preformance of world capitalism has been the brainchild of economists aided and abetted by wise political leaders. Economists may like to think that they are powerful, and political leaders that they are wise. But the sad truth is that there is precious little evidence to support these amiable conceits. True, they play a role, but not the one they think they play or would like to play; rather their role is that of instruments and agents of elemental forces generated by a blind and self-contradictory economic system which no one can control.

---

*Heinz Abosch, *The Menace of the Miracle* (Monthly Review Press, 1963), p. 79.

**Shigeto Tsuru, *Essays in Economic Development*, Economic Research Series No. 9 (Tokyo, 1968), p. 168.

"Special Procurement" was the name given to U.S. purchases for military and related purposes. According to Professor Tsuru's figures (pp. 156-157) this item averaged 34.2 percent of Japan's total receipts from foreign sales of goods and services in the years 1951-1953.

The real question to which economists ought to address themselves, but consistently refuse to do so, is why capitalism in the twentieth century has such a powerful tendency to stagnation that it requires increasingly massive forms of public and private waste to keep itself going at all. (As every reasonably sensitive observer of contemporary capitalism knows, military spending is only the leading species of a large genus.) Basically, the reason was stated by Marx with both eloquence and clarity more than a hundred years ago when he wrote : *"The real barrier of capitalist production is capital itself.* It is the fact that capital and its self-expansion appear as the starting and closing point, as the motive and aim of production, that production is merely production for *capital,* and not vice versa, the means of production mere means for an ever-expanding system of the life process for the benefit of the *society* of producers."* To put the point in another way, as long as the driving forces of production are profit and the expansion of profit-making enterprises, and as long as the incomes of working people are held down pre-

Capital, vol. 3, Kerr edition, p. 293. Italics in the original.

cisely to make possible an increase in profits and a more rapid expansion of enterprises, so long will the growth of society's power to produce tend to outstrip its power to consume. And if this contradiction is deeper and more pervasive today than it was in Marx's time, the reason is that in the intervening period the process of concentration and centralization of capital — which he recognized as inevitable features of capitalist development — has gone so far that dominant monopolies today have the power not only to exploit their own workers but all other strata of society as well, thus expanding the gap between wealth at one pole and poverty at the other, at the very time when there is, or soon could be, ample productive power to provide everyone without exception with the means to a decent human livelihood.

Under these circumstances economists have taken upon themselves the task of hiding the facts, of making the uncontrollable appear under control, of rationalizing a system which condemns hundreds of millions of people to lives of despair and starvation, and which through its unrestrained profligacy and violence threatens the very continuation of life on earth. It is not a task I envy them.

CAPITALISM, FOR BETTER OR WORSE

Kenneth J. Arrow

*In the following essay Kenneth J. Arrow, professor of economics at
Harvard and 1972 Novel laureate in economics, examines six
fundamental contradictions of capitalism, not all of them put
forward by Marxists, and concludes that they need not be fatal, at least
in the foreseeable future. Indeed, capitalism may be strengthened
for resolving them.*

There is little warrant for the belief that we
know the laws of history well enough to make
projections of any great reliability. Most of the
turning points of history, great and small, were
surprises to both their participants and the
analysts of the day, whatever their doctrine.

That the capitalist system excels at productive
efficiency is not to be denied. In the United
States, Western Europe, and Japan, at least, the
rate of increase in efficiency is much higher now
than it was when the authors of the Communist
Manifesto included a fulsome panegyric on the
productive accomplishments of the bourgeoisie.
But no social institution has ever felt justified
solely by material product. Moreover, the inequalities in the distribution of this material
wealth and in the power and control over the
activities by which it is created constitute a
steady indictment.

This indictment has, among several different
groups of social analysts, taken the empirical
form of asserting that the development of capitalism has given rise to "contradictions" that
imply its eventual extinction as a matter of
historical law. As I have said, I do not believe us

From Kenneth J. Arrow, "Capitalism for Better or
Worse," from *Capitalism, The Moving Target,* ed.
Leonard Silk (Quadrangle, The New York Times Book
Co., 1974), pp. 105-113.

capable of discerning inevitable contradictions
and, in any case, capitalism has survived long
enough in advanced countries to show that the
contradictions can hardly be fatal, though they
may have been avoided only by the development
of new institutions, such as labor unions and
government intervention.

It is still useful to list some six of the leading
proposed contradictions, for they do all point to
real problems for social policy and criticism. No
doubt the idea of a contradiction in the capitalist
system is Marxian in origin, but some of the
following contradictions have been put forward
by non-Marxists only and some by both sides.

1. *Ideological weakness.* Capitalism relies for
its operation on selfish motives. Its prized efficiency depends on the greed of the owners and
managers of firms, on their desire for increasing
profits. Further, the success of capitalism
depends on careful calculation, on a nice balancing of costs and benefits. The reliance on
selfishness is defended as a realistic evaluation of
human motivations. But neither selfishness nor
calculation are goals for which men are willing to
make deep commitments. It is a fear of many
conservative thinkers, the late Joseph Schumpeter
being perhaps the best known and most thor-
oughgoing and Irving Kristol being the latest,
that the ideological commitment to capitalism is
too weak to resist the idealistic appeal of

socialism or similar doctrines, which promise a daily contribution to the common good.

2. *Alienation.* A closely related critical theme holds that capitalism, with its emphasis on the impersonal-exchange relationship, leads to destruction of personal and communal relations. If these are fundamental needs of mankind, then alienation ultimately undermines the social relations that define the capitalist system itself. This thesis, put forward vigorously by conservative and romantic thinkers of the early nineteenth century, was adopted by Marx, but with an added characteristic element: the worker is alienated from the product of his labor, his work becomes merely a means to income, not the satisfaction of a need to be productive. The human-relations movement in industry illustrates how the same critique can be put to defend and improve personal hierarchical relations in industry.

3. *Increasing concentration.* Marx and many others have argued that competition and technological development force a growing concentration of economic power into fewer and fewer hands. Among other alleged consequences: the size of the class that benefits from capitalism would be steadily shrinking, and therefore the system would be more vulnerable, and the transition to a centrally controlled socialist economy would be made easier.

The actual development has revealed some factors that modify these effects. The hypothesis of growing concentration and the two consequences just drawn were based on observations in the industrial sector of the economy. But the degree of concentration in the industrial sector seems to have reached a stable level and has not changed greatly in fifty years or more; the exercise of control in giant firms itself requires an increasingly large fraction of the employees, who become identified in some measure with the directing groups; and the proportion of employment in the industrial sector is decreasing, as rising incomes cause more expenditure on services, which tend to be operated by smaller firms.

4. *Working-class solidarity.* The grouping of workers for effective production, as in factories, reinforces the sense of their common position as against the employers. The sense of solidarity gave strength to the tendency to unionization and, in Europe, to the socialist and syndicalist movements. The intensity of feeling in these movements, exemplified in the sit-down strikes in the United States during the late thirties, certainly appeared to justify the notion of intense class conflict.

In fact, several factors have mitigated the thrust of working class solidarity: the conflict between unions and employers has become institutionalized and legitimized wherever unions have become strong enough to reach a level of security; not only are the economic conflicts fought out in ways that pose no threat to the social order, but politically organized labor plays a relatively more conservative role than in the past.

There is, however, one unresolved strain in labor relations which has come to surprise us: the determination of wages and working conditions in the public sector. In recent years we have moved to unions and strikes in this region. We clearly have not come to an institutional equilibrium here; laws against strikes are not enforced, not even in the case of police, where striking has some especially severe consequences. Labor relations in privately owned public utilities pose some of the same special problems. This development can hardly be called a contradiction of capitalism, to be sure.

5. *Unemployment.* Over the last hundred and fifty years by far the most serious criticism of, and threat to, the capitalist economic system has been the recurring cycles of unemployment. Here was a clear malfunctioning of the system itself, not attributable to external causes imposing misery on its victims. Further, not only was it to be expected that insecurity and patently un-

necessary poverty would create resentment and violent antagonism on the part of the working class, but also each depression was accompanied by a destruction of profits, the lifeblood and raison d'etre of the capitalist system. It seemed a reasonable extrapolation to foresee a collapse of the system, both economical and political. But no such collapse occurred. Not even the Great Depression caused a serious question to be raised, except perhaps in the special case of Germany. Perhaps the clearly evident growth in the real incomes of all members of the society more than compensated for the recurrent economic disasters.

The new economic ideas of Keynes and his disciples have been translated into policy with almost unprecedented speed. The idea that the state, through its decisions to spend, tax, and regulate the supply of money, could reduce unemployment to levels far lower than those in the depths of previous depressions was accepted among both economists and political leaders and has shown itself to work in practice with great success. In every advanced country the post-World War II economic record is like that of a new economy. Sophisticated radical economists, such as Paul Baran and Paul Sweezy, quickly recognized that the Keynesian solution would work but argued that in a capitalist system the government could spend enough to insure full employment only on socially wasteful and even destructive ends, such as war and preparations for war. Socially constructive spending would necessarily compete with and eventually undermine t.ie private sector. The example of Japan suggests some reason to doubt this argument, though the Japanese circumstances are somewhat special. At home over the last decade it has been found possible to achieve a much higher level of government spending on social purposes and to decrease defense expenditures at least relatively. We do have higher unemployment rates than are desirable, but that is because of inflationary fears rather than a shortage of ways to spend money.

There is little reason, therefore, to accept the Baran-Sweezy variation of the unemployment contradiction though perhaps it is too soon to regard it as definitely controverted.

6. *Inflation.* There appears to be this element of truth in the idea of a contradiction: the resolution of any problem always creates a new problem. From the beginning of the Keynesian era the fear has been expressed that vigorous full-employment policies will lead to inflation. Standard economic theory has been built in large measure about the idea of equilibrium, that an exact balancing of supply and demand on all markets, including the labor market, will lead to steady prices, while an excess of supply leads to a downward pressure. Thus, unemployment ought to lead to wage declines; they manifestly have not done so in recent years. The coexistence of inflation and unemployment is thus an intellectual riddle and an uncomfortable fact.

But in my judgment the contradiction here hardly compares with some of the others to which capitalism has adapted.

First of all, the rates of inflation with which we have had to contend impose no insuperable problem or even major difficulty to the operation of the economic system, nothing comparable to the major depressions of the past. Individuals will learn, and have learned, to deal with inflation, making their plans to take expected inflation into account. The economic system and the government will create and are creating methods of mitigating the effects, such as variable-annuity plans and cost-of-living clauses in savings bonds. What the future will bring is of course a matter of conjecture. Some analysts feel that inflation will inevitably accelerate, but others will note that in the past peacetime inflations have tapered off. The present rates are historically high but not totally unprecedented; it appears from the record that even in peacetime, over the period 1897-1902, prices rose more rapidly than they have in the last five years.

Second, we may have some reasonable hope that economic research and experimentation in policymaking, between them, will evolve more sophisticated means of managing the overall economy. Research into monetary economics is at an unprecedented level of activity, and better and more abundant data are available than ever before. With the variety of policy instruments now available and better understood, I think it most likely that the reconciliation of full employment and price stability can be significantly improved in the future.

We find that capitalism, like any very complex system, contains within itself contradictory tendencies, but there is no reason to suppose they are fatal, at least in the foreseeable future. We do find implied in these contradictions some social tasks: the completion of the tasks involved in the achievement of macroeconomic stability, the redistribution of income and power to improve the sense of justice in the arrangements of society, by which I mean the inseparable elements of the liberty and equality of individuals, and, perhaps hardest, the increase in the sense of individual and local control over one's destiny in the workplace and the small society. These aims are mutually reinforcing, not competitive.

42

An Introduction to Statistics and Econometrics

We are not going to present a test, a review, or readings on statistics. The subject is simply too large to be covered adequately, and our statistical section is meant to introduce you, not to train you, in its complexities. For someone who is interested in the problems of statistics let us suggest a good first reader where the matter can be pursued a little further: *A Primer on Statistics for Business and Economics* by Irwin Miller (Random House, 1968). Or for the more adventurous, any good beginning text on the subject. Your instructor can help you make a wise choice.